Constructions of Literacy
Studies of Teaching and Learning
In and Out of Secondary Schools

Constructions of Literacy
Studies of Teaching and Learning
In and Out of Secondary Schools

Edited by

Elizabeth B. Moje
University of Michigan

David G. O'Brien
Purdue University

 LAWRENCE ERLBAUM ASSOCIATES, PUBLISHERS
2001   Mahwah, New Jersey   London

T 75664

Lawrence Erlbaum Associates, Inc., Publishers
10 Industrial Avenue
Mahwah, NJ 07430

Cover design by Kathryn Houghtaling Lacey

Library of Congress Cataloging-in-Publication Data

Constructions of literacy : studies of teaching and learning in and out of secondary schools / edited by Elizabeth B. Moje and David G. O'Brien.
    p. cm.
    Includes bibliographical references and index.
  ISBN 0-8058-2948-2 (cloth : alk. paper)
  ISBN 0-8058-2949-0 (pbk. : alk. paper)
1. Language arts (Secondary)—United States—Case studies.
  2. Language arts—Correlation with content subjects—United States—Case studies.   I. Moje, Elizabeth B.
  II. O'Brien, David G.
LB1631 .C667   2000
418'.0071'273—dc21

                                   99-089996
                                       CIP

Printed in the United States of America
10 9 8 7 6 5 4 3 2 1

*To the secondary school teachers
and adolescents who allowed us to represent
the complexity and richness
of their teaching and learning lives*

Contributors

Donna E. Alvermann, *University of Georgia, Athens, GA*
David Bloome, *Vanderbilt University, Nashville, TN*
Deborah R. Dillon, *Purdue University, West Lafayette, IN*
Victoria Parsons Duling, *Fairfax County Public Schools, Fairfax, VA*
Kris Fassio, *University of Utah, Salt Lake City, UT*
Barbara J. Guzzetti, *Arizona State University, Tempe, AZ*
Robert E. Hall, *Woodbridge, VA*
Kathleen A. Hinchman, *Syracuse University, Syracuse, NY*
Michelle M. Kelly, *State University of New York at Cortland, Cortland, NY*
Allan Luke, *University of Queensland, Brisbane, Australia*
Elizabeth B. Moje, *University of Michigan, Ann Arbor, MI*
David W. Moore, *Arizona State University West, Phoenix, AZ*
David G. O'Brien, *Purdue University, West Lafayette, IN*
Scott F. Oates, *University of Wisconsin, Eau Claire, Eau Claire, WI*
John E. Readence, *University of Nevada–Las Vegas, Las Vegas, NV*
Rebecca Springs, *Lafayette Jefferson High School, Lafayette, IN*
Roger A. Stewart, *Boise State University, Boise, ID*
David Stith, *Lafayette Jefferson High School, Lafayette, IN*
Elizabeth G. Sturtevant, *George Mason University*
Mark Volkmann, *Purdue University, West Lafayette, IN*
Debra J. Willes, *Granite Park Junior High School, Salt Lake City, UT*
Patricia Zalewski, *Liverpool Central Schools, Liverpool, NY*

Contents

Cases That Seek to Reform

Cases That Seek to Interrupt

Part III
Commentaries

Foreword

In a recent *USA Today* report on the anti-trust suit against Microsoft, one of the consulting economists claimed that the breakup of the dominant technology corporation would "create competition up and down the value chain." The metaphors of the financial pages of cable business reports, on-line stock reports and news broadcasts tell us a great deal about which discourses count, about which kinds of textual representations are powerful in the economies and cultures of New Times. Here we find two interesting ideas at work. First is the idea that the aim of rule of law is to open up possible worlds to "create competition." Second is the idea that the complex markets where software and communications media (and the very word processing package that I'm using now) are part of a hierarchical ("up and down") and singular "value chain." However oblique the connection to literacy might seem to you, consider the social arithmetic of globalized capitalism: one world = one marketplace inhabited by mobile players with generalizable capital.

How apt would it be to extend these metaphors to our understandings of literacy? Are there singular cultural, economic or social fields (e.g., "markets") against which the efficacy of literacy and literacy education can be measured? Is literacy education simply an issue of "constructing" functionally literate adults capable of using transferable cognitive and textual tools for "competition up and down the value chain?" Is the goal of literacy education to produce more effective and competitive players in colleges and universities, bureaucracies and businesses?

As teachers and teacher educators most of us are poised to argue against crass economic reductionism. The principal response of secondary English teachers over the years has been to reassert the claim that the literate, her or his "voices," sensibilities and refinements are ineffable and immeasurable—escaping the calculation of behaviourist skill descriptions, cognitive operations or, indeed, numbers games about the value of functional literacy.

Yet these defenses of literacy—defenses of the intellectual and aesthetic autonomy of literacy from the social and economic—must explain or survive two conditions of postindustrial societies.

First, young people in mass-mediated cultures face a complex, continually mutating field of texts and discourses (and reports such as the one cited above). They have to contend with an environment where economic, medical and scientific/technical discourses are used to normalize and guide virtually all aspects of everyday life, often in less than publicly accessible and criticizable ways. They have to manage themselves in environments where cultural identity, where the personal, the spiritual, and the emotional likewise are constructed through the texts and textures of institutions like schools, churches, and corporations but as well through talk shows, online communications, cinema and consumer designs.

In these economies those secondary and middle school students struggling with aspects of traditional print literacy are in serious trouble, particularly in the jobs-rich sectors of digital-boom economies. It is an unsurprising and powerful lesson that "reluctant learners" may be re-engaged through educational use of new media, online materials, and popular cultural texts.

Second, these same cultures—now built around the exchange of discourses for material artifacts, the exchange of goods but as well of symbols and signs—are complex social fields where our capacity to sign, to produce, read and interpret signs become central means of livelihood. In semiotic economies, literacy is labor. And a critical literacy is necessary not just to engage in that labor, as a tool for capital exchange and value, but as well to understand how that labor is described and represented, shaped and controlled—a kind of meta-literacy, if you will. A critical literacy could be: a self-reflective tool for the analysis of the shapes, designs and relations of these same fields where literacy is made and used. A critical literacy could be: the capacity to name, shape and remediate your relations to the dominant modes of information in knowledge-based economies.

Yet we continue to work from a number of naïve assumptions about literacies old and new, their place and significance. Even where we have made the move away from narrow psychological approaches, as the contributors here have, much of our work is based on the assumption that literacy is a universal form of capital for entry into a complex but singular cultural, economic and social domain. Such premises are up for grabs. The power of literacy for adolescents is field specific, depending on complex webs of exchange in classrooms, in workplaces, on the streets, on the Internet. Work in the field of cultural studies has shifted our understandings from a view of cultures as singular, homogeneous rule-bound social organizations, to a view of cultures as plural, contingent, heterogeneous sites, ridden throughout by difference, conflict and tension. Learning communities, then, are not necessarily benign spaces or power-free zones.

Elizabeth Moje and David O'Brien have assembled a refreshing and broad minded look at literacy practices affiliated with that strange form of life called 'adolescence'—the term itself less than a hundred years old. The papers here begin to locate adolescent literacy squarely in the lived social realities and experiences of what British cultural theorist Stuart Hall (1996) has termed "New Times." In globalized economies, and polyglot nation states, via new communications technologies, adolescents encounter complex and partial forms of social identity, work and agency, new forms of political and cultural affiliation and alliance. This doesn't look like adolescence as many of us knew it (or "teen spirit" for that matter). We aren't sure exactly what to call it, but it certainly isn't postwar adolescence, any more than it can be accounted for by the seminal descriptions offered by psychologist G. Stanley Hall (no relation to Stuart whatsoever) and colleagues a century ago.

More and Readence's beginning essay lays out the 'field' of "secondary school literacy research," looking at 4 paradigmatic approaches with different metaphors and goals. Each is itself the product of a particular political economy. Each is an historical construction of literacy tied to a normative version of how discourse and discourse practices should be distributed, to whom, for what ends. In this sense, we would be wasting our time to debate which of these models' 'truth claims' about adolescent literacy is correct. Rather they should be read as competing attempts to define and delimit what might count as school literacy. Each is tied, respectively, to an idealized life world of texts, and each attempts to design and designate, however successfully or unsuccessfully, a set of practices that children *should* acquire.

Yet at the same time More and Readance's paper names the field as "secondary school literacy." In this way, it accepts as unmarked and leaves uncriticized the 'naturalness' of the institutional box of the secondary school. This is the kind of move that is critiqued by middle school advocates. We could cleave the field up differently, attempting to map the territory as "adolescent literacy," as "youth literacy," or, to use a throwback from trade publishers, "teen literacy." Foucault would be the first to point out that how we 'name' a field in question is telling.

Other categories and terms go unmarked or unremarked in the chapters that follow. Specifically, the disciplines of secondary school teaching remain

beyond criticism. In their initial formulation, O'Brien, Moje and Stewart refer to these as "subject area divisions," noting that they are "subcultures and
discourse communities." Yet many of the subsequent studies do not follow
through on this key insight: that disciplines, fields of knowledge are in fact
constituted by discourses. In sum, doing "physics," "biology" or "mathematics" is about introduction into a form of life, with contestable and malleable
discourse practices, conflicting positions and ideologies (Halliday & Martin,
1996). A failure to engage with discipline as discourse leads us back to the
very epistemological basis of the failure of "literacy across the curriculum:"
the assumption that literacy practices are simply skills, tools or cognitive operations that can be superimposed, or laid over non-problematic or stable
fields of knowledge and fact. As any practicing scientist or sociologist of science will tell you—disciplines are only static as they are represented and
freeze-dried in textbooks. In the field and the laboratory, they are dynamic,
shifting, and contested. 'Truth' is played out, argued, written up and over by
scientists. If we accept as stable and non-problematic the 'content' of a secondary discipline—we are left with educational approaches that superim-
pose activities or genres or skills onto fields and into courses. Literacy across
the curriculum typically means the more efficient delivery of content
knowledge—not a critical engagement with the disciplinary discourses and
textual practices of a field.

Without a critical literary—self-critical, multidiscursive and multivoiced,
discourse analytic and textually focused-content area literacy simply becomes an adjunct technology for the domestication of students into non-ne-
gotiable fields of knowledge. It fails to see how science, history, engineering
and other cognate fields are constituted by multiple and contending discourses. *Constructions of Literacy* presents some classrooms that leave discipline untouched, thereby maintaining a strong binary divide between
literacy and the field; and it presents some that use literacy to engage with
and interrupt disciplinary discourses. In so doing, these classrooms
reconceptualise disciplinary training as critical discourse practice.

According to sociologist Pierre Bourdieu (1992), the institutions that we
live and work in are social fields. These are fields of dynamic cultural and
economic exchange, where different kinds of literate practice, texts, and
discourses have variable value when combined with economic and material
goods, and social access and infrastructure. There are rules, rigid and flexible, determining and determined, structuring and structured that enable
the translation of the kinds of literacy acquired in classrooms to out of
school environments—and vice versa. Literate practices have differential

conversion value into material resources, into other kinds of symbolic and semiotic codes. These conversions and translations, thus, are at the heart of life in semiotic economies, and they begin to bind together cultural with economic with social practice.

Is this vision of literacy economistic and reductionist? Let's return to the rather obscure USA Today textual metaphors that we started this introduction with. These worlds of texts that adolescents occupy are neither singular "markets" nor "value chains," nor are they necessarily ruled by competition. In globalized economies and cultures, they are complex, multiple, and characterized by rapid change, uncertainty, and complexity. The teaching of literacy is an introduction to a semiotic economy where identities, artefacts, texts and tokens are exchanged in predictable and unpredictable ways, ways that may fly with and against attempts by governments, corporations and teachers to regulate them. Curious indeed. But this means that a critical literacy isn't necessarily about learning to read and critique a text or discourse that is given—it could be about critically understanding the variable rules of exchange, the social and material relations of power that operate in the social fields where such texts and discourses are used. If there is such a thing as "secondary" or "adolescent literacy," it could be about working and designing the relationships between discourse and discipline, identity and social field.

—*Allan Luke*
University of Queensland
Brisbane, Australia

REFERENCES

Bourdieu, P. (1992). *Language and Symbolic Power*. G. Raymond & M. Adamson, Trans. Cambridge: Polity Press.

Hall, S. (1996). The meaning of New Times. In D. Morley & K. H. Chen (Eds.), *Stuart Hall: Critical Dialogues in Cultural Studies* (pp. 223–237). London: Routledge.

Halliday, M.A.K., & Martin, J. R. (1996). *Writing Science*. London: Taylor & Francis.

Preface

In this volume, we explore and represent, through a series of cases and commentaries, how and why secondary school teachers and students—also known as adolescents—use literacy in formal and informal learning settings. Throughout the volume, when we speak of *literacy*, we are referring to speaking, listening, reading, writing, and performing written texts, with the acknowledgment that texts can be broadly conceived. However, we also refer to how these literacies are negotiated and used for specific purposes (Scribner & Cole, 1981). We see literacy, as being used in particular ways, in particular places and times, for particular reasons in secondary school contexts, and we believe that it is important to develop deeper understandings of how the contexts of secondary schools shape and reflect different literacies. These ways of using literacy—or literacy practices—lead to particular constructions of literacy. Thus, when we discuss constructions of literacy, we are referring to how people generate and bring practices of literacy to particular events of reading, writing, speaking, and listening, particularities that are shaped at least in part by the context of the secondary school and by adolescence as a period of development or as a way of being and knowing the world.

Another important aspect of this book is that as a group of authors, we believe that secondary literacy theory and research must move beyond a focus on print. We conduct our research from the perspective that literacy can be conceived of as a sociocultural practice (cf. Scribner & Cole, 1981), and that in an increasingly diverse and changing world, we are encountering multiple forms of print literacy, including visual, spatial, performative, and electronic literacies (cf. New London Group, 1996). What's more, literacy is integrally connected to oral and visual forms of communication and representation that are not necessarily print-based. Thus, we see literacy as the reading and writing of text, but we define text broadly to include any rendering of experience into a systematic and communicable form. We also see literacy as inseparable from orality and other forms of representation.

The cases included in this volume share a common focus on secondary or adolescent literacy, but the theoretical perspectives and research methods used in the cases are diverse. Although a number of quasi-experimental studies have been conducted on literacy teaching and learning strategies, fewer critical, cultural, feminist, interpretive, or postmodern studies have been conducted on how and why literacy is used by teachers and students. Nor are there many studies of how teachers and students negotiate and construct understandings of literacy in various secondary disciplines or content areas (e.g., Myers, 1992; Santa Barbara Discourse Group, 1994). As Moore (1996) suggested in his National Reading Conference research address on the future of secondary literacy research, a new era of research is emerging in secondary literacy. Recent interpretive studies have made important contributions; studies currently being conducted from feminist, critical, cultural, and postmodern stances offer new insights for the field. Because of the diverse perspectives offered in the different cases and commentaries of this volume, a guiding principle for each contributor was to make explicit how theoretical perspectives influenced each contributor's interpretations of the social construction of literacy, and how findings in each study influenced theoretical perspectives.

Additionally, the cases presented here are drawn from a diverse group of secondary classrooms, content areas, and communities across the United States. Some of the cases focus on the complicated nature of *teaching* or *learning to teach* secondary literacy; others focus on how students *learn* literacy, use literacy to learn in secondary schools, or use literacy to make sense of their lives. Some cases focus on specific pedagogical innovations, others on analyzing what made a particular classroom work as it did, and yet others on how young people are invited into or marginalized from learning experiences in and out of secondary school settings.

Finally, although focused on contributing to theoretical understandings of secondary literacy, the contributors are all teachers and researchers who are committed to changing teaching and researching practices. The goal here is to encourage theorists, researchers, and teachers to analyze the complexities of secondary literacy teaching and learning, and to examine their own understandings of literacy within their own literacy contexts, whether in research settings, universities, or secondary school classrooms. As a result, we each strove to write in ways that extend, rather than obfuscate, theoretical, empirical, and practical understandings. We agree with Hooks (1994), who wrote, "It is crucial that critical thinkers who want to change our teaching practices talk to one another and collaborate in a discussion that crosses boundaries and creates a space for intervention" (p. 129). Our intention, then, is to cross boundaries and create spaces for theorists, researchers, teachers, and students to talk to one another about what literacy is and how literacy teaching and learning are shaped in classrooms, schools, and communities. Consequently, we have presented not only research, but also our emerging theories and questions about literacy. In each of the chapters—whether introductions, cases, or commentaries—we reflect on how our research or the research of others has pushed us to question our own conceptions of literacy, as well as our research and teaching practices.

THE ORGANIZATION OF THE VOLUME

This volume is comprised of 13 chapters: Two chapters that provide frameworks for thinking about secondary/adolescent literacy, 9 include cases of research with teachers and adolescents, and 2 present commentaries discussing the contributions, contradictions, and potential problems represented in and among the different perspectives. In chapter 1, Moore and Readence provide an analysis of research goals and stances that serve to situate secondary and adolescent literacy research, and analyze new directions and changing focuses in the field. This chapter places the studies collected in this volume in the context of existing studies of secondary literacy and provides a frame for thinking about the diverse theoretical perspectives that are represented. In the second chapter, O'Brien, Moje, and Stewart present a sociohistorical analysis of contexts of secondary/adolescent literacy as well as the issues in the teaching and learning of literacy at the secondary level. O'Brien, Moje, and Stewart examine the macrocontexts and microcontexts of secondary schools and adolescents' lives to advance the idea that secondary/adolescent literacy research must move beyond the study of strategies for teaching young people to use literacy in content areas, toward research that helps teachers and researchers better understand how contexts shape literacy learning and use. In particular, the authors emphasize the importance of studying how everyday practices of people in microcontexts both reflect and reproduce or contest larger structural practices of the macrocontexts.

The cases included in the next section of the book represent a variety of secondary (middle, junior high, and high school settings) content areas, including the sciences (biology, earth science, and physics), English literature and composition, social studies, mathematics, and a literacy lab classroom for learners who have been identified as being at risk of failure in high school. Each of these content classrooms is comprised of students from diverse ethnic, cultural, and socioeconomic backgrounds. As we attempted to organize these diverse chapters, we explored several possibilities, including arranging them according to the content area being studied, to the theoretical perspectives identified, and to the participants on which they focused (teachers or young people). Finally, we turned to the perspective of Moore and Readence articulated in chapter 1 on how the goals of any study shape its stance, methods, analysis, and assertions. Thus, we have organized the book around what we viewed as the goals of each project. We found this a bit difficult, however, because many of the studies seemed to pursue overlapping goals, as illustrated in Table P.1.

Nevertheless, we forged ahead in our attempt to provide a general sense of organization for the reader. We found that every study made interpretation its basic goal, but that several of the studies also engaged in the other goals of predicting, reforming, and interrupting. However, because only one study even touched on prediction, we did not include prediction in

TABLE P.1

Studies Organized by Goals of the Research

Predicting	Interpreting	Reforming	Interrupting
Guzzetti	Guzzetti, chap. 6	Guzzetti, chap. 6	
	Dillon et al., chap. 3		
	Hinchman and Zalewski, chap. 8		Hinchman and Zalewski, chap. 8
	Kelly, chap. 11		Kelly, chap. 11
	Moje et al., chap. 9	Moje et al., chap. 9	Moje et al., chap. 9
	Oates, chap. 10		Oates, chap. 10
	O'Brien et al., chap. 5	O'Brien et al., chap. 5	
	Stewart, chap. 7		Stewart, chap. 7
	Sturtevant, chap. 4		

our organizational scheme, and thus we begin the section with cases that interpret teachers' and students' practices.

In the first *interpretations* case, Dillon, O'Brien, and Volkmann analyze the oral and literate interactions of young people in a high school biology class. Dillon and her colleagues weave together the teacher's and students' practices in this classroom, showing that through their interactions the teacher and students generated texts for learning. Chapter 4 represents the one case on literacy and mathematics teaching in the collection. In this case, Sturtevant, Duling, and Hall interpret the process of learning to use literacy to teach mathematics while also learning to teach. Sturtevant followed the teacher represented in the study—co-author Hall—through his preservice teaching and into his first year. As Sturtevant, Duling, and Hall illustrate, the contexts of secondary school, especially the disciplinary contexts, dramatically shape what teachers are able to do in regard to literacy teaching.

The next section includes the two cases that we have categorized as having an ultimate goal of *reforming* classroom practice. In chapter 5, O'Brien, Springs, and Stith examine a high school literacy lab designed to support struggling learners in learning literacy. These authors approach their research of these young people in the literacy lab context from a perspective on at-riskness that argues that youth are placed at risk rather than having internal qualities or home experiences that lead to school struggles. In chapter 6, Guzzetti presents an analysis of gendered interactions that occur when teachers and students are engaged in talk about physics texts. Guzzetti's analysis focuses on how teachers implicitly engaged in gendered practices and on how one teacher attempted to reconstruct those practices, while students struggled to maintain them.

The next section contains cases that seek to interrupt understandings of literacy teaching and learning. Chapter 7, by Stewart, represents a re-analysis of data that the author collected in a high school earth science classroom. In re-analyzing his data, Stewart provides a glimpse of the complexity in engaging in research on teaching and learning in any setting. Although his first analysis is compelling, his re-analysis illustrates that his first analysis was only one representation of how the teacher and students used literacy in the classroom. In chapter 8, Hinchman and Zalewski examine the teaching of global studies from the perspective of two students. Their chapter interrupts conceptions of literacy teaching in the social studies by raising questions about how the students' interpretations of the classroom practices might have been shaped by race, class, and gender relations. Moje, Willis, and

Fassio present findings in chapter 9 from a study of two seventh-grade literacy workshops. Moje, Willis, and Fassio use two cases of adolescents' writings, readings, and oral language to raise questions about how the literacy workshop supports reading and writing processes but does not make room for reading and writing practices. In chapter 10, Oates also presents cases of students in an English classroom, in this case a high school classroom. Oates illustrates the social purposes that undergird the literacy practices of these young people and illustrates how various Discourses (cf. Gee, 1996) are woven throughout their literate practices in the English classroom. The final chapter, Kelly's case, explores one students's literacy learning across content areas and outside of school in a community church–school program. Kelly illustrates how the church–school program extended the learning provided in the public school program by explicitly drawing from the young man's ethnic, cultural, and raced experiences in society and by teaching him literacies not privileged in school. Her work interrupts traditional conceptions of literacy learning by highlighting the various literacy and learning communities in this youth's life.

In the final section, Alvermann and Bloome comment on the various cases presented in the book. Alvermann reads the cases from a feminist poststructuralist position, synthesizing the various interpretations by wondering in print what the interpretations, reforms, and interruptions might have looked like had a feminist poststructuralist perspective been adopted. Her chapter highlights the various perspectives while contrasting them with her own stance. Bloome's commentary takes a critical perspective, in which he argues that as secondary and adolescent literacy teachers and researchers, we need to be explicit about how reading, writing, and other representational forms should be taught and used to develop a just and democratic society. Bloome offers four moves that we must all engage in to further the goal of equitable and democratic literacy education for all youth.

ACKNOWLEDGMENTS

Collecting these cases and commentaries would not have been possible without the support and extensive efforts of a number of people. Jamal Cooks and LeeAnn Sutherland, two doctoral students at the University of Michigan provided extensive critical feedback on the manuscript as we worked through the editing process. Dianne Haft painstakingly proofread the entire manuscript and fixed a number of technical difficulties that we encountered. We would have been lost without her assistance.

The staff at Lawrence Erlbaum Associates has been tremendously supportive. Lori Hawver guided us—with great patience—through the process of preparing the manuscript for publication. Our editor, Naomi Silverman, provided substantive feedback, moral support, and good humor. And Nadine Simms spent countless hours with this manuscript. Her diligence, patience, and support is much appreciated. They were a pleasure to work with.

Deborah Dillon, Erin O'Brien, John Moje, and Avery Moje put up with us at home, as we wrote, edited, proofread, and struggled with technical difficulties. Thank you for giving us time, support, and pleasant distractions as we put this book together.

And finally, the young people and teachers who let us study in their classrooms, homes, churches, and communities deserve our gratitude and respect. This book, of course, would not be possible, and indeed, would be pointless without them.

—*Elizabeth B. Moje*
—*David G. O'Brien*

I

Framing Secondary and Adolescent Literacy Research

1

Situating Secondary School Literacy Research

David W. Moore
Arizona State University West

John E. Readence
University of Nevada–Las Vegas

Since the early 1980s, scholars have advanced multiple approaches for examining teaching–learning processes. Inquiries into literacy now take many forms, and multiplicity and pluralism are emerging as characteristics of the field (Beach, Green, Kamil, & Shanahan, 1992). Secondary school literacy research possibilities have increased along with this overall movement.

Published debates about the different approaches to educational research in general (e.g., Smith & Heshusius, 1986) and secondary school literacy research in particular (e.g., Alvermann & Dillon, 1991; Anderson & West, 1995; Myers, 1995; Roller, 1991) have led to concerns about the nature of scholarly discourse. After advocates began asserting the legitimacy of particular approaches—and challenging the legitimacy of others—members of the research community expressed anxieties about paradigm wars (Gage, 1989; Stanovich, 1990), insular fragmentation (Howe & Eisenhart, 1990), and balkanization (Smith, 1997). Some feared that researchers would gather in like-minded camps, communicate primarily among themselves while talking past others, and consider the contributions of others only with dissent and contempt or indifference and apathy. Indeed, as we wrote the first draft of this chapter during July 1997, postings on the National Reading Conference (NRC) e-mail listserv attested to the vehemence among some literacy researchers working with disparate approaches. One participant worried that NRC members were becoming hostile toward researchers employing traditional approaches. Another quickly replied that

NRC members had been hostile to many, if not most, qualitative researchers and that the traditionalists' concerns were ludicrous.

Like many, we value openness in a world of multiplicity. Demonizing researchers from alternative approaches is counterproductive. Being open to diverse research enhances the potential for improving insights and making visible currently unseen aspects. An inclusive attitude improves opportunities for enriching ideas about secondary school literacy, making sense of its complexities, and generating action.

Valuing the overall idea of multiple research approaches is one thing; understanding them is another. Research comes from diverse traditions and perspectives. Blithely assimilating genuinely different ideas into preconceived categories is professionally irresponsible. Taking seriously what others are saying and engaging their thinking on their own terms is a professional responsibility (Donmoyer, 1996). Situating research is an important part of understanding it.

The remainder of this chapter contains four sections. The first section presents a way to situate secondary school literacy research according to four approaches. The approaches are distinguished by their underlying metaphors and goals. We sketch historical backgrounds of each approach, describe a study that exemplifies it, and comment on the exemplification. The second section shows how secondary school literacy research can be situated by examining perspectives suggested by studies' terminology. The third section catalogues numerous additional possibilities for situating secondary school literacy research. We conclude with a final word.

RESEARCH APPROACHES

Think of the Grand Canyon. You can think of this natural wonder's 1-mile depth, 10-mile width, and 275-mile length in multiple ways. You might concentrate on its physical dimensions, or you might celebrate its aesthetics. People such as air-tour operators, land developers, and hydroelectric producers seem to think of the canyon differently than amateur river rafters, backpackers, and photographers. Geologists and poets examine the canyon in fundamentally different ways. Looking at the Grand Canyon as a revenue source, an excursion site, a sublime inspiration, a land formation, a laboratory of climate variation, and a record of human settlement are some of the possibilities. Like those who examine the Grand Canyon, secondary school literacy researchers approach phenomena differently.

In this section, we concentrate on metaphor and goal as devices for situating secondary school literacy researchers' approaches to phenomena. We think of metaphor and goal as basic navigational aids, as ways to enter and explore intellectual territories. They provide entry points and help establish directional bearings. We find metaphors and goals to be manageable and productive tools; they get us off to a good start when making sense of the overall theoretical orientations, research questions, methodologies, and outcomes of secondary school literacy research.

Metaphors are vehicles of thought and communication that chart mental domains by comparing phenomena (Lakoff & Johnson, 1980; Ortony, 1993). To name a few possibilities, teaching–learning processes can be thought of metaphorically as master–apprentice relationships (Brown, Collins, & Duguid, 1989) and as scaffolding (Langer & Applebee, 1986); language can be viewed as a conduit (Reddy, 1993) and as a transaction (Rosenblatt, 1978); and readers can be thought of as builders, lifelong learners, and participants (Moore, 1998).

Goals indicate researchers' general intentions. They address the purpose, or aim, of a study. Just as knowing the goal, or object, of a card game reveals much about it, knowing the goal of inquiry reveals much about a researcher's language game. Goals suggest where a study is headed.

Metaphors and goals readily combine. To illustrate, the Grand Canyon can be thought of metaphorically as a treasure, and one's goal could be to preserve or exploit it. The Grand Canyon can be considered as an excursion site, and one's goal could be to limit or maximize experiences there.

As two individuals involved with secondary school literacy since the early 1970s and interested in its history since the early 1980s (Moore, Readence, & Rickelman, 1983), we sequence our description of the four research approaches presented here in the chronological order in which they became readily visible to us. Our interpretation of secondary school literacy research published in mainstream outlets is that the tendency to predict patterns dominated from the early 1900s through the early 1980s. A shift occurred in the 1980s as many researchers adopted ethnographic and hermeneutic modes of inquiry and began interpreting literacy experiences. Emphasis on the reform of power relations also rose in the 1980s as literacy educators began resisting and contesting oppression. The 1990s began witnessing research efforts to interrupt the turbulence of literacy practices and create spaces for multiple possibilities. Alignments between the metaphors and goals that characterize the four research approaches we present in this section are as follows:

Goal	_Metaphor_
Predict	Pattern
Interpret	Experience
Reform	Power
Interrupt	Turbulence

Predicting Patterns

Predicting patterns is based on the metaphor of ordered systems. Researchers who embody this approach attempt to discern the regularities of literate actions and literacy learning. They seek to learn the design underlying humanity and nature. Knowing the consistent patterns of literacy helps educators anticipate the effects of future actions.

Researchers seeking to predict patterns view the world in mechanical terms, searching for insights into the running of teaching–learning procedures. They might look at education as a complicated assembly line and their role as discovering the levers that control certain functions. They might see the mind as a computerlike information-processing device that encodes, stores, retrieves, and outputs data. Or they might see the teacher–student relationship as a medical doctor–patient one, with the doctor diagnosing conditions and prescribing treatments.

Those who predict patterns set out to produce generalizations that are universally applicable. They act on a scientific basis, applying when possible principles and methods of research such as randomization, controlled settings, and hypothesis testing that are found in the natural sciences. Researchers intending to predict patterns among actions and conditions concentrate on cause–effect relationships, searching for variables that reliably determine or at least regularly occur with one another.

Background Sketch

Educational researchers began predicting patterns in the early 1900s when they sought the most efficient ways to run schools, looking for connections between instructional inputs and outputs. Those promoting efficiency in secondary school literacy, such as William S. Gray (1948), devised survey instruments to assess the achievement of students. Following the educational-measurement dictates and advocacy of Edward L. Thorndike (1917), social efficiency educators produced numerous tests, scales, and formulas to determine instructional practices that resulted in the highest achievement. The search today for best practices and what works is in line with this search for behavioral patterns that lead to the most efficient learning.

Along with the school efficiency movement, early psychological research in internal reading processes sought to predict patterns. The belief that thinking consisted of patterned connections that needed to be separately triggered and trained was dominant in educational research throughout the first half of the 1900s. Researchers intended to reduce thought processes such as reading into predictable components. Thorndike's *Reading as*

Reasoning, a very influential report published in 1917, expressed this patterned, mechanistic view as follows:

> Reading is a very elaborate procedure, involving the weighing of many elements in a sentence, their organization in the proper relations one to another, the selection of certain of their connotations and the rejection of others, and the cooperation of many forces to determine final response. (p. 323)

In the past, secondary school literacy researchers have sought numerous patterns. They have looked for consistencies underlying the technical vocabulary of reading materials in academic disciplines, eye-movement training, programmed learning, speed reading, and cloze testing (Baldwin et al.,1992; Moore et al., 1983). They have examined recurring effects on literacy produced by factors such as intelligence, self-concept, and family position along with the effect of instructional interventions such as remedial and accelerated reading classes, mechanical devices, and varied readability of materials (Artley, 1968).

Pattern predictions that predominated in the 1970s and early 1980s emphasized the effects of teaching strategies such as questioning and advance organizers, the effects of learning strategies such as notetaking and imagery, the influence of text and knowledge structure, the role of prior knowledge on inferring text ideas, and metacognitive processing (Alvermann & Moore, 1991; Berger & Robinson, 1982; Pearson, 1992). For instance, studies of adolescents constructing graphic organizers (Barron & Stone, 1974), completing study guides (Vacca, 1975), participating in reciprocal teaching (Palincsar & Brown, 1984), and previewing stories (Graves, Cooke, & LaBerge, 1983) have emphasized patterns of instructional procedures, thinking strategies, and achievement. Researchers hoped to learn how these strategies worked so they could predict their outcome in future situations. The following study exemplifies research oriented toward predicting patterns.

Exemplar.   Dillon (1983) linked the duration of individuals' classroom utterances with the cognitive complexity of their utterances. He transcribed 10-minute samples from each of 27 classroom discussions among high school teachers and students to produce a corpus of 1,364 utterances. Dillon timed the duration of each utterance and, using a taxonomy from Bellack, Kliebard, Hyman, and Smith (1966), he categorized each utterance according to level of cognitive complexity (e.g., defining, explaining, justifying). He implemented a procedure so that scorers' interrater agreements were acceptably high.

Results indicated that duration of classroom speech is related to level of cognition. For all speakers, teachers, students, males, and females, utterances were increasingly longer at successively higher levels of cognitive complexity. Defining a term lasted about 5 seconds on average, whereas justifying an opinion or judgment lasted about 20 seconds on average. Dillon (1983) closed with implications of his results for classroom instruction and management as well as for further research.

Commentary.   Dillon (1983) used his results to predict classroom actions. He claimed a pattern among duration of speech and level of thinking that educators could count on finding in other situations. He implied warrant for this claim through the application of systematic scientific inquiry procedures. This somewhat brief report exemplifies the numerous attempts to predict patterns that dominated secondary school literacy research.

Alvermann and Moore's (1991) review of secondary school reading research demonstrates the predominance of the pattern metaphor typified by Dillon's (1983) study. This review concluded in one part that: "The experimental research on secondary reading practices suggests moderate support for most of the teaching and learning strategies reviewed here when they are used under conditions similar to those employed by the research" (p. 964). In other words, the behaviors and outcomes of questioning, graphic organizing, notetaking, and so on followed a predictable pattern—as long as classroom conditions approximate research conditions. Alvermann and Moore's (1991) review also examined reading practices actually occurring in secondary classrooms and divided the practices between *Universals* and *Regularities*, pointing to recurring patterns such as emphases on factual information and teacher governance of information. Predicting patterns clearly predominated secondary school literacy research from its beginnings through the 1980s.

Interpreting Experience

The metaphor of literacy and literacy learning as experience began entering the research scene in the 1980s. The metaphor of experience focuses attention on lived-through events and the meanings people make of them. Researchers who interpret experience seek insights into how people define the situations they undergo. These researchers gain access to educational situations and issues by explaining how people see themselves participating in them. Rather than looking at people as following patterns that structure their literate actions and classroom dynamics, interpretive researchers look at people as artists or workers who construct literacy worlds and act accordingly.

One highly visible set of interpretive studies centers about readers' aesthetic experiences. Stimulated by Rosenblatt's (1978) work, researchers focused on readers' thoughts and feelings about the experience—the lived event—of reading more than on what they carried away from the reading. Examinations of literary experiences focused on the present tense; researchers sought insights into what readers personally and vicariously thought and felt during the act.

An even larger set of interpretive studies concentrates on readers' social experiences. Based on pioneering treatises derived from the social sciences (Erickson, 1986; Green, 1983b), these studies portrayed the meanings individuals make of their interpersonal face-to-face actions. A basic assumption of these studies was that people act according to the meanings they construct, taking up roles as teachers, students, readers, and writers according to their definitions of the situation. For instance, students who answer teachers' factual questions about passages construct particular ways of thinking about what teachers want, why it is wanted, and how to reply.

Background Sketch

The treatment of students interacting in classrooms by the American Educational Research Association's *Handbooks of Research on Teaching* offers good benchmarks for the emergence of interpretive research. In the first handbook, Medley and Mitzel (1963) reviewed studies reporting how patterns of classroom interactions such as question asking and answering influenced the time students had for learning. The second handbook contained Rosenshine and Furst's (1973) review of how observed teaching functions affected what students learned. The third handbook contained three chapters indicating the beginnings of classroom experience interpretations. Cazden (1986) summarized work on classroom discourse, showing how perceptions affected classroom interactions. Erickson (1986) presented a thorough account of the conduct of qualitative research, and Evertson and Green (1986) reviewed work on the nature of observational research in classrooms.

Other benchmarks for the emergence of this research involve specific publications. For instance, Barnes, Britton, and Rosen (1971) showed how students in Great Britain shaped their language to fit their school situations, and Lincoln and Guba (1985) published an influential guide to conducting research in natural settings. Specifically with regard to secondary school reading, Bloome (1987b) presented a communication frame teachers and students jointly constructed for interacting with text that was characterized by text reproduction, procedural display, cataloguing, and a passive stance toward extended text. Hinchman (1987) showed how secondary teachers differed in their classroom uses of print. And Dillon (1989) described a teacher and his students in a low-track English classroom jointly construct-ing an effective learning environment.

As noted in the introduction to this chapter, authorities have criticized and debated the value of alternative approaches to research. Several re-searchers have portrayed the personal and professional turmoil they en-countered during the middle and late 1980s when moving from the dominant approach of predicting patterns to the emerging one of interpreting experiences (Collins & Collins, 1992; Fleischer, 1994; Heshusius & Ballard, 1996). Erickson (1986), who frequently is cited as an authority on interpre-tive research, shared a telling story of the turmoil accompanying interpretive research's emergence in education. Erickson reported that a well-known re-searcher devoted to predicting patterns took a common one-liner of the times, "Real men don't eat quiche," modified it to "Real men don't do ethnog-raphy," and sent it out for his colleagues' amusement. Erickson (1996) re-ported finding the one-liner funny because it ironically called attention to the power wielded by those devoted to "prediction and control" (p. 158); he called interpretive research on teaching "not only an alternative method, but an alternative view of how society works, and of how schools, classrooms, teachers, and students work in society" (p. 158); and he pointed to interpre-tive research as an alternative "form of continuing education and institu-tional transformation" (p. 158). The following study exemplifies the interpretation of secondary school literacy experiences.

Exemplar.   Prentiss (1995) posed the question: "How do students view their lived experiences in an advanced high school English class?" (p. 27). To answer this, she conducted a three-stage multilayered analysis. Prentiss first traced the general pattern of literacy events made available to students during one semester. She identified regularly occurring events such as storytelling, writing letters, and discussing novels. During this stage of analysis she noted that the teacher's stated goals for the events and the re-sources made available for accomplishing the goals contextualized what happened. For instance, the goal for storytelling was to explore interpreta-tions of text. The resources made available for accomplishing this goal in-cluded in-class and outside-of-class reading assignments, small-group production of an oral story, and a field trip to a musical production.

In the second stage of analysis, Prentiss (1995) portrayed students' specific opportunities for participating in the events. Such portrayals are important because people become environments for each other during interactions. Considering participation structures led Prentiss to determine norms such as when students asked questions, what counted as reading and writing, and who had the authority to verify the meanings participants produced.

Prentiss' (1995) third stage of analysis drew on data from interviews and student essays to present student beliefs about the literacy events. She showed that some students believed they could interpret text differently than the teacher, while others believed that their interpretations needed to match that of the teacher. In addition, many students reported that the class was comfortable and supportive, with no intimidation by the teacher or other students.

One final feature of Prentiss' study (1995) deserves mention. Prentiss—like many other interpretive researchers—described forces that can shape and be shaped by contexts for literacy. The shaping force she highlighted was students' previous experiences. She showed how students invoked past literacy experiences when producing current social situations, and she suggested how, in cyclical fashion, these current situations then were invoked later on. For instance, one student's prior experiences connecting her life with what she read led her to view her current classroom reading and writing assignments as fragmented and meaningless. Prentiss ended the report by underscoring its contribution to understanding students' literacy opportunities in class and students' perceptions of the opportunities.

Commentary.   This study portrayed secondary school literacy events three ways, general patterns (e.g., writing letters), participation structures (e.g., teachers offering final answers to questions), and individuals' definitions of the situation (e.g., some believed that textual interpretations needed to match that of the teacher). Additionally, this study showed how students' experiences in another situation influenced how they took up literacy in this one.

Many other secondary school literacy interpretive research studies reported in the 1990s could serve as exemplars of the field. For example, Alvermann, O'Brien, and Dillon (1990) portrayed what teachers do when they say they are having discussions of text. Myers (1992) called attention to the differences and similarities of adolescents' school and personal literacy practices. Moje (1996) focused on the relationship a teacher established with her students and how it, combined with beliefs about subject matter and schooling, mediated classroom literacy practices. Sperling and Woodlief (1997) examined the creation of classroom communities that supported writing in an urban and a suburban school.

As literacy researchers in the 1980s were influenced by social psychologists and cultural anthropologists such as Vygotsky, Cole, Lave, and Heath, more and more secondary school literacy research attention turned to the social contexts of literacy (Moore, 1996). However, many researchers tended to predict patterns among these contexts rather than interpret experiences associated with them. For instance, three research-based efforts to promote reading comprehension through students and teachers jointly verbalizing their thought processes include reciprocal teaching (Palinscar & Brown, 1984), collaborative strategy instruction (Anderson & Roit, 1993), and questioning the author (Beck, McKeown, Worthy, Sandora, & Kucan, 1996). These efforts capitalize on social interactions, but they do not report what the students make of the situation. These research emphases are on optimizing patterns of social interaction more than on interpreting how students are experiencing them. When situating secondary school literacy research, it is important to realize that many studies emphasizing social contexts do not emphasize individuals' interpretations of them.

Reforming Power

The metaphor of literacy as power foregrounds issues of control, authority, and privilege. Thinking of literacy as power calls politics to mind; it emphasizes ideology and factionalism. Researchers who embody this metaphor often assume that they should work to change the world, not just analyze it or improve the mainstream. They believe in reform, in having an agenda for social action, in planning to reconstruct social situations.

Many working to reform the power relations of literacy do so explicitly in a critical mode. Critical researchers generally work from the premise that certain groups in any society are privileged and that the privileged ones oppress others (Kincheloe & McLaren, 1994). Oppression is especially forceful when subordinates accept their unequal status as natural, necessary, or inevitable. Given this assumption, critical researchers challenge the status quo. They proclaim an openly ideological edge to their efforts as they confront injustice and seek to empower individuals who have been marginalized and silenced. They address societal, political, legal, and economic barriers to literacy.

Background Sketch

Revisionist educational historians of the 1970s presented much early work emphasizing power relations that had indirect effects on literacy. For instance, Katz (1971) connected privileged and powerful members of society with school administration. He portrayed bureaucratic school structures, compulsory attendance, and curricular tracks as oppressive policies of the middle 1880s imposed on poor and ethnic minorities to provide industrial workers.

Secondary school literacy research examining power relations and ac-companying reform efforts often trace their roots to the writings of Freire (1993; Freire & Macedo, 1987). An adult educator and social activist, Freire worked for empowerment. He invited learners to write and read about their experiences in relation to their subservient positions in the world. In order to read the word, then, students needed to read the world. Scholars in the United States such as Henry Giroux and Ira Shor followed Freire in seeking opportunities for marginalized people to liberate them-selves by resisting, contesting, and transforming subjugation.

Contemporary writers who have characterized literacy as power argue that it mainly is about the hidden construction of unequal identities and re-lationships. Street (1995) named this view of literacy *ideological*, contrasting it with an *autonomous* view, to emphasize how technical individualistic as-pects of reading and writing always are embedded in the power relations of the larger society. The critical discourse analysis work reviewed by Luke (1995/1996) represents much of this thinking. Additional prominent writ-ers who implicated literacy in power relations include Anyon, Apple, Fairclough, Gee, Grumet, hooks, and McLaren.

Secondary school literacy studies embodying the metaphor of power be-gan appearing sporadically in research outlets in the late 1970s and early 1980s. Most of this research has been published in the 1990s. For instance, Barbieri (1995) reported her ongoing efforts to help her students use literacy while questioning stereotypical gendered roles. Schultz (1996) described how she initially set out to focus on the literacy practices that female stu-dents brought with them into their future workplaces but redirected her re-search questions with a critical orientation to look at the ways students use literacy to help them imagine and plan for their futures. Fecho (1998) re-ported his experiences as a Euro-American teacher who explored complex and often contradictory relations between language and power with his Af-rican-American students. And Cohen, Christman, and Gold (1998) studied how listening to students' voices supported school change efforts and how having students participate in these efforts supported their literacy learning. The following study exemplifies a reform-minded examination of power re-lations during talk about texts in a secondary school.

Exemplar.   Gutierrez, Rymes, and Larson (1995) examined a class-room literacy event that centered on a teacher quizzing students on current events taken from the day's newspaper. Students were to raise their hands when they could answer the teacher's questions about the news. This in-structional format reflected common hierarchical teaching procedures ac-centuating individuals' efforts.

The newspaper contents identified for quizzing defined information about the world that the teacher considered worth knowing. For instance, one question aimed at a story of a whale swimming upriver from the San Francisco Bay and staying near Petaluma, California. This happening was presented on the front page of the newspaper, a condition that spoke more about attempts to sell newspapers than to provide meaningful information and insights about the world. When some students indicated that they knew about a recent kidnaping and murder in Petaluma, the teacher continued probing for a different answer because the crimes were not described in the day's paper. This practice indicated the role the teacher assumed as the controller of events as well as the relayer of knowledge.

Not all students participated in the routine of trying to guess what was in the newspaper; a few participated in an underlife that blocked the academic roles expected of them. A few students began joking about what might have happened in Petaluma ("they peed in the river"), indicating that some had moved away from the teacher's intentions to their own. Some students began associating terms from the teacher's discourse with terms that fit their worlds. When asked about the 1954 *Brown versus Board of Education* ruling, some students began associating with another *Brown*, James Brown the musician. Two separate discourses then functioned concurrently: The teacher's search for right answers to current events questions occurred along with the students' wordplay about what the teacher mentioned. These two discourses, defined by Gutierrez et al. (1995) as *script* and *counterscript*, limited an exchange of ideas.

Although the teacher and student scripts typically remained distinct during the current events quizzing, a new script occasionally became apparent. At one point during the *Brown versus Board of Education* talk, a student asked, "What if the kid's half White and half Black where do they g- what school do they go to?" (Gutierrez et al., 1995, p. 465). At this point, the teacher changed his discursive practice and explained school segregation policies of the time. This sequence fit neither the pattern of the teacher's quiz nor students' word associations. It was a transformed context that both the teacher and student produced. The researchers noted that this new *third space*, neither script nor counterscript, was responsive/collaborative and provided teachers and students an alternative to traditional classroom patterns defined by typical power relations.

Commentary.   This study challenged "the critical social scientist to move more fluidly between theory and classroom life to understand more richly how the power relations in classrooms unfold in routine activity" (Gutierrez et al., 1995, p. 448). It showed minority students being disenfranchised through hierarchical monologic language patterns that escaped the notice of the study participants. It offered third space as a solution to the limited exchange of ideas about what had been read.

Attempts to enfranchise those on the margins of society by changing classroom conditions no doubt will continue, although the direction is unclear. As Lesley (1997) reported, "Critical literacy simply does not come about in a predictable, orderly fashion" (p. 423). Lesley compared critical literacy instruction to a difficult dance, calling attention to the many unintended, unforseen, and complicated moves associated with her attempts to empower those in her class. For instance, she remained silent during class discussions about race because she did not want to impose her views. But her silence only complicated issues about why she chose a politically charged text to discuss. Her report suggests why many who addressed literacy as power in the middle 1990s began refining the underlying metaphor as turbulence.

Interrupting Turbulence

Thinking of literacy as turbulence accentuates uncontrollable, unpredictable, and unstable conditions. This metaphor emphasizes chaos and dissonance. It carries a sense of contingent and provisional realities, a world continually shifting. Many have commented on the buzzing, booming confusion of life, but early efforts typically focused on producing guides like systems analysis to classify, explain, and eventually predict heretofore unseen patterns. Those who interrupt turbulence scorn efforts to characterize literacy processes as knowable and unified systems; these researchers celebrate the mutable and tentative nature of literacy. They disdain efforts to present mental and social processes as coherent unified wholes. Researchers who set out to interrupt the turbulence of literacy momentarily freeze-frame reading and writing events, interrogating the moment from multiple perspectives.

Researchers who interrupt ask "What's wrong with this picture?" and attempt to unmask the power that underlies what is happening (Brodkey, 1992). For instance, researchers interrupt attempts to empower students by inquiring into unintended consequences. What happens during well-meaning attempts to give girls a greater voice during classroom discussions? What happens during process writing events when teachers publicly display students' deep-seated personal expressions about issues such as race relations and friendships? Efforts to empower others can be seen as ways of actually perpetuating oppression because power is a force that people appropriate rather than something that can be handed over (Orner, 1992). Change agents ironically might assume power over the disenfranchised.

Researchers intent on interrupting the turbulence of literacy practices assume human discourse represents the world and the representation always serves someone's interests. Consequently, change-oriented researchers who interrupt turbulence continually interrogate discursive practices, including their own. They seek "to keep things in process, to disrupt, to keep the system in play, to set up procedures to continually demystify the realities we create, to fight the tendency for our categories to congeal" (Lather, 1992, p. 96). For instance, poststructural researchers wonder who should speak for those being studied. They see great indignity in speaking for others, wondering who has the authority—much less the capacity—to render another's life appropriately. They also wonder what is lost when offering consistently tidy accounts of phenomena.

Background Sketch

Studies interrupting turbulence began appearing in secondary school literacy research outlets in the 1990s as poststructuralist theorizing entered the picture. Many who position themselves this way refer to early work by Ellsworth (1989), who told of a university course she designed and taught on racism and sexism. Bothered by the silences and muted voices of her students, Ellsworth posed a key poststructuralist issue in the title of her paper, *Why Doesn't This Feel Empowering?* She examined what happens when people wield emancipatory authority, the power to empower others.

Those who interrupt turbulence in literacy draw on postmodern thinking. Inspired by the philosophical treatises of writers such as Derrida, Lyotard, and Foucault and related educational work by writers such as Davies, Lather, Orner, and Usher and Edwards, postmodern poststructuralist theorists problematize notions of progress and improvement, wondering about whose agenda is being forwarded (Anyon, 1994). The following study illustrates how researchers interrupt the turbulence of literacy reform.

Exemplar.   Alvermann, Commeyras, Young, Randall, and Hinson (1997) focused on the difficulties encountered when attempting to alter gendered inequities during text-based discussions. The study participants examined their own practices in a graduate-level content literacy class and in a seventh- and an eighth-grade language arts class. Three members of the research team were university-based women interested in feminist theories of teaching and research, and two members (one male and one female) were middle school teachers willing to participate in a feminist-based study without necessarily considering themselves feminists.

The researchers collected and analyzed data in a way that was "recursive, layered, multi-voiced, ideologically revealing, and personal" (Alvermann et al., 1997, p. 100). They included data such as fieldnotes, journals, videotaped transcripts of classroom events, personal histories, and interviews. Each time data were analyzed, texts were generated in the form of narrative vignettes, memos, and preliminary reports. This layering of data promoted writing as a mode of learning throughout the project rather than just during the final write-up. It resulted in the team identifying four discursive practices manifested in the classroom talk about texts they observed (a) self-deprecating talk (e.g., "Ellen announces that she's 'not very good at this.'" p. 86), (b) discriminatory talk (e.g., "Our friend from Taiwan … who is a super sweet person," p. 86), (c) exclusionary talk (e.g., "It's a proven fact women are smarter," p. 89), and (d) talk desiring neutrality (e.g., "Where do I cross the line between discussing literature and discussing family values and marital relationships that in this community I better stay away from?" p. 92).

As stated in the title of this chapter, addressing the inequities of gendered discursive practices during classroom talk about texts was easy to think about but difficult to do. One difficulty involved seeing gendered communications as emanating from power differentials rather than only from what males and females produced. Another difficulty was with intervening in interpersonal processes that some viewed as inalienable rights. Participating in a plan of action that teachers had second thoughts about and experiencing self-doubts about teaching and researching from feminist perspectives also posed problems during the study.

The researchers' parting insights, which contained sections attributed to each individual author, presented first-person accounts of what each considered significant about his or her research experience. Some of the significant outcomes included (a) realizing the potential ironies when people in authoritative positions downplayed their authority; (b) questioning the ways gender and power roles mixed with individuals' personalities; (c) holding concerns about the premiums placed on comfort in teaching and research settings; (d) appreciating opportunities to overcome traditional academic hierarchies and work as friends and equals; and (e) acknowledging the magnitude of the resources and the personal and professional risks entailed in interrupting traditional social practices. In reflecting on the value of the research, Alvermann et al. (1997) stressed how it helped them make more sense of their lives as teachers, researchers, and students and encouraged others to begin similar experiences.

Commentary.   This study featured many ways to interrupt the turbulence of traditional teaching and research practices. The research team's studying *across* to themselves rather than *down* to their students indicates concern with power. Having each member of the research team write and be credited with separate sections rather than presenting a unified voice throughout the report portrays additional concerns about exerting power over the representation of others. Attempts to unmask power relations embedded in the project are evident in the concerns expressed about attempting to change others' deeply held beliefs and about moving forward in a plan that some began to question.

As of this writing, few studies have interrupted and interrogated secondary school literacy teaching—learning processes, although we suspect that more will be coming. For instance, Dressman (1993) presented a fictional portrait of teaching that called attention to ways literacy workshops privilege the discursive practices of mainstream students. Finders (1996) uncovered inequities, lack of ownership and engagement, and the negation of girls' personal identities in a mainstream middle school language arts classroom with reading and writing workshops. These findings led her to pose questions about the impact of student-centered pedagogy on students' literacy. Hinchman and Moje (1998) call attention to the contingencies associated with turbulence by their frequent references to multidimensional human beings and multiple literacies, forms of representation, discourses, and memberships and positions in social groups.

PERSPECTIVES

Examining perspectives that are reflected in the terminology of secondary school literacy research is another way to situate the field. The meanings of terms are tied closely to particular perspectives on what is being examined. Knowing that the name people give something often shapes—and is shaped by—their thinking about the phenomenon allows insights into the orientations they hold. For instance, Grand Canyon is a name tied to people's aesthetic sensibilities toward the magnificence of this particular land formation; alternative names historically used such as *The Abyss* and *Canyon of the Colorado* are connected more with pioneers' animosity toward this natural barrier to exploration, settlement, and transportation (Pyne, 1998).

Scholars working in disparate specializations such as cultural psychology (Whorf, 1956), semiotics (Eco, 1984), and critical discourse analysis (Luke, 1995/1996) have called attention to how naming, or wording, ideas is in accord with particular perspectives. For instance, the names secondary school literacy researchers use to represent people in a study imply particular roles and relationships. Calling those who were studied *subjects* indicates that the research had hierarchical relationships and possibly hidden manipulations. Calling those who were studied *informants* implies that those being studied knowingly gave information. *Participants* suggests that those who were studied had a somewhat reciprocal role in the research. *Collaborators* indicates joint involvement and equality in the researcher–researched relationship.

Unlike our taxonomy of research approaches, we do not categorize sets of perspectives reflected by particular terms. In this section we intend only to suggest a way of thinking about a particular aspect of secondary school literacy research because it contains all manner of perspectives. To illustrate, a term used in the early 1900s, *laggards in our schools* (Ayres, 1913), signals an emphasis on the innate slowness of low-achieving students. An early 1980s' label, *students placed at risk*, indicates mismatches between students' cultures, learning preferences, and school environments (Garcia, Pearson, & Jimenez, 1994). The perspective moved from examining learners' shortcomings to examining problems with teaching–learning conditions. *Learning from text* studies in the 1970s emphasized ways for teachers to transmit information or for students to download information as efficiently as possible from single sources. A related term that came later, *learning with texts*, signaled a perspective of students actively constructing and acquiring new ideas from multiple sources (Tierney & Pearson, 1992).

Secondary classrooms devoted to reading instruction moved from housing reading *clinics* and reading *labs* to housing communities of learners. Perspectives changed from medical to sociological ones. As educators in the middle 1990s began to see potentially adverse effects of power and privilege in student-centered situations, classrooms were called sites for *coalitions* or *affinity groups* rather than *safe havens* or *communities* (Hynds, 1997).

Researchers' uses of the terms *sex* and *gender* when accounting for reading vividly illustrates different perspectives (Patterson, 1995). In 1968, Artley included *sex* as a heading for factors related to secondary school reading achievement and summarized reports of reading test score differences between boys and girls. The studies Artley summarized represented attempts to predict patterns of achievement by boys and girls. Moore's (1996) review of secondary school literacy research included a related—yet different—term, *gendered positionings*. This heading indicated researchers' newer inquiries into how teachers and students construct female–male positions during classroom literacy events. It suggested emphases on the literacy experiences, politics, and turbulence associated with boys and girls. Past researchers' perspectives on gender resulted in the mention of test score differences without examining how girls and boys experienced literacy differently, how the differences in experiences and achievement occurred, or what they signified about societal conditions.

During the first half of the 1900s, researchers developing standardized tests had students answer questions and recall passages to indicate their prose comprehension. The educational community then determined which of these modes counted as the best evidence of comprehension. The continuation of multiple-choice question-answering and the demise of recalling information attests to practical decisions about scoring and socially sanctioned views of reading more than to correspondence with reality (Readence & Moore, 1983). Multiple-choice formats became known as *objective* tests, and comprehension research until the mid-1970s concomitantly was characterized by a focus on text-based distanced interactions more than on subjective personal responses to text. For instance, researchers examined the propositions retrieved from artificially structured expository texts more than the feelings elicited from naturally occurring stories. Being objective helped concentrate attention to the aspects of comprehension that were named and diminished attention to aspects not named. Objectivity produced—and was a product of—researchers' perspectives on reading comprehension assessment.

The segments of classroom life that even are named help situate researchers' perspectives. Determining literacy events in the ongoing cycles of classroom action is not a straightforward cut-and-dried enterprise (Green & Meyer, 1990). For instance, *orally reading a short story* might be labeled as an event, but if students discussed the story's contents, then orally read/discuss might be the event and be labeled something like *passage interpretation*. Furthermore, if students wrote responses before and after reading, then the event write/orally read/discuss/write might be called a *reading workshop*. And what if the story immediately followed a related movie? Researchers—usually in concert with classroom individuals—might segment oral reading's identity in the ongoing flow of teaching–learning processes to suit their purposes, but they do not have access to it as an isolated prepackaged entity with preset names.

OTHER POSSIBILITIES

The two preceding sections of this chapter summarize features of the landscape useful for situating secondary school literacy research. However, examining approaches and perspectives as presented here are only two ways among many to situate research. This section notes other possibilities for situating research commonly found in the professional literature. We mention common heuristics, specializations, generalizations and so on mainly to alert readers to these possibilities. Again, we find approaches and perspectives to be manageable and productive devices for situating research; others might value devices such as the following.

Common Heuristics

Several common heuristics are available for marking intellectual territories. One common heuristic is paradigm (Soltis, 1992). Paradigm has been called "the basic belief system or worldview that guides the investigator" (Guba & Lincoln, 1994, p. 105). Positivism, critical theory, and constructivism are paradigms available for categorizing research that have received considerable attention. Other heuristics for distinguishing research include agendas (Mosenthal, 1993), dimensions (Constas, 1998), postures (Wolcott, 1992), rhetorical traditions (Hayes, 1992), and stances (Beach, 1992).

Epistemology, a branch of philosophy that addresses what counts as knowledge, where knowledge is located, and how knowledge increases, offers still another device for mapping research efforts. Studies can be clustered among groups such as hypothetico-deductivism–formalism, realism–essentialism, and poststructuralism–postmodernism (Cunningham & Fitzgerald, 1996).

Specializations

A possibility for situating research that we passed over earlier involves distinctions between quantitative and qualitative research. The following presents some of the major differences between these research categories:

Quantitative	*Qualitative*
• searching for universal laws	• searching for unique meanings
• reductionistic perspective	• holistic perspective
• manipulated setting	• naturalistic setting

Despite these major differences, we did not distinguish quantitative and qualitative domains earlier because the specializations within each one are so striking. To illustrate, quantitative research has been divided convincingly among experimental, ex post facto, and survey designs (Kerlinger, 1964). Qualitative research has been categorized convincingly among biographical life history, phenomenology, grounded theory, ethnography, and case study (Creswell, 1998). Furthermore, researchers affiliated with interpretive anthropology, symbolic interactionism, and interpretive interactionism are joined in their efforts to express the meanings people make of their experiences, but they differ somewhat in the roles they attribute to social and historical influences (Schwandt, 1994). Additionally, one qualitative researcher might tell of member checks and audit trails to verify assertions' trustworthiness, whereas another might publish self-reflexive disruptions of the master narratives controlling her or his thinking. Some qualitative researchers argue for thick description of particular events, and others seek broad views. Considerable differences in qualitative research also are evident in the debate about whether or not novels should count as dissertations (Saks, 1996).

We also did not call attention to feminist research, a possibility that has contributed substantially to theorizing literacy actions. Many feminist researchers share commitments to reflecting on and transforming gender-based power differentials (Fine, 1992), although there are many types of feminisms. The interrupting turbulence exemplar by Alvermann et al. (1997) serves as a good model of one type of feminist research.

Another specialization not mentioned earlier involves teacher-researchers' reform efforts. Teacher-researchers often assume that inquiries will result in insights and suggest practical actions applicable to immediate classroom concerns (Patterson, Santa, Short, & Smith, 1993). For instance, Cone's (1994) research questions came from the experiences and concerns she encountered in a high school English class she taught. Cone reported how reflecting on her practices helped her create an environment where readers of all abilities could succeed.

Disciplinary specializations are additional ways to situate research. For instance, Green (1992) told how researchers from three disciplines examined how one teacher and group of students read and discussed stories. A sociolinguist showed that students' different perceptions of how they were to accomplish the tasks led to differences in their recalls. A literary theorist showed that some students interpreted the basic story lines differently and, in effect, heard different stories. A researcher using propositional analysis concluded that the stories' different memory and inferencing requirements resulted in recall differences. Three different disciplinary specializations led to three different—yet complementary—explanations for the varied amounts of information each student recalled.

Generalizations

Noting the degree to which researchers generalize relationships among phenomena is another possibility for situating research. Much early research can be grouped according to explanatory principles. For instance, numerous studies of the 1960s and 1970s indicated that overtly responding to questions following reading best influenced long-term learning of a passage's gist (Anderson & Biddle, 1975). Many researchers explained such an effect through a levels-of-processing explanatory principle (Craik & Lockhart, 1972).

In another instance, reports of teacher–student interactions revealed highly controlled routines, authoritative governance over what was said, and emphases on factual information (Edwards & Furlong, 1976). Many researchers accounted for such patterns through a social reproduction explanatory principle, claiming that classroom practices reproduced the social class distinctions found outside classrooms (Everhart, 1983).

A possibility for situating research that is similar to grouping studies by explanatory principle involves grouping them by whole–part topical relationships. Outlining whole–part relationships is a common practice especially with early research. For instance, Alvermann and Moore's (1991) headings show three main topics that secondary school literacy researchers pursued, teaching strategies, learning strategies, and actual reading practices. Within each topical domain, more specific topics emerged such as questioning, outlining, and reading practice variation. And within the questioning teaching practice, for example, researchers examined effects with readers of varying abilities, with questions of numerous types placed differently in texts, and with various outcome measures. An outline would look like this:

I. Teaching strategies
   A. Advance organizers
   B. DRA and DRTA
   C. Guided reading and writing
   D. Questioning
      1. Readers of varying abilities
      2. Types placed differently in texts
      3. Outcome measures
II. Learning strategies
   A. Imagery
   B. Notetaking
   C. Outlining
   D. Summarizing
III. Actual reading practices
   A. Reading practice variation
   B. Textbook predominance
   C. Governance of students' encounters with print

Generalizations expressing explanatory principles and whole-part topical relationships can range from elegant wide-ranging ones such as intertextuality (Demory, 1994) and semiotics (Suhor, 1994) to more modest figurative ones such as curricular postholing (Glatthorn, 1994) and webbing (Ogle, 1994). Large-scale, somewhat elegant expressions that have been applied specifically to literacy processes include constructivism (Spivey, 1997), schema theory (Anderson & Pearson, 1984), and transactional theory (Rosenblatt, 1978). Expressions related to instruction include assumptive teaching (Herber, 1978), engagement (Guthrie, McCann, Hynd, & Stahl, 1997), and scaffolding (Langer & Applebee, 1986). Comparing and contrasting studies according to their expressions of explanatory and topical relationships can go far in making sense of the field.

Methodology

This chapter barely mentions research methodology even though methodological decisions are important. Deciding to interview people or to administer a multiple-choice achievement test are decisions made in line with the theoretical perspective that is followed (Jaeger, 1997) and often demarcate types of research.

However, viewing secondary school literacy research initially in terms of metaphors, goals, and perspectives emphasizes content, and we find this emphasis to be productive because it focuses attention on studies' ideas, which are at the heart of the matter (Wolcott, 1992). The contribution of research to secondary school literacy theory, practice, and basic knowledge in large part depends on the quality and significance of the ideas that are presented.

Research Processes

Another possible way to situate research involves emphasizing the ongoing processes of a study. Researchers might be construed as having single unified orientations even though blending frequently is practiced. As Lather (1991) explained, "I place my work in the emancipatory column with great fascination with the implications of deconstruction for the research and teaching that I do in the name of liberation" (p. 7). Interpretive researchers often seek patterns in the actions of people, although these researchers rarely predict future actions. A view that is more nuanced than what we presented here might clarify how researchers merge goals, metaphors, and perspectives over time.

We represented research in terms of polished published reports, but—as literacy educators well know—inquiry products that are written differ substantially from ongoing inquiry processes that are enacted. When recounting her work as a literacy teacher-researcher, Fleischer (1994) noted, "It is not always neat; it tends not to be linear; it cannot be summarized easily; its conduct and its findings are, at times, confusing, and even contradictory"

(p. 86). Representing the ways different approaches and perspectives actually play out during the conduct of secondary school literacy studies is a promising possibility for future efforts.

A FINAL WORD

Many theorists say that people collectively construct reality (Gergen, 1985). People in a community are said to construct their worlds collaboratively by selectively attending to and interpreting events and situations. Researchers, for instance, are said to form possible worlds politically and pragmatically by jointly constructing, naming, and authorizing the contents of their studies.

Thinking of secondary school literacy research as a social construction casts it as inventions and creations rather than discoveries. It positions researchers as producing and conveying impressions of the world rather than uncovering and displaying the realities of the one real world. It helps explain the dynamic fluidity and overlap evident in researchers' efforts—and in observers' efforts to situate such research. We find that using this root metaphor of social construction when viewing the secondary school literacy research landscape clarifies its ever-shifting terrain.

2

Exploring the Context of Secondary Literacy: Literacy in People's Everyday School Lives

David G. O'Brien
Purdue University

Elizabeth B. Moje
University of Michigan

Roger A. Stewart
Boise State University

Since the late 1960s, secondary literacy research has sought to inform rather than to be informed by practice. Cognitively based experimental studies have served as a rationale for a wealth of instructional strategies used to promote and integrate reading and writing into various content disciplines. This body of experimental research has made an impressive contribution to our understanding of basic reading comprehension processes, and we owe a debt to the researchers who contributed to that corpus. Nevertheless, the research—true to the positivist epistemology undergirding it—largely ignored or neutralized the contexts in which secondary school teachers and adolescents live and learn as it attempted to analyze cognitive processes. In fact, practices related to curricular, pedagogical, cultural, assessment, classroom, and disciplinary contexts—contexts that are highlighted throughout this book—were treated as variables to be controlled.

In this chapter, we argue that literacy is negotiated and constructed by people in the contexts of their lives inside and outside of secondary schools, keeping in mind that the secondary school is a socioculturally and historically situated institution. We have divided our discussion of contexts of secondary school literacy into three sections. In the first section, we discuss what we call macrocontexts, or broad contexts, of schools: curriculum, school culture, pedagogy, and assessment. Next, we discuss the microcontexts of schools, centered in what happens in classrooms, but also in what happens in adolescents' interactions and practices out of classrooms, in the hallways of the school, in their extracurricular activities, and in their homes. In the final section, we discuss how changing technologies and information systems have changed our world and, consequently represent a context for examining secondary literacy.

In practice, of course, each of these contexts is present in the others; teacher–student interactions, for example, cannot be separated from curricula, pedagogy, or school culture. Consequently, there is some overlap in our discussion, but we believe that examining each of these contexts allows us to become aware of the complexities of theorizing, teaching, and researching secondary school literacy.

MACROCONTEXTS OF SECONDARY SCHOOL LITERACY

We begin this section by discussing the context of the secondary school curriculum and then move to school culture, pedagogy, and assessment.

Literacy and the Curriculum

Reports addressing secondary education (Boyer, 1983; Cusick, 1983; Goodlad, 1984; Powell, Farrar, & Cohen, 1985; Sedlak, Wheeler, Pullin, & Cusick, 1986; Sizer, 1985, 1992, 1996) show that the enacted and experienced secondary curriculum (Gehrke, Knapp, & Sirotnik, 1992) is relatively routine and standardized across the country. Despite this constancy within the walls of classrooms and schools, curriculum scholars view curriculum in diverse ways (Pinar, 1988; Pinar, Reynolds, Slattery, & Taubman, 1996). This range of perspectives on curriculum has significant impact on how teachers and students view literacy, but perhaps the most predominant perspective is shaped by technocratic rationality—the view that curricular components can be identified, related to one another, and put into a system to predict uniform outcomes like achievement test performance (Giroux, 1988b; Pinar et al., 1996).

Technocratic Rationality.   In general, a technocratic rationality drives curriculum planning, design, and implementation in schools in the

United States (Apple, 1993). Curriculum, when defined within a technocratic rationality framework, includes a body of knowledge and ways of teaching knowledge that are officially sanctioned and managed by content subcultures (Hargreaves, 1994; Pinar et al., 1996). Technocratic rationality is evident not only in the substance of the formal curriculum but the way in which it is framed, especially in secondary schools: Six or seven 50-min class periods provide forums in which an approved knowledge base, divided into subject classes, is dispensed. The success of the curriculum is gauged by the efficient coverage of content (Boyer, 1983; McLaughlin & Talbert, 1990; Powell et al., 1985; Sedlak et al., 1986).

Technocratic rationality positions literacy as a tool to help students acquire information represented in officially sanctioned texts that legitimatize certain kinds of knowledge and particular ways to teach that knowledge (Apple, 1988, 1993, 1996; Apple & Christian-Smith, 1991; Giroux, 1988b). The primacy of content coverage assigns literacy to the level of a technician's tool that can be used to accomplish prescribed institutional ends. Students are assigned reading in board-certified textbooks, and secondary literacy specialists serve as technicians who show content teachers how to use strategies that help teachers teach and students learn the content in those textbooks. Within the context of a technocratic rationality, literacy is a tool for students and teachers to replicate the prescribed knowledge base. For example, acronym strategies (e.g., Survey, Question, Read, Recite, Review [SQ3R]; Robinson, 1941; Predict, Organize, Rehearse, Practice, Evaluate [PORPE]; Simpson, 1986) and instructional frameworks (e.g., pre-, during-, and post- phases) are designed to increase the efficiency with which students process information contained in textbooks. The focus on efficiency and replication has also shaped the research base that supports strategies instruction in the secondary content areas.

Content literacy research and strategies, when appropriated within this curricular and pedagogical context, also become tools for meeting the broad technical goals of the secondary school curricula. As long as curricula were viewed as relatively homogeneous and remain underpinned by technical rationality, secondary literacy educators were able to remain comfortable in their belief that universal strategies could be universally applied within homogenized curricula (O'Brien, Stewart, & Moje, 1995). Thus, simply informing teachers of the availability of these strategies on the premise that they would speed content coverage and acquisition has seemed to be a logical means for infusing content literacy strategies into secondary classrooms. In the context of an increasingly fragmented, information-based society, however, perspectives on curricula have broadened and diversified, the complexities of teaching and schooling have become more evident, and the infusion model has struggled (O'Brien et al., 1995; Ratekin, Simpson, Alvermann, & Dishner, 1985), making alternative models necessary.

For example, rather than being viewed as a prescribed core of knowledge, curriculum can be viewed as a hidden set of values, expectations, and routines. Within this perspective, literacy and language are integral to helping students understand themselves and construct their racial, ethnic, and gendered identities within school culture. On yet another level, curriculum is viewed as a set of lived experiences of teachers and students (Pinar, 1988). Within this perspective, literacy is also viewed as a vehicle through which students construct their social and cultural identities (Finders, 1996; Rubin, 1995). Most recently, curriculum has been conceptualized as discourse, specifically as discursive practice that follows certain rules to construct the objects it studies (Pinar et al., 1996).

The many different ways of conceptualizing curriculum have a significant impact on whether literacy is viewed as a beneficial learning tool applied to typical curriculum texts, a socially constructed vehicle for circumventing or undermining politically dominant views of legitimate knowledge, a vehicle for constructing meaning, or an avenue for shaping the total school experience. How the curriculum is enacted by teachers and taken up by students, then, can be thought of as a context that shapes how literacy gets used in secondary school classrooms.

Subject Area Divisions.   A number of scholars assert that subject matter is the most comprehensive organizer and determiner of the secondary school curriculum (cf. Alvermann & Moore, 1991; Gehrke et al., 1992), and that subject area divisions are seldom questioned (Goodson, 1994; Lee, Bryk, & Smith, 1993). The unquestioned dominance of a curriculum divided into subject areas is grounded in the positivistic assumption that knowledge can be objectified, verified, and best disseminated via clearly compartmentalized disciplines to meet two goals: (a) to transmit knowledge judged as important by academics, and (b) to inculcate certain discourses, or forms and methods of seeing, arguing, and discussing the content indigenous to disciplines (Gee, 1996; Popkewitz, 1991; Posner, 1988).

The first goal, most closely aligned with technocratic rationality, is the one to which content literacy practices have been traditionally associated. Literacy educators strive to fit various strategies (based on readers' prior knowledge, interest in the subject, an underlying adaptable set of comprehension processes, strategic thinking, and human language capabilities) to the content area by targeting certain features of the texts or teaching and learning practices common within a discipline. This model, however, where content literacy experts provide content teachers with strategies from afar without attending to the particular discourse community in which the strategy is to be deployed, has met with resistance from pre- and in-service teachers alike (Holt-Reynolds, 1992; O'Brien & Stewart, 1990; O'Brien et al., 1995; Ratekin et al., 1985). The primacy of subject areas, the status hierarchy of subject areas (cf. Ball & Lacey, 1984; Grossman & Stodolsky, 1995), and the expectations these engender in students and teachers have inhibited attempts at infusing literacy into secondary school classrooms (O'Brien et al., 1995). Moreover, as Holt-Reynolds (1999) argued, many content-area teachers have subject matter expertise but do not have the knowledge of how to model and share that expertise with their students, in other words, to develop pedagogical content knowledge (Shulman, 1987). Thus, a new model or perspective on secondary literacy is needed; such a model will need to foreground the exploration of subject divisions as subcultures, or discourse communities. We discuss the concepts of subject subcultures and discourse communities further and offer ideas for new research directions in the section devoted to school culture.

Literacy and School Culture

Schools, like the broader communities in which they exist, have their own bodies of cultural knowledge and ways of communicating and legitimizing that knowledge (Mercer, 1992). We define secondary school culture as the representation of how individuals in the secondary institution construct their teaching and learning lives within a system based on partially shared beliefs, practices, symbols, and knowledges (Marcus, 1986).

This cultural perspective is based on the premise that all secondary schools share some organizational, political, and philosophical foundations (Cuban, 1984; Cusick, 1983; Lieberman & Miller, 1992; Sedlak et al., 1986) even though each school has a distinct cultural stamp due to its unique social organization, expectations, administrative structure, community members, and values of the community in which the school is situated (Metz, 1990). Hence, any efforts at changing or reconceptualizing the curriculum or its pedagogy, such as introducing various literacy practices or creating situations favoring certain literacy practices, must attend to the broad cultural aspects common to the secondary school institution; the beliefs, values, and practices of people who work there; and the unique cultural aspects of individual secondary school settings. To understand how we might construct and better conceptualize literacy practices in these schools, we must understand the compatibility or incompatibility between the intentions and values of change agents like content literacy specialists and persons who work in the schools and hold membership in its cultural beliefs and practices.

Teaching and Studenting as Work.   Secondary teachers, like
other workers, shape their beliefs and actions in relation to the structures,
policies, and traditions of the workday and the school as an historically situated institution (Cuban, 1984, 1986; Cusick, 1983; McLaughlin & Talbert,
1990; Rosenholtz, 1989). As a result of institutional constraints and interactions with students, peers, and administrators, teachers construct unique
work cultures. Their work is primarily conducted within one room, with
multiple classes of students. Daily, teachers are faced with the contradictory
objectives of teaching large numbers of students while attending to students' individual needs (Lieberman & Miller, 1992), all the while trying to
protect the little autonomy they have.

Students' lived experiences in school are often neglected when educators
talk about curricular reform because students are positioned as compliant or
resistant in the face of behavioral and curricular manipulations by teachers
(van Manen, 1990). Pedagogy is something done to students, and students
are positioned as responsive rather than as acting subjects (Hinchman,
1998). So-called successful students often are those who comply with authority but question or even dismiss the value of the subject knowledge they
are asked—or told—to learn; they are members of what Myers (1992) called
the "achievement club," rather than learners invested in particular concepts, skills, or learning processes (cf. Cusick, 1983; Moje, Brozo, & Haas,
1994). In an achievement orientation students and teachers often establish
work ethics based on perceived payoffs (cf. Boyer, 1983; Cusick, 1983;
Sedlak et al., 1986).

Furthermore, like teachers, students bring unique personal and academic
histories to school that shape how they view their work in school (Dillon &
Moje, 1998; Kelly, chap. 11, this volume; Fordham, 1996; Moje, Willes, &
Fassio, chap. 9, this volume; Oates, chap. 10, this volume; O'Brien, 1998).
Personal and academic histories also influence with whom students socialize and whether they and their friends value academic work (O'Brien,
Dillon, Wellinski, Springs, & Stith, 1997). Whereas some students match
their work ethics to what teachers value academically because they perceive rewards after high school, many students respond more to social interaction with teachers even when they are aware of the achievement
ideology in which their school work is embedded (Lieberman & Miller,
1992; O'Brien, 1998).

Thus, even if teachers change pedagogical and curricular goals, such as
introducing new content literacy practices and strategies into curricular
planning, students who have been enculturated to value typical artifacts of
instruction, such as reading without guidance to answer homework questions, define school work in typical ways. These students may comply but
may not embrace the teacher's revised agenda (Myers, 1992) because it

holds no promise for making their work easier or more efficient. Thus, an important part of the secondary literacy research agenda needs to focus on student reactions to content literacy practices—and to schooling in general—to better understand what is adopted and why (Hinchman, 1998; Hinchman & Zalewski, chap. 8, this volume).

Subject Subcultures.   Academic departments are more than organizers of curricular content. They are also subject subcultures, shifting subgroups who compete for status, power, and territory (Ball & Lacey, 1984; Goodson, 1994; Goodson & Anstead, 1994). Competition, amidst continual demands on their existing resources, causes each subject subculture to withdraw further into their content areas and reject what are perceived as novel pedagogical practices such as small-group work, discussion, or interdisciplinary projects (Ball & Lacey, 1984; Goodson, 1983). This subcultural identity affects how literacy practices are used to promote learning. That is, each subject department, communicating through department meetings, curriculum guides, textbooks, and supplements, defines and delimits what is pedagogically possible (Johnson, 1990).

Decisions made within subject subcultures about what constitutes knowledge, instruction, and learning—whether explicated in curriculum guides or implicitly understood within a subject area discourse community—are as socially and politically driven as they are intellectually driven. Since content knowledge is the primary academic and social grounding shared by persons in a department, traditional ways of framing content and representing knowledge may be deeply ingrained through shared beliefs or traditions. Literacy strategies promoted by content literacy theorists will be met with varying degrees of enthusiasm based on how a particular practice meshes with ways of believing, thinking, and acting within a subject subculture. In particular, the interdisciplinary nature of content literacy research and practice brings with it a unique set of discursive practices that are not necessarily at home in any mainstream discipline.

If we view content areas as subcultures within the secondary school—subcultures that are socially constructed and historically substantiated—rather than as representations of how knowledge is actually divided in "reality," we can think about how literacy practices get constructed and negotiated by people who teach and learn within these subcultures. Curricular subject areas, as discourse communities or subject subcultures, influence the forms of knowledge and the processes, including literacy processes, validated for accessing and using knowledge in a particular group (cf. Crawford, Kelly, & Brown, 1999; Kelly & Green, 1998). Recognizing the importance of subject subcultures in secondary literacy research allows each

discipline to be studied as a community with unique discourse forms for conceptualizing and discussing knowledge and making knowledge available
within and outside the community (Foucault, 1972; Lemke, 1990). This
perspective is based on the belief that instructional strategies can be adapted
to disciplinary discourse communities only if the respective discourse communities are better understood as dynamic subcultures. This perspective
also emphasizes the importance of teaching youth to become aware of the
multiple discourses they must negotiate both in and out of school in an information-based society (Hicks, 1995/1996; New London Group, 1996).

Such a model simultaneously foregrounds the interests and needs of students and teachers because it casts the disciplines, or content areas, as human constructions. Consequently, approaching secondary literacy from this
perspective makes it possible to address oppressive social structures, discourses, and practices reproduced in particular representations of the discipline (cf. Moje, 1997).

Literacy and Pedagogy

Three conceptualizations of pedagogy have had an important influence
on secondary literacy research: teaching as telling and controlling, teaching as celebrating experience and developing competence, and teaching
as transforming or transgressing.

Teaching as Telling and Controlling. The technocratic rationality of the secondary curriculum supports a pedagogy of control in which
secondary teachers efficiently "cover" content (Boyer, 1983; Bullough,
1989; Goodlad, 1984; Powell et al., 1985; Sedlak et al., 1986; Sizer, 1985).
Secondary teachers control the content and pace of classroom interaction
because this control enables them to respond to organizational and time
constraints of the institutionalized curriculum. A consequence of the pedagogy of control is the pedagogy of telling (Sizer, 1985) in which teachers engage in the time-saving explanation of concepts and processes to students
rather than engage students in reading, writing, discussion, and performance. Numerous studies and critiques of secondary literacy practices have
illustrated that secondary teachers use lectures or question–answer sessions
(in an Initiation–Response–Evaluation format) as their primary teaching
practice (cf. Alvermann & Moore, 1991; Alvermann, O'Brien, & Dillon,
1990; Lemke, 1990; Ratekin et al., 1985).

It is a curious paradox that content literacy strategies both contest and
support the pedagogy of control and telling. Although ostensibly designed to
engage students in a conversation about what they know and what they will

learn or have learned, many of the strategies (such as what do you know, want to know, and learn [KWL], Ogle, 1986; or Directed Reading-Thinking Activity [DR-TA], Haggard, 1988) are also designed to support the efficient learning of predetermined information from text and, as such, are compatible with the technocratic rationality on which the secondary curriculum is based.

Secondary content literacy pedagogy conflicts with the pedagogies of control and telling because strategies often promote reading, writing, and discussing—discursive practices that do not mesh with those valued in the discourse communities of the disciplines, at least as they are enacted within school settings. What is more, the strategies are viewed as inefficient means of achieving the same ends—the transmission of predetermined information. By using the strategies, teachers lose control over the efficient production and reproduction of knowledge. Finally, although designed to help students learn information with and from text (cf. Alvermann & Moore, 1991), content literacy strategies have socio-constructivist underpinnings that ostensibly transfer control from teachers and place it in students' hands.

Teaching as Celebrating Experience. Expressivist and progressivist literacy pedagogies represent alternatives or complements to content-area strategies instruction. The expressivist–progressivist tradition emphasizes the expression and exploration of the "inner self" (cf. Elbow, 1976) through the exploration of individual experience. Such pedagogies are most often embodied in reader response approaches (Rosenblatt, 1978) and in reading and writing workshops (cf. Atwell, 1987; Elbow, 1976).

Whereas strategies instruction often seems more appropriate for discipline-based learning in classes like social studies, science, and mathematics, expressivist and progressivist pedagogies are often incorporated in some form into English literature and writing classes at the secondary level. Unlike strategies instruction, expressivist pedagogies do not rely on a series of steps (although many of the frameworks for implementing expressivist and progressive pedagogies like writing process or writers' workshop suggest a series of steps). For the most part, these pedagogies run counter to the technocratic rationality of strategies instruction because expressivist and progressivist pedagogies depend on student experience and student control of learning rather than on the authority of the teacher.

Despite the suggestion that expressivist and progressivist pedagogies represent ways to decenter teacher authority and to inspire students' self-expression and self-exploration, these pedagogies have also been characterized as potentially oppressive pedagogies that privilege the literacy practices of White, middle-class students and promote the status quo (cf. Berlin, 1987; Dressman, 1993; Lensmire, 1994). Students whose experiences are valued in the culture of power (Delpit, 1988) are rewarded and validated in the practice of these schooled literacies (cf. Willis, 1995). However, students whose experiences are not valued continue to be alienated from and othered by these school literacies.

Moreover, the exploration of individual experience valued by expressivism and progressivism fails to challenge students to critically examine their experiences and texts in relation to larger social and cultural experiences and texts. In fact, because the expressivist tradition emphasizes the expression and exploration of the "inner self" through the exploration of individual experience, it actually precludes reading or writing that depends on or acknowledges group identity or experience (Lensmire, 1994; Moje & Thompson, 1996). Adolescent students who write and read within these approaches do not engage in writing that helps them think about how their individual experiences are situated in larger social groups, practices, and structures. Instead, it is quite possible that they will learn that their experiences are unique because each individual is unique, thus potentially reproducing color, gender, and class blindness and an individual achievement ideology (MacLeod, 1987, 1995). Additionally, Usher and Edwards (1994) argued that so-called child-centered pedagogies actually serve to control students more effectively than those based on technocratic rationality (i.e., teacher–subject-centered approaches) because the emphasis on student choice and control places responsibility for students' success or failure on them and fails to acknowledge social and cultural context.

These critiques suggest an interesting avenue of research for secondary literacy scholars, one that acknowledges the value of students engaging in reading and writing about their own experiences, but that also documents and challenges the individualism and mainstream underpinnings of expressivist and progressivist pedagogies. It is interesting to speculate, for example, on the different literate and discursive practices learned by students in a classroom context in which strategies pedagogy prevails compared to a context in which expressivist pedagogy dominates. How are adolescents' literacy practices shaped not only by the content area and teacher–student interactions in which they engage, but also by the pedagogy they are offered?

Teaching as Transforming or Transgressing.   Unlike strategies instruction and expressivist–progressivist pedagogy, transformative, or transgressive pedagogy—what we call radical pedagogy—does explicitly attempt to build on and challenge students' experiences as members of both mainstream and marginalized social groups. Pedagogies derived from critical theory in the 1970s and 1980s focused on developing critical consciousness (Freire, 1993) about the privileges of upper class, elite groups and oppression of lower classes.

More recently, critical and poststructural theorists have suggested pedagogies of difference or border pedagogies (Aronowitz & Giroux, 1991), in which students and teachers engage in the reading and deconstruction of various texts, including canonical and popular cultural texts. These texts, however, should be read not simply as tools of information or of expression; rather the texts should be critiqued and questioned for their limits, partiality, biases, and influences on the ways we come to know the world and act in it. Aronowitz and Giroux, like the members of the New London Group (1996), argue for a pedagogy that helps students create language (the New London Group talks about a meta-discourse) "for critically examining the historically and socially constructed forms by which they live" (Aronowitz & Giroux, 1991, p. 131).

In *Teaching to Transgress*, Hooks (1994) offered a different pedagogy that engages students in the development of critical consciousness and praxis (Freire, 1993), but also engages them in the joy and pleasure of the learning. Thus, Hooks took a relational, embodied stance on pedagogy, arguing that teachers must consider the knowledge that their students bring to the classroom, take risks with their students (as opposed to encouraging their students to take risks while they watch from some safe place), and become involved in the process of learning with students.

When she argued that a safe classroom is not necessarily a goal of engaged pedagogy, Hooks implicitly acknowledges Ellsworth's (1989) recognition that a pedagogy of difference must recognize difference, rather than subsume it under a banner of a common goal. Hooks suggests that there is a shared commitment, a commitment to learning, and that each person's voice must be heard—at least by another person—if differences are to be acknowledged, valued, questioned, and challenged. Accordingly, there are no blueprints for developing engaged pedagogies because to offer blueprints would "undermine the insistence that engaged pedagogy recognize each classroom as different, that strategies must constantly be changed, invented, reconceptualized to address each new teaching experience" (Hooks, 1994, pp. 10–11).

Although these border or difference pedagogies are often discussed by radical (critical, feminist, and poststructural) theorists, such pedagogy is seldom practiced in schools, especially at the secondary level. In part, the lack of blueprints and concrete strategies tied to these pedagogies challenges teachers already burdened beyond their limited time and energy resources. In part, the broad contexts of curriculum and school culture serve to stifle the generation of such pedagogy. The technical rationality that drives curriculum and the hegemony of control pedagogy constrain critical, border, or difference pedagogies; these pedagogies are enormously difficult to undertake within dominant institutional structures. They represent a threat to the security and order of the school as an efficient and rational institution—and, thus, to a teacher's tenure; they are also difficult to carry out because they aim to deconstruct the very discourses in which they are immersed. Documenting and perhaps supporting the process of radical secondary literacy pedagogy represents a rich research agenda for secondary literacy scholars.

Literacy and Assessment

The paradox and irony in content area literacy extends into the realm of assessment. On one hand, content literacy expands the assessment options of a teacher (Moje & Handy, 1995; Palmer & Stewart, 1997). On the other hand, it supports the hegemony and autocracy of objectified knowledge and the pedagogy of control. So how do we address this duality and find an assessment agenda that will place content literacy squarely and firmly in the middle of all content-area classrooms? Addressing and managing this duality poses a significant challenge given the complexities outlined throughout this chapter.

Historically, assessment has mirrored the dominant curricular model of technocratic rationality and the dominant pedagogical model of control. Standardized tests and quasistandardized tests of teacher making showcase objectified knowledge that has been transmitted from teacher to student in linear and authoritarian ways. Bubble sheets filled in by students and efficiently fed through scoring machines by teachers epitomize this movement. The computer scoring sheets and machines are still with us and will most likely be with us far into the future, but alternative assessment has made some significant—and surprising—inroads given that the alternative assessment movement attacked the hegemony—and by some peoples' reckoning the tyranny—of standardized and quasi-standardized forms of assessment in the United States.

The alternative assessment movement has roots that go deep into the beginning of this century with the rise of progressive education, but its latest incarnation gained momentum in the 1980s with the call for authentic assessments and the concerns raised about the value of standardized tests. Portfolios are probably the best exemplar of this movement, with numerous books and articles published on the topic (e.g., Tierney, Carter, & Desai, 1991). Vermont's portfolio initiative, in which the entire state adopted a version of portfolio assessment to measure student progress, illustrates the deep inroads the alternative assessment movement made into the educational community. The zenith of this movement has perhaps been reached, and a resurgence of standardized testing is emerging as states and school districts adopt exit measures to augment their traditional standardized testing cycle, and the country as a whole mulls over the idea of national standards and testing. What results is a precarious and shifting balance between the two types of assessments.

The secondary content area literacy field is late to the table but is now beginning to reap some benefits from this movement. Moje and Handy (1995) underscored the paucity of research into alternative assessments in secondary content classrooms before exploring a variety of contextually meaningful assessment structures in a high school chemistry classroom. Similar research could contribute to building a knowledge base of alternative assessment possibilities for content-area classrooms, in which large numbers of students make performance and portfolio assessments much more difficult to implement. These assessments should span the continuum from standardized to the most unique and contextual, and researchers should explore them from multiple perspectives and time frames. Longitudinal perspectives should be sought in which assessments are studied over time to see how they evolve, how and what knowledge they represent, and stakeholders' opinions of them as time passes.

The need for this reconstitution and revitalization is underscored by the emerging multitextuality and multivocality of a postmodern world (Slattery, 1995). This multivocality belies an even deeper transformation in the nature of the known and knowing when we acknowledge the absence of absolute or universal truths. The static, inert, stable, and objective veneer that covers traditional assessment practices in content-area classrooms seems to have cracked under the microscope of postmodernity. Assessment is now recognized by many as a socially mediated process that both reflects and refracts the larger social and political structures around it and yet demands for accountability and standards that support continued use of traditional measures.

Those calling for national testing and the primacy of standardized measures do so with the belief that standardization and efficiency of information processing will ensure the quality of adolescents' learning experiences. By contrast, those calling for authentic assessments wish to acknowledge the unique, contextual, and contingent nature of all learning and knowing. A challenge for content literacy in the future will be to develop a palate of assessment strategies and complementary instructional approaches that will be responsive to multiple ways of thinking about knowing and learning. The success of such an undertaking will require a coordinated research and de-

velopment process that can become part of the larger secondary school discourse and still contribute unique discursive practices that emphasize
interdisciplinary connections and multiple literacies and discourses.

MICROCONTEXTS OF
SECONDARY SCHOOL LITERACY

In the next section we turn to microcontexts, which we define as the contexts that directly influence how curriculum is enacted, how classroom culture is constructed, and how pedagogies and assessments are practiced.
These contexts include the everyday practices of teachers, students, parents, and administrators. To understand secondary literacy through these
contexts we need to look closely at how people engage in microprocesses in
classrooms, schools, and communities as they construct and negotiate
meaning in the school curriculum—within the school and community culture—when using various pedagogies and assessments. This
microcontextual focus necessitates a study of both the material conditions
of and the discursive practices and interactions that occur in classrooms,
schools, and communities. In the following sections, then, we examine
these interactions by looking at teachers' and students' discursive practices,
beliefs, and relationships, all of which are shaped by issues of race, class,
gender, age, and ability.

Literacy and Classroom Interactions

Although strategies research and instruction has dominated the secondary
content literacy landscape since the late 1960s, several studies that highlight the influence of secondary school classroom interactions on literacy
teaching and learning have made important contributions to the field (cf.
Bloome, 1987a, 1987b, 1989; Dillon, 1989; Hinchman & Zalewski, 1996;
Moje, 1996; Myers, 1992; Santa Barbara Discourse Group, 1994; Stewart,
1990a). Conducted from interactionist perspectives, these studies illustrate
how teachers and students construct understandings of each other, of literacy, and of content material as they interact with one another.

Specifically, these studies highlight how acts of literacy are embedded in a
network of social relations based on the premise that people use literacy as a
way to make meanings for themselves and for other people. As these literacy
acts take on particular meanings and as they are used to gain particular social ends, they become literacy practices (Barton, 1991). Within classrooms,
teachers and students define and negotiate rules, norms, and values that
create a unique classroom culture (Erickson, 1984; Mercer, 1992; Santa

Barbara Discourse Group, 1994). Interactionist studies have helped us understand that classroom cultures are not preformed or static; rather, they are defined as teachers and students interact. Although not preformed, the practices, discourses, and structures that shape the classroom cultures and constructions of literacy are interpreted and reinterpreted through the process of interaction within a dynamic classroom culture and in light of broad social and cultural discourses that surround and structure secondary schools and classrooms.

The interactionist studies just listed have been critical in helping us rethink what it means to talk about secondary literacy teaching and learning; these studies, however, have not investigated the ways that potentially oppressive practices of the macro-context (broader school and social contexts) are linked to the microcontexts of classroom literacy interactions and practices. More recent studies of classroom interactions have focused on how macrocontexts are linked to and reproduced by microcontexts. In the remainder of this section, we discuss this relationship between the macrocontexts and microcontexts of secondary literacy teaching and learning to provide another means of framing the nine case study chapters that follow this chapter. In each of those nine cases, the relationships between microcontexts and macrocontexts are evident, with the authors taking various theoretical perspectives on whether these relationships should be highlighted explicitly or implicitly.

Literacy and Discursive Practices

One of the most obvious—and most analyzed—aspects of classroom interaction is the talk that occurs among classroom participants. Analyses of classroom talk—or discourse—have made a significant contribution to educational research and practice since the late 1960s. In her recent review of research on discourse, learning, and teaching, however, Hicks (1995) defined discourse as more than talk. She called it "communication that is socially situated and that sustains social 'positions': relations between participants in face-to-face interactions or between author and reader in written texts" (p. 49). Similarly, in his examination of ideological assumptions about discourses and literacies, Gee (1996) defined *Discourses* as socially constructed ways of using language that signal people's memberships in particular groups and provide them with *identity kits*. Gee asserted that these uses of language are imbued with ideological assumptions and commitments. Thus, Discourses can be conceived of as socially, politically, and historically mediated texts—whether oral or written—that shape and are shaped by the way people think about knowledge in social and material relations. In schools, discursive practices are situated in the activity of the class-room, as well as in the activity and social relations of school, a particular discipline or professional community (as discussed in the previous section on macrocontexts), and the broader society. Thus, we need to ask what students are learning about how to be, act, think, value, speak, listen, read, and write in different contexts (Gee, 1993; Gee, Michaels, & O'Connor, 1992; Lemke, 1990; Luke, 1995).

One consequence of a broadened perspective on literacy and discourse is an awareness of the social situatedness of literacy and discourse and the accompanying relations of power in which all literacy and discourse practices are embedded. For example, a number of studies have revealed that people engage in different kinds of Discourses as part of the process of making meaning in social settings (e.g., Erickson & Schultz, 1981; Gee, 1996; Green, 1983; Lemke, 1990; Mehan, 1979; Sinclair & Coulthard, 1975; Tharpe & Gallimore, 1988). Because a number of different kinds of discourse practices abound in social interaction, youth from non-mainstream backgrounds—those not privileged in schools—can struggle to make sense of the disjuncture between the discursive practices valued in their homes and communities and those discursive practices that are accepted as an invisible norm for classroom Discourse (e.g., Cazden, 1988; Gumperz, 1977; Heath, 1983; Phillips, 1972).

Additionally, Discourses create identities for people and how people unconsciously shift and negotiate Discourses as they participate in different communities and activities (e.g., Gee, 1996; Gee et al., 1992, A. Luke, 1993). For example, several literacy scholars have examined how gendered discourse practices position adolescents in certain ways that either open or constrain their learning opportunities. In some cases, those studies examine how often both female and male students are brought into classroom conversations and the nature of the interactions in which they engage (e.g., Guzzetti, chap. 6, this volume), whereas other studies examine the discursive practices for the ways in which the classroom talk is marbled with hierarchical and binary relations that reproduce gendered—and often oppressive—positionings (e.g., Alvermann, Commeyras, Young, Randall, & Hinson, 1997; Moore, 1997).

Literacy and Relationships

An often overlooked context for literacy researchers in secondary school settings is the relationships constructed among students. As Finders (1996) illustrated, groups or cliques are important sites for literacy teaching and learning. The adolescent girls in her study engaged in literacy practices that served to support their identity construction, while also reproducing dominant—and asymmetrical—class assumptions. Heath and McLaughlin (1993) studied a number of out-of-school learning sites in which young people come together to dance, play sports, or put together theatrical productions, showing that these learning sites represent some of the most important literacy learning moments in these adolescents' lives, and yet the literacy learning and practices that develop in these sites are rarely acknowledged in formal school settings. Moje's (in press) study of the unsanctioned literacy practices of adolescents affiliated with street gangs also illustrates the importance of youth relationships in the identity construction and representation of young people, especially among adolescents typically marginalized in school settings. Moje argued that the adolescents' desire to be part of a group (or "part of the story" in the words of one of the study participants) led to their engagement in gang-connected literacy practices, practices they employed both in and out of school as ways of making meaning, claiming space, and identifying with a group. Several of the cases in this book (e.g., Dillon, O'Brien, & Volkmann, chap. 3, this volume; Oates, chap. 10, this volume) illustrate the importance of understanding adolescents' relationships with one another.

Material Conditions of School and Classroom Life

Material conditions of classroom and school life shape classroom interactions and relationships but represent a microcontext often overlooked in secondary literacy research. Rarely do we acknowledge how physical, material conditions shape and reflect the discursive practices of classrooms, which in turn shape and reflect the ways people use and practice literacy. And yet, classroom interactions are shaped not only by the meanings about school, literacy, or content that participants bring to classroom life, but also by the ways classroom participants position themselves in space and how they use time and materials in the classroom.

For example, certain spatial arrangements in the classroom also seem to support different kinds of discursive and literate practices. Moje et al. (chap. 9, this volume) argue that the use of a circular arrangement of desks for a whole-class group sharing of writing served to silence students. The circle became a panopticon-like structure (cf. Foucault, 1980), which allowed the gaze of the teacher—as well as every other peer—to be directed upon all students almost simultaneously. Students in the class actually seemed to be more engaged—and more comfortable—when sitting in traditional classroom rows. Instead of the comfortable group sharing and writing atmosphere the teacher tried to achieve, students felt monitored and controlled by the teacher's gaze when in the circle. Whereas the circular arrangement in and of itself did not construct regulation and control, it served to reinforce already-existing asymmetrical power relations in the class and allowed particular tactics of power to be enacted (Foucault, 1980). Uses of space and body are always tied to other discursive practices and structures. Simply using a circle arrangement within a pedagogy of control and telling does not make power differentials disappear.

Similarly, small-group peer interactions, although often supported as a way to decenter teacher authority and encourage students to take control over their literacy learning, can also serve to reproduce oppressive power relationships and stereotypical assumptions, while silencing the voices of those marginalized by their peers. Alvermann (1995/1996), Evans (1996), and Guzzetti (chap. 6, this volume), for example, found that girls were often silenced in peer literacy groups dominated by boys; Moje and Shepardson (1998) found that a boy of low academic standing rarely had the opportunity to handle the materials necessary for an inquiry lesson in science and was left behind as he attempted to read and fill out a worksheet designed to guide the inquiry lesson.

Such physical and spatial arrangements are not the only material conditions that shape classroom interactions and concomitant literacy practices; seemingly trivial environmental conditions such as temperature or visual aspects of the classroom and school may shape how literacy is practiced or how particular pedagogical innovations are taken up by students. Although teachers often acknowledge the ways that these material conditions constrain their teaching decisions and practices, rarely does secondary literacy research examine what these conditions mean for literacy practices, teaching, and learning in schools and classrooms.

Literacy and Difference:
Experience and Positionality

As implied in the preceding sections, contexts of secondary schooling are shaped by differences among teachers and students. Although there are many aspects of difference (gender, class, race, ethnicity, sexual orientation, culture, age, and religious affiliation, to name a few) to be examined in conjunction with secondary literacy research, we have chosen to talk about difference in terms of experience and positionality, emphasizing how people are different on the basis of their experiences and the ways they have been positioned or positioned themselves in their social worlds. We find locating difference along the lines of experience and positionality powerful because this allows us to acknowledge aspects of difference such as race or gender (or any of the other aspects we listed previously), but to avoid essentializing these aspects with the assumption that all people with particular physical markers (e.g., race or sex characteristics) or who identify in particular ways (e.g., gay or lesbian; Catholic or Mormon; gangsta or skater[1]) have the same thoughts, dreams, experiences, and needs.

Thinking about difference in terms of experience and positionality also allows us to think about intersections among categories of difference as well. That is, we can acknowledge that the experiences of a middle-class African American adolescent in Salt Lake City, Utah (cf. Kelly, chap. 11, this volume) are different from those of a poor African American adolescent in Los Angeles, California. At the same time, the concept of positionality encourages us to ask how people are positioned and position themselves, and how these positions shape their practices. Because physical markers such as race, gender, class, and dress are often used to position people, we can acknowledge that two African-American youth may share experiences of being positioned in similar ways by virtue of their race without essentializing how they take up those positions and how their race intersects with other aspects of their experiences.

Why are these differences in experience and position among teachers and students important to secondary literacy research? The ways that people experience the world and are positioned in it shape both their access to literacy and how they engage in various literacies and other discursive practices. Thus, in our increasingly diverse secondary schools, researchers should ask what difference means for the education of all adolescents. Should we ignore difference, choosing a perspective of color, class, gender, or other blindness? Or should we engage in a politics of difference, in which we seek to understand how difference shapes and reflects identities and how different identities require and construct different literacy practices? If we follow the second stance, then we must recognize that students and teachers move in and out of different communities and subject positions, and thus use multiple literacies in multiple ways. Recent theoretical arguments in literacy have highlighted the ideological nature of literacy and literate practices (Gee, 1993; Graff, 1987; Luke, 1995; Street, 1994; Volosinov, 1973). Street (1994) argued, "the meaning and uses of literacy practices are related to specific cultural contexts; ... these practices are always associated with

---

[1]A member of a loosely organized youth group whose central identifying practice revolves around skateboarding. Street-gang kids argue that skater groups are a type of gang, but skaters, who are generally White members of the middle class, do not self-identify as gangstas, nor are they identified by the media as gang members. Community groups organized to study or eradicate gangs do ostensibly identify skaters as gang members, but they do not target their practices.

relations of power and ideology" (p. 139). In other words, the ways that our students use literacies—and the literacies to which we provide them access—shape their future experiences and positions in the world.

A number of scholars have begun to explore these aspects of difference (e.g., Athanases, 1998; Hartman, 1997; Henry, 1998; Kelly, 1998, chap. 11, this volume; Moje, 1999; Noll, 1998; O'Brien, Stith, & Springs, chap. 5, this volume). Kelly (chap. 11, this volume), for example, explores the intersections between African American adolescents' literacy learning in public school and their literacy learning in their church-based "Saturday School." She illustrated how the church-based Saturday School generated opportunities for them to learn literacies as tools for examining their positions as African Americans in the world, while also helping them learn literacies necessary for school success. Fewer such opportunities existed in their public school classrooms.

CONTEXTS OF TIME AND HISTORY: SECONDARY LITERACY IN THE POSTMODERN MOMENT

The period of time that has been popularly termed *the postmodern moment* has dramatically shaped and will continue to shape our conceptions of literacy, our literacy research, and our teaching and teacher education practices. Postmodern perspectives and practices dismantle the modernist notion of absolute truth and epistemologies centered on the inherent power of human reason. Hence, postmodernism questions definitive theories such as the cognitive theories that support much of secondary literacy research and that privilege certain forms of science and methodologies. In a postmodern (and post-postmodern) era, blurred genres and boundaries are valued; irony, indeterminacy and contingency are replacements for closure, unity, and order, all of which erase our security in the absolute and rational (Natoli & Hutcheon, 1993).

In particular, a profusion of information technologies has brought social and cultural groups closer in *cyber proximity*. This closeness influences the way we must think about literacy theory, research, and teaching. Consonant with postmodern perspectives, the fragmented and frantically paced nature of our information systems promise both great potential and great problems for the future of secondary literacy. As we encounter one electronic image after another, it becomes difficult for us to know what is real and what is a sign (Baudrillard, 1988); this confusion may be positive in that it will force us to examine closely long-held truths. However, such confusion can also lead to gaps between what researchers and teachers believe or between what teachers and students believe. It seems important then, that as content literacy theorists, researchers, and educators, we begin to expand our sense of what it means to be literate, moving beyond the privileging of print literacies, toward an acceptance of "multiliteracies" or an awareness that "the textual is also related to the visual, the audio, the spatial, the behavioral, and so on" (New London Group, 1996, p. 64). We must grapple with the "hyperreal" (Baudrillard, 1988) nature of our increasingly textual world in which both electronic print and images are increasingly popular media and objects of our work. The New London Group (1996) writes that "Effective citizenship and productive work now require that we interact effectively using multiple languages, multiple Englishes, and communication patterns that more frequently cross cultural, community, and national boundaries" (p. 64). As we recognize the diversity of our world—and even of our local communities—we must rethink our privileging of particular literacy practices—usually print literacies—in theory, research, and practice.

Such a move is important because in our rapidly changing and shrinking world we are encountering many different modes of sense making. If we think of literacy as ways of representing and communicating, then we have to acknowledge these multiple modes or forms of representation. In other words, literacy practices—or meaning making—can involve more than doing something with print; they can include making meaning through visual or oral representations, such as drawing, performing, or dancing. Literacy practices may revolve around electronic hypermedia where print, visual, and audio images merge to create a form of representation different from unidimensional and monomedial print matter. Or, literacy practice can involve using multiple media to interpret or *transmediate* (Siegel, 1995) understandings. An expanded perspective on literacy does not require that the teaching of print literacy be discarded; it does suggest, however, that we need to think about changing our pedagogical and research approaches to understand and make use of multiliteracies (New London Group, 1996).

SUMMING UP AND MOVING FORWARD

As secondary and adolescent literacy research have evolved since the 1960's, we have moved from a focus on controlling contexts in order to understand cognitive processes, to a stance in which we recognize that cognitive processes are shaped by and reflective of social, cultural, historical, and political practices in which people engage in their everyday lives (Michaels & O'Connor, 1990). These practices cannot be ignored if we wish to use our research to make a difference in the lives of adolescents and their teachers.

Secondary and adolescent literacies are complex processes and practices, enacted by complex human beings.

Having generated secondary and adolescent literacy perspectives in which exploring contextual variables is as important as controlling them, a next logical or useful move would be to articulate more carefully the intersection between the macroprocesses and microprocesses and practices of secondary and adolescent literacy education. Microlevel, everyday literacy practices and processes construct what we have come to think of as macrolevel, broad, virtually untouchable structures such as curriculum, culture, pedagogy, and assessment. They are built, maintained, and reconstructed through the everyday practices of teachers, adolescents, and community members in and out of school. Similarly, macrocontexts or structures constrain the amount of reconstruction members of a particular school or social culture are able to enact, especially for those who are marginalized in these settings. Thus, we cannot afford to leave our research at the level of exploring the complexity of macrosystems or of everyday, micropractices; we should move forward to an examination of how the two support, reproduce, and contest one another, with an emphasis on how we might begin to reconstruct those contexts that are oppressive or marginalizing in the lives of adolescent learners in the secondary school.

II

Cases of Secondary and Adolescent Literacy

3

Reading, Writing, and Talking to Get Work Done in Biology

Deborah R. Dillon
David G. O'Brien
Mark Volkmann
Purdue University

In this chapter, how reading, writing, and talk are used to complete assignments in a secondary school biology classroom are examined. Instead of evaluating these literacy acts from a perspective outside of schools, the are described and interpreted from the participants' lived experiences as they socially construct meaning in day-to-day lessons. Before the study is presented a conceptual framework is provided to explain why the traditional functionalist perspective on secondary school reading and writing across the curriculum should be extended to a social constructionist perspective and an expanded view of texts and text structures or genres.

CONCEPTUAL FRAMEWORK

Content literacy broadly defined is using reading and writing to learn the content of various disciplines. In reading, the traditional term *content area reading*, and in writing, the expression *writing across the curriculum* (more broadly termed language across the curriculum [Bullock, 1975; D. Dillon, 1990]), have denoted how literacy intersects with learning. Traditionally, content reading, based on a cognitive perspective, has focused on how the teaching of strategies can improve the way teachers teach and students learn from text materials (Alvermann & Swafford, 1989; Moore, 1996; O'Brien, Stewart, & Moje, 1995). Since 1974, the research base and interest among university researchers in content literacy has influenced policy. For example, the majority of state departments of education in the United States require secondary school preservice teachers to gain knowledge, experience, or both in content reading (Bean & Readence, 1989; Farrell & Cirrincione, 1984). Similarly, English language arts professionals have devoted considerable attention during the last decade to studying the benefits of writing as a learning tool (Hayes, 1987; Martin, 1983; Schumacher & Nash, 1991; Tierney & Shanahan, 1991; Young & Fulwiler, 1986); they have also studied how writing is used to promote learning in content-area classrooms (Applebee, 1981; Langer & Applebee, 1987; Newell, 1984).

What is Functionalism?

A functional perspective of reading is when teachers help students adapt and modify reading processes to various texts for various purposes using a variety of instructional strategies (Bean & Readence, 1989; Herber & Herber, 1993). This predominant perspective on reading and writing, which has been constructed outside of schools, has focused on teaching students reading and writing strategies to improve the way they learn. For example, the functionalist perspective looks at the extent to which students, with teacher modeling and guidance, use reading processes dictated by the texts they are reading. Similarly, a functionalist perspective on writing focuses on how students write a variety of texts and explore a range of discourse for various purposes in multiple subject areas (Applebee, 1981; Beason, 1993). Within an ideal functionalist view—the best of all possible literate school worlds—students would flexibly adapt their reading and writing to fit a wide range of functions using a range of discourse.

However, the infusion of content reading strategies into the curriculum has been resisted by content area teachers (O'Brien et al., 1995; Ratekin, Simpson, Alvermann, & Dishner, 1985; Stewart, 1990). The same reluctance applies to writing (Langer & Applebee, 1987). Content teachers have found the use of a range of functions and instructional strategies, as promoted by reading and writing specialists, incompatible with their training, deeply seated content-driven goals, assignments, and assessments (for a detailed discussion see O'Brien et al., 1995). In earlier chapters in this volume, the functionalist view of reading to learn is discussed in detail. Thus, in the following section we elaborate further on the theoretical and philosophical bases of functionalist views of writing. Following this explication, an alternate view based on the social construction of meaning is presented.

Functionalist View of Writing-to-Learn

Two major forces impacted functionalist notions of writing in secondary schools, specifically the work of Britton and his colleagues of the London School (Britton, Burgess, Martin, McLeod, & Rosen, 1975) and the work of Applebee and his colleagues in the United States (Applebee, 1981, 1984b; Langer, 1984; Langer & Applebee, 1987). In England, Britton and his colleagues shifted from traditional rhetorical evaluations of ideal written products produced according to set conventions (e.g., models of writing set by professional writers) based on traditional discourse types (e.g., narration, exposition, description, and argument), to examining how students in school write within particular functions in various subject areas. Based on theories of the function of language (Jakobson, 1960), Britton and his colleagues studied over 2,000 pieces of writing from students between 11 and 18 years of age. These researchers examined students' writing completed in five subject areas, focusing on the dimensions of audience and the function of the writing. Conclusions from the study indicated that 63% of the writing students completed in school was transactional or informational and that students did little expressive writing where they might use a more personal, informal voice to reveal themselves and to explore ideas.

Durst and Newell (1989) noted the large impact that Britton's function categories had on other writing researchers because of the work's focus on what writers actually do with language in school. Applebee (1981, 1984b) extended Britton's work by focusing on the purposes of school writing, examining writing assignments in textbooks, and gleaning students' interpretations of these tasks. Applebee found that most school writing served restricted purposes: Students used writing to fill in answers or to answer questions with abbreviated responses. Moreover, Applebee's work supported the work of the London School researchers in demonstrating that the writing students were asked to do in school was informational—rarely personal and imaginative. Similar to reading-to-learn, writing across the curriculum has not been embraced within the dominant school culture defined by various school subject areas (Langer & Applebee, 1987; Britton et al., 1975).

Like reading, theoretical perspectives developed within the last two decades on writing have been largely based on experimental or empirical research (Hillocks, 1986) and cognitive psychology (Schumacher & Nash, 1991). In contrast, qualitative case studies, which gained popularity in the 1980s, have attempted to embed writing in daily school contexts or to view writing from a social constructivist view. However, these studies have been critiqued according to traditional standards of quantitative empirical research such as causality, sampling, and analytical evidence (Hillocks, 1986). For example, the bulk of writing research has targeted specific composition variables associated with particular writing tasks (e.g., planning, revision, and text features), in controlled experiments. Nonexperimental research has also focused on specific instructional situations in which secondary school students write across the curriculum with attention to tasks, teachers' writing assignments (Applebee, 1981) or observational studies of the effects of introducing writing tasks on student learning in various subject areas (Langer & Applebee, 1987). In short, this line of research is limited in that it has targeted specific writing assignments and tasks related to assignments. As McGinley and Kamberelis (1996) noted, with only a few exceptions such as the work of Dyson (1989), most of the functionalist views of writing are limited because they have primarily been concerned with categorizing the functions accomplished via writing. To address this limitation, McGinley and Kamberelis called for research that examines the "multiple functions of writing as they occur in relation to other language practices within complex social activities" (p. 78). Until recently, relatively little attention has been paid to the in-depth study of how writing is constructed and defined through students' social constructions in day-to-day school assignments across the curriculum (Beason, 1993; Fulwiler, 1988; North, 1987).

Social Construction as a Functional View of Content Literacy

School-based research targeting reading (e.g., Alvermann & Moore, 1991; Alvermann, O'Brien, & Dillon, 1990; Ratekin et al., 1985; Smith and Feathers, 1983a, 1983b) and writing (e.g., Applebee, 1981, 1984b; Langer & Applebee, 1987; Healy & Barr, 1991) has illustrated convincingly that these literate practices are seldom systematically used by students to understand concepts, and students are seldom given opportunities to use reading and writing to learn content. Additionally, the two processes are largely neglected in instructional planning and, hence, students have little opportunity to improve their reading and writing skills across the curriculum. In short, content literacy, as enacted daily in classrooms, bears little resemblance to the ideal generated from outside of classrooms (Fulwiler, 1987; Vacca & Linek, 1992).

This discrepancy is easily explained from a social constructionist view. Whereas the ideal functionalist view looks at reading and writing with a preconceived notion of how reading and writing should intersect with learning, or how teachers should construct specific assignments focusing on reading and writing, a social constructionist view looks at reading and writing as defined by the social contexts in which language is used (Bloome & Egan-Robertson, 1993; Dyson & Freedman, 1991; Healy & Barr, 1991; Willinsky, 1990). This perspective also focuses on how language and literacy acts structure social interaction (Bloome & Green, 1984), how schooling itself defines literacy (Bloome, 1989a, 1991), and how language is inseparable from social context as it is in the actions and reactions of participants and social relationships are possible only through language (Bloome, 1985; Bloome & Egan-Robertson, 1993). Moreover, literacy functions are not only defined by the social contexts in which they occur, but are constrained by the structure of tasks and materials with which students engage (Dyson & Freedman, 1991).

In addition, reading, writing, and talking as literate acts are deliberate social activities that are inseparable from the world in which they occur (Purves, 1991). These acts are cultural practices (Bloome, 1991; Cook-Gumperz, 1986; Scribner & Cole, 1981). Specifically, the "meanings and uses of literacy are deeply embedded in community values and practices" and focus on "the varied social and cultural meanings of the concept and its role in power relations in contemporary society" (Street & Street, 1995, p. 75). Finally, reading and writing should be viewed not as teacher-directed assignments but as the meaning constructed and negotiated by teachers and students as they construct understandings of literacy (Gee, 1996; Willinsky, 1990). Unfortunately, reading and writing practices in secondary school content classrooms are seldom viewed as events that guide social interaction.

In addition to broader cultural contexts, social functions are embedded in the institutional culture of the school (Goodlad, 1984; Hampel, 1986; McLaughlin, Talbert, & Bascia, 1990; Sedlak, Wheeler, Pullin, & Cusick, 1986; Sizer, 1985) and the forms and functions of content literacy are part of this culture. For example, writing serves a combination of intellectual and social functions; it can be viewed as a social tool constrained or enabled by the norms of the school institution (Cook-Gumperz, 1986; Florio & Clark, 1984). Likewise, reading is socially constructed and shaped by the demands and values of the institution in which it occurs (Bloome, 1989a; O'Brien et al., 1995). Responses to what one reads depend not only on the text itself but on the culture of the reader and the textual contract the reader fulfills within a given culture (Purves, 1991). This textual contract, applied to secondary schools, posits that the socially constructed functions of reading and writing result in texts written by students that are explicitly and implicitly demanded by the institution, the curriculum, teachers, and, more specifically, individual assignments.

In addition to the sociocultural perspectives previously presented, an expanded view of texts is provided by Halliday and Hasan (Halliday, 1985; Halliday & Hasan 1976; Hasan, 1995). In this view, a text is a semantic unit and a social exchange of meanings; it is also "an instance of the process and product of social meaning in a particular context of situation" (Halliday, 1985, p. 11). Pappas and Pettegrew (1998) outline the questions posed by Halliday and Hasan for any context of situation: What is happening? (What is the social action, setting, subject matter, topic or focus?). Who is taking part? (Who are the participants, and what are their roles and relationships with each other?). What role or part is language playing? (What do people expect language to do for them; what is the goal and function of the text—is it written, oral or both?).

In examining the three aforementioned contextual factors, it is clear that language users make different linguistic choices that result in different text structures (Pappas & Pettegrew, 1998). The overall structure of communicative events or texts, through which meaning is made, is referred to as a genre. The concept of genre is important because "in learning how to mean in any situation, one learns how to construct the discourse appropriate to that situation" (Christie, 1989, p. 20), as language mediates and maintains relationships and is used to negotiate content (Lemke, 1990). Thus, the role of multiple texts and genres of text are critical to our understanding of how students interact together and learn in content area classrooms.

The study outlined in the remainder of this chapter is based on the assumption that function, defined as the use of language in particular texts and in relation to those texts, is socially negotiated, constructed, and perceived within a particular classroom culture. The texts read and written in school are viewed as enabling texts (Heap, 1992). That is, texts are composed to facilitate an action beyond the literate act itself. For the purposes of this study, the literate act is using reading, writing, and talk to complete assignments. Specifically, the focus is on how and why students read, talk about, and construct (write) various forms of texts, based on their appraisal of assignments and completing assignments, and the influence of the sociocultural context on students' interactions as they work in classrooms. The function (from the emic or participants' perspective) varies but primarily focuses on getting work done so that assignments can be turned in and students are prepared to take tests based on the work.

BACKGROUND OF THE STUDY

This study is a topic-oriented analysis (Hymes, 1972; Zaharlick & Green, 1991) based on a broader ethnographic-collaborative study (Dillon,

O'Brien, & Ruhl, 1988). The theoretical framework of holistic ethnography and symbolic interactionism (Blumer, 1969) guided the research. In the broader study we examined the culture of a biology classroom, focusing on how the teacher and his students jointly constructed the social organization that enabled learning. The cultural context of the classroom was the bounded whole, and all of the aspects of the study, including the current analysis, were related to the whole (Patton, 1990; Zaharlick & Green, 1991). The overall purpose for the study was: How do the students and teacher jointly construct the sociocultural environment in the classroom and work together to make meaning during biology lessons? In this chapter, the focus is on one facet of the larger study—how reading, writing, and talk were enacted and functioned to help students complete work during lessons. The following research questions guided the inquiry:

1. What texts, within the day-to-day routines of classroom life, do teachers and students construct to complete class assignments and how are they constructed?
2. What does students' use of texts look like? Why are texts constructed as they are?
3. How do students mediate their construction of texts and understanding of reading and writing through talk and interactions with the teacher and peers in particular literacy events (Bloome & Bailey, 1992)?

Selection of Site and Participants

The school site, the teacher, and the students in the observed classroom were purposefully selected (Patton, 1990). Specifically, we wanted to collaborate with a science teacher who had been identified as effective while working with academic track students. We also wanted to work with a teacher whose administrators would allow us to work in the school on a daily basis for an academic year. Mr. Joe Ruhl was selected as the teacher we wanted to collaborate with after we read a newspaper article detailing how he had won a state-wide teaching award. He also won numerous awards including the 1989 Presidential Award for Excellence in Science Teaching, awarded to 50 science teachers nationwide. We met with Mr. Ruhl, explained the purpose of the study, and he expressed interest in working with us on the project.

Mr. Ruhl is a teacher at Jefferson High School. At the time of the study, this school had an enrollment of 2,250 students; it is located in a midwestern community with a population of 121,702 persons from a wide cross-section of socioeconomic levels. The employment level in the community is one of the highest in the country with a mix of blue and white collar jobs in diverse manufacturing and service industrial positions. We attended one section of biology; this section was comprised of 25 academic-track students, 14 females and 11 males. All students in the classroom were White as was Mr. Ruhl and all of the researchers. Students were from a variety of socioeconomic backgrounds and included a range of ability levels.

Researcher Roles, Data Collection, Analysis, and Interpretation

Deborah Dillon and David O'Brien assumed the role of participant observers (Patton, 1990) on a daily basis for one school year, observing students, talking with them about lessons, and occasionally working with them on study group and lab activities. We also observed and interacted with Mr. Ruhl who participated as a teacher researcher, collaborating with us in posing research questions and collecting data. Mark Volkmann and Mr. Ruhl worked with Deborah and David on data analysis and interpretation.

Primary data, in the form of fieldnotes and transcriptions of audio and videotaped lessons were triangulated (Denzin, 1978; Patton, 1990) with secondary data in the form of structured and informal interviews with Mr. Ruhl and key-informant students, artifacts (e.g., curriculum materials and student products) and students' academic records in biology. Fieldnotes, transcripts of audio and videotapes, and videotape-viewing session notes were analyzed using the constant comparative method (Glaser & Strauss, 1967). This strategy ensures that data are collected and continually compared with new data in an attempt to generate categories and properties depicting patterns of actions in the data. Data collection and analysis for interviews relied on a within and cross-case analysis strategy (Patton, 1990). Document analysis strategies were used to make sense of artifacts and other documents (Patton, 1990). Our team of researchers continued to interpret data and write up findings over a 2-year period beyond the data collection year. In this chapter, the focus is on our analysis of the teacher and student interviews, triangulating these data with fieldnotes and transcripts of videotaped lessons of whole-class and groupwork sessions.

RESULTS AND DISCUSSION

From our analyses we generated a descriptive-interpretive picture of how students perceived and enacted literacy events as they pragmatically completed various class assignments and activities. Our interpretations of the activities are embedded in the culture of the classroom, including a look at the influence of the social and academic subcultures within the classroom on acts of literacy related to learning. We also examined events by working to understand the specialized language patterns or genres used to communicate within the classroom.

In the following section, we address the research questions, presenting overall assertions about enactments of reading, writing, and talk supported by categories.

A Closer Look at Enactments of Reading

Similar to findings of previous studies of secondary school classrooms, reviewed in the opening section of this paper (e.g., Ratekin et al., 1985; Langer & Applebee, 1987), we found that students did not read texts for the purpose of learning concepts. Rather, students used reading as a tool to obtain and share information in order to complete written products. What was more compelling within the theoretical perspective of this study was *how* students socially negotiated and constructed a definition of reading, and how they valued reading within the context of completing tasks. Before presenting the first assertion, we provide background information about Mr. Ruhl's classroom.

Most class periods began with an overview of the day's activities (often written on the chalkboard), a greeting and announcement time conducted by Mr. Ruhl with the entire class, an occasional whole-class introductory or minilesson on a science concept, followed by groupwork. The last few minutes at the end of the class period was reserved by Mr. Ruhl for whole-class sessions where he taught difficult concepts or determined the progress groups had made and reviewed what was to be completed in the future. The majority of class time was organized around cooperative groups comprised of approximately five to six students. Individuals in groups worked together on the unit study guides Mr. Ruhl had designed (the primary text for the class). These guides contained key concepts and objectives for the unit, important vocabulary, diagrams, questions, and activities students were to complete with the help of the textbook and other sources. At the conclusion of each unit, students were asked to study the guide and complete Form A of a multiple-choice test. If they passed Form A, students engaged in enrichment activities. If they did not pass Form A with an 80% mastery level, they restudied content and took Form B. During most of the semester, individuals were allowed to self-select small group members. Mr. Ruhl wanted the students to work in study groups and with lab partners because he believed they could learn more if they struggled collectively to solve problems (see Dillon, O'Brien, Moje, & Stewart, 1994 for information on Mr. Ruhl's philosophy of teaching and science as well as his classroom organization beliefs). Mr. Ruhl preferred this group struggling process to delivery of information in lectures. Groupwork was social, involving camaraderie, competition, and cooperation. Hence, groupwork provided a forum for weaving social and academic work together as students completed assignments.

The two assertions that follow focus on the collaborative, social nature of reading used to complete work while accentuating how individual students, even within groups, preserved their individual work styles and responses to tasks.

Assertion #1

Reading to get work done is a collaborative social act shaped and enacted through language, the dynamics of groups, students' work styles and ethics, and their goals in completing assignments. Much of what students implicitly define as reading (i.e., through their actions) in doing schoolwork is getting information, consolidating it, and sharing it to complete assignments.

Two categories were generated that support this assertion and are subsequently detailed.

Group Reading as a Social Act.   This category includes enactments of reading as students worked in small groups. The groups were self-selected study groups, lab groups, or *ad hoc* groups formed to complete specific assignments. Within this category, we found incidents of students reading collaboratively to look up information leading to group consensus and using this information to write a shared text. In addition, our interpretation of a variety of data indicates that students' gender and social status impact their reading and writing practices in groupwork (see Dillon et al., 1988; Dillon & Moje, 1998). The reading enactments we observed were characterized by cooperative learning in which group members completed lab activities, study guides, or practice activities. In some instances, this group collaboration was used to create a shared text. For example, students read sections of textbook chapters to fill out the study guides, looked up vocabulary, and wrote definitions. This process often involved the concurrent reading of multiple texts (e.g., textbook, study guide, and handouts). An example of this collaborative social process is portrayed in a vignette and observer comments from the following small-group meeting:

> Carolyn, Tina, and Jeff are working on a practice activity (a review of previously learned concepts, completed as a precursor to taking Test B) in which they label parts of a spider. Carolyn, who is popular in school, is perceived by Tina and Jeff as having more social status than they do. Carolyn appears to use her social advantage to try to lead the group. She looks up the term *silk gland*

and reads aloud [Observer Comment (OC): Perhaps Carolyn reads aloud to help herself understand what the term means while at the same time reading to ensure that group members hear the definition she reads from the book]. She writes the definition down; the others write down versions of what she said, asking for clarification. Jeff has his book open but does not look at it. Tina takes Jeff's book and looks at the diagram of the spider in the book. Carolyn is now looking up a word in the glossary. Tina looks at Carolyn's study guide and corrects Carolyn's spelling of a term. Tina reads a definition from the book, with several miscues. When Tina praises herself for finding the definition, Carolyn jokes with her, in a somewhat cynical manner, about how Tina must really feel proud of herself. The whole time Tina is trying to attend to the ongoing discussion of terms, she is also copying a page of Carolyn's worksheet that Carolyn had already completed before class.

[OC: The section of the text needed to complete questions on the study guide is discovered by Tina only when the diagram in the book and the one on the worksheet do not match. The first tactic, though, is to call Mr. Ruhl over for help. The group members are sitting together, yet working individually to fill out the worksheet.]

(Viewing session notes of videotape, 3/22)

Reading, as illustrated in the aforementioned excerpt, is implicitly defined by the task, which is intimately connected to the relative social status and power exercised by group members. Social and political status mediated who did which tasks, who was excluded, and how the contributors' work was valued. Because Carolyn was perceived by both Tina and Jeff to have more social status than they did, her words were used primarily as the basis for all three students' answers on the study guide. Jeff, who from our observations appeared to understand most of the biology concepts better than his group members, rarely spoke during interactions. Usually he was excluded from discussions about answers that would be written on the study guide. We speculate that this was because Jeff recently joined the group and the other students did not know or trust him enough to place a great deal of faith in his responses. He was also not well accepted socially: Students perceived him as being somewhat overweight and opinionated. Tina tried to gain favor with Carolyn by helping to find information but was sarcastically put in her place when she attempted to correct Carolyn's answers. Driving the whole work-related interaction was the pressing need of each participant to get information so they could complete work and turn it in to Mr. Ruhl.

Reading as Production.   Groups often strove to finish reading tasks to get answers and complete the guide or worksheet. This production was often spurred by competition with other groups, and groups sometimes strove to produce answers before other groups could find information. These cooperative efforts within groups, or what we call production competitions across groups, resulted in an impromptu division of labor within groups. In some cases, tasks were duplicated by members of a group, with everyone rushing to finish the work. Tina's reflections provide insight into how group production sometimes functioned inefficiently with redundancy across members:

Tina: Yeah [we compare answers], and then we'll find out what the right answer is. One time we had to get two or three labs done in one day.
Deborah: So what did you do then?
Tina: We just did what we really had to do.
Deborah: How do you guys get it done, when you just have to get it done. You have to meet deadlines. What do you do?
Tina: We just looked up specifically what we have to do and then just hand it in.
Deborah: So everybody finds information—some part of the guide or the lab or someone looks up stuff?
Tina: No. We all, we all do it. We all look for [the same] stuff.

                                                                (*Interview*, 5/10)

In this excerpt, Tina stated what most group members believed—that it was important to do the work necessary and get the biology study guides (the product) completed in a timely fashion. As noted, most of her comments focus on completing product and getting the right answer. Other groups were quite efficient in this process, dividing up different tasks across group members. As Tina noted, however, all members of her group looked up the same information ("we all look for stuff"). Despite being perceived by other groups as an inefficient strategy, students like Tina, who had more difficulty academically in biology, tended to trust only answers that everyone had collaboratively constructed. This process allowed group members to check themselves against others and validate the group response before moving on to the next question. Furthermore, this practice allowed all group members to appear equal in ability and effort—no one did more work than someone else or sought to be the leader.

Assertion #2

Individual goals for reading are closely tied to instructional goals, materials, and priority of assignments. However, in spite of the classroom climate and established explicit and implicit curriculum related to reading, students still maintain individual work styles related to reading that they have adopted through years of schooling.

Two categories were generated during data analysis that support this assertion.

Reading to Study.   Although reading the textbook was not encouraged by Mr. Ruhl as a study technique, students who trusted reading as a long-used and practiced study technique read the textbook to study for tests. These students stated that they believed reading the textbook enabled them to pass tests. Additionally, some students used the textbook to understand concepts during various whole-class activities as evidenced in the videotape viewing notes that follow:

> Mr. Ruhl is reviewing invertebrates with the students. He asks them questions. He has alerted the students to a pie chart showing what percentage of invertebrates are insects as a prelude to their introduction to insects. Tracy immediately retrieves her book from her backpack, opens it, and turns to page 415 in the book where the pie chart is printed. She believes that Mr. Ruhl has identified the chart as being important, so she copies it into her notes. Tracy often copies material from the book, in note form, as a way to learn the material.
>
> *(Videotape viewing session notes, 3/4)*

Tracy relied on the textbook in and outside of class. She related that she also routinely read and outlined the textbook. We often observed her reading it during class and outlining what she felt was important information. Other students told us during interviews that they regularly read and studied the book at home. In fact, some used it almost exclusively despite the fact that Mr. Ruhl did not place much emphasis (if any) on studying the textbook. As Jay noted in the following interview excerpt and other conversations we had with him, he read the book in this class and other classes because it allowed him to be successful on tests:

> Deborah: If you do study, or if you have studied biology, how do you study, say for the test?
> Jay: I just read over the chapters.
> Deborah: In the book you mean?
> Jay: Yeah. And that's it.
>
> *(Interview, 5/10)*

Later in the interview, Jay mentioned that he sometimes used the study guides to study, but that he used the textbook as his primary source. Because of students like Jay who read the book at home regularly to study but in class participated in the implicitly sanctioned study guide activities, we came to refer to perusal of or reading from the textbook as a subversive activity. Although Mr. Ruhl did not disapprove of using the textbook, he viewed it as one way to complete the study guides, which then could stand alone as the primary text for the class. Students who read the textbook outside of class realized that this activity was relegated to a secondary status in comparison to using study guides. Students knew that the guides outlined important objectives and information because Mr. Ruhl noted this and told them to focus on the guides as they studied for the test. Hence, we found that the use of the textbook persisted as a matter of institutionalized personal comfort and because students felt that they learned from it, rather than as a response to the explicit curriculum or Mr. Ruhl's statements.

Reading to Look Up Information. At times, knowledge of certain vocabulary was required of students to understand how to label diagrams, or to understand how various components of a system function. Students scanned the textbook for this information as well as other concepts they needed to pass tests. The overall goal here was a combination of reading-to-complete-assignments and reading-to-study-for-tests. Jennifer's comments provide an example:

> Deborah: Tell me about when you study for test A. How do you study?
> Jennifer: I go through the study guides and I look up everything that it says in there … like, the vocabulary words, sometimes I'll go through, if I don't understand one, I'll mark it; then after I've marked all of them, I'll go through the back of the book and look them up [in the index] or even in a dictionary if they have them in there, too.
> Deborah: What do you do when you look them up?
> Jennifer: I try and memorize what they mean.
> Deborah: Do you ever write them down?
> Jennifer: I just read them. I understand most of them. If I don't understand some of them, I'll usually either go ask my mom or dad or sister.
> (*Interview,* 5/10)

In this interview excerpt, Jennifer outlined her strategy for learning vocabulary. She noted that she used the guide to find key words and mark those she did not know, and then used the glossary in the textbook to obtain definitions. Her response indicated that this strategy did not work for her in all instances so she also relied on the dictionary. Part of her strategy was to read and then memorize the words—she did not use other methods to understand the words. However, understanding was important to her memorization process as she prepared for tests because she resorted to talking with family members if she needed help in this area.

When asked how they study, students reported selectively reading information they perceived as important. *Looking over* or *looking up* were typical terms students used in reference to skimming or scanning. In the following excerpt Matt described how he used these processes.

Dave: Now tell me about when you study. What do you do? Like, what materials do you use?

Matt: Well, if we do any labs, I look through those. Because sometimes they got some stuff on it.

Dave: The labs do?

Matt: Yeah, well they fit in, you know, kind of like that. Especially when you have diagrams because they define stuff and you've got to know.... And so we try to look at all of the objectives and then after that, I don't worry about studying the objectives first. I go to the study guide again. Just, you know, clipping through and reading everything once. And then I go back to the objectives and then I read off those and I try to answer them in my head.

Dave: Oh.

Matt: And then if I can't do it, on a few questions, I'll go back and study the study guide again and go through my labs again and I'll try it again.

(*Interview*, 5/10)

Matt and other students' references to *looking through* or *reading over* as study strategies represented students' perceptions of how information could be learned. Most students we interviewed expressed a relatively high level of confidence in their ability to use selective reading techniques to complete assignments. Such selective reading ventures focused on looking for important vocabulary and selectively reading diagrams that contained information that had to be verified on a test. Students also reported reading portions of the text chapter that they thought might contain important information. Similarly, they repeatedly read various texts because they found that repeated reading helped them learn and retain information they needed to pass tests.

The view of the role of the textbook as a resource was reinforced for students throughout the semester by Mr. Ruhl, as noted in the following excerpt:

After working with students on the meaning of *arthro* to see if students can derive the meaning of the term *arthropods*, Mr. Ruhl refers the students to the textbook: "Turn to page 415," he tells the students. After the students turn to the pie chart he referred them to, he asks questions about it. Some of the students thumb through pages near the reference. After the reference to the pie chart, Ruhl and the students close their books.

(Videotape viewing session notes and transcripts, 3/22)

In this clip, we see that Mr. Ruhl believed that using the text as a reference to find particular information or to view a graph for clarification is important. At the same time, however, he implicitly conveyed to students that systematic reading of the textbook to understand concepts was not important or helpful.

A Closer Look at Enactments of Writing

We generated two assertions about writing. For each assertion, we will present categories with data clips.

Assertion #1

Writing is viewed by students as a way to share or acquire a common pool of information, drawn from the textbook, teacher-created texts, and the teacher and other students. The pool of information is viewed as necessary in completing assignments and passing tests and the information shared is defined or shaped by specific types of tasks and accompanying materials. Three categories support this first assertion.

Collaboration Through Joint Construction of Texts. This category includes enactments of writing in which students worked together to construct texts. The writing was collaborative, representing a consensus of opinion about what the written product should include. Because of the concern for joint construction of texts, the collaborators felt ownership of the product. The first category is illustrated in the following excerpt where Tim's group worked on an enrichment activity. Their goal was to work together to conduct an experiment, write up the results, and give an oral report based on the write-up:

Tim, Chip, and Chris are working on an enrichment activity. They are all observing meal worms placed in the center of a pan to see which kind of food the meal worms prefer to eat (various cereals or potato flakes are deposited in each corner of the pan). The three group members act like scientists. Their enactments are matched to stereotypical lab researchers who wear white jackets and talk to each other using technical jargon. They observe the meal worms and time how long the worms take to reach each type of food. Tim writes down the observations, usually in his own words. He reads orally what he is writing down as he writes it. Sometimes Chip and Chris verify what he is writing; sometimes they correct him, or advise him about what to include and how to organize the information; periodically they remind Tim about things he has left out. Hence, to an extent, what Tim writes is negotiated among the three. At times, though, Tim writes what he wants—the text is his version of what transpired in the experiment. Chris and Chip read questions from the activity sheet that outline the experiment while Tim continues to write the report.

(Videotape viewing session notes, 3/21)

The aforementioned excerpt displays a collaborative effort in which students drew on their individual and shared ideas to contribute to the construction of a report. Tim was identified by his group members as the leader in the group and as such was designated to write the report. Specifically, Chris and Chip deferred to Tim because they believed that he was the better student. Nevertheless, because the three males were friends, they all took an active role in contributing to Tim's efforts, correcting him when they felt it was necessary and helping him co-construct the written text. A group effort created the final product and yet remnants of the student "in power"—the one writing the report (Tim)—superseded several group members' ideas.

Acquiring Work Completed by Others.   This category contains enactments of writing that illustrated the students' definition of sharing information. Sharing meant giving information to persons who had not invested time in working on assignments either in or out of class. The students rationalized copying others' work or allowing others to copy their work by stating that shared work provided everyone with information to study. However, students stated that once information was acquired, it was up to an individual to be responsible and study for the test (i.e., use the information or not). Tina explained this definition of sharing:

Deborah: We've noticed that sometimes people show up to class with their study guides all filled out ahead of time. Why do you suppose people do that?

Tina: So they can help their friends out. I did that once. And um, so that way I have more time to study—that way I have more time to study for tests. So I can help everyone else.

Deborah: So some people do the guide at home to get it done ahead of time, so when they show up it's gonna be all done?

Tina: And so they can help. 'Cause that's—I did that. I did it [the study guide] all so that way it'd give me more time to study and help my friends and I'd pass that one [test].

Deborah: Well, one of the things we've seen related to this—sometimes peo-
            ple will show up with something done or they'll get something done
            before somebody else will. And they'll just pass their guide around so
            other people can get the answers written down on their guide. What
            do you think of that?

Tina: I do that. But we do it sometimes like when we'll write it down.
            Then sometimes I study mine. I mean I go home and just sit there
            and study mine. I think it's okay [to copy] if like you're gonna study,
            but if you're just sitting there writing it down to write it down, you
            shouldn't do it. I write mine down so I can study it.

Deborah: So it's good—it's okay [to copy] as long as you're just writing it
            down?

Tina: If you're gonna take it [the study guide] home and study it.

                                                                (*Interview*, 5/10)

An interesting pattern that emerged from the data was the belief that is
was acceptable to fill out the study guide at home despite Ruhl's desire that
students work on the guide in groups struggling over the material together.
Several students in the lower academic groups that we observed tended to
arrive to class with all of the written work done before they met in their
group, knowing that other group members would not have completed this
task. The practice of sharing one's work with students who had not completed it prior to class, represented a desire to be a good friend but also to improve one's social status or academic acceptance in a group. This need for
social acceptance is evident in Tina's statement about how you help your
"friends" by giving them answers you've already obtained on the guide.
However, we speculate that Tina had other reasons for completing work or
studying at home. For example, extra time to work on the study guide in the
privacy of her home allowed Tina to take her time when looking up information. It also provided her with "more time to study" and learn the material.
And having the academic work completed at home allowed Tina the time
she needed to concentrate on the social aspect of learning when she was at
school. Another interesting observation about the study guides was that
students felt little ownership for the writing that went into them or concern
for punitive action from Mr. Ruhl if the guides where not complete or accurate. The act of sharing texts, which could be called copying, shows how little value the students placed on the texts as individual, original
compositions. We speculated that students were unconcerned about ownership of their written products because they saw the function of such texts as
collaboratively sharing information for individuals to use, if they so choose,
to prepare for tests. Additionally, the guides were not graded by Mr. Ruhl
and thus did not impact overall course grades like tests did.

Transcription From the Textbook.   This category includes enactments of writing that show how students disregarded explicit instructions from the teacher in favor of efficiently getting information. The students, therefore, focused on product over process:

> The groups are all writing something—actually, they are copying out of the book. They are copying rapidly to get the information transferred to their study guides. Mr. Ruhl observes this practice as he visits one group—he wants students to take what they have read from the text and write it in their own words—not copy from the book.
>
> [OC: These are some time constraints on quantity and quality of writing due to limited time in class and the need to get sections of the guide completed by particular due dates prior to tests.]
>
> *(Fieldnotes, 8/28)*

In this excerpt, we see that students disregard Mr. Ruhl's instructions that they look up answers in the text and paraphrase these, or construct an oral text that they would then write on the guide. He believed that their synthesis, rather than copying, would help them learn the information. Nevertheless, the students rapidly copied statements directly from the book onto their study guides. From the students' perspective, they had little time to find information, discuss it, synthesize ideas, and write answers on the guide. Thus, what they wrote, they did not compose—they transcribed.

This category of transcription from the text also includes enactments of writing reflecting how the product orientation implicit in the larger curriculum superseded the process orientation that Mr. Ruhl tried to instill in the students. Following we illustrate one example of how the students figured out the implicit curriculum. Clearly, the implicit definition of the purpose of writing—to get information to complete study guides—won out:

> Jason, Chris, and Tony are using their books now to help them fill in the study guides. They have figured out, after Tony's question to Mr. Ruhl, that they can copy definitional information from the textbook to their study guides.
>
> *(Fieldnotes, 9/3)*

After asking Mr. Ruhl for help on a study guide question dealing with key vocabulary, students took Mr. Ruhl's advice and used the textbook to find the information. However, they used it a bit differently than he suggested. They skipped over discussing the terms and merely copied the definitions verbatim from the index. Students found this practice more efficient as it resulted in their early completion of the guide, allowing more time for social conversation. Completing work early was also a sign of being smart and many groups quietly competed to be the first to finish work. Groups that chose to engage in talk about the concepts (i.e., struggling), often worked at a slower pace. These groups also tended to merge social and academic agendas, talking and laughing as they moved between out-of-school and in-school topics of conversation. Unfortunately, individuals in these groups were often viewed as being off task and as having lower academic ability because they required more time to complete assignments. As the groups who struggled realized that they were behind everyone else, students adapted their actions so that they were similar to those described in the transcription from textbook fieldnotes (see Dillon & Moje, 1998 for a more complete description of these events). Thus, what we see is that despite Mr. Ruhl's desire for students to focus on the process of learning via struggling to complete the study guides during groupwork, he still implicitly expected (and to some extent explicitly) rewarded production—getting the work completed in an efficient, complete, and accurate manner. The students figured out this tension or discrepancy in Mr. Ruhl's expectations and opted to follow the broader context of schooling (production) and their own social needs.

Assertion #2

The types of writing that small groups engage in are both a function of and a contribution toward the relative social and academic status of students. Relative social and academic status, sought by some students via participation in certain writing tasks, is indicated by the types of tasks a student assumes or is assigned. Three categories were generated during data analysis that support this assertion.

Low Social Status Excludes Participation. This category represents enactments in which persons with low social status were excluded or excluded themselves from participating in group writing activities. In the following activity, Jason chose not to participate with his peers but members of his group helped him complete the task nonetheless.

> Mr. Ruhl tells Group B students [students who did not pass the first test and have to take a second test or Test B] to work on homework they may need to work on when they are finished with the test. Jason is one of these students. After completing the test he sits with a blank worksheet in front of him while Chris and Tony collaborate on the "science in the newspaper" activity. Chris and Tony do all of the writing on the worksheet. Jason waits until they finish and copies from Chris and Tony anything that will have to be handed in later.
> (*Fieldnotes*, 9/2)

Through a semester of observations, we were never sure what Jason was actually capable of doing because he regularly allowed other members of his group to write up labs, practice activities, or written segments of study guides which he then copied. He did not appear to want to help with the work, have a voice in answers, or take an active part in groupwork interactions. Interestingly, his peers allowed him to assume this nonparticipatory role in groupwork and did not look to him for help with academic work. Furthermore, Jason did not participate in any social conversations with his peers. Based on our observations and comments made by students, we believe that students viewed Jason as having lower social and academic status.

High Status Gives Participatory Rights.   This category includes enactments in which persons accorded relative high social status wrote answers for the group or otherwise shaped what the group wrote. In the fieldnote excerpt that follows, Mike's actions indicate how writing for the group is connected to social status. As background, Mike was asked by Mr. Ruhl to leave his self-selected group (comprised of high social–high academic achieving students) and provide leadership for a particular group comprised of averaging to lower achieving students. Despite the fact that Mike had higher social status than other members of this new group, his grades in biology were similar to those of his new group. However, in his role as leader, Mike set the pace and direction of activities and assumed the role of academic leader:

> Mike, Jeff, Carolyn, Tracy, and Joey are working on a study guide. Mike, because of his perceived high social status and group leader role, tells other members what to write on the guide and how to construct and label a diagram of a spider. In spite of the fact that other group members ask legitimate questions about his mislabeling of the spider, he appeals to Mr. Ruhl to support his group leader status stating, "My group members won't agree with me." When Mr. Ruhl questions Mike's labeling and agrees with the way Jeff, a low social status member has labeled it, Mike leaves the group shouting, "Okay, put it into your own words."
>
> *(Videotape viewing session notes, 3/8)*

To Mike, writing for the group, and having the group accept his oral and written texts, solidified his social and academic position as group leader. When Jeff, a low social status student, questioning Mike's practice of constructing and dictating the writing of answers, Jeff was essentially questioned Mike's position as leader. When Mr. Ruhl affirmed Jeff's concerns, Mike left the group to save face. He departed telling the others to go ahead and "put it in your own words", which he clearly perceived to be inferior to his words. Mike's actions are a counter move to reposition himself as having power over his group by leaving them. What is also evident in Mike's actions and statements was that students selected by Mr. Ruhl as group leaders perceived that they had more academic knowledge and the license to expect others to acquiesce to their views. Additionally, Mike selected tasks for himself (e.g., reading answers from the book for his group members to copy down), as a way of positioning himself as powerful and as a way of disempowering others in the group (see Dillon & Moje, 1998 for a detailed analysis of Mike and his group members). This positioning of others is also evident in the next category that outlines how students were aware of the relative social position of persons in their groups. Also implied in the next category is the idea that relative status was related to the types of writing, reading, or talk that group members were allowed to do or were assigned to do.

Group Members Are Positioned by Others.   This category includes enactments of writing in which persons who have low social position are given work to do by members who have more power in the group. In the interview that follows, Matt outlined how his work within the group was related to his position:

> Dave: You mentioned your role in the group.
> Matt: Yes, Chris would look stuff up in the book. Like the vocabulary—he'd almost always looked up the vocabulary stuff. And the other three were responsible for screwin' around and talking. And they did that quite well. And I did the rest of the stuff, pretty much [writing up the labs and activities].
> Dave: Well, you got to the point where, in some cases a certain amount of stuff had to be done by a certain time. What would happen then? How would you work it out to get stuff done on time?
> Matt: Oh, I did it—ha!
> Dave: And what did the other people do?
> Matt: Copy it.
> Dave: So, another thing we've noticed about these groups is that someone kind of assumes the leadership role. Did you guys have somebody like that in your group?
> Matt: It was—I sort of did all of the work, but um, but the guys I was with um, well two of 'em are freshmen, and they were real popular so they kind of led [the group].

(*Interview*, 5/10)

The aforementioned interview clip excerpt illustrates the complexity of the interaction between academic and social position and who wrote up assignments. In this particular group, any task related to completing work was considered to be a low-level activity relegated to persons with low social position. In Matt's case, he was academically equal to his group mates. However, his peers knew that he would do the work because he was concerned about the academic consequences of not completing it. They also knew that Matt wanted to be part of their social group. The high social status attained by the popular males in this group allowed them to position Mike into the role of worker. Meanwhile, the rest of the group leisurely talked and relaxed, eventually copying the answers down so that they could use the completed guide to study for and pass the tests. Throughout group interactions they gave enough positive strokes to Matt—allowing him to be part of their social group in biology class (only) because they needed someone to do work they considered uninteresting but necessary.

CONCLUSIONS

Our analyses and interpretations allowed us to generate a conceptualization of reading, writing, and talk related to specific contexts of situations. In this paper, we presented a descriptive–interpretive picture of how students perceive reading, writing, and talk as they pragmatically applied these literacy skills to complete various class assignments and activities. Our interpretations of the activities are embedded in the culture of the classroom and the social interactions between students and their teacher. Finally, we sought to understand the interplay between the cultural, social, and academic influences and how these impact literate acts related to learning.

As a result of our findings, we conclude that reading, writing, and talking, as they occurred on a daily basis in the biology classroom we studied, bear little resemblance to the ideal uses proposed by literacy researchers (e.g., reading and writing to process and learn new concepts). Students did use a variety of literacy skills to complete assignments, but these enactments, as particular events, must be viewed as socially situated to appreciate their significance (Bloome & Bailey, 1992; Pappas & Pettegrew, 1998). For example, reading and writing events were constructed and enacted by participants with attention to the social and academic positions students assumed or were given, as well as their assessment of teachers' actions and demands (Delamont, 1983). Second, literacy events are historically situated within the school culture. Students in the study used reading and writing to complete assigned tasks. Nevertheless, they based their literacy actions historically on their previous experiences in school (e.g., using the textbook as the primary source of information) and by constructing agendas that met their needs (e.g., a combination of social and academic work) but also met the requirements of the organizational structure in which they worked (Bloome & Bailey, 1992). Third, reading and writing practices cannot be studied separately from the language patterns or genres (Christie, 1989) that surround and comprise these practices. For example, when working in groups, the students we studied attempted to understand information and collaboratively reinterpret and relate information to their experiences (Barnes, 1990). What they read, discussed, and wrote was inextricably tied to the discourse patterns or genres of this collaborative process. Furthermore, from our observations we concur that what counts as a text should not be restricted to the physical text but should include the result of *textualizing* (Bloome & Egan-Robertson, 1993): "People textualize experience and the world in which they live, making those phenomena part of the language system (broadly defined)" (p. 311). The textualizing perspective on reading, writing, and talking implies that what counts as a text must be determined within the particular context of situation (e.g., setting, participants, topic and purpose) and where textualizing occurs (Pappas & Pettegrew, 1998). Although the textbook counts as a text, texts are also spoken, or spoken and then transcribed.

IMPLICATIONS

What can be learned from examining the students' experiences and perspectives in Mr. Ruhl's biology class and what implications can be drawn for instruction? First, it is useful to examine the events that occur in our classrooms each day and to consider whether they have been constructed around our agendas as teachers (e.g., the content we want students to learn) or with input from students' agendas. It is clear that despite our love for learning and the subject matter at hand, adolescents have their own agendas. These include the need to learn, socialize, make friends, feel a sense of community in a classroom, and develop a relationship with their teacher. Also, students want school to be enjoyable—they want to have fun. Often educators cannot envision how to merge students' needs and agendas with their own. As educators, we worry that if students socialize or have fun while completing classwork, then important content may not be covered. We also worry that classrooms filled with talk and laughter may indicate weak teaching instead of indicating an active learning process. To his credit, Mr. Ruhl tried to make biology class academically meaningful while also allowing students to intertwine their social agenda—having fun in self-selected groups and whole-class settings—with the need to complete tasks and learn.

Second, in examining students' actions in this biology class we found that most students used reading, writing, and talking in functional ways to complete tasks as quickly as possible, with little time spent on struggling to learn concepts. Curiously, it was often the more academically able students who did not talk much during groupwork, dividing the reading and writing tasks up in efficient ways to complete work. In contrast, average and lower ability students, when grouped together, often did not trust their individual academic efforts. Instead, they relied on talking through the study guide questions with peers prior to offering answers. However, these students who talk and laugh while completing work, may not match our definition for engaged, thoughtful learners. We believe that our findings may prompt teachers to closely examine the reading and writing practices of students in their classrooms because events may not be what they appear to be on the surface (e.g., working quietly and efficiently in groups may not be collaborative learning; talking and laughing may be an indicator of engagement in a task). These conflicting ideas—wanting students to be actively engaged in their learning yet efficient and serious in completing schoolwork—pose one of many tensions for many educators.

Finally, the way students position themselves or are positioned by their peers during groupwork, shapes the literacy practices of individuals and of the group. The concept of positioning is important for teachers to consider. Too often teachers think about students as a unit—a class. And often when teachers do think about individual students we see them as one-dimensional beings. Yet every classroom contains many students, each with multiple positions that they assume and move in and out of in a fluid fashion. Working to understand each student in our classroom and closely observing individuals as they work with peers will allow us to better understand students as individual learners. It is our hope that the research presented in this chapter shows how teachers might better understand the sociocultural construction of reading and writing events in classrooms. This knowledge can serve as a foundation for teachers as we reconsider our pedagogy in light of students' academic, social, and emotional needs.

4

"I've Run a 4,000 Person Organization—and It's Not Nearly This Intense": A Three-Year Case Study of Content Literacy in High School Mathematics

Elizabeth G. Sturtevant
George Mason University

Vicki Parsons Duling
Fairfax County Public Schools

Robert E. Hall
Bishop Denis J. O'Connell High School

Secondary mathematics has infrequently been studied by literacy researchers, and literacy has infrequently been studied by mathematics researchers (Sturtevant, 1997). Indeed, in many schools and universities, literacy and mathematics are located in totally different departments or buildings, with little cross-communication. Recently, however, each group has begun to explore and advocate a variety of literacy related teaching strategies for mathematics education. In its national standards documents, for example, the National Council of Teachers of Mathematics (1989) emphasized the benefits of a constructivist curriculum in which students use both real-life materials and oral and written language to learn and communicate about mathematics. Likewise, literacy educators have moved from conceptions of content area reading that emphasize textbook comprehension and retention of facts to definitions of literacy that view reading, writing, and other forms of communication as tools for learning in every content area (International Reading Association [IRA]/National Council of Teachers of English [NCTE], 1996).

Examples of classroom practices suggested by both fields include cooperative group work for solving nonroutine problems, informal writing for exploring and extending mathematical ideas, and student interpretation and creation of graphics and symbols (Sturtevant, 1994). Written language is defined broadly, to include visuals, graphics, and symbols. Mathematical literacy is seen both as a goal of instruction (that students will develop competence as readers, writers, and communicators of mathematics), and as an instrument students and teachers can use for thinking and learning in the mathematics classroom (Vacca & Vacca, 1999).

Despite this apparent convergence in the theories and goals of mathematics and literacy educators on a national level, very little is known about secondary school classroom teachers' actual experiences or perspectives related to the implementation of literacy-related strategies in mathematics. Secondary school mathematics teaching practices may differ radically from the instruction recommended by researchers and national standards documents, because positivistic principles that support lecture–recitation methods, or a "pedagogy of telling" (Sizer, 1985) has guided much secondary school teaching because the early 20th century (Cuban, 1986). Teachers who attempt change may encounter a variety of constraints or dilemmas that are only superficially understood by those outside their settings.

Case studies of individuals can help illuminate the complexities of specific situations and provide "insight into an issue" or a "refinement of theory" (Stake, 1994, p. 237). Over the past decade, case studies of secondary school science, social studies, and English teachers have increased our understanding of their instructional literacy practices (Hinchman, 1987; Moje, 1993; Stewart, 1989; Sturtevant, 1992, 1996a). This study was designed to extend this work to mathematics, with a particular focus on nontraditional beginning teachers. Although the entire project involved five teachers (Sturtevant, 1996b, 1997), the focus here is on Bob Hall, who began teaching high school mathematics at age 49 after retirement from the United States Navy.

Guiding purposes for the overall study were to explore (a) how the teachers described their mathematics instruction and uses of literacy from preservice teacher education through the first 3 years of teaching, and (b) how the teachers perceived that various influences interacted and affected their instruction over this time period, including their uses of literacy. Influences on instruction were defined very broadly (Sturtevant, 1996a), in the general domains of influences the teacher brought to the setting (beliefs, knowledge, personal experiences, etc.), and contextual influences existing in the setting (including students, other teachers, administrators, required curriculum, facilities, and so forth).

Bob's case was unique among the original five because he became a coresearcher for his own case study toward the end of the study, after he had left the classroom to take a position with a technology firm. As coresearcher, Bob read data from his entire case and assisted in the development of conclusions. Therefore, with Bob's case an additional guiding purpose was to explore how Bob viewed his own preservice education and teaching experiences when looking back, after he left the classroom.

THEORETICAL FRAMEWORK

This study was designed from a social-constructivist perspective, which holds that reality is socially and symbolically constructed (Berger & Luckmann, 1967; Schwandt, 1994). We agree with O'Brien, Stewart, and Moje (1995) that it is important to " … understand teachers, learning, and school life from the perspectives of the participants and to write about schooling in ways that represent the everyday lived experiences of teachers and students" (p. 458). In addition, we hold that a greater understanding of and respect for the local knowledge of teachers and other participants in secondary settings is vital. This local knowledge includes teachers' understanding of their teaching situations and their perceptions of their own beliefs and decisions.

We conceptualize this study as supported by two related bodies of literature: studies of teachers' belief development and of secondary school literacy practices in content area classrooms. Although both literatures are too large to consider fully here, we were specifically interested in work that addresses how teachers' beliefs develop over time and interact with other influences to affect literacy in secondary schools.

Teachers' Belief Development

We define *instructional beliefs* very broadly, as ideas, perceptions, and knowledge that teachers have about teaching. In particular, beliefs and knowledge were not considered separable, as some authors suggest, but rather as interwoven concepts teachers construct within their own frameworks, contexts, and cultural situations (see reviews, Anders & Evans, 1994; Pajares, 1992).

Teachers' instructional belief systems have been the focus of studies from widely differing perspectives (Pajares, 1992). Whereas many studies have found that teachers' beliefs influence instruction (e.g., Anders & Evans,

1994), it also has been found that teachers must weigh the importance of many factors, including their own pre-existing beliefs, when making instructional decisions (Knowles, 1992). In addition, studies from anthropology, psychology, sociology, and education support the premise that teachers' beliefs about instruction often begin to develop early in life and therefore, may resist change (Sturtevant, 1996a). However, even deeply held personal beliefs can be affected through an individual's gestalt shift (Pajares, 1992) or changes in the school culture (Van Fleet, 1979).

Knowledge of the process of instructional belief development, belief change over time, and interconnections between beliefs and instructional decision-making is still very limited (Pajares, 1992). For example, while several encouraging studies have found that preservice teachers in well-designed content literacy courses may develop positive beliefs about using content literacy strategies (e.g., Armstrong, Dubert, & Drabik, 1995), few studies have followed new teachers into the secondary school environment to see how they connect literacy related beliefs with practice during the first few years. Although the induction years of teaching are considered crucial to teacher development (Gold, 1996), most recent studies of secondary school literacy practices have focused on either experienced or preservice teachers.

Secondary Literacy Practices

During the 1980s, both large- and small-scale studies (e.g., Goodlad, 1984; McNeil, 1988) described secondary instruction in the United States as characterized by lecture and recitation, as it had been for the past century (Cuban, 1986). At the same time, a number of content literacy researchers began to explore relationships between school contexts and secondary teachers' uses of content area reading methods (e.g., Ratekin, Simpson, Alvermann, & Dishner, 1985; Smith & Feathers, 1983b), in part because both preservice and in-service secondary school teachers often seemed resistant to the value of content area reading (O'Brien, 1988). Scholars theorized that numerous aspects of secondary school contexts—from heavy required content coverage to colleague opinion—may dissuade teachers from using methods that encourage student discussion and decision-making, which is characteristic of many content literacy strategies (O'Brien et al., 1995). In addition, it was suggested that new teachers often model their instructional behavior after their own former teachers, which may perpetuate traditional ways of teaching (Kagan, 1992). Overall, it was recognized that efforts to improve secondary school literacy required a much more in-depth knowledge of the contexts of secondary schooling, the types of instruction that actually occurred in these settings, and the role of various influences on teachers' beliefs and decisions (Alvermann & Moore, 1991; Moore, 1996).

A number of studies have since documented influences on a few secondary school teachers' uses of literacy, finding that influences may emanate from a wide variety of sources both within and outside of the school setting, including a teacher's own philosophy and personal history (e.g., Dillon, O'Brien, Moje, & Stewart, 1994; Sturtevant, 1996a). Although these studies have, not surprisingly, found relationships between school contexts and teaching practices, they did not, as Moore pointed out (paraphrasing O'Brien et al., 1995), find teachers and students to be mere cogs in an institutional wheel: " … people did not passively react to systems; rather, people actively constructed, through negotiation and context, their lives within systems" (1996, p. 17).

In focusing our attention on beginning mathematics teachers, part of our interest was to expand knowledge of this specialty. Within secondary school literacy research, studies of mathematics are essential because modes of teaching and learning in this domain may differ from those in others that are less well-structured (Alexander, 1997). An additional goal was to provide a more situated view of the experiences of beginning teachers than has been provided by secondary school literacy case studies to this point. Whereas previous work has asked experienced teachers to reflect retrospectively on their early teaching (e.g., Moje, 1993; Sturtevant, 1996a), the hope in this study was to capture the beginning teacher story as it happened.

THE PROJECT

Beginnings

Three coresearchers participated in this project: Betty, a teacher–educator with an interest in secondary school literacy; Vicki, a graduate assistant and middle school teacher; and Bob, the beginning teacher introduced earlier who is the focus of the case.

Betty and Bob first became acquainted in the spring of 1993, when Betty was teaching a course entitled "Reading Across the Curriculum" at a small, private university near Washington, D.C. The course was part of a licensure program offered to military personnel who wanted to become secondary school teachers. The university had a government contract and special permission to offer the classes at the Navy Annex of the United States Military Headquarters (the Pentagon) in Arlington, VA. Bob, who at the time was a Captain in the United States Navy, was a student in the class.

The "Reading Across the Curriculum" course was required of all secondary school majors with the intent that they would learn methods of teaching reading and writing strategies appropriate to their content areas. Text materials included a basic text (Vacca & Vacca, 1993) and assignments specific to the needs of math and science teachers, since many students had these specialties. Betty also included reading and discussions that she hoped would help students understand the context of high school instruction, including reasons why high school teachers sometimes find it difficult to implement content literacy strategies.

At the end of the "Reading Across the Curriculum" course, Betty asked students to complete anonymous open-ended surveys designed to gain information on their beliefs about the usefulness of content area reading and writing strategies for their disciplines. Over two semesters, 93% of students indicated positive attitudes and identified specific strategies they hoped to use in their future teaching (Sturtevant, 1993). Many also indicated willingness to participate in interviews during student teaching. Of these, five class members, who would be student teaching in mathematics the next semester, were selected. The project then continued through the end of the 1996–1997 school year. Vicki joined the study in 1996 during her work as a graduate research assistant.

Personal Perspectives

The coresearchers had personal reasons for participating in the study, which we share to give a sense of our individual perspectives (Alvermann, Commeyras, Young, Randall, & Hinson, 1997). At the start of the study, Betty was a new assistant professor with an interest in literacy and the context of secondary school instruction. For both theoretical and practical reasons, she wanted to connect her research and teaching in a logical way. She also hoped to gain more knowledge about mathematics instruction in order to inform her work with mathematics teachers. During the course of the study, she changed positions, moving from the small university Bob had attended to a larger one in the same region.

Bob now recalls that when Betty originally asked him to participate in the study, she said "she wanted to follow the paths of military officers who chose teaching as a second career." During the year after he left the classroom, Bob recalled having three reasons for his initial interest in participating:

> "To get feedback and advice on how to use reading and writing across the mathematics curriculum I was about to teach....
>
> I saw the interaction with Betty as a forcing function to prod me to try some of the reading or writing activities prior to our discussions.

… I also saw this as a valuable source of guidance from someone who was naturally interested in and very knowledgeable in this subject area."

Interestingly, it seems in retrospect that Betty and Bob had potentially conflicting agendas at the start of the study: Whereas Betty was intending to explore what happened to new teachers in a natural school context, Bob was hoping that his own participation would provide additional "feedback" and "guidance" that he imagined a new teacher might find valuable. This difference in agendas may be quite natural given the perspectives of the "researcher" versus the "researched" at the time. Data were interpreted with this difference in mind. For example, data from class observations indicated that Bob always used literacy strategies during Betty and Vicki's visits. Because conversations with Bob indicated that he did this purposefully to get feedback and sometimes tried strategies he did not often use, it was never assumed that observations were revealing typical instruction.

Vicki first joined the study as a paid research assistant during her master's degree program. She later entered the university's doctoral program and decided to continue with the project on a voluntary basis because it related to her literacy major and provided "a unique, hands-on experience in aspects of qualitative research." During the final stage of the larger project, Vicki also joined a research team that analyzed data across cases (Sturtevant et al., 1997).

Design and Data Collection

This case study was designed as a qualitative, longitudinal case study with data collection at specific points in time (Merriam, 1988). Data collected included the following: (a) a written open-ended questionnaire at the end of the "Reading Across the Curriculum" course; (b) a total of six transcripts from hour-long interviews and related notes from teaching observations (twice during student teaching and the first 2 full years of teaching); (c) transcripts from two additional interviews during the year after Bob left teaching; and (d) electronic mail responses Bob composed and sent after reading his original 6 transcripts and summaries of these transcripts.

Class observations were made just prior to all interviews at Bob's teaching sites; these were used primarily to generate relevant questions for the interview sessions that followed. Since the focus of the study was on Bob's perceptions and descriptions of his own beliefs and decisions, the primary data sources were the interviews and Bob's written comments rather than observational data. All interviews were tape-recorded and transcribed.

Analysis Procedures

Analysis included on-going constant-comparative procedures in which data (the preservice phase questionnaire and essays, interview transcripts, observational notes, and classroom documents) were read and analyzed on an on-going basis in order to guide the next step in data collection (Glaser & Strauss, 1967). After the 2nd year of teaching, data were sorted, with computer assistance, into categories that emerged as significant after reading and rereading by the first and second authors (Merriam, 1988). This sorting process was completed and summaries written, first for each year separately, and then across years.

During data analysis in the last 6 months of the study, data collection was layered in the sense that written comments and transcribed interviews that related to discussion of previous interviews became new data (Alvermann et al., 1997). For example, in March 1997, Betty, Bob, and Vicki participated together in a 2-hour conversation related to Bob's new position and his reflections on entire teaching experience. Just after this point, we invited Bob to participate as a coauthor on this chapter, indicating that he could participate anonymously if he chose. Bob indicated a preference for using his own name rather than the pseudonym ("Will") that had been used to present his case in earlier reports (Sturtevant 1996a; 1997). Each of us then reread all of the data from the case, making written notes. In July 1997, we met again to compare our notes and discuss questions that had arisen during our rereading of the data. We tape-recorded this meeting. Transcripts of this meeting and the earlier one (spring, 1997) were sent via e-mail to all parties, as were summaries Vicki wrote of the six transcripts from the interviews during teaching.

Throughout July, August, and September, each of us then wrote more comments based on our reading of the meeting transcripts and Vicki's data summaries. These comments were downloaded and became another layer of data. Bob's comments from different points in time were kept separate so that we would clearly differentiate statements he had made during a particular year of teaching from those he had made at a later time while reflecting on his own experience. E-mail assisted with keeping the data sorted as the e-mail always was marked with a date and time.

THE STORY

Bob's Background and Decision to Teach

On his first day in Betty's class in the spring of 1993, Bob wrote on an index card that his ultimate goal was: "To become a great math teacher!" Four years later, during his postteaching interviews, Bob explained that he had decided to become a math teacher after so many years in the Navy partly because he had enjoyed working with young people for many years while raising his own three children and through involvement with church youth groups. Teaching "seemed like a natural thing to do." In 1990, the idea for his career change, however, really came into focus and was solidified for Bob when he read *Do What You Love, The Money Will Follow* (Sinetar, 1987). Bob remembers that this book asks readers to consider what they would want said as a eulogy after death, and he decided he wanted to be remembered as a teacher and positive role model for young people. Bob said he chose mathematics as a field because he had enjoyed mathematics throughout his life. He remembered that as a 6-year-old, his parents "would ask me to demonstrate ... addition skills in front of their friends ... I enjoyed the attention and found mathematics fun." Bob's bachelor's degree was in mathematics (Iowa State University); he also earned a master's degree in operations research–system analysis (United States Naval Postgraduate School of Monterey, California).

Bob's naval career included a variety of positions, including a 2-year assignment as a mathematics instructor at the United States Naval Academy in Annapolis, Maryland. Although he enjoyed this teaching experience, Bob now regrets that he did not have any knowledge of teaching strategies at that time. He explained that his Academy teaching involved mostly lecture and review of problem assignments, with instructors of various sections keeping to the same schedule. Later, Bob worked for 15 years in aircraft carrier construction and aircraft depot maintenance. This culminated with a 2-year assignment (1989 to 1991) as the Commanding Officer of the Naval Aviation Depot in San Diego, California, which employed 4000 military and federal civilian personnel. In 1991, he moved to northern Virginia, where he was head of the Total Quality Management Office at the Defense Logistics Agency. At this time, he began preparing to retire from the Navy and took the licensure courses for teaching offered at a local university.

During his first interview in student teaching, Bob was asked to describe one of his own teachers he admired, and another he did not. He spoke highly of one of his high school English teachers, a Christian Brother who "had high standards" but was "fair" and encouraging with a "you can do it" attitude. Bob said students "just knew if [they] followed this person it would lead to good stuff." Bob mentioned that he found the English course difficult, although the teacher gave extra credit to students that "read whole books." Bob had kept in contact with the teacher ever since high school, for 36 years.

When asked to recall a teacher whose instruction he did not like, Bob immediately recalled a high school math teacher who interacted little with students, was not challenging, and gave a final that required only memorization of steps in a problem. When asked about his decision to become a math teacher despite what he saw as some poor math instruction in his own background, Bob said, "Well, yeah, because I'm dissatisfied with the way a lot of math teachers teach … I'm just dissatisfied."

Career Transition and Student Teaching

During 1992–1993, Bob's last year in the Navy, he completed the five graduate-level education courses that were required for secondary licensure in his state-approved program. The coursework included the "Reading Across the Curriculum" course and a general secondary methods course, but no specific mathematics methods course. Bob then retired from the Navy and began 12 weeks of student teaching during the fall semester, 1993, in a large public high school about 20 miles south of Washington, D.C. This school, with about 3000 students, is located in a rapidly growing suburban area.

Bob's cooperating teacher, Sandy (a pseudonym), was a 20-year veteran teacher who had previously served as department chair. Her teaching load included both 9th graders (two sections) and 12th graders (three sections). All classes were at basic or average levels of achievement; the two ninth-grade classes were taught in a snack-bar area that was used temporarily as a classroom due to school overcrowding.

At the time of Bob's student teaching, Sandy had recently participated in regional workshops related to the implementation of National Council of Teachers of Mathematics National Standards (1989) in her school district. Sandy said she was experimenting with strategies she had learned in these workshops such as journal writing and small group discussions. Sandy also was implementing a new text in Grade 9 that included an emphasis on math communication (one goal in the NCTM Standards). Bob told Betty in his preliminary student teaching interview that he found the ideas Sandy was implementing similar to strategies he had heard and read about in his education courses and was glad to have the opportunity to try them during student teaching.

Literacy Practices.   Throughout his 12 weeks in the school, Bob said he and Sandy worked closely together and that she always encouraged him to try new things. Examples of the types of literacy assignments that Bob used in Sandy's classroom were teacher–student dialogue journals, writing out problems step-by-step ("we … encourage them to write the steps … so that nothing's missed because usually in any math problem there might be ten different steps … "), and asking students to translate mathematical expressions into words (" ... [what is] 25N?"). Bob indicated that students wrote in their journals about once a week. However, due to time constraints he and Sandy were only able to collect, read, and comment in the journals every 9 weeks. Journal topics ranged from reflections on the movie *Stand and Deliver*, to mathematical comparisons ("How are the 'real numbers' like a family?") to requests for student feedback on instruction ("What are your suggestions about how I have been teaching?"). Bob also sometimes asked students to give him written feedback on his instruction at the end of class. During the interviews, Bob indicated that he found this feedback very helpful, and gave an example of several students who requested that he slow down when introducing a new concept.

Cooperative Grouping. Bob also developed some lessons in which students worked in small groups to solve mathematical problems. He expressed a continuing interest in cooperative grouping, based in part on his Navy experiences: " ... because of the last two years of my job in quality management [Total Quality Management] in the Navy ... I could see the benefits of people working together, and the difficulties and the dynamics." Bob said he and Sandy used a cooperative exercise "about every three to four weeks" in their teaching. In contrasting these exercises with his Navy work, Bob explained:

> We're not taking these kids aside in a training class and [teaching them] the dynamics of forming a team ... because they barely know each other's names, and yet we are encouraging them [by saying] "Hey, why don't you share that a little bit."

An example of a cooperative activity occurred one day when Betty visited Bob's ninth grade class. Students were assigned to work in small groups to read word problems, make data charts, and share with the class using overhead transparencies. Bob said he developed this activity from a lesson in the new ninth grade math textbook.

Concerns. Despite Bob's high motivation during student teaching, he did experience some problems. Discipline seemed to be a constant concern for both Bob and Sandy, especially with ninth-grade students. During his second student teaching interview, Bob discussed this problem, explaining that both he and Sandy had "the same personality ... neither of us are real hard-nosed type people, and we have a tough time with discipline in the classroom." He indicated at the time that he wanted to do "something different in order to keep ... things under control." When speaking of the ninth grade, he identified the problem as partly students' "maturity level ... which is very low."

Concerns about discipline dissuaded Bob from using cooperative activities more frequently, as he found students' behavior worse when working in groups. During Betty's observation, she noted that students seemed very distractible and that it was very hard to hear during their presentations because of poor acoustics in the snack bar-classroom. Bob indicated later that at least one group was very frustrated by their assignment: "One group over here was really hung up on this one problem ... perhaps in reading the problem ... they were getting it all kind of mixed up."

By contrast, Bob described a cooperative activity his seniors had previously completed with two classes of another teacher, in which there was "a lot of interaction, teaming, learning, and wonderful feedback." Bob felt the senior classes' behavior was better because they were older and also because the classes occurred in the morning rather than after lunch. In addition, Bob explained that the ninth graders seemed generally more "edgy" than the 12th graders and were much more likely to "[get] up and walk around or [go] over and pick a fight" with other students. Bob expressed his frustration succinctly: " ... [it's] very frustrating, very scary ... when I hear from seasoned teachers who are tired ... frustrated ... just angry at the behavior of a lot of students ... Woa, what about a new guy?... What am I supposed to do?"

Bob also believed that his students' difficulties with reading and writing affected his ability to implement some teaching strategies. Sandy described the English reading achievement of students in their ninth grade "basic" classes as ranging "anywhere from 4th grade reading to no English at all because we have ESL students." Bob later said that while in a sense the new math book's inclusion of "more writing activities [and] reading activities" was positive, he was concerned that " ... a lot of the kids can't handle [the book] ... there's more writing and reading in a math course than I've ever seen before ... which makes it harder for the students." Giving an example of an ESL student who had been in the United States about 2 years, Bob said the student had interpreted the phrase "twenty-six" as "20 minus 6." Bob said that school policy was to place new ESL students directly into regular math classes, because it was thought math was universal. However, both Sandy and Bob worried that the use of reading and writing activities in the mathematics curriculum might make math learning harder for both ESL students and native English speakers who found reading and writing difficult.

Bob's Reflections.   At the end of student teaching, Bob was asked to reflect on what he thought would be the ideal environment for teaching math. He responded that he would request a room and appropriate desks where students could work either individually or cooperatively in groups of four or eight. He explained that despite some problems with cooperative groups, he still disliked lectures and wanted students involved in doing things as their primary method of learning.

When asked if his beliefs about teaching changed during the student teaching experience, Bob explained that he really became more convinced that teaching was what he wanted to do. He also said that one important belief he held was "that students and teachers learn simultaneously; we learn as we go."

Bob's Entry Into Full Time Teaching

In January 1994, Bob accepted a position in a high school about 10 miles from his student teaching site, in the same district. With about 1500 students, this school was much smaller than his previous school but had a more diverse population. During the spring, he taught a full load of students taking Algebra I, Applied Algebra, and Applied Geometry. The next fall, when he began his first full year of teaching, Bob remained in the same school. He was assigned to a ninth-grade team, with students split between Applied Algebra (Pre-Algebra) and Algebra I. Interviews took place during Bob's first full year assignment (1994–1995).

Bob's team was interdisciplinary and shared the same students. The district and school were using site-based management practices that gave teachers some freedom in decision-making. For example, at the beginning of the year, Bob arranged his students into mathematics classes based on achievement test scores. Within the school, teachers of the same subject also worked together to select textbooks for purchase. In addition, the ninth-grade team had decision-making power in scheduling. Although at the start of the year they had traditional 45-minute classes, in March, they decided to change to block scheduling so that classes came less frequently, but for 90 minutes. Bob initially hoped his team also would work closely together for instructional planning. However, at the end of the year he explained this had not occurred, due, he felt, to personalities, a lack of knowledge about how to work as a team, and lack of a regular team-planning period.

Teaching Situation.   Bob's classes ranged from 20 to 28 students, with an average size of 24. His classroom was very small for the number of students, with student desks all the way to the back and sides of the class and only a small space between the rows. Bob thought his assignment to a small room was mainly due to the "pecking order" in the school, with new teachers assigned to the smallest rooms. Overall, however, Bob described the school administration as very supportive and said he felt very "comfortable" with them.

When discussing curriculum, Bob indicated that while he felt he had overall freedom in how to teach, the district curriculum had recently been rewritten with required math objectives that were "pretty heavy." The department designed a test for each course at the end of the year to measure students' mastery of the objectives, although sometimes teachers who worked with lower achieving students were allowed to "delete parts of [the test]." Bob thought that common goals for the Algebra I classes were a good idea: "We're all trying to have the kids at a certain level [so when we] turn [them] over to the other math teachers [we can say] 'yep, they're ready for geometry.'"

Bob described his students as "nice kids" who were sometimes difficult to teach because they "like[d] to socialize." He said, as he had earlier during student teaching, that he did not have "the personality ... of really ... coming down hard" but instead found that he needed to "come up with more and more exercises ... in order to keep their interest." He described the teaching experience with these ninth-grade students as "incredibly intense," making a succinct comparison to his previous role as a Commanding Officer:

> I've run a 4,000-person organization before, and it's not nearly as intense as coming in here and trying to figure how to orchestrate 25 kids that come in every day with different agendas, different things on their minds, some good and some bad. There is all this variation and change, it's just incredible.

Bob said that while he was "trying to get very tough" he also kept "looking for the easier way, or the more efficient way" to manage his classes. He also tried to teach behavioral standards through discussions about values with students: "I also take liberty in talking about life, and talking about behavioral standards—language—being a gentlemen—[a] lady ... so I am on their case a lot about that, at the same time that I'm teaching ... "

Literacy Practices.   Visits to Bob's classroom occurred prior to both scheduled interviews. Students completed math-related writing activities during a part of each observed class. As mentioned earlier, Bob specifically used literacy activities during Betty's visits in order to gain her feedback. When interviewed in November, Bob said that he had used a writing activity about once a month, or three times to that point.

Bob often selected his writing activities from a book on mathematics writing (Gray, 1993) that he said he ordered for about $15 from a NCTM advertisement. For example, he used two writing prompts from this book: "write a 25-word definition of multiplication" and "explain in writing the mathematical terms 'rise' and 'run.'" Bob described that his "main purpose" in giving writing assignments was to help students learn "to be able to write something about mathematics that is clear, that is understandable." He also hoped that, as a teacher, he could learn more about what students "know and understand" by reading their writing.

Bob found students' written products widely varied, and gave an example of one struggling student who wrote: "Rise is the amount up, run is the amount over." Bob explained that while short, this answer was correct and "to the point." Other students wrote lengthy accurate descriptions including diagrams, but some students' written work was very short or incomprehensible: "some of them put down [answers] … I didn't have a clue [as to] what they [were] talking about." Bob worried that sometimes writing exercises may be "not a measure of [students'] math ability, so much as of their writing ability." Later, he explained that he thought that some students could calculate a slope, but found the writing difficult: "It's one thing to sit down and work a math problem; it's another thing entirely to explain it in words." Nonetheless, he indicated that he thought this was an important goal.

Bob also expressed uncertainty about how to grade students' writing, indicating he planned to show the papers to the team's English teacher "to get an assessment of how I [should] grade these." He speculated that the question might not have been a good one for some students, and wondered if he should have students rewrite the papers as a follow-up exercise. Overall, Bob said he was "looking at [the day's writing activity] as a signal to myself on what … they know."

When discussing his uses of reading, Bob explained that most reading assigned was from the textbook, which students were asked to read at home or in class: " … periodically I will say … let's … read the opening of this section." In the fall interview, Bob described his textbook as "big [and] colorful" with a "tremendous amount of applications," or real-life situations. However, by spring he noted that he did not think the book was really effective because the author "failed … to provide a sufficient amount of practice problems of the traditional type … [and sometimes] puts two or three concepts in a single day's assignment." On reflection, Bob said, "At first I fell in love with this text … but then students kept having more and more problems with it." For his applied classes, Bob supplemented the text heavily with worksheets: "[I] don't use the book as much … [but rather] a lot more … worksheets." These provided the extra practice he felt students needed; in addition, he found that students in the applied classes focused better on completing an assignment when it was on a single worksheet rather than embedded in the text. Another difficulty Bob found was that many students could do calculations but had difficulty with interpreting and solving word problems:

What we're finding is that kids are able to work a traditional algebra problem set up with variables and coefficients ... [but] they have a very difficult time with ... a word problem ... trying to decipher what is being asked ... then applying a mathematical model to it.

Bob also used other types of mathematical reading and writing activities, such as charts, graphs, and visual representations. His department had enough graphing calculators for students to use in class, and Bob said they completed related exercises in "every chapter" of the textbook. In the fall, he developed some charting activities, such as a project in which students made charts showing the correlation of height to shoe size of themselves and classmates. During the spring, students completed a unit on probability that Bob described as his most successful teaching activity during the year. This unit included activities with playing cards, dice, and M&Ms that were recorded and described through graphing. Another visual activity Bob designed involved students drawing sketches of "Mathland," including fantasy items such as a "subtraction slide" or a "fraction flyer." Students were expected to explain a mathematical concept or principle in their drawings. He also used art during a cartooning activity in which students enlarged cartoons to scale using a grid. Bob explained that he "got [the cartoon activity] from another teacher" and that "the kids really enjoyed [it]."

Cooperative Grouping.   For a few of his classroom activities, such as the probability unit, Bob said he had students work in pairs or groups. However, despite his previous interest in cooperative grouping strategies, during this school year he did not feel ready to start any extensive group work. While he thought that "the kids would probably enjoy working with each other, and [would learn] from each other as well," he was concerned about potential disciplinary problems: " ... the thing I've been afraid of so far, is the behavioral thing, and keeping things under control, especially [with students] at this age." He went on to say that he felt he "[needed] to figure out the cooperative learning" but that he was "afraid to let go ... [because] I don't know what's going to happen." Bob did indicate that his school administration supported the use of cooperative learning and was providing some training that he planned to take advantage of: "I'm still learning how to do that, I really am ... I'm going to a workshop they're having here in school tomorrow ... that's probably going to be my next thing to get a handle on ... besides [more] writing exercises ... " He went on to say that overall, in his teaching he was just "trying to figure out what makes sense ... "

Bob's Reflections on the First 18 Months.   At the end of the year, Bob was asked to compare his first 18 months of full-time teaching with his student teaching experience. He said that while he believed his ideas about teaching had not really changed from the student teaching experience, he had become more versatile in different techniques. Bob explained that both his wife and his department had helped him a great deal. Bob's wife, Nancy, had experience in several part-time teaching positions, including work with preschoolers and prison inmates. Bob said he and Nancy sometimes discussed teaching ideas and that one of her friends lent him some manipulative materials he hoped to use the next year.

With regard to his department, Bob said he often gained ideas from other math teachers and that the department was compiling a book of teaching strategies for their own use. He also admired the teaching of several department members, and hoped that a particular teacher would be able to work with him as a mentor the following year:

> I want to see how she introduces the class, how she guides the class without being an ogre. She allows kids flexibility in doing things certain times, but I want to see how she pulls it back together again. I want to see how to deal with the kids and [how to] motivate a kid from class clown to someone engaged.

When asked what he wanted to do differently the next year, Bob's first response was "get a little more sleep!" He also said he would "like to have more students gain a sense of increasing their mathematics skills" and that he "would like to have a better behaved class with more students engaged" and that he needed "to learn more how to get student centered, you know, [become] more of a facilitator."

Summary.   During this time period, Bob tried a wide variety of teaching strategies, including some that involved reading, writing, and interpretation of mathematical symbols and graphics. He believed his department and school administration were supportive, although he wished that teachers on his interdisciplinary ninth-grade team had worked more closely together. He taught a full load of Grade 9 in a crowded classroom, and expressed continuing frustration over student behavior. These difficulties dissuaded him from trying much cooperative learning, although he continued to express interest in these strategies.

Throughout the year, Bob worked toward improving his own knowledge about teaching, as evidenced through his seeking of advice in his department and from his wife, in his attendance at workshops, and in his continued participation in this study. He also was working to arrange a mentorship for himself the following year as he thought it would be very valuable to learn from an experienced math teacher. Overall, it seems that while Bob found the year intense and exhausting, he also felt he was increasing in competence in his new career.

Bob's Second Full Year of Teaching

For the 1995–1996 school year, Bob returned to the same high school. By this time all grade levels had adopted the same school-wide block schedule, with full-year courses taught in half a year. Classes meet five times a week for 85 minutes and students completed four courses each semester. Teachers' schedules included three classes and one preparation period each day. Bob moved to a larger room, located upstairs near other math department classes rather than within an interdisciplinary team setting.

Teaching Situation.   At the beginning of the year, Bob was again teaching mostly ninth graders, with two classes of Algebra I and one class of Pre-Algebra. For second semester, he had two Pre-Algebra classes and an elective statistics course for juniors and seniors. This was the first time Bob was assigned to teach an upper level class, which he described as "the closest thing to heaven that I've had." It also was the first time since student teaching that he taught a class that was not primarily ninth graders. When asked about this, Bob indicated that school tradition seemed to dictate that new teachers were assigned ninth grade and lower level courses. He gave an example of another math teacher who had just joined the staff and was teaching all ninth graders. Bob explained: "This is something called rank has its privileges … the experienced teachers have already gotten to a certain level … they've developed the courses and it's sort of [an] unwritten [policy]." He did mention that some experienced teachers chose to teach at least one lower level class per year.

When describing the statistics course, Bob indicated that he especially enjoyed the course content, saying it was "the stuff I taught before at the Naval Academy … I have a master's in it, almost." Bob explained his perception of the effect of his content knowledge and enjoyment of the subject: "I just love it, to begin with … [and]… I'm comfortable with the course content, so it's just [a matter of deciding] … what to teach … or what objectives." In this class, 20 of the 26 students were identified as gifted.

Students in the Pre-Algebra classes were generally below average in math achievement, as most students in the district took Algebra in Grade 9 or Grade 8. In addition, about five students identified as having special needs (Learning Disabled and Emotionally Disturbed) were mainstreamed into one of the Pre-Algebra classes. A special education teacher worked in the classroom 2 days per week to assist these students. Bob commented that he thought "most of [the mainstreamed students] are able to do the work, they're just slower.… "

Bob found behavior management difficult in the Pre-Algebra classes, especially for the third-period class that occurred after lunch. Bob worried that behavior problems affected instruction, mentioning one day, for example, that this class "had less lesson today than what I had hoped for." He developed varied presentation strategies ("I use the overhead and look at them, or if they are calmed down enough, then I can go and use the board"). He also included a variety of short activities within each 85-minute class period: "[with the] lower-level class[es], I have to have about 5 different [activities] for a routine class just to have any success ... its very challenging ... " Activities Bob mentioned included textbook problems, worksheets, "a variety of visuals," computer math games, and some "writing exercises." One goal was "to give the kids ... variety in working these problems, because it's essentially the same [mathematical] process but looking at it ... slightly [differently]."

Literacy Practices. Mathematical reading and writing were embedded within much of what Bob's students did in class and for homework; this included solving of equations, interpretation of word problems, and reading and creation of charts and graphs. Bob also made specific attempts to teach students how to read and solve written problems. When asked if students found word problems difficult, Bob replied "yes, very much so, they don't want to tackle them ... so [this term] I'm trying to [say] 'come one, let's take these apart a little bit at a time.... '" He placed a chart on the classroom wall showing steps for solving math word problems, and said that about every 2 or 3 weeks he worked with Pre-Algebra students on related lessons. Bob's instruction in problem solving differed between the two Pre-Algebra classes due to adjustments he made related to student behavior. For example, on the day of one observation Bob said that with the first period Pre-Algebra class he had gone "over all the answers" and led students through an inquiry process "[asking students] what does that [problem] say to you?" However, the third-period class did not get through this activity because they "were disruptive."

Students in both upper- and lower-level classes were involved in the creation of charts and graphs. The statistics students were observed in a computer-graphing project, while the Pre-Algebra students participated in an unusual multiclass activity in which marines from a nearby military facility came to the school and took students' pulse and blood pressure. Students then recorded the data in chart format and used them for problem solving. The statistics students worked in groups for their project. As in the 1st year, Bob said that disciplinary concerns dissuaded him from using group activities with the lower-level classes.

In addition to writing equations and charts, Bob said he asked students to write brief explanations of mathematical concepts about "every two or three weeks." These activities were similar to the types of writing Bob used in the 1st year, such as asking the statistics students to write an (unsent) letter to a friend that explained the terms "mean," "median," and "mode." As in the previous year, Bob had concerns about evaluating writing. He met with members of the English department who advised that he mark errors in grammar but grade only for content. Bob's goals in encouraging writing included helping students:

> To be able to write coherently ... [to] write a sentence with nouns and verbs and be able to express themselves in the Kings' English.... I read some of this stuff and it's just horrible ... I would like for them to be able to read or ... write better....

Bob also used student writing for diagnostic purposes: "I ... think that writing gives me an idea of whether they understand [math concepts]. If I can read a story [they wrote] ... I can tell if they used the process right.... " When asked if he saw writing as a means of learning for students, Bob was unsure: " ... as far as whether it's a learning vehicle ... I suppose [it might be] ... especially when they get a paper back [from me] and it says [to the student] 'yep you do understand the concepts here.'" Overall, Bob saw writing as "another way of reinforcing [concepts]" and found that with his lower level classes, especially, he was "at the stage of [just] encouraging them to write anything."

Making Connections.   Throughout the year, Bob described numerous instances of teachers working with other teachers on instruction, both within the school and across schools in the district. For example, within the mathematics department teachers who taught the same course had occasional meetings, with one serving as lead teacher. Informally, Bob had sought out a mentor. As mentioned earlier, at the end of the 1st year he had located a mentor and was looking forward to working with her. However, he said this "fizzled out" because the teacher was assigned to teach a different course. Nonetheless, Bob persisted and located a different mentor, whom he found helpful. Unfortunately, their time to meet was very limited due to different planning periods.

During the 2nd year, Bob also was clearly doing some informal mentoring of at least two new teachers in the math department. On the day of one observation, for example, he had several brief hallway conversations with one new math teacher about instruction and later assisted another in planning a writing assignment. Bob also mentioned school-to-school connections that went back several years. For example, he used one activity in statistics that involved use of cookies for measurement. Bob explained that he first saw this activity in the class of a teacher at a nearby school about 3 or 4 years earlier during an observation for one of his graduate classes. He called this teacher the "statistics guy in this county" because the teacher offered help to others and had developed an Advanced Placement Statistics course that had recently gained district approval.

The district also provided instructional support that Bob found useful. For example, in the summer of 1995 he attended a writing-related inservice and learned the Role, Audience, Format, Topic (RAFT) writing strategy (Rusnak, 1994). Bob later said RAFT was "probably the best [strategy] I used in writing across the curriculum" and explained that since other teachers in his school were not aware of the strategy, he "spread it around among teachers during the school year."

Bob's Reflections at Mid-Year.   In early winter, Bob discussed with Betty and Vicki how his 2nd year of teaching had been different from the first. He mentioned the value of increased experience: "You know, just being there ... it's easier in looking for resources, having seen where they are ... and feeling more comfortable with the administrators and other teachers ... it just [comes] with time." Although he still found teaching challenging ("I really don't know how to deal with ... [some] kids, like in third period"), he thought he would stay at the school: "I like it here. What I really like is ... the support of the staff and the teachers ... [and] the principal ... he works very hard in hiring people that fit well ... that means a lot to me."

Change of Assignment.   When Betty visited Bob late in the 1995–1996 school year, she was surprised to find that he had changed teaching positions. In April 1996, Bob switched jobs with another teacher in his building who tutored individual students under a grant-funded program. Bob explained what occurred:

> In a nutshell, I found it very frustrating teaching to this one class in particular, and I approached the principal and he asked me to think about it.... In the meantime I knew of a [first year] teacher in the building who taught basically as a tutor to groups of students who had come for help [from classes]. I approached her and asked her if she wanted some classroom experience.

After this change, Bob reflected that he had repeatedly sought help related to disciplinary problems in Period 3 and felt his administrator had done his best to assist: "I've had many talks with my administrator. He [knew] I [was] struggling in there. I asked him to come up and sit in my class [to] give me some ideas.... I just haven't been able to internalize [the ideas] and change my own mode of how to work in the classroom." Bob said that his administrator also had tried to reassure him by saying that " Historically, one out of your classes will be really bad," but that he did not want to "go on with that ... [because] ... I [spent] more time worrying about how to teach the class and keep kids under wraps ... than I [did] ... trying to focus on the good kids, and how to become more creative for them ... and it shouldn't be [like] that."

In the new position, Bob worked with students who asked for extra help in both mathematics and other courses. With teacher permission, these students could leave their classes and go to the tutoring center. Overall, Bob enjoyed the one-on-one work with students and felt they made progress in the program. In June, however, he was unsure if he would return to the school the next year, in part because the grant funding was running out. At this time, he said that he had applied to the local Catholic school system and also was inquiring about jobs with consulting firms. He indicated that if he worked for the private sector he hoped to continue as a teacher or trainer of adults.

Post Script

Bob left teaching and went to work for a technology company during the summer of 1996. When interviewed in the spring of 1997, he said that while his new job was not teaching-related, he had continued teaching as a private math tutor and as a Sunday school teacher for young adolescents. During this interview, Bob reflected extensively on his teaching experiences, and later agreed to join the study as a coresearcher.

DISCUSSION AND IMPLICATIONS

In fall, 1998, Bob returned to teaching and currently is a faculty member at a private high school. This study focused on one "nontraditional" beginning teacher as he changed from Naval officer to mathematics teacher. Over a 3-year period, Bob welcomed one, and later two, literacy researchers into his classroom. He openly shared his experiences, successes, frustrations, and dilemmas. He spent hours in conversation about his life and his instruction. Although Bob eventually left teaching, he still continued participation in the study, as a coresearcher on his own case.

But what is the ultimate value of a case study of one teacher? Merriam suggested that a single case study may offer "insights and [illuminate] meanings that expand its readers' experiences" (1988, p. 32). In addition, case studies can build theory grounded in the specifics of human experience, especially when considered together with other studies (Glaser & Strauss, 1967). In this section, we share issues Bob's case raises for us, with the hope these issues will serve as springboards for the reflections of others.

Uses of Literacy

As explained in the beginning of this chapter, few studies have explored the classroom literacy practices of mathematics teachers. Table 4.1 briefly summarizes Bob's uses of literacy in his teaching. It seems notable that he maintained an interest in reading and writing in mathematics instruction over time, although implementation varied. For example, although Bob did not continue some practices (such as journals) that he began in student teach-

TABLE 4.1

Influences That Bob Perceived Affected His Instruction Over Three Years

	Positive	Negative
Personal Influences	Teacher education program.	Prior misconceptions about teaching.
	Previous work and life experiences.	Inexperience in teaching.
	Conversations with family–friends.	Personal exhaustion from teaching.
Contextual Influences	Helpful colleagues in school and district.	Interdisciplinary team not trained in teamwork.
	Administrative support.	Schedule primarily of Grade 9 and low-track classes.
	School and district in-service program.	Behavior of students.
		Size of classes.
		Overwhelming paperwork.
		Limited time and space.
		Uneven quality of textbooks.

ing, he attended in-service meetings and learned other strategies that he used more extensively. Overall, he seemed to use an eclectic variety of teaching methods, bringing in whatever he thought would help students learn the material. This purpose seems consistent with previous findings related to other secondary teachers' uses of literacy. Over a decade ago, for example, Hinchman (1987) reported that secondary school science, social studies, and English teachers thought of reading and writing mostly as means of conveying content.

Influences on Instruction

Influences on Bob's instruction can be categorized (Table 4.1) as those that were more personal versus those that were more related to the context of teaching, with the caveat that because influences often interact, borders between them are fuzzy. In our analysis, we coded personal influences as those that affected Bob prior to his mathematics teaching experiences, or those that were related primarily to his personal life, family, or his own personal belief system. Contextual influences were those that occurred or originated in his teaching contexts, including both people (e.g., students, colleagues, and administrators) and conditions (e.g., time constraints, curriculum, and textbooks).

Personal Influences.   An overarching theme that emerged from Bob's story is that high school teaching is incredibly complex—even for someone who has successfully run a large military base! Bob entered teaching with many background experiences that could certainly be considered positive. These included a successful career, positive experiences working with young people, prior teaching experience, and success in a teacher education program and student teaching. However, he later said that he originally had "incredibly naive" conceptions of what high school teaching would be like, as he thought he would have "time to plan exciting lessons, students who exhibited proper behavior, " and students who would be reading at the eighth-grade level or higher." In looking back, Bob described his teacher education program (including the "Reading Across the Curriculum" course) as "extremely useful" but too limited. He recommended more coursework on classroom management, teaching methods, and assessment, as well as full-year student teaching with "three or four mentoring teachers." Bob's state-approved graduate-level teacher education program included 15 credit hours of education courses before student teaching. It did not include a course specific to methods of teaching mathematics or a course in behavior management, although related topics were included in some of his other courses.

It seems that Bob's story illustrates concerns that should be addressed by teacher education programs, school districts, and state policy makers. Although teacher educators may see Bob's coursework as very limited, the trend in the state where Bob worked was toward alternate routes to teacher certification that provided even less preparation than his state-approved university program. New models of teacher preparation that help students build an in-depth knowledge of teaching and learning, that provide bridges from teacher education to school classrooms, and that help new teachers identify and modify their misconceptions seem urgently needed. In our view, high quality programs are intensive and time-consuming, and cannot be developed as a quick fix to teacher shortages. Promising programs such as various professional development school models (Holmes Group, 1990) with full-year internships are worthy of further study.

Contextual Influences.   As illustrated in Table 4.1, Bob experienced many contextual influences that he found both positive and negative. With regard to his interactions with colleagues and administrators in his school settings, Bob uniformly described these individuals as friendly and helpful. He did, however, regret that his interdisciplinary team in Year 1 did not work together more effectively, and he believed that training in team work would have been useful. Bob also took initiative in trying to locate mentors for himself—although he did not achieve as much success in this area as he wished, because of changing schedules. However, he reported that two "informal" mentors in his school gave him valuable assistance, such as "ideas … for hands-on experiences" and help with how to teach "various math concepts."

A contextual situation of major influence, that Bob described as "tradition," was the practice of assigning new teachers to the low-track classes or to classes of ninth-grade students, which teachers tended to find more difficult to manage. Although reasons for these management difficulties are beyond the scope of this report, related issues were the inclusion of special needs students in the classes and the generally large size of the classes. The tradition of assigning the most difficult classes to new teachers is, in our experience, common in high schools and also was reported by Goodlad (1984) in his large-scale study of secondary education. Another tradition in Bob's school was that of assigning the newest teachers to the smallest classrooms. Combined together (the largest, most difficult to manage classes in the smallest rooms, with the newest teachers) these practices seem a recipe for difficulty for beginning teachers. Studies of teacher development indicate that teaching knowledge develops gradually as new teachers learn to combine their personal theories with classroom realities, and new teachers need substantial support as they enter the profession (Gold, 1996). An additional, very serious concern is that these practices seem to totally disregard the needs of the students with the greatest educational difficulty, blatantly marginalizing them not only to lower tracks within the school setting but also to the most difficult instructional circumstances. In our view, this situation, which may be pervasive in high schools, requires the urgent attention of school administrators and policy makers.

Contextual Interactions.   Interactions between various contextual influences, and between the contextual and personal, also were important. Jacob (1999) provided a useful image for considering context: that of a forest, in which parts of an ecosystem mutually influence one another. Bob's decisions about cooperative grouping are illustrative of this perspective. The value of cooperative grouping seemed to be an important part of Bob's belief system when he entered student teaching, as he explained that he had taught group methods as part of his Navy position and strongly believed in their value. He even frequently wore a button that said: "None of us is as strong as all of us." In addition, Bob was aware that grouping methods had been stressed in the "Reading Across the Curriculum Course," since many literacy-related teaching strategies require group discussion, and current conceptions of literacy include oral as well as written communication (Vacca & Vacca, 1999).

In the early parts of student teaching, Bob tried to implement group strategies, with the support of his cooperating teacher. However, over his 3 years of teaching he reduced his use of group methods, so that by the last year he said he only used group methods with his (one) upper-track class because of disciplinary problems in the other classes. As noted earlier, the conditions for teaching and learning in Bob's lower-track classes were difficult, which related to a complex interplay of contextual traditions and decision-making at the school level and beyond. Although Bob still professed a belief in the potential value of cooperative grouping methods, he felt unable to implement them.

In our view, future research on the ways various personal and contextual influences interact and affect instruction is essential. Teacher educators, school-based educators, and administrators need much more information about how instructional decisions are made, including why some very promising teaching strategies may go unused. If, for example, Bob's experiences with grouping are played out in other settings, then a great many students in low-track classes may never experience the value of instruction that includes discussion.

In the end, we hope this study serves as an impetus for further inquiry and that it encourages all those interested in the education of both young people and their teachers to work together. Teaching is challenging, especially for the new teacher. Although Bob's story is his own, and unique in that sense, the issues raised here also affect the teaching and learning of numerous others.

5

Engaging At-Risk High School Students: Literacy Learning in a High School Literacy Lab

David O'Brien
Purdue University

Rebecca Springs
David Stith
Lafayette Jefferson High School

In this chapter, we present a case based on a 4-year project in which we developed an innovative curriculum for *at-risk* high school students and studied its effectiveness. The project, The Literacy Lab, is located at Lafayette Jefferson High School, in Lafayette, Indiana. The school is a comprehensive high school that is attended by 2200 students. The Literacy Lab enrolls students who are the lowest achievers in reading in the school. These students, who are traditionally known as *remedial readers*, provided us with academic histories in which they chronicled a series of negative school experiences rooted firmly in elementary school and amplified through the grades. From their earliest encounters with schooling, they were predestined to fail in an unbending system reluctant to invite them into its community.

We initially studied the students' literacy engagement as part of the broad organizing theme of the National Reading Research Center (Alvermann & Guthrie, 1993) using frameworks from achievement motivation and historically and institutionally generated definitions of at riskness (O'Brien, Dillon, Wellinski, Springs, & Stith, 1997). Within this theoretical framework of engagement, we accepted the way these students had been positioned and helped them be more successful in school, although we critiqued traditional notions of at-riskness that placed blame for their circumstances on students and their families. However, after constructing the program and spending 2 years studying its efficacy, we realized that our perspective on engagement must be broadened to include more of the fabric of their experiences rooted in school culture and popular youth culture.

Terms like *at risk* or *remedial* permit the institution of the school to position these adolescents as failures and as persons likely to continue to fail, unlikely to fit into the system, and, inevitably, persons who will suffer sanctions for nonconformity. As we constructed the program and researched its effectiveness, we cautioned ourselves not to peer into the students' academic lives, past or present, without examining critically or naming (Fine, 1991) the institutional constraints and practices that marginalize them in relation to the mainstream school community. We realized the limitations of constructing a program that elevated slightly the status of these students while continuing to position them as inadequate in terms of school-based notions of literacy (official forms of reading and writing) and traditional notions of text (print). We tried to create a motivating and intellectually challenging curriculum that allowed the students to develop literate practices as a social and cultural process mediated by their interest in and expertise with popular culture, particularly media.

In this chapter, we first discuss theories that frame our work with these marginalized adolescents. We define low literacy attainment from two perspectives: (a) perspectives grounded in the institutional response to being at risk for failure or dropping out of school; and (b) the engagement perspective, particularly the position articulated in motivation theory and studied recently by literacy researchers (e.g., Alvermann & Guthrie, 1993). Then we explore how socially and culturally mediated perspectives on literacy, particularly multiple literacies (Alvermann, Hinchman, Moore, Phelps, & Waff, 1998; Barton, 1994; New London Group, 1996; Street, 1984) defined from a popular cultural perspective, particularly literacy practices linked to the popular media culture (Buckingham & Sefton-Green, 1994; C. Luke, 1993), can counter traditional notions of literacy failure and expand positively on school-based notions of literacy and text. The study was guided by the following questions:

1. What is literacy engagement in a program in which students situate their practices as social and cultural practices, particularly as practices electronically mediated within popular youth culture?

2. How does the program mitigate against traditional notions of school failure and remediation supported by traditional school culture and its attendant definitions of literacy and text?

THEORETICAL FRAMEWORKS

In this section we discuss briefly the traditional theoretical perspectives on so-called at-risk adolescents who struggle in school, particularly as they are defined within the institutionalized structure and practices of secondary schools. Then we use engagement as a lens to critique the predominant theoretical perspective on at-riskness grounded in institutionalized practices. Finally, we discuss a perspective that defines literacy as a socially and culturally mediated practice.

Literacy Campaigns:
At-Risk Students or At-Risk Schools?

Programs for at-risk students, particularly students who struggle with reading and writing, are propped up by the same literacy campaigns as national and international campaigns that inflate the numbers of illiterates to overdramatize the social and economic consequences for these people (Street, 1984, 1995). The campaigners construct a political agenda using war, crime, and disease metaphors that position illiterates as naive victims and societal burdens (Ilsley & Stahl, 1993). Such campaigns secure funding for programs rather than opportunities for clients.

For example, at-riskness, which is often directly or indirectly tied to low literacy attainment, is blamed for billions of dollars in lost productivity, social programs, and incarceration of adolescents who become so disenfranchised in school that they drop out (Garcia & de Felix, 1995). Granted, high school graduates in the United States have trouble with the literacy demands of the workplace (Lewis, 1990; Mikulecky & Drew, 1991; SCANS Report, 1991) and the community (Alvermann & Guthrie, 1993; O'Brien & Dillon, 1994, 1995). But the most disturbing aspect of the problem is not its magnitude, which depends on the political faction characterizing it, but our inability as educators to adequately address it in school despite its early identification (Allington & McGill-Franzen, 1993).

The current campaign is the campaign against *aliteracy*—when students who have the ability, choose not to engage in reading (Foertsch, 1992; Guthrie, Bennett, & McGough, 1994; Mikulecky, 1978). These aliterate adolescents spend more time watching MTV and *Beavis and Butthead*, playing video games, or listening to music than reading. None of these activities, although genuine literate practices within a broader definition of literacy, is accorded the status of traditional practices endorsed by the institution of the school. These adolescents are engaging in complex literate practices crucial to how they read and write their world and construct their identities in it.

Any study of the literacy engagement of adolescents must consider institutional perspectives on schooling and literacy learning. In spite of unique features that distinguish individual schools, secondary schools share institutionalized organizational structures, practices, and beliefs (Boyer, 1983; Cusick, 1983; Goodlad, 1984; Lieberman & Miller, 1992; McLaughlin & Talbert, 1990; Powell, Farrar, & Cohen, 1985; Sedlak, Wheeler, Pullin, & Cusick, 1986; Sizer, 1992, 1996) that impact student learning and define the values placed on various literacy practices (O'Brien, 1998; O'Brien, Moje, & Stewart, chap. 2., this volume; O'Brien, Stewart, & Moje, 1995). The secondary school, as an institutionalized experience, shapes the way students perceive themselves and influences how they assign value to activities in which they engage. We examine this experience for adolescents who are classified as at risk.

When we use the term at-risk, we understand its ambiguity and political implications. The prevailing definition of at-riskness castes it as an environmentally linked malady: The students and their families are at fault—students are predisposed to fail due to factors beyond the scope of schools' control (Donmoyer & Kos, 1993; Ralph, 1989). For example, at-risk students have been defined as persons likely to fail in school because they (a) are educationally disadvantaged, exhibit low achievement, and have trouble adapting to school; (b) show outward signs of distress and failure due to alcohol and drug abuse, unwed pregnancy, attempted suicide, crime, delinquency, or truancy; (c) are children of the urban poor or members of racial minorities that have been recognized historically as problematic to the larger society and particularly needy in terms of education and special resources (Cuban, 1989); and (d) have genetic or psychological inadequacies in their preschool lives that predispose them to failure in school (Bitting, Cordeiro, & Baptiste, 1992).

Ostensibly, programs designed to help these students are intended as humane niches that nurture the adolescents back to good academic health. In reality, the programs often remove the students from the classroom and school community through technical etiologies and restrictive placements based on complex psychometrically derived input variables, and politically motivated funding schemes (Wang, Reynolds, & Walberg, 1995). Publicly, the programs are acclaimed by school officials in promotional brochures as extraordinary attempts to meet the needs of diverse student populations. Privately, discussions of the actual effectiveness of the programs are silenced (Fine, 1991) when school officials are painfully reminded that students enrolled in such programs can not or would not achieve, can not be brought up to grade level, and fail to acquire even the most basic literacy strategies and skills before graduating or dropping out of high school.

We prefer the alternative perspective on at-riskness that disrupts the institutionalized view of schools as supportive, nurturing places. Schools either intentionally or unintentionally support the values, beliefs, and actions of some students while excluding, marginalizing, or punishing others (Fine, 1991; Spear-Swerling & Sternberg, 1996). Schools, not students, are at risk. Students in at-risk schools are positioned to fail and disenfranchised by the inflexible institution (O'Brien, 1998; Waxman, 1992). These at-risk schools are characterized by programs that are responsive to neither the students' current needs nor their future needs beyond high school; moreover, these schools have little tolerance for students who deviate from rigidly institutionalized rules (Pugach, 1995).

To this point, we have defined at-riskness in terms of the institution and its practices related to at-riskness and school failure. Next, we focus on the literacy engagement of the at-risk students.

Literacy as Engagement

The institutional perspective that defines at-riskness, situates these adolescents as persons marginalized by the institution. The engagement perspective, on the other hand, provides a sociocognitive complement that explicates how adolescents approach schoolwork, task by task, using strategies successfully or unsuccessfully, constructing self-perceptions, deciding to persevere or not and, ultimately, accepting or rejecting failure. In explaining literacy engagement, we drew largely from broad theories of motivation (Anderman & Maehr, 1994; Covington, 1992, Dweck & Leggett, 1988; Nicholls, 1989; Pintrich & Schunk, 1996) and theories explaining the relation between motivation and literacy engagement (Guthrie et al., 1994; Guthrie & Wigfield, 1997; McCombs, 1996; Paris, Wasik, & Turner, 1991).

Informed by these theories, we concluded that (a) engaged learners are motivated to persevere with a task; (b) they choose to engage in similar tasks in the future because they are interested in what they are learning; and (c) they feel successful in using the strategies they are using. Early in their academic histories, students who are currently labeled as at-risk experienced failure and developed early dispositions toward school that helped them avoid failure and preserve their self-esteem. One way to preserve self-esteem is to avoid tasks they realize through experience that they can not succeed at (Paris, Wasik, & Turner, 1991). Moreover, if they know that they cannot succeed and they cannot attribute their failure to lack of effort, you realize the futility of engaging in those tasks (Covington, 1992).

In sum, traditional notions of at-riskness blame the students (and, implicitly, their environment) for their relative lack of success in school. Both assessment and instructional practices put a premium on compliance. Students are at-risk because they can not or choose not to meet the goals of the institution; the students, not the institution, must bend. And the socio-cognitive perspective on engagement, although sensitive to immediate learning contexts and learner self-perceptions, largely ignores the social and cultural contexts that confound learning. To change the school experience and curriculum for marginalized adolescents we need to disrupt the institutionalized authority that supports routinized schedules and practices, question what counts as schoolwork and, most importantly, systematically affront print-based, textbook dominated forms of literacy that are privileged over other forms (Gee, 1996; New London Group, 1996).

This eroding of print culture, particularly that aligned with an approved cannon of schooled literacy, and the acknowledgment that literate practices are always context specific, paves the way for a view of multiple literacies, rather than a singular literacy. These literacies take the form of various practices that define and are defined by the social and cultural contexts in which they are embedded (Alvermann et al., 1998; Barton, 1994; Gee, 1996; New London Group, 1996; Street, 1984, 1995). Some of these literacies are rooted in the popular culture and the understanding, creation, and appropriation of cultural texts as a way to critique the world and construct a social identity (Buckingham & Sefton-Green, 1994; C. Luke, 1993).

Celebrating At-Risk Students' Practices

Socially and culturally mediated perspectives, rather than marginalizing these adolescents, invite them as expert consultants to draw on their experiences and to participate with a community of peers in exploring those experiences in constructing a relevant curriculum. In celebrating rather than subjugating practices that are atypical in the institution, socially and culturally mediated perspectives encourage these adolescents, as agents of social action, to construct and affirm their social identities by appropriating popular cultural forms and creating hybrid forms represented by a variety of media texts, including, but by no means limited to, printed texts (Buckingham & Sefton-Green, 1994; Luke, 1995).

The perspective of the New Literacy Studies era (Gee, 1996) capitalizes on cultural theories of school and classroom life to look more broadly at engagement. Cultural theories informed by popular youth culture, can redefine engagement by moving away from individual learners encountering tasks to collective reading of a variety of shared media texts (Buckingham & Sefton-Green, 1994).

Engagement in the literate practice of reading these texts is closely connected to engagement with a social community in which the texts are understood; and, engagement with the texts is motivated by the fact that the texts provide access to a social community while allowing a person to define him or herself as a member of that community (Finders, 1996, 1997). We discuss some of those community texts later.

Methodologies

The purpose of the 4-year project was to study the literacy engagement of adolescents in a program designed for low achievers. The focus of this analysis was on how these adolescents produced and critiqued media texts rooted in popular youth culture.

We conducted the research as participant observers (Patton, 1990). Rebecca Springs and Dave Stith are teachers in the Literacy Lab. David O'Brien spent a semester-long sabbatical leave from Purdue University and a year-long research fellowship in the lab as a teacher–researcher and was assigned the role of teacher by the students. David, during years 3 and 4 of the project, on his regular university schedule, spent about 5 or 6 hours per week in the lab. Throughout the study, he spent about half of his time taking fieldnotes and videotaping various literacy events from day to day while working with the students. Rebecca and Dave, although they occasionally helped with data collection, spent most of their time working with the students.

The findings from the study, as it progressed, were used to reshape the program and to inform the development of a grounded theory that addresses how these students' engagement, defined by socially and culturally based theories of literacy, mediates traditional notions of literacy that have failed them.

We observed students working individually and collaboratively on lessons and recorded fieldnotes. About one-fourth of these lessons were videotaped and about one-fourth of lessons not videotaped were audiotaped. We transcribed selected lessons, collected student work, and transcribed selected portions of videotapes and digitized multimedia productions.

The fieldnotes and taped records allowed us to document the activities the students engaged in, students' and teachers' interactions during lessons, and strategies students used during various tasks. We also constructed academic histories of students who had been in the program from 1–3 years. The histories include interviews that focus on the students' perceptions about their academic experiences and their perceptions of the impact of the program on their reading and writing.

As noted previously, the substantive theoretical base of this project is a critique of institutionalized notions of at-riskness, and literacy engagement. The data were analyzed using a lens in which the students' enactments in the program were viewed as socially and culturally embedded practices (Barton, 1994; Gee, 1996; Street, 1995). The broad 4-year study was guided by the theoretical frameworks of symbolic interactionism (Blumer, 1969; Denzin, 1992) and hermeneutic phenomenology (van Manen, 1990). Symbolic interactionism posits that meaning is constructed, assigned, and modified through social interaction. Specifically, as individuals interpretively assume others' perspectives they construct new meanings and modify their actions based on those meanings. This framework helped us interpret the actions and interactions of teachers and students as they worked within the program. Hermeneutic phenomenology focuses on the textual expression of lived experience. This framework provided both a descriptive and interpretive methodology, that is, it allowed us to hear the participants' voices via the textual representation of their lived experiences (phenomenological), and understand and interpret the texts of their lived experiences in terms of our own experiences (hermeneutic). We used this framework to understand the teacher-researchers' and students' experiences in the innovative program.

Setting and Participants

The Literacy Lab is set up with four tables, each seating four to six students, set in the middle of a room with 16 networked computers around the perimeter. Several other stand-alone machines are set up as multimedia workstations, and a laser printer occupies one corner. Students can work in small groups or on individual projects at the tables. Classes in the block-8 schedule meet for 92 minutes each day (each student attends the lab every other day). The atmosphere of the lab reflects mutual respect among teachers and students. We typically move around the room, helping students on computers or guiding group work.

The 9th through 12th-grade students enrolled in the Literacy Lab, have been administratively enrolled rather than choosing the program as an elective. The Literacy Lab is a regular English class, not a pull-out program. The students enrolled in the program have performed in the range of the lowest 5–8% of reading achievement in the school according to the state-mandated standardized achievement testing. Some of them are incoming freshmen who scored below frustration level in three subject areas on content-reading inventories constructed and administered by us. Some of the students have been referred to the Literacy Lab by guidance counselors or teachers or have been identified through special education assessment as mildly handicapped with a particular deficit in literacy and language skills and strategies. Hence, the program includes students with a history of low academic performance who have failed consistently in literacy.

Maxine, who is representative of the clientele of the Literacy Lab, noted that she has had trouble with reading since elementary school: "Learning how to read was hard. I didn't want to focus on it. I thought I could just blow it off and get through. But now, I'm like, 'Oh no!' And it's been trying to catch up with everyone."

Due to the referral process, the program also includes persons who have been unsuccessful because of a complex variety of factors including academic, social, and emotional issues. Jennie is representative of this group. Her reading achievement is good enough to place her at about the sixth or seventh-grade level. She was administratively referred to the program because of her identification as learning disabled and a host of other problems, including moving frequently to different schools, and a history of behavior problems. She is in her 2nd year in the program. Jenny perceives herself as a troublemaker, so much so that she claimed one of her English teacher's resigned to escape her obnoxious behavior. "I was always in the principal's office. I was too immature, and everyone else was wanting to study and stuff. I was always goofing around, you know, flipping teachers off. I'd get in fights every day, beat 'em up and get suspended, get Saturday school, and wouldn't go." She said that she hates school, other than socializing with her friends, and she hates reading and the Literacy Lab in particular:

> Like, every day you do the same old thing—every single day. You sit down, listen to the announcements [on the PA], free time reading. It is so stupid. You do the same thing every day. Group one and group two, whatever the heck that is. And, like last year, you do the reports every day, that last, like, four weeks. And you had to get it done before four weeks, and you have to have it, like twenty pages. And, if not, then you flunk. You have to be perfect to get an A.

We screen all new enrollees at the beginning of each year to assess literacy performance. The proportion of minority students and students from poor families, according to federal eligibility requirements for free and reduced lunches, is proportional to the larger school population. Hence, about 4% of the enrollees are African-American and Hispanic students and about 29% of the students are from lower socioeconomic-level families. Most of the students have had negative experiences in school and many of them are not motivated to engage in many school tasks. About 20% of the students drop out of school.

The staffing resources in the Literacy Lab determine the number of students enrolled. The program typically houses 120 students (15 students per class period in a block-8 schedule) to maintain the current teacher–student ratio of about one teacher per eight students.

The Literacy Lab Curriculum

In the Literacy Lab, students engage in activities that integrate text with other media and, hence, other forms of textual representation, including a variety of computer-based, multimedia authoring activities. Based on their interests, the students select from a menu of possible projects. For example, in the Violence Project, which we discuss later, students conducted ministudies and constructed documentaries, including persuasive pieces about the impact of violence in the media on adolescents and children. In essence, it was a media-based study of media. The students chose topics within the broad topic of violence as portrayed or constructed in the media, selected media they found most compelling, and constructed presentation formats that fit their projects.

Some of the activities could be completed in a class period; others, like the violence project, took several weeks to complete. In other multimedia productions, students wrote about people or events important to them and used various visual media such as scanned pictures, images downloaded from Web sites, or video clips complemented with computer graphics and drawing tools. At times, they developed narratives or informational texts after reading on topics of interest. For example, after reading stories in *Current Events* or *Newsweek* students wrote about teen pregnancy, smoking, crime, and gangs. They sometimes wrote about themselves, their friends, or families by augmenting print with visual media.

At the beginning of the program, we structured assignments, particularly longer multimedia projects, using steps and checklists to monitor the progress and completion. From our early observations, we noted that the students often lost track of their progress unless assignments were laid out in a linear order with clearly articulated steps. When we were able to acquire more computers, we moved more toward multimedia projects that permitted much more freedom in terms of choice of topics and the form the products would take. In this analysis, we focus on the multimedia projects.

Most students reacted positively to the setting and curriculum of the Literacy Lab. For example, Becca sees the Literacy Lab as a place where she gets individual attention, a place where her interests and personality are considered. She sees the Literacy Lab as a contrast to regular curriculum where she feels like she is homogenized by teachers:

> Being compared to other people is a problem. I am not them. I have teachers who say, "Well, if this person can do it, you can do it too." I am not gonna do it! I tell them, "The last time I checked, my name is not the same as theirs, I do not think the same as them—so don't compare me." Mrs. Springs is really good at instead of comparing me to other people, she'll compare me to what

she's seen me do. I gave her one of my reports that I had done. It was kind of a rushed job, and she said, 'You've done better than this" and she gave me half credit for it. I have had a bunch of teachers that can't do that.

Eric is also positive about the Literacy Lab:

They have a good plan going. I like working on the computers and stuff. I like the teachers. They are different. They try to help you. The atmosphere is sort of peaceful and I know just about all of the kids in here.

Josh also likes the atmosphere of the Literacy lab. He noted, "It is laid back." But he has reservations about the curriculum. He stated, "I read all of the time. That gets boring." He likes to read on his own outside of school but hates to work with others in groups: He emphasized, "I don't like working with other people, and I don't like working with computers."

INTERPRETATIONS

In this analysis, we focused on literacy engagement as situated practice focusing on how the Literacy Lab students used print and other media to reposition themselves beyond traditional notions of at-riskness and school failure. The assertions that follow are based on patterns induced from the data.

Literacy Engagement Can Be Best Defined by Looking at How Individual Students Construct Their Social Identities and Share in Cultural Meaning Through Various Literate Practices.

Many of the at-risk learners with whom we work are reluctant to participate in schoolwork as it is typically defined by the institution of school. Nevertheless, they willingly engage in activities that help them construct and affirm their social identities. They enthusiastically write and read about topics grounded in their popular culture.

When Given Choices, These Students Will Almost Always Avoid Schoolwork.

They choose activities that look least like the activities and materials they have encountered through their years in special programs. They avoid materials such as anthologies with questions, high interest–low vocabulary paperbacks and skill sheets, regardless of some of the merits of these activities. They like computer-based activities because of the visual media, the novelty, or simply because the computers provide an escape from the traditional materials they have learned to dislike. They read and write for longer durations and write more elaborated texts if they are working on projects of their choice in which the text serves to augment visual media—for example, writing a description of a picture or a video clip in a report.

For example, Don composed a documentary on heavy metal bands, but only after he scanned in the most outrageous images of the bands that he found in magazines and album covers. He placed the scanned files chronologically and used the pictures to help him construct the story of each group's formation, evolution, demise, and sometimes rebirth. In a later section of this chapter, we highlight one of Don's productions on heavy metal artist, Ozzy Osbourne.

In a similar fashion, Greg and J. T. wrote extensively about vampires, but before they wrote anything they scanned in the most bizarre pictures they could find in books they checked out of the library. Using each picture as a jumping off point, they constructed text and paraphrased from the books.

In both of these projects, visual media was the primary text and visual media resulted in a more interesting, critical use of printed text. In the next section, we illustrate this juxtaposition of media texts and printed texts in more depth through a focus on the Violence Project, a project in which students explored aspects of violence in media that impact adolescents. Ironically, the project asked the students to use integrated media to critique media itself. The students were required to use a variety of media forms including text to express their ideas and beliefs.

The Violence Project

In this project, some students explored the issue of violence in television. Donny and Ashley authored a persuasive project, "Can Violence be Cured?" In the introduction of their piece, they wrote:

> Television and movies promote violence. The purpose of the presentation is to inform people about how TV violence affects the way people act, specially children.

Then they presented evidence using a variety of media and intertextual links. Following the introduction, they juxtaposed a Quicktime© video frame of Beavis and Butthead with a scanned magazine photo of 2-year-old Jessica Matthews, a tragic victim of a house fire. Below the video frame and scanned picture they inserted text:

> The death of two-year-old Jessica Matthew was blamed on the MTV show Beavis and Butthead. Her five-year-old brother watched a Beavis and Butthead show on fire. He set fire to their house, while their mother was gone.

Rather than using the printed text to persuade the audience about the impact of violence, they launched into the next media assault, noting how the movie, *The Program* was the possible cause of a teenage fatality:

> The movie, "The Program," persuaded a teenager to lay in the middle of a highway like the character in the movie, but unlike in the movie, he was killed. A boy named Michael Shingledecker tried the little stunt and was killed. Marco Birkhimer was also killed. The movie was recalled and they cut that part out. But there are probably uncut movies out there in people's hands.

Like in the previous evidence segment, they juxtaposed two images. On the left, a scanned picture of the night scene of Michael Shingledecker's fatal accident; on the right, a high school photo of Michael that appeared in a magazine. Below the two photos, they placed a scanned text of the story on the impact of the media on young viewers, which discusses both the incidents they portray in their presentation.

Donny and Ashley then discussed the *Ren and Stimpy* cartoon's impact on children and pleaded with parents to pay more attention to what their kids watch on TV. They ended the presentation with an MTV© video clip showing three gangster-like characters with Panama hats, sunglasses, and white ascots.

Donny and Ashley's printed text was not polished. Their written argument served as a bridge to each image. Their statement about violence was made with the combination of the abruptness of the written text and the power of the images. Whereas Jessica Matthews stares eternally from her photo, Beavis and Butthead make their authority-defying grunting noises as they play with matches in the video clip. The authors of this piece used an intertextual link that allowed them to manipulate our sensibilities and fracture the temporal order. The tragedy that followed the television airing of the episode and the video clip of the fire-starting episode occur together in the production.

Donny and Ashley's writing is powerful in its subversion of the printed text to the textual images. Their lack of technical sophistication with conventional genres of writing promotes a documentary style in which the written text plays out in the background while the images capture our attention and emotions. Donny and Ashley understand the power of the media. They have studied *Beavis and Butthead*, one of most popular shared media texts of popular youth culture, and they empathize with victims of violence in media. The pictures, particularly their editing of the pictures and print—their composite text—tell us so.

Beavis and Butthead and *The Program* were shared media texts in the project. During The Violence Project students passed around magazine and newspaper articles detailing these incidents, although various project authors took different approaches to them. Cindy and Shanna, like Donny and Ashley, referenced incidents related to the *Beavis and Butthead* episode and *The Program* film, but unlike their colleagues, they first launched into a more predictable documentary lead-in:

> The average child sees something like 8,000 television murders by the time he is 21. The purpose of this presentation is to advise that parents should not be letting their kids watch too much T.V. violence, because it could cause them to act violently.

Rather than show the violence in media referred to in newspapers and magazines, they lead readers to a video clip in which parents talk about the impact violence in television has had on their kids. Instead of presenting the video clips, they refer readers to a magazine article from *U.S. News and World Report* portions of which they have digitally scanned into their presentation.

But before the reader gets to the scanned article, the authors offer a synopsis of the article by mixing paraphrasing with a conversational style and repeating the warning to parents. Their argument drifts from the responsibility of parents to the responsibility of TV programmers, to responsibilities of lawmakers. The documentary genre in the beginning is transformed to a typical schooled literacy report. Albeit a shared text in terms of the stories and what they represent within the popular culture, this version of the shared text is sharply contrasted to Donny and Ashley's composite text, which is constructed mostly of images. The reader must traverse their winding synopses before getting to the scanned article. The article has a moving picture of the friends of teenager, Michael Shingledecker, hugging as they mourn him at the cemetery in which he was buried after he was run over by a truck. Nevertheless, the picture is almost inconsequential because of where it appears—and because Cindy and Shanna let *U.S. News and World Report* contextualize it for the reader. They let the existing media contextualize their perspectives and emotions about the events.

In contrast to Donny and Ashley, Cindy and Shanna are ineffective at using visual media to communicate, they are unable to manipulate the media tools they have to do so, and struggle to break out of the typical schooled literacy genre. As readers, we are captured by their struggle with conventional writing rather than their prowess with media texts even though Cindy and Shanna use media to critique media, for example, magazine articles critiquing TV and film.

The topic of choice for other authors of the Violence Project was school violence. Lupe, Dusty, and Bill opened their presentation:

> The purpose of this presentation is to inform the readers about school violence. We will discuss kids killing teachers, kids killing kids, and gang violence. Kids are coming to school with guns and knives. Scott Pennington of Kentucky allegedly shot and killed Deanna McDavid, a 51-year-old teacher. Pennington got the idea from the book *Rage*.

Below the lead-in is a picture of McDavid, rotated to the left off a perpendicular axis partially overlapping a picture of Pennington, coat draped over his head, being taken from the shooting scene by police. Below the caption of Deanna McDavid's picture, the authors scanned an excerpt from a magazine, a quote from one of McDavid's friends: "After her family, her students were the most important people in her life." After the images, Lupe, Dusty, and Bill listed a series of recent incidents similar to the McDavid shooting:

> On August 31, a ninth grader was killed and a tenth grader wounded when another student allegedly opened fire in a crowded cafeteria at Atlanta's Harper High School. On September 16, a 17-year-old at Immaculate High School in Somerville, NJ was charged with attempted murder after allegedly shooting another student. On September 8, a 14-year-old student at rural South Iredell High School north of Charlotte, NC was arrested for shooting a classmate on the sidewalk in the back and chest as school was dismissed.

In addition to the national stories, students wrote about local stories, like a 17-year-old Indianapolis youth who was stabbed to death in the cafeteria of Arlington High School. They also wrote about the Indianapolis Schools' new random weapons search policy, including photos of students being searched, to augment the text.

The Lafayette Jefferson students, like their peers around the country, were concerned about violence. Their concern was reflective of the media's preoccupation with it. When they wrote about violence using print and media text, they discussed the national trend and local exemplars of it. Ironically, they used their own media in the Literacy Lab to critique the broader cultural text of a media that reported, critiqued, and sometimes overdramatized the scope of the problem.

In addition to the Violence Project, the students explored a variety of other topics embedded in their popular youth culture. Some students who were most reluctant to read and write in the traditional sense, engaged in a variety of literate practices related to important facets of their lives outside of school. Music was such a facet.

Media Documentary:
Diary of a Madman

Don is an avid music fan and possesses a compendium of information about several generations of artists. He knows the names and biographies of every member of every band he listens to, attends as many concerts as he can, reads *Rolling Stone* religiously, and has a wardrobe of promotional T-shirts from concerts and music stores. He is an expert biographer of a few favorite artists. For one of his projects in the Literacy Lab, Don put together a multimedia presentation on Ozzy Osbourne. In this assignment, he used print, scanned images, and digitized video to create a composite media text that chronicled Osbourne's life and musical career. The media text is anchored in Don's assumption that a chronology of the themes of Osbourne's music—at least as the themes are evident in his album titles and images on album covers—reflect the epiphanies of the musician's life. He is intensely interested in Osbourne's life because he sees contradictions between Osbourne's performance persona and his real life. Don highlights the madman of heavy metal as an irreverent, daring, and outrageous performer only to assure the reader that in actuality Osbourne is a sensitive family man. The printed text in his narratives is an interesting composite of paraphrasing from a variety of sources (e.g., *Rolling Stone, Modern Guitar,* MTV) and Don's own text. His project began:

> Ozzy Osbourne was born on December 3, 1948 in Ashton, a blue collar section of Birmingham, England. Ozzy credits his strange behavior on heredity, coming from a family in which lunacy was not uncommon.

He continued the narrative about Ozzie's brief prison time for burglary and some of the artist's work experiences before he embarked on the music business. Don wrote about the first band Osbourne formed, "Earth,"which after a brief unsuccessful stint, became the well-known band "Black Sabbath", named, Don noted, "from the Boris Karloff film." Under a scanned picture of the album cover *Blizzard of Oz*, Ozzie's first solo album released in 1981, Don wrote:

> Since the start of Black Sabbath, Ozzy had an alcohol and drug problem. He was constantly drunk or stoned. After the release of "Blizzard of Oz" Osbourne arrived at a meeting at Columbia Records in Los Angeles. Being drunk, Ozzy was handed two doves and told to walk in and toss the doves into the air. The first dove he tossed into the air. The second, trying to crack a joke, he bit into it and chewed its head off. After that, the second Ozzy album, "Diary of a Madman," was released in 1981.

From Don's chronology, it is sometimes difficult to figure out how events are contextualized or connected. He highlights the bizarre and weaves in crucial incidents in Ozzie's life in a way that romanticizes the unpredictability of the eccentric musician. Clearly, he admires Osbourne for his unconventional attention-getting antics.

Next in the project, the *Diary of a Madman* album cover appears. As the reader–viewer is drawn into this image, we are suddenly immersed in a video clip of Osbourne talking with animated gestures, in a black T-shirt sitting on a sofa, telling about how he bit into a bat on stage, assuming it was a Halloween prop and then underwent a series of rabies shots And with alternating scanned images, video clips, and printed text, Don follows Ozzy through a series of other negative experiences including the death of his lead guitar player, and a wrongful death law suit in which his song, "Suicide Solution" was blamed for the death of John McCollum, a teenage fan.

Don loves music—particularly heavy metal. Many of his heroes are musicians. But in the spirit of connoisseurship, he looks beyond their glamorized public images into their personal challenges and tragedies. He and his friends experience music as entertainment; but equally important, music is a shared text of their youth culture. They buy CDs, go to concerts, wear music T-shirts at school. They read about artists, and try to connect the artists' lives to their music. Some of them view music as a sort of romantic escape from their daily routines. Some want to be like their musical heroes. But most, like Don, want to live part of their youth through music. Nevertheless, in spite of the appeal of importing popular youth culture into school, we must temper the advantages with the reality that these adolescents will ultimately need to be equipped to deal critically with print literacy (Hinchman & Moje, 1998).

SUMMARY AND IMPLICATIONS

There are three issues in this project on which implications can be based: (a) technology is a useful educational tool for motivating reluctant learners to read and write; (b) media and media literacies, as culturally shared texts, may be more powerful than traditional print texts in engaging these adolescents; and (c) the use of technology and media are inextricably connected to issues of power, control, and reinforcement of certain economic, social, and cultural values. We will discuss implications within each of these issues.

We can examine the Literacy Lab curriculum and practices from the practical stance of technological determinism (Bromley, 1998). If we set aside the social and cultural forces and contexts in which technology is used, and ascribe power to the technology itself to change practices, we can make the case that technological tools provide a way for adolescents who avoid traditional schooled literacy practices to engage in interesting, meaningful practices. From this perspective, we can make the case that access to the hardware and media authoring software in the Literacy Lab provided these adolescents with opportunities to read and write that they would not have otherwise explored. Similarly, from a task analysis perspective we contend that media-based projects and the accompanying media literacies are challenging enough to be interesting, yet flexible enough to provide adolescents leverage in controlling the level of difficulty (Covington, 1992; Nicholls, 1989). These tasks, which can include a variety of textual representation, through a range of print and other media, stand in stark contrast to the low-incentive, high-risk, competitive, ability-based tasks valued in the predominant school culture.

Second, media texts, as popular cultural texts, embody the shared interests, experiences, and paths to personal identity these youth have in the broader culture outside of school. As with the task structure mentioned previously, these texts stand in contrast to the relatively weak shared experience of reading the typical school canon (Buckingham & Sefton-Green, 1994; C. Luke, 1993; Tierney, 1997). To improve the quality of at-risk students' literacy engagement we must dispense with the belief that popular youth culture, particularly as it is constructed through the media is, by nature, antithetical to students' academic growth and school-sponsored preparation for adult life. This relaxation of imposing school cultural values on students should be accompanied by revising considerably the view of the school institution as a way to inoculate students against the influence of the popular culture (Buckingham & Sefton-Green, 1994). Rather, we need to embrace these adolescents' literate lives that thrive in their popular culture—the same literate lives that are suppressed in school by understanding that the opportunity to critically examine and construct media texts may result in more complex expectations for all texts (Hobbs, 1997).

The third issue, which is the caveat, is that neither technology nor media can be viewed only pragmatically as motivating instructional approaches. We cannot use technology without considering issues of power, politics, and the extent the technology is representative of and reinforcing of certain social and economic structures (Bromley & Apple, 1998; Tierney, 1997). The pragmatic and deterministic view of technology typically embraced by educators in general, and literacy educators, particularly reading educators (e.g., Reinking, Labbo, & McKenna, 1997), often downplays the social, cultural, and political implications in the various contexts in which the technology is used in the interest of exploring ways the technology will change how we read, write, and view those processes.

Media, especially the electronic variety, is both controlling—shaping our views of ourselves in our culture—and empowering, enabling us to access information and take a more direct role in charting our culture within the "mediashpere" (Rushkoff, 1996). A critical stance warns us, however, that adolescents are particularly interested in media or electronically mediated popular culture because they are, among all human beings, most in search of an identity that popular media partially provides. That same media represents a powerful market force that co-opts adolescents' alienation as a marketing strategy (Epstein, 1998). The media-focused strategy serves to further cement the alienation and youths' identification with certain subcultures whose artifacts like music, dress, and ways of acting, are commercialized. Hence, we can provide Don the opportunity to author multimedia presentations on Ozzy Osbourne, but we have to realize that, because of the commercialization of the image and persona of Osbourne, Don buys his recordings, attends concerts, and has purchased a wardrobe of T-shirts with a barrage of commercialized images of Osbourne. Don has, in effect, invested much more financial and personal capital in Ozzy Osbourne and other music artists than he has in school.

Two implications, which have surfaced during our conference presentations of this project, can be raised as questions: First, to what extent does our official sanctioning of importing popular culture into school promote the further commercialization of popular youth cultural identities, many of which are antithetical to the institutional symbol of the hegemonic culture, if not the instructional goals of the institution of school? Second, to what extent does this substitution of popular youth culture and media for the traditional literacy curriculum limit these adolescents' visions for moving beyond their current plight and restrict their chances to learn literate practices that are valued in the broader community? These are indeed complex implications of the project with no easy answers. And we have taken the position, as stated within the second issue previously mentioned, that we are willing to explore the disruption of institutional values and practices to provide opportunities for these adolescents to engage in a more relevant curriculum connected more to their literate practices outside of school.

Finally, the most important implication for literacy researchers and educators is that we must expand our conceptions of text and literate practices from print to multiple forms of representation. Inevitably schools, as institutions in the broader community, are becoming more connected to the electronically mediated popular culture via the Internet, CD-ROM, DVD, and Satellite TV, to mention only a few of the current technologies. We must consider how to teach with and study how to use a variety of forms of symbolic expression, which we can call media literacy (Hobbs, 1997) to redefine what is meant by engagement and literate practice.

6

Texts and Talk: The Role of Gender in Learning Physics

Barbara J. Guzzetti
Arizona State University

Prior research in content reading has investigated discussion in classrooms, treating students' discourse about the concepts in texts as literacy (e.g., Alvermann, Dillon, & O'Brien, 1987). Content reading and literacy methods textbooks include discussion as a literacy activity designed to promote students' understanding of concepts in texts, build knowledge, clarify ideas, explore issues, and share perspectives (Alvermann & Phelps, 1998; Anders & Guzzetti, 1996; Vacca & Vacca, 1996). In content areas, treating discussion as literacy is based on Gee's (1996) notion that learning the talk of a discipline is part of becoming literate in a field.

Past investigators of discussion in classrooms have identified the types of discussion that occur (Alvermann et al., 1987), and the ways in which teachers can facilitate and guide discussion (Kindsvatter, Wilen, & Ishler, 1991). Recently, investigators have begun exploring imbalances of power and gender bias in classroom discussions of literature (Alvermann & Commeyras, 1994) and in discussions of content reading methods (Alvermann, Commeyras, Young, Randall, & Hinson, 1997). Krockover and Shepardson (1995) requested investigators turn their attention to science classrooms to identify how students are oppressed as they engage in scientific literacy. Such studies are needed because males have typically outperformed females in science classes and have maintained better attitudes toward science (American Association of University Women [AAUW], 1992; Kahle & Lakes, 1983).

One reason typically cited for this disparity is differential opportunity to engage in academic tasks and talk about those tasks, commonly referred to as gender bias in science classrooms (NBC News Dateline, "Failing in Fairness"; Tobin & Garnett, 1987). Within the past decade, researchers have identified behaviors that characterize gender bias in classrooms (Sadker & Sadker, 1994). For example, Morse and Handley (1985) found that teachers allow males to dominate science talk, whatever the structure or activity. A student's argument is taken more seriously by the teacher if the position is asserted by a male (Lemke, 1990). Males receive more attention from teachers than do females, and tend to call out answers in whole-class discussions (Sadker & Sadker, 1994).

Investigations into gender inequities have had several limitations. First, most investigations were conducted primarily by recording percentage tallies in categories on predetermined observation guides, and have focused primarily on teachers' behaviors. These studies have resulted in the common finding that teachers typically are unaware of gender bias, both in their interactions with students and in their methods of instruction (Sadker & Sadker, 1994; Tobin, 1988). Hence, researchers have tended to make suggestions for raising teachers' awareness, and for changing teachers' behavior, particularly teachers' talk. Typical recommendations to teachers have included calling more frequently on females to answer questions, asking them more higher-order questions, and giving more elaborate feedback to females about their responses (Tobin & Garnett, 1987). Others have suggested or tried all-girls classes in science (Kumagai, 1995; NBC News Dateline, "Failing in Fairness").

Second, most research on gender and literacy has not considered culture or ethnicity as influences on the development of literacies (Orellana, 1995). While the well-accepted finding (in both the popular press and in academic literature) has been that males dominate classroom interaction (Tannen, 1992), studies like these were criticized for their assumptive nature. Specifically, findings from these studies have been generalized from European American, middle-class students to students of other cultures, races, and socioeconomic levels (Orellana, 1995; Swann, 1988).

Recent investigations have shown, however, that other influences, like ethnicity, do interact with gender and impact students' instructional interactions. For example, contrary to findings from studies of Euro-American females, there is evidence that African-American females often dominate whole-class discussions in dual-sex science classrooms (Luster, Varelas, Wenzel, & Liao, 1997). African-American females also dominate discussions in other content classrooms when the class is comprised predominately of African Americans (Kyle, 1996). Mitigating influences (generally referred to as context), like a person's age and generation (Gritsavage, 1997a; 1997b) or geography, like urban or rural origins (Guzzetti, 1997), can also impact the content and delivery of class members' talk.

Third, few investigators have focused primarily on the interactions between students that constitute gender bias. There have been few studies describing how students in their dealings with each other (and with their teachers) allow, promote, and reinforce gender inequities in the science classroom (Jones & Wheatley, 1990). In addition, few researchers extended their studies of teachers' gendered language beyond quantitative tallies of verbal behaviors (e.g., percentage counts of call outs, questions, and responses by gender) to actually identify the language patterns that disenfranchise students or describe the conditions that allow gender inequities to prevail. Hence, researchers like Alvermann and Commeyras (1994) called for research that reveals the asymmetrical power relationships between males and females that perpetuate inequities.

Finally, few researchers have attempted to intervene by raising students' awareness or by changing students' behavior that characterizes asymmetrical opportunity and differential power relationships (Tobin, 1988). When these attempts have occurred, they have usually been limited to one-time interventions, like sharing with students the results of research on gender inequities in classrooms (e.g., Sadker & Sadker, 1994).

To expand these investigations and interventions, our conducted studies (as coresearchers with the teachers in whose classrooms we worked) focused on students' learning. We explored gender disparity in science literacies (i.e., speaking the talk of a discipline, using that language to construct and represent understandings, and acquiring vocabulary or concepts through text and talk about text). In doing so, we focused on students' perspectives and interactions with each other, as well as with their teachers. Although most of the students we studied were Euro-American, we did identify and consider the ethnicities of all the student informants.

In addition, we attempted to change patterns of asymmetrical power relations among students and between students and their teacher in several unique ways. First, we conducted our investigations by recording and analyzing the gendered language patterns and behaviors we observed among students, as well as between teachers and students. Second, we asked our informants to talk with us about their talk in classrooms. Third, we changed grouping patterns for instruction, provided more opportunity for females in whole-class activity, and gave our student informants feedback about their interactions. These methods constituted the action research component of each year's study.

Hence, our descriptive and action research consisted of studying students from two different academic years at three levels of physical science. In the 1st year, we described teachers' and students' behaviors that perpetuated gender inequities in Physical World (a basic class for noncollege-bound freshmen), Physics, and Honors Physics. Students in physical science classrooms were chosen for study because physical science is traditionally viewed as a man's field, more so than earth or life science (Kahle & Lakes, 1983). Males have been shown to have higher self-efficacy (confidence in their abilities) in physical science than do females (Smist, Archambault, & Owen, 1997).

Most of our 1st and 2nd years were devoted to describing gendered behaviors and documenting why and how these patterns existed. A portion of each of these years also consisted of action research in which we explored ways to address gender bias. Two of the questions that guided these inquiries were: What behaviors and language patterns do teachers and students display that create and maintain asymmetrical participation in learning science? And, what can teachers do to address gender bias that occurs among students and between students and the teacher?

THEORIES THAT FRAMED OUR WORK

Several cross-disciplinary perspectives guided the focus, data collection, and data analysis. The first of these was social constructivism. From this theory, the learning process is influenced not only by students' prior ideas, but also by the context in which students find themselves and their ideas, and by their interactions within that context. Vygotsky (1978) cited the importance of interplay between language and action as students learn in social settings, like classrooms. Activities like open-ended questions, students' explanations, writings, and classroom dialogue involve interactive and reciprocal use of language to both construct and represent understanding. Students' understandings evolve through a meaning-negotiation process in which they discuss and test their own and others' ideas through talk. Hence, we turned our focus to language, and how instructional discourse might be influenced by gender.

A second theoretical perspective that influenced these investigations came from sociolinguistics. Given the influence of language on learning from social constructivism, the literature from sociolinguistics that examined gendered forms of language became relevant. Researchers like Edelsky (1981), Tannen (1992) and Tromel-Plotz (1985) identified language patterns (like interruptions, call outs, and loud vocalizations) that characterize asymmetry in opportunity to participate in discussions. These descriptions assisted us in focusing our observations and expanding extant characterizations of instructional interactions that marginalized either gender.

A third theoretical orientation that framed these studies was taken from a typology of feminist theory, since there is no single feminist theory, but rather multiple points of view within feminism (Alcoff, 1989; Stanley & Wise, 1993). The views of feminism conveyed in the studies reflect our personal views. This position may be best described as social feminism or a feminist sociology (Stanley & Wise, 1993), which emphasizes that "women can't do it all alone" (p. 53). Men must also be involved in recognizing and addressing asymmetrical power relations that marginalize one gender or another. Hence, we looked for expanded notions of masculinity (e.g., how males can learn and be valued for active listening, which females are typically known for [Dubois & Crouch, 1975; Edelsky, 1979]). From this framework, these studies identify how males are also disenfranchised when gendered discourse occurs in science classrooms.

OUR PROCEDURES OF INVESTIGATION

Harding (1987) distinguished methodology from methods by defining methods as techniques for gathering empirical evidence, and methodology as a theory of knowledge or as an interpretative framework that guides a study. The orientation of the study embraced qualitative research as critical inquiry, a method more amenable to challenging the power and structure of privilege (Giroux, 1992) to change and understand the world (Fay, 1987). This perspective influenced our attempt to interrupt the asymmetrical power imbalances we identified in the classroom.

The types of qualitative research that these studies exemplify are case study, the complete study of a bounded and integrated system (Stake, 1994) and naturalistic inquiry. The first investigation, conducted with the male teacher over nearly the complete cycle of the school year, was a case study. The follow-up investigation that spanned a 4-month period of the next academic year was naturalistic. Both studies, however, were characterized by data triangulated through direct observations captured in fieldnotes, formal and informal interviews, audiorecorded and videotaped lessons, photographs, questionnaires, and documents like lesson plans, seating charts, and worksheets.

These investigations focused on gender as a social influence on learning through literacy practices (i.e., listening, speaking, reading and writing, but primarily orality or classroom discourse). During the first year, data were collected in three physics classes taught by two teachers (one male and one female) representing three levels of physics (Physical Science or Physical World, Physics, and Honors Physics). These teachers were selected purposively, on the basis of their reputations as effective teachers (as evidenced by their teaching awards), and their willingness to be coresearchers by assisting in formulating related questions for study, developing questionnaires, and reacting to and analyzing data.

Observations occurred daily in the Euro-American male teacher's (Mr. Williams) Physics and Honors Physics from the 1st day of school in August until the end of the third quarter in April. Students in these classes were generally alike in their ethnicity (85% Euro-American, 9% Asian, 4% Hispanic, and 2% Native American, with 16% foreign-born), chronological age (juniors and seniors, age 15–17), and socioeconomic status (upper-middle to middle-upper class). The Physics section consisted of two-thirds males and one-third females, while Honors Physics was about evenly divided between males and females. There was essentially no difference between the sections as students could be placed into Honors Physics simply by parent request and many who would have taken Honors Physics were enrolled in the regular section due to scheduling conflicts. Hence, the teacher's lesson plans were essentially the same for both sections.

Observations of the Euro-American female teacher's (Miss Smitts) Physical World class occurred daily from the 1st day of school in August until February of that academic year. Observations of this class ceased when the teacher's absences, due to illness, became so frequent and long in duration that a realistic picture of her students' interactions and her instruction could no longer be captured. Although enrollment and attendance fluctuated, the 25 Freshmen in Physical World enrolled the first day of school were about evenly divided between minorities and Euro-Americans. Ethnic composition of the class was 44% Euro-American, 32% Hispanic, 12% Native American, and 4% African-American, with 56% male and 44% female students. Of the female students, 55% were Hispanic, 12% were Native American, 6% were Asian, and 6% were African-American. These students generally represented upper-lower to lower-middle class socioeconomic levels.

The 2nd year's study was conducted with two sections of the male teacher's Physics students, and one section of his Honors Physics students. These sections were evenly divided by gender, and were comprised of approximately the same percentage of ethnic groups as the prior year's classes. Observations of the three sections occurred daily for 5 months.

All qualitative data, including video and audio recordings of interviews and class sessions as well as fieldnotes, lesson plans, questionnaire responses, and journal entries were transcribed to written record. Data were analyzed for patterns through constant comparison (Glaser & Strauss, 1967), and by discrepant case analysis. Member checks were conducted with informants (teachers and students) through their readings of and reactions to the data to ensure ecological validity.

How Gendered Language is Evidenced in Classrooms: Interactions Between Teacher and Students

We found the same teacher–student interactions in science class previously identified in the literature from studies of other content areas in which teachers gave males more opportunity to participate in classroom activities. In Physical World, these behaviors included males shouting out answers, asking immediate questions after the teacher paused, dominating whole-class discussions, and interrupting. Males also tended to hold the floor by illustrating their points or refuting.

Perusal of our observation notes from Physical World showed that in addition to allowing males to dominate the class, Miss Smitts permitted the same boys each day to control whole-class discussions. She reinforced particular male students' participation (Rufus, an African-American male; Julio, a Hispanic male; and Byran, a Euro-American male) by elaborating on and validating their remarks, by complimenting these boys on their questions and responses, and by showing the class the projects they did as examples to illustrate her lecture. This pattern was illustrated in a lecture–discussion on mechanical advantage:

Miss Smitts:	We've been talking about mechanical advantage.
Observation:	A Euro-American male student [Tom] asks the researcher what an inclined plane is used for.
Miss Smitts:	You want a truck with a ramp. Why?
Boys, including Julio:	So you don't have to pick it up.
Miss Smitts:	Work is force times the distance moved.
Byran:	In the back of the truck, the door that opens is a pulley.
Miss Smitts:	Your car door opens and shuts on a lever. What's your light switch?
Julio:	What about your remote?
Miss Smitts:	Maybe the mechanisms inside it would. I saw a NOVA presentation on Channel 8. How they were pulling pyramids. All they used were levers and wedges. They didn't have a pulley. Imagine those stone blocks. How did they get those blocks way up high?
Julio:	How about the wheel?
Miss Smitts:	You know, I saw them trying to use logs, but I'm not sure. It wasn't like the wheel and axle principle. But just imagine those stone blocks of the pyramid …
Julio:	They were perfect. They said that the experiment was so geometrically perfect.

Byran:	And they tried to put them on logs and roll them. Yeah, they were trying all different kinds of things. They said that back in those days they didn't have a pulley. They didn't use pulleys so all they used were wedges and levers and ropes to pull.
Miss Smitts:	They did it with precision to get it perfectly square, like Julio said. I was told they're not off more than 1/4 inch if you measure. That's amazing!
Rufus:	Didn't it take them 100 years to build it?
Miss Smitts:	No. I think it took about 30 years to build one of the pyramids. But think about how many people were working on that ... [Miss Smitts continues her lecture].
Rufus:	[Interrupting] I have a book on the Nile.
Byran:	If it took 30 years for the pyramids to be built, it must have started when the king was born.
Miss Smitts:	King Tut? They would start building monuments right away with all kinds of gold inside. You can spot all the simple machines in everyday life.
Julio:	There's an ancient mine with doors. On certain days light would shine through the doors.
Miss Smitts:	That's right. Stonehenge was like an astronomical clock. People could tell when to plant, when winter would come. Part of the difficulty in making a machine is coming up with the idea. The hardest part is to get started. To come up with the idea and then once you start to work out all the bugs when things go wrong. That's why I wanted you to start with this. Jerry had the ultimate killing machine. I can't get over how your machines mutilated things. Where's the gerbil? [The teacher begins showing poster drawings of the male students' machines that included a live gerbil as part of the machine]. In all of them, everyone wanted to kill this little guy. Everyone somehow either ground him, mutilated him, dismembered him, took his head off and put it some place else. Whichever way it comes out, I think he's done.
Julio:	Mine made money. [Student refers to his project].
Miss Smitts:	I noticed a lot of you made machines that dismembered the rat that was operating the machine. You used a pulley ...
Rufus:	The longer it is, the more force you have. The fulcrum is like when you take a screwdriver to get a wheel off. What part is the fulcrum?

Julio:	[Asks a balance question—inaudible phrasing].
Miss Smitts:	What part is the fulcrum? Look up here …
Rufus:	I thought that the fulcrum on a teeter-totter was the end where the pressure is.
Miss Smitts:	Write this down for 2A. [Note-taking directions]. The second one is the moveable pulley. That's called the block and tackle.
Julio:	I mean one where they were … [inaudible].
Observation:	The class ends with a video that ties machines to force. Three girls of mixed ethnicities at the table next to me draw during the video.

Whereas the males in general (and in this scenario specifically) can be characterized as active, the females in Physical World were generally passive. As this vignette shows, only rarely did females speak in class discussions. Usually, the girls would draw, talk among themselves, or put their heads down and go to sleep during lectures. The girls would wake up when it was time to do seat work. Typically, when a female did speak in these situations, it was only in response to the teacher's query. Females were not observed asking questions or initiating a topic in whole-class discussion. Males, however, were consistently recognized for their participation. Boys received repetition of their responses (e.g., "They did with precision to get it perfectly square, like Julio said"), and positive reinforcement or elaboration on their responses and questions (e.g., Julio asked a one sentence question about using wheels to build the pyramids; Miss Smitts responded with a paragraph referring to the wheel and axle principle).

Data like these from our repeated observations in Physical World indicate the ways in which teachers sustain and promote gender bias in science classrooms. Although, like these students, males may have more favorable attitudes toward physics, no deliberate efforts were made to develop females' interests and curiosities. At this level of physics, the female teacher, as well as her students (who also made little or no attempt to solicit and reinforce females' participation) perpetuated gender bias in the science classroom.

Gendered Language in Classrooms: Interactions Among Students

Findings from the 1st year's investigation provided evidence that despite a teacher's intentions to be gender fair, the culture of the classroom may subvert or override these attempts. The male Physics teacher thought he was being equitable in his Physics and Honors Physics classes by calling on proportional numbers of males and females, and by appointing females as discussion leaders. Despite these interventions, debate-like formats favored males, and males dominated activity and talk about that activity in whole-class and small-group interactions.

The debate-like format that Mr. Williams used in his whole-class discussions was a form of refutational discussion he called Inquiry Training. Mr. Williams would choose a counter-intuitive concept and pose a question about it. He would then secretly select a member of the class to be a "shill"—someone who would supply the scientifically unacceptable but logical answer along with a seemingly plausible explanation. If shills could convince others to their way of thinking, they received double points for extra credit, creating a competitive environment. Fieldnotes show that as Tannen (1992) found, debate-like formats in whole-class discussion favor males. In a typical instance, only a male would assert his opinion and argue for it. In this case, a Euro-American male student was able to persuade the majority of the class to his position: [Physics Observation, 1/24, 10:10 a.m., Inquiry Training, 1994]

Mr. Williams:	I'm going to start the fan up and the fan will go as fast as it can. Note the direction it's going. [Mr. Williams turns out the lights and turns on the strobe].
Mr. Williams:	I'll stop the fan blade and start turning the frequency higher and higher. Will the fan blade turn clockwise or counter-clockwise or will it still look like it's stopped? Let's discuss it.
Evan:	It will go clockwise because it is already going in that direction.
Mark:	Counter-clockwise!
Mr. Williams:	If no one knows for sure, then your comments are just as valid. That's what we do in science. We sift out ideas and find those that are valid.
Mark:	It's counter-clockwise. When you're driving on the freeway, it looks like the tires are going backwards even though they really are going forward.
Mr. Williams:	What does it look like to you? I'll take the majority answer. [Mr. Williams asks for a show of hands in response to the three choices. Most students vote for counter-clockwise].
Mr. Williams:	I won't tell who the shill is!
Observation:	Several boys seated near me ask me for the answer. I decline to participate.

Aside from instances like these in refutational discussion, the teacher also noticed asymmetrical participation in other whole-class discussions. Mr. Williams also noted (in a formal interview) gender disparity in activity where small groups report to the whole class, using posters to illustrate their explanations of their solutions to a physics problem, an activity he called "Wells Boards":

> I think the girls are a lot less likely to argue with me. I think if we get arguments, it's usually the boys arguing. The girls feel, it seems like to me, when I have them doing Wells Boards, a lot more like letting the boy explain everything. They like to sort of hide behind the board or stand back, especially with the math concepts. They seem to shy away from it.

In the past, Mr. Williams had used the seating chart to select the student who would explain the group's Wells Board solution to the whole class. We agreed during this interview that the next time he did Wells Boards, he would allow the groups to pick their own spokesperson. We would observe together to see if the groups would consistently choose males from their members to explain the concepts to the class. Transcription of this video-taped observation reveals this pattern: [Observation: Students are Euro-American].

Mr. Williams:	Get in your teams, and I'll assign you to Wells Boards. You pick this time who will speak for your group. [Observation: Marcey tells her group she's not doing it].
Marcey:	[Talking to Oz, whose father is a physicist]. You're the only one in here that knows what's going on.
Ellen:	We like you, Oz!
Oz:	Would you like some Starburst? [Oz offers candy to the group members and they each accept]. [Observation: Bernice presents for her group. Connie presents for her group. Her group chose Connie because she's a strong speaker, according to one boy in the group].
Mr. Williams:	Oz, are you the presenter for that group?
Oz:	Yeah. [Oz presents for his group].
Mr. Williams:	Shannon, are you the presenter for that side?
Shannon:	Yeah.
Mr. Williams:	O.K., Shannon, you talk about E for us. [Observation: Shannon discusses his group's solution].
Mr. Williams:	Let's have groups for 2 a and 2 b. Steve, who's responsible in your group? [Group was split between Sam and Brian]. In case of a split, make it Brian.

Mr. Williams:	Mike, explain B to us.
	[Observation: Jon reports for his group. No disagreements or questions].
Mr. Williams:	Dean, do you agree? I can't see the numbers on yours.
Dean:	The main number is here. [Dean explains his group's solution].
	[Observation: Groups finish their presentations. Bernice tells me later that their group actually had chosen Phil for the presentation, but Mr. Williams called on her. This means that Connie was the only girl appointed by a group to do the talking in front of the class].

Because females in this class were often reluctant to actively participate in whole-class discussions, researchers like Tannen (1992) have recommended that teachers use small groups for discussion. Hence, we were interested to note if females' participation would increase in a small-group activity and in talk about that activity, like a lab experiment. Contrary to expectations from the literature, however, females, when placed in small groups with males, did not talk more than they did in whole-class discussions. Girls' roles in these groups were generally confined to recording and reading aloud the data the boys supplied from their set-ups, manipulations, and observations. This pattern was evidenced by an observation of a lab group composed of Euro-American students, Ericka, Kurt, and Sam who were conducting an experiment on friction:

Ericka:	O.K., What do we do?
Sam:	Let's do a nice list of our surfaces.
Sam:	Foaming carton, egg carton, plastic bag ... [Sam states the items aloud; Ericka records what he says].
Sam:	[to Ericka] You scribe today.
Kurt:	One half Newton. [Kurt is observing results of pulling the garbage bag on the weight].
Sam:	[to Ericka] I guess I'd put the towel down [on the list]. I am so tired!
Ericka:	Why?
Sam:	I was up til one o'clock last night.
Ericka:	The smart one's tired.
Observation:	The towel is now placed on the board. Kurt pulls it across the board, and Sam makes a verbalized observation.
Ericka:	[Speaking to the researcher] Sam wants to be a physics teacher.

Researcher:	Sam wants to be a physics teacher?
Ericka:	Yes, he does.
Researcher:	[Speaking to Sam] Really?
Sam:	Yeah.
Researcher:	So you let him do it? You let him make the observations?
Ericka:	Yeah.
Researcher:	[to Ericka] And you act as secretary?
Ericka:	Uh huh.
Researcher:	And Kurt does the manipulating?
Ericka:	Yeah.
Sam:	[Directing Ericka] When you write bubble wrap, be sure to write bumpy side.
Researcher:	Who's not here [today in the group]?
Ericka:	Jenna.
Researcher:	So, she's in your group?
[Observation:	Ericka nods affirmatively].
Researcher:	Is Jenna smart, too?
Kurt:	No.
Researcher:	No, Kurt? You said no. Why?
Kurt:	She whines too much about her opinion.
Ericka:	Sometimes she's right, though.
Sam:	She got us 10 points extra credit on one lab.
Researcher:	So, does she disagree with you a lot?
Ericka:	She's skeptical, but not overly skeptical.

It is interesting to note that the one female who did voice her opinions and debate ideas with the males in this group was regarded by a male in her group as whiny. This dismissal of a female's contributions to a small group attempting to learn science principles was also evidenced by Moje and Shepardson (1998). Patterns of females' nonparticipation in small groups of mixed gender were also observed by Mr. Williams, as noted in a formal interview:

> I found out sometimes the best thing I can do as far as lab assignments, and that's what I'm doing on the last one to a large extent, is to split the girls together, and see if I can put them together. When there's any boys on the team, they defer to the boys, and let them set up equipment, and do stuff like that. Whereas if we have all the girls working together, they seem like hey, no problem. They go ahead and do it [on their own].

Data like these have shown us that simply putting students into small groups for instruction does not solve the problem of asymmetrical power relations that lead to differential opportunity for participation. This finding has been confirmed by other researchers (Evans, Alvermann, & Anders, 1998; Moje & Shepardson, 1998). At all levels of physics, with both sexes of teachers, in either small group or whole-class activity and discussion, female students played a much more passive role than males did in learning science. These stereotypical roles were reinforced by some of their textbooks that predominately showed photos and illustrations of males engaged in active roles that demonstrated physics principles.

WHY GENDERED LANGUAGE IS MAINTAINED IN CLASSROOMS: PERCEPTIONS AND EXPECTATIONS

After observing lesson after lesson with these types of interaction patterns, we were able to document ways in which gendered language is reconstructed in classrooms. We then explored why these norms were allowed to exist. In doing so, the teachers and their students were questioned about their perceptions of gender differences in academic performance or attitudes toward science.

It became apparent that expectations and perceptions on the part of the teachers, the students, or both, in their classes, fostered stereotypical and marginalizing behaviors. In the Physical World class, we found that both the teacher's and the students' assumptions about female students were framed in one of two ways—either by their preconceptions of females' roles in society, or by their perceptions of the female students' own role expectations for themselves. In the case of the Physical World teacher, her assumptions about the position of a female within a particular culture also framed her expectations, as revealed during a formal interview:

Researcher:	Have you noticed in the interactions of students any gender differences in your classroom?
Miss Smitts:	Do you mean ratio wise or what?
Researcher:	Not just in terms of numbers, but in any way.
Miss Smitts:	Well, like out of a class of 30, I'll have 5 girls.
Researcher:	And then, within the numbers, have you noticed any gender differences?
Miss Smitts:	I'm not following you.
Researcher:	Gender differences in terms of the way they learn or the way they behave.
Miss Smitts:	O.K., I see. No. Maybe on a rare occasion I have in the Hispanic girls. Not in their ability to learn, but on their

stereotypical attempts to learn. Like if they're paired up with another Hispanic boy, they'll culturally believe that it's the boy's place to do certain things. So they leave it up to them without really realizing that they are doing it, and that it's O.K. to be stupid or not do the work because I'm female, and I'm going to have kids and raise a family, and I don't need to know that. But, push come to shove, if I show them that they can do it and encourage them, and because I'm female, I think I see that there really isn't a difference. It's strictly motivation, cultural experience, background.

It is interesting to note in Miss Smitts' response that she reports that only about 15% of her class size is comprised of females, when, in fact, this section was almost one-half females, or 40%. It did seem, however, as if there were fewer females in the class due to their invisibility. Females' lack of presence was evidenced by the absence of their voice in class discussions, their physical seating away from the teacher, their withdrawal from class activity, and, in some cases, by absenteeism. One female Hispanic girl was suspended from school for her truancy. Another female was suffering from Down syndrome and was absent, or when present, never did participate in discussions. Only two or three girls who sat together ever seemed to ask a question in small-group activity or contribute a response in whole-class discussion. These Euro-American and Hispanic girls often put their heads down and went to sleep during lectures and whole- class discussions. These findings are similar to those of Hynd, McNish, Qian, Keith, and Lay (1994) who studied Euro-American and African-American students also enrolled in a low-level physical science class.

The teacher's role expectations for females alluded to her beliefs about the way in which girls in her class were positioned within their culture and socioeconomic status. Responses from male students, however, alluded not to culture, but more simply to gender. When informed that, from the analysis of our questionnaire data, male students showed better attitudes toward physics than the females in their class did, the boys had ready explanations. These males attributed the nature of their own personalities and early experiences (which they perceived girls did not typically have) to present attitudes toward physical science. For example, Julio, a Hispanic male, stated, "Boys are more mischievous, and that grows into interest [in science]." Rufus, an African-American male stated, "Guys like to mess around and get dirty. Girls don't."

The female Physical World teacher also assigned some of these males' attention-getting behavior to one male's (Rufus') self-consciousness about his cultural difference from the others. Rufus' aggressive behavior was evidenced in several ways, as indicated by observation notes from a Research Assistant:

African-American male student [Rufus] continually interrupts a Hispanic girl next to him until he is called to the front of the room by Miss Smitts. I didn't hear what she said, but he came back quiet and continued with his experiment without further interruption.

My fieldnotes from an observation read:

Rob approaches Rufus like a fight will erupt. Miss Smitts walks over using her cane. She advises Rob to take a deep breath and count. Miss Smitts tells Rob it is not worth it to get in trouble.

My notes from an informal interview with Miss Smitts cited the teacher's rationale for Rufus' disruptive behavior:

Miss Smitts and I discussed Rufus' flirtatious behavior. He was done with his questionnaire long before the researcher had finished reading it aloud, and he began to distract the females near him. Miss Smitts felt he did this to be noticed for his behavior, and to avoid being singled out "because he's the only Black student in the class." She perceived that "it's his way of getting attention for another reason besides being Black."

Although stereotypical, this teacher's beliefs about why students display gendered behaviors in classrooms at least bring to mind the notion of being positioned in multiple ways. Some researchers have pointed out that a person is "multi-layered" (e.g., Weiler, 1988). An individual acts not only from a position of gender, but also from a myriad of other influences as well. Bing and Bergvall (1997) noted that:

There is considerable evidence that variables such as race, social class, culture, discourse function, and setting are as important as gender and not additive or easily separated. (p. 5)

STUDENTS' GENDERED PERCEPTIONS AND EXPECTATIONS FOR EACH OTHER

In addition to the comments made by some male students in Physical World regarding role relations, we had a plethora of other evidence that students' perceptions and expectations about gender and race maintain gendered role relations in science classrooms. Our informants themselves in our 1st year's study attributed cultural differences to one male's dominance in small-group activity and talk about that activity. Two Euro-American girls in Honors Physics perceived that a boy in their class had marginalized one of them due to his position as a Euro-American male raised primarily in a foreign country:

> [Observation: Honors Physics, 3/7, 1994. Researcher is observing Elaine's lab group. Marcey from another group comes over to Elaine and begins to confide something in her. Marcey appears upset, as she is red in the face, and her voice is stressed].

Marcey:	He treats me like I don't know anything knowledge wise.
Researcher:	A boy in the group?
Marcey:	Umm humm.
Researcher:	Does he take over the group?
Marcey:	No, not really. There's two people who do all the calculations and controls.
Researcher:	Who are the two people in the group?
Marcey:	Bill and Oz. Everybody seems to be fine except Oz. This is the first time I've ever felt discriminated against because I'm a woman. I'm not the only one that thinks that. I thought maybe I was just imagining it, so I was like kind of ignoring it, and I said something to Rob and he agreed.
Researcher:	Rob agrees? Is Rob in your group?
Marcey:	Yeah. He noticed it, too.
Researcher:	So, what does Oz do?
Marcey:	Every time I offer to do something, like if I offer to record the data, he has to do it, too. The vibes I get from him is that he has to do it to do it correctly. Something like that.
Researcher:	Why do you think he has that attitude?
Marcey:	I don't know. But, he doesn't do it with anyone else in the group. So, it makes me feel like he does it with me because I'm a girl. That's what I think.
Elaine:	I think I know why he does it. Because Oz is from a different culture. He wasn't raised in the United States. That crossed my mind.
Marcey:	Yeah. That crossed my mind, too.

Other data in which students talked about their talk in classrooms, were gathered from Physics and Honors Physics during both years. For example, students were given questionnaires assessing their observations of their own and others' participation in discussions and activities. Individuals were asked to identify the student who talked the most in class, how willing they were to participate in whole-class or small-group discussions, how likely they were to debate a position, and any differences they saw in how males and females talked in class. In addition, a purposive sample of 22 students in our second year responded to related queries during formal, audiorecorded interviews.

These data revealed in several ways that students of both sexes were well aware of the forms of gender bias we had identified. First, during both our 1st and 2nd year's investigations, the majority of males and females in both levels of Physics nominated males as students who talked the most in class. Second, responses to the questionnaire item, "Do you notice any differences in the way boys talk in class versus the way girls talk in class? If so, what?" showed that differential language patterns were observed by both males and females at both levels of physics. In the 2nd year of our study, males in Physics wrote responses like, "Most of the girls seem more timid and shy compared to the boys"; "I think the boys generate ideas faster than the girls"; "Boys are more opinionated—they say what they think"; "Boys are always right"; "Boys make it seem more technical"; and, "The boys are louder and more confident—they talk more." In Honors Physics, males made comments like, "Boys usually have reasons to back up their hypotheses"; "It's probably not true, but it seems like the boys understand the new concepts more easily"; and "Girls usually ask questions. Boys usually express what they think will happen"; "Girls seem to ask the questions and guys just argue"; and, "Boys are more funny and creative. Girls are more serious and whiny."

Females in Physics during Year 2 made remarks like: "The boys talk like they know what they're talking about, whereas girls always seem unsure of their ideas". A National Merit Scholar female in Honors Physics reported, "The girls gibber-jabber and try to talk their way through answers and are more likely to be swayed. [They are] easier to persuade. The boys have more substantive, empirical ways to prove things." Other Honors females' remarks included, "Boys talk without being called on. The girls wait to be called on"; "Guys tend to be hostile—if you're wrong, you're stupid, according to them. Girls are more likely to listen to an opinion."

Responses from females in the Physics section in Year 1 (which had the greatest ratio of males to females) focused on intimidation, including remarks from females like, "The boys are loud and obnoxious, and they try to show off, so it intimidates girls from asking questions because they might get made fun of"; "The boys make stupid comments on everything—the girls keep quiet and to themselves." The males in this section typically self-reported aggressive behavior in discussions, making comments like,

"Guys talk more—they're more outgoing and outspoken"; "Girls say the stupidest things"; and, "The boys are louder."

When confronted with these findings, the males appeared to be proud of their oppressive behavior, while females seemed to be accepting. When the researcher returned to the site at the end of Year 1 to share these data with the classes, including remarks like, "The boys haven't grown up yet"; "They [the boys] rule the class", a group of males in Physics broke out in unified song. They sang the Toys R Us jingle, which has words alluding the desire to never grow up. Rather than being embarrassed, males celebrated their pride in their oppression of the females.

In response, these females generally agreed that such behavior was to be expected. Females expressed their fears of repercussion in attempting to challenge or violate these norms. Girls tended to accept the boys' behaviors which marginalized them. They spoke of concern for their reputations and their popularity. Even those who had complained to us on an individual basis refused to discuss their observations in a whole-class setting. One female stated, "It just isn't worth it."

HOW GENDERED LANGUAGE IN CLASSROOMS CAN CHANGE: REPORTS OF INTERVENTIONS

Given these conditions, Mr. Williams and I attempted various interventions during the last quarter of our 1st year's study and during the entire second year. First, students were grouped by gender for small-group activities, like labs. Observations of these interactions showed that when females were grouped with females, groups were characterized by collaborative and equitable participation in activity and talk about that activity.

Interviews with students during same-gender labs revealed that female students appreciated the opportunity to work exclusively together. Two Euro-American females voiced their opinions:

Roberta: When I'm with boys, I feel really threatened, like I'm there to collect the data and write it down. The boys get to do the hands-on stuff. Last semester I had an all-girls group. I prefer it that way. I get to voice my opinions. No one is dominating the group. You don't feel threatened that you will say something stupid.

Tammy: Yeah. [Nods her head affirmatively]. I went to an all-girls school before I came here. The learning environment was more relaxed. Then I came here last year and took chemistry. I had 2 girls and 1 boy in my group. He pretty much took over our group.

Although females did participate actively and equitably when placed in same-gender groups like this one, females placed in groups where they were the only one of their gender or where only one of the opposite gender was present again experienced asymmetrical opportunities for instructional activity and discussion of that activity. Because there were uneven numbers of males and females in a class, some lab groups in each section were comprised of mixed genders. In these cases, females often were observed to be or reported being marginalized. And, although we did note females who were more dominant than others in same-gender lab groups, we did not see any female being marginalized in any same-gender lab group.

Despite increased proclivity to talk when placed in small group, single-gender labs, females did not become more verbal in whole-class discussions. Girls who did speak in these forums were usually those few who did so prior to our interventions. These girls (all Euro-American) also tended to be the same female voices heard in each whole-class discussion. Females' increased participation in small-group discussions, whether same or mixed gender groups, did not lead to increased participation in whole-class discussions.

SUMMARY

What have we learned about gender bias from 2 years of observation in secondary school science classes? Findings from these studies can be summarized as follows:

1. Behaviors that characterize gender disparity in science include those previously identified in the literature for other content areas. These include males' interruptions, call-outs, and loudness. Females are typically less active in experimentation and discussions.

2. Teachers may not be aware of gender bias in their classrooms, but their students are. Both teachers and students maintain the norms required for its existence.

3. Expectations for and performance in learning science are influenced by the perceptions and expectations of both teachers and students.

4. Gender disparity in classrooms will be difficult to change because of the benefits Euro-American, middle to upper-middle class students of both genders receive from maintaining the status quo. Males may continue to enjoy their power and privilege through their superordinate interactions. Comments from the females in the study like, "It just isn't worth it" [to try to change the status quo] indicate that females are able to act on their desire for popularity by enacting traditional female roles (e.g., being good listeners and subordinate to males). The general consensus among students is that gender bias in the classroom is the norm. Attempts to change

that norm are either not worth the risk (for females) of popularity or not worth the loss (for males) of power.

5. Simply placing Euro-American and Asian females (as typified in this study) in small groups does not increase their participation. Placing females in small groups by gender does increase their participation for that event, but does not carry over to whole-class activity.

Implications for Future Research and Practice

Although students in the 2nd year's study were grouped by gender for instructional activity, we realized that same-gender groups are unrealistic in preparing students to work together in the future. For when students do not learn to listen to each other, males who typically do the talking are disenfranchised from acquiring an important educational learning strategy (listening), and do not benefit from hearing the ideas of others. Females are disenfranchised because they do not get opportunities to work through their thinking aloud, or to verbalize questions that would stimulate further thought.

If researchers have failed to counteract gender bias in classrooms, how can teachers do so? Based on our observations and reports of other teacher researchers who have attempted interventions (e.g., Alvermann et al., 1997; Gallas, 1995), the key is to involve students. Students must recognize gender disparity as a problem and be active in creating solutions to that problem within their own contexts. Science education researchers like Tobin (1988) agreed that teachers should involve students in creating solutions to the problem of gender disparity in science activity and in talk about that activity.

How can teachers attempt interventions when they are often blind to the existence of a problem? Teachers can raise their own awareness of gender inequities by observing for the behaviors we have identified, and by designing and administering questionnaires to their students. The questionnaires could be designed with items that ask questions such as, "Which student talks the most in this class?" and "Do you notice any differences in the ways males and females participate in class?" By asking questions like these (through questionnaires or informal interviews with students), and by collecting, tallying, and analyzing these data, teachers can become action researchers in their own classrooms.

If teachers discover gender bias, then they may involve their students in interventions that will address their own specific needs. These interventions might include involving students in tracing activity and discussion patterns, critiquing and rewriting texts and materials, writing self-reflections, or monitoring whole-class and small-group discussions, as Gallas (1995) an elementary science teacher did. As we did, students might also be involved in developing metacognitive awareness of and metacommunication about talk that marginalizes others in classrooms.

What are the implications of this research for future research? Whenever I have talked about these findings with my students or with other researchers, I have been asked the following questions:

1. Would these same patterns of gendered discussion occur in other subject areas, like Social Studies, or in subjects thought of as more feminine, like an English or literature class?
2. What do male–female interaction patterns look like in science classes at various grades (e.g., elementary classrooms) and with different cultures (e.g., primarily Hispanic or African American?
3. How and for how long would the suggested interventions change gendered interaction patterns?

Aside from these queries, in reflecting on the results of these 2 years of documentation and intervention, I am left with findings that puzzle me. First, like Alvermann (1993), I am intrigued by the implications of changing gendered patterns of discussion. I am still struck by the resistance on the part of both males and females to confront the problem publicly, despite their complaints to me privately. Like Alvermann and her colleagues (1997), I have found that changing gendered literacy practices is more difficult to do than I imagined. I am also reminded that there are costs or risks in doing so.

My research also leaves me with unanswered questions to be addressed by future intervention studies. For example, will males be willing to relinquish power to gain valuable literacy strategies (i.e., active listening to benefit from females' questions and thought processes)? Will females be able to be less concerned about their reputations and popularity, and become more concerned about their academic opportunity? In what situations are students most likely to make these changes? Finally, like Alvermann (1993), I wonder what repercussions these changes may bring. These are a few of the questions that I hope that I and other researchers will be able to explore in our future efforts.

7

Looking Back at Mr. Weller: A Personal Retrospective

Roger A. Stewart
Boise State University

In the late 1980s, I studied Mr. Weller (pseudonym) and his high school earth science class using microethnographic methods (Goetz & LeCompte, 1984; Stewart, 1990a). The study explored text use and reading in Mr. Weller's fourth period class. Mr. Weller was in his fifth year of teaching at the time and had been teaching for two years at Lincoln High School where the study took place. Lincoln High had roughly 2,300 students and was located in a city of approximately 60,000 people. During a spring semester, I was a participant observer for 60 days in Mr. Weller's 4th-hour earth science classroom. I assumed the role of a student as much as a balding, mid-30s, former high school teacher could. I had an assigned seat and textbook, and I participated in laboratories, lectures, and small-group work. I completed homework, quizzes, and tests alongside the 20 tenth graders and two eleventh graders in the class. When I was not in the classroom or "hanging out" with Mr. Weller in the science department office, I was hanging around the cafeteria eating lunch with students and talking to the teachers who monitored the cafeteria and hallways.

Apart from it being interesting and fun, this study was necessary because of an identified need in the field of secondary content-area literacy. In the 1980s, the field of content-area reading, as it was called then, needed thick descriptions of secondary school classrooms revealing the what, how, and why of text use and reading. Hinchman's (1985, 1987) early work exploring reading and text use in secondary school classrooms exemplified the qualitative research called for by the content-area reading scholarly community. This need came about because of growing awareness that content-reading instruction was not becoming a part of day-to-day pedagogical routines, as had been anticipated when state certification offices began requiring course work in content-area reading for secondary teachers (Farrell & Cirrincione, 1984; O'Brien, 1988; O'Brien & Stewart, 1990; O'Brien, Stewart, & Moje, 1995; Ratekin, Simpson, Alvermann, & Dishner, 1985; Rieck, 1977; Siedow, Memory, & Bristow, 1985; Smith & Feathers, 1983a, 1983b; Stewart, 1990b; Stewart & O'Brien, 1989; Vaughan, 1977). In addition to the content area reading scholarly community, a few scholars in science education published research and opinion on the subject of text use and reading in science classrooms (e.g., Yore, 1986, 1987, 1991; Yore & Denning, 1989). In aggregate, the two fields, content-area literacy and science education, produced a body of theory and research that created the conditions for a study such as mine.

Awareness of the lack of integration of content-area reading into secondary school classrooms grew during the 1980s, and specialists in the field suggested two primary means for addressing the problem: (a) long-term association between teachers and content-reading specialists to affect permanent incorporation of content reading into secondary school classrooms (Conley, 1988; Herber, 1988) and (b) gathering detailed knowledge about the day-to-day workings of content classrooms to better understand how to insert reading instruction into existing classroom milieus (Moore, 1988; Smith & Feathers, 1983a, 1983b). The microethnography of Mr. Weller was born in the latter. The study provided detailed descriptions of the day-to-day workings of a single high school earth science classroom with particular attention to the roles of text materials and reading.

METHODOLOGY, THEORY, SETTING, DATA SOURCES, AND ANALYSIS

"Microethnographic work depends upon a combination of participant observation (direct, continuous observation and reflection, recorded in running field notes) and microanalysis of films and videotapes of everyday happenings in schools" (Erickson & Wilson, 1982, p. 43). Microethnographers focus on the patterns of social interaction among members of a cultural group or among members of different cultural groups. They are interested in specifying the processes of face-to-face interaction and in understanding how these "micro" processes are related to larger "macro" issues of culture and social organization. (Jacob, 1987, p. 18). I explored interactions within Mr. Weller's 4th-hour classroom and how text materials and reading shaped and were shaped by those interactions. The exploration revealed aspects of classroom culture and the roles of text materials and reading within the culture.

Theoretical Underpinnings of the Study

Symbolic interaction theory underpinned the study (Blumer, 1969; Woods, 1992). Symbolic interactionists believe that people construct meaning through social interaction. Symbolic interactionism (SI) has three primary premises: (a) "that human beings act toward things on the basis of the meanings that the things have for them" (Blumer, 1969, p. 2); (b) that the meanings of these things are derived from social interaction; and (c) that meanings are modified within an interpretative process employed by people as they interact with their worlds. Thus, meanings form and change as individuals interact with things (i.e., symbols) and people in their environment. Importantly, as meanings change for symbols so do actions toward those symbols (Stewart, Paradis, & Van Arsdale, 1995). SI dovetails nicely with microethnographic fieldwork in that both focus on the interactions between people and how meaning is constructed as a consequence.

Setting

Lincoln High School had four grades (9–12). Students were predominantly White and middle class, although there was a wide range of socioeconomic status. Students were tracked in primarily two levels: general and academic. Criteria for placement were student performance on standardized instruments and grades. Mr. Weller's 4th-hour earth science class was considered academic, meaning students scored in the 5th stanine or above on standardized measures of science knowledge and had achieved C or better grades in previous science classes. There were 11 males and 11 females in the class. All were White except one student of Hispanic origin. I began participant observation on the first day of the spring semester. All but a few of the students were new to Mr. Weller's class since most changed schedules at the semester, which involved switching earth science teachers. The earth science curriculum was structured so that all teachers covered the same content during the first semester.

Mr. Weller was in his 5th year of teaching, his 2nd year at Lincoln High School. Although his primary teaching assignment during his teaching career had been earth science, he had taught mathematics, physical science, and astronomy. He was within 6 credit hours of earning a master's degree in Secondary Education.

Mr. Weller was purposively chosen (Merriam, 1998; Patton, 1990) from a pool of three earth science teachers, all from different local high schools, who upon telephone contact had expressed interest in participating in the study. After interviewing the three teachers, Mr. Weller was chosen because of his enthusiasm for the project and two other important criteria. First, one of the other teachers was in her 1st year of teaching, and experience was a selection criterion. Second, the earth science course in the school where the third teacher taught was in a state of flux because of changing state graduation requirements. Although studying this transition would have been fascinating, it did not provide the stable environment that this study required.

Data Sources and Analysis

In addition to participating in Mr. Weller's 4th-hour classroom and spending time in Lincoln High School conversing and interacting with a wide variety of faculty and staff, I conducted informal and formal interviews with a variety of students, staff, faculty, and administration. Formal interviews were conducted with Mr. Weller, six students in 4th hour (i.e., key informants and others), other teachers, a counselor, and a building administrator. Numerous informal interviews occurred spontaneously as I spent time in the school. All classroom observations and formal interviews were either audiotaped or videotaped for later transcription and analysis. Additionally, I collected all handouts in Mr. Weller's class including laboratories, worksheets, tests, and study guides. I also collected all administrative correspondence disseminated to the teachers and the daily school-wide attendance lists.

My observations were not limited to Mr. Weller's classroom. My regular schedule was to arrive before 4th hour and remain in the building through the lunch hour. Throughout the study, however, I kept talking, listening, asking questions, and seeking novel environments in which to do so. Thus, I was in and out of the building at a variety of times. I attended convocations and a teacher luncheon. When I was not in the student cafeteria, I ate lunch with the science teachers in the department office. Mr. Weller and I traveled to a regional conference together, and I attended a party at his home. Thus, I amassed a body of data from diverse observations and experiences. As my interpretation of what I was experiencing took form, I checked it against the variety of data sources, the multiple perspectives sampled, and my key informants (Goetz & LeCompte, 1984).

I had informal conversations and interactions with many of the students in 4th hour; however, several students became especially important to me. They were articulate individuals who exhibited insights into Mr. Weller and his classroom and who were willing to talk with me. I relied on these students when checking my emerging interpretations. In addition to informal conversations, I formally interviewed them. They represented a breadth of achievement and interest in the class. I also formally interviewed several other students in the class who had not become key informants so that diverse perspectives were represented.

Data were analyzed using the constant comparative method (Glaser & Strauss, 1967, 1978; Strauss & Corbin, 1990). In constant comparative analysis, data are analyzed as they are collected. Preliminary results are used to inform and guide subsequent data collection and analysis. As new data are analyzed and compared to previously collected data, explanatory and interpretive categories and properties inductively emerge. As the categories and properties evolve from the iterative data collection and analysis process, the researcher reenters the field to test hypotheses and to explore, modify, and subsequently saturate categories and properties.

Negative case analysis (Erickson, 1986; Glaser & Strauss, 1967; Miles & Huberman, 1994) was also an important part of this study. A negative case was a disconfirming instance of student or teacher behavior that directly conflicted with a tentative research hypothesis. For example, Scott represented a negative case. All the other students I talked with in Mr. Weller's 4th-hour class reported that Mr. Weller was their primary source of information, however Scott said the textbook was his main source. Why was he different? Maybe my hypothesis that Mr. Weller was the primary provider of information did not have as much explanatory power as I originally thought? I started observing Scott more carefully, and I made an extra effort to maintain our acquaintance. In time, he became one of my key informants.

What I learned was that Scott did not like Mr. Weller or earth science, slept or read car magazines through most every class, and relied on the textbook for what little information he picked up from the course. He narrowly passed the class. Thus, Scott did not negate my hypothesis. On the contrary, he caused me to broaden and refine it. I came to realize that Mr. Weller was the primary source of information, but the textbook contained a lot of what was covered in the class, and a student such as Scott could get at least a portion of what he needed by using the book.

RESULTS AND DISCUSSION

In this section, I describe and discuss the categories and properties that represent salient characteristics of Mr. Weller's classroom. These categories and properties reveal the foundation of social interaction around which definitions for text and reading developed. Four categories and attendant properties will be explored.

Category #1: Mr. Weller's Philosophy of Earth Science Teaching

Mr. Weller's philosophy of earth science teaching framed his goals as an earth science instructor and his demeanor toward students. Thus, the properties under this category include: (a) Mr. Weller's goals and (b) Mr. Weller's demeanor.

Mr. Weller's primary goal was to get students to perceive the world about them in a more critical and inquiring fashion. He believed knowledge of earth science became a tool in the hands of a discriminating perceiver of the natural world. He did not necessarily want students to label their world with the correct geological terms, but he did want them to have a heightened awareness of their natural surroundings. In an interview, he said:

> I am trying to draw out verbally an understanding of their environment. Not some specific thing about earth science, but I try to draw out from them a relaxed attitude but attentive attitude about their surroundings. But that's the whole purpose of the earth science class as far as I'm concerned: to build awareness.

Although Mr. Weller never explicitly stated his goals to the class, students were implicitly aware of them. Students reported that Mr. Weller really did not care about the details. He wanted them to learn concepts. Megan, a student in the class, provided an example of this when she said, "Mr. Weller wants us to know that if you go to California you won't slide off into the ocean." She went on to say that naming the fault and its type was of secondary importance.

Mr. Weller's jovial and personable demeanor became a primary means for achieving his goals. Mr. Weller believed if he could convince students that he was an "all right guy," they would listen to him and perceive him as a viable role model. During an interview, he articulated this belief:

> But I'm trying to get them to open up to me to see my attitude. Okay, if they can open up rather go—He's a teacher. He's a jerk. We hate him. Don't say anything. Don't look at him. No. Instead of that kind of attitude, I want them to think well he's not a bad guy. He does that. That sounds neat. Maybe I'll try that. I'm trying to project. I guess I'm trying to get them to see me as a decent role model.

Mr. Weller projected his personable and approachable demeanor through his sense of humor and theatrical flair. He had performed in high school plays and the glee club in college. The students enjoyed his sense of humor and his ability to act. For example, Megan said about Mr. Weller's occasional impersonations, "He does a good Nixon." Students in 4th hour, with the exception of Scott, reported liking Mr. Weller and looking forward to attending because the class was considered fun.

Category #2: The Culture of Control
at Lincoln High School

The category of Culture of Control at Lincoln High School encompasses both Mr. Weller's classroom and the school-at-large. There are two properties within the category: (a) School and classroom control and (b) Influence of control on curriculum and pedagogy.

Although Lincoln High School was far from a violent school, it suffered its share of vandalism, mischief, and fighting among students. Consequently, an air of control permeated the building. Unarmed, off-duty policemen, whom students called "rent-a-cops," patrolled the school and grounds throughout the day. The school had a closed lunch hour during which time students could not leave the grounds. Nine teachers monitored the cafeteria and the doors and hallways around the cafeteria during the three lunch periods each day. Teachers were released from teaching duties throughout the day to monitor hallways and restrooms, and there was a strict hall pass system.

I had several first-hand experiences with the culture of control. I was stopped in the hallways and asked what my business was. I was also confronted by an assistant principal while I was interviewing one of my key informants in the commons area adjacent to the cafeteria. He approached us and asked us where we were supposed to be. After I explained to him what we were doing, he thanked me for the information and gave us permission to continue.

Teachers talked with me concerning control. Mr. Reed, an intensely perceptive teacher, characterized Lincoln High School in the following way:

> Mass education so that kids don't start to think that they are individuals and can do whatever they want and have their own opinions because nobody wants the late 60's and early 70's again. (Informal conversation)

The concern with control extended into the classroom. Evidence accrued throughout my stay at Lincoln High School that classroom control was on the minds of Mr. Weller and his colleagues, both those in his immediate department and those in other departments. For example, Mr. Standifer, a science teacher, commented how it was difficult to separate the police function from the teaching function even after the classroom door was closed. I became acquainted with Mr. Standifer through conversations we had during lunch as he monitored a hallway adjacent to the cafeteria that was a student escape route.

The culture of control influenced what was taught and how it was taught. For example, Mr. Weller carefully orchestrated his class through strategic selection of materials and activities so that disruption was minimized. When asked how he chose activities, Mr. Weller said that he had a file full of resources that he leafed through and picked something appropriate. When asked what was appropriate, he said he was careful to pick something of moderate difficulty. He said that if he picked something too difficult or too easy the students would get silly on him. Silly meant that they would start talking, lose interest in the activity, and subsequently become difficult to manage.

Further insight into the power of students to influence what was taught, how it was taught, and thus, the way in which classrooms were controlled came from a variety of conversations and incidents. A counselor, Mrs. Snead, corroborated what I had heard from Mr. Weller and his colleagues concerning both school and classroom control. During an interview, Mrs. Snead talked about the difference in behavior between the two tracks: academic and general. She believed that most teachers were reluctant, no matter the track, to give students more freedom and voice in their learning because they might not maintain control.

This distinction between academic and general was underscored one day as Mr. Weller and I walked between the science department office and his classroom. The following is an elaborated and edited excerpt from my field notes from that day:

> On our way to Mr. Weller's classroom, we walked through Mr. Tadance's [another earth science teacher] classroom. Today half of the chalkboard was covered with 20 or more vocabulary words over the same content that Mr. Weller was currently teaching in fourth hour. As I passed by the board and noticed the list of vocabulary, I mentioned two things. First, I commented on the large number of words. Second, I commented that I never saw that number of vocabulary words in Mr. Weller's classroom. Mr. Weller quickly responded that this was probably a class of "generals," and with a short laugh and a smile he said, "Gotta keep those generals busy."

Other teachers and staff provided additional insights into classroom control and its influence on curriculum and pedagogy. One day, while in the cafeteria during lunch, I talked to Mrs. Clark, a business education teacher. She was stationed as a sentinel in a hallway leading to the main parking lot. Mrs. Clark explained that students who want to pursue a business career in college cannot take business courses offered at Lincoln High School because of college entrance requirements. She commented that, in some of the classes she taught, she felt like a baby-sitter trying to "entertain and contain." She summarized her feelings when she said, "Well, you know, we [i.e., teachers in the business department] would like to get some of the good students, too."

The culture of control that dominated Lincoln High directly relates to the next category, classroom choreography. Mr. Weller carefully orchestrated his class to operationalize his philosophy, achieve his goals of earth science teaching, and maintain control of his students.

Category #3: Classroom Choreography: Divide and Conquer

The category of Classroom Choreography delineates the ebb and flow of classroom activity. This ebb and flow helps describe text use, reading, and some of the influences on literacy practices. This category is closely related to the control category because Mr. Weller orchestrated his classroom with control in mind; but the Classroom Choreography category adds layers of complexity because it takes into account Mr. Weller's philosophy along with his content objectives. The category has two properties: (a) Activity base and (b) Locus of interaction.

Activity base is a catalogue of all the activities and their sequence in Mr. Weller's class including lecturing, corrective feedback, seat work, laboratory activities, and downtime. For each day of observation, I reviewed my fieldnotes and audiotapes or videotapes to catalogue the day's events. Figure 7.1 is one day's activity base analysis log.

In conjunction with the activity base analysis logs, I kept a subject matter time line cataloguing the topics covered. Thus, I accumulated a record of the amount of time spent in various activities and the topics covered.

Locus of interaction involves whether the activities were teacher-focused or student-focused. For example, teacher-focused activities included lecturing and corrective feedback sessions. Student-focused activities included individual and small-group seat work, reading, and laboratories. Through careful selection of activities, Mr. Weller regularly altered the locus of interaction from himself to the students and then back. This occurred within class periods and also across days. As part of my analysis, I catalogued the total amount of observation time where the locus centered on Mr. Weller (56.14% of total time) and the total amount of time centered on the students (43.86% of total time).

As the percentages reveal, Mr. Weller carefully choreographed his class, making sure that he did not lecture too much or give the students too many independent seat-work activities. In short, Mr. Weller was cognizant of the locus of interaction and how often it needed to be altered. He never lectured for more than one class period, and he would often shift the locus two or

Time After Bell Activity	Activity	Activity Category	Total Time of Activity
0 – 4:05	Announcing quiz today. Will spend some time studying. Announces local gadget contest.	M	4.08
4:05 – 9:20	Reviewing for quiz.	QTS	5.25
9:20 – 10:30	Preparing for quiz #4 (i.e., putting books away and getting out pencils). Handing out quizzes.	M	
10:30 – 27:20	Taking quiz. Working on worksheet (grids).	SW	16.83
27:20 – 52:40	Going over worksheet. This almost turned into a lecture on grid systems.	CF	26.33
52:40 – 53:00	Bowling pun sequence.	DT	.33
Total taped classroom time			52.82

M = management; QTS = quiz study; SW = seat work; CF = corrective feedback; DT = downtime; L = lecture

FIG. 7.1 Example of activity base analysis log for one day of classroom observations.

three times during a class. For example, he would start with a brief lecture, move to some corrective feedback on a quiz, and then finish with a small-group seat-work activity. In this way, he kept the class moving forward with variety. I recorded in my fieldnotes Mr. Weller saying in his office one day, as he was thinking out loud, deciding on the next thing to do in earth science, "We've done enough of that for now, we better move on to something different." He was referring to a series of seat-work activities the students had recently completed. The day following this comment, he spent some time providing corrective feedback and lecturing. Thus, he moved the locus of interaction back to himself.

Mr. Weller carefully selected a variety of activities for each unit of instruction; however, the units exhibited similar general patterns. A unit lasted from 2 to 4 weeks and was constructed around a topic such as plate tectonics. Each unit began with one class period devoted to students reading corresponding chapters or sections in the textbook and answering textbook questions. The remainder of the unit involved iterations of the following:

lecture followed by one or more seat-work activities or laboratories applying the lecture content, corrective feedback over the completed materials, and a quiz. Interspersed was an occasional video. The unit was finalized with a comprehensive unit test. Figure 7.2 provides a break down of the percentage of observed time devoted to various classroom activities.

Figure 7.2 reveals that Mr. Weller lectured about 14% of classroom observation time. His lectures had a characteristic flair about them. He used multiple colors of dry-erase markers to outline his lecture on the board as he progressed. He was careful to make all the headings of a certain level the same color. The students became adept at catching him when he was about to use the wrong color. It was a source of interaction and humor in the classroom.

When I asked Mr. Weller about his selection and sequence of activities, he said, "Well, you gotta mix it up." He felt that a variety of carefully selected activities, none of which took dominance over the others, kept the students' attention and the instruction moving forward. Concerning the consistent

Classroom Activity Category	Percentage
Management (Attendance, giving instructions, transitions, announcements)	19.57
Seat Work	
Studying Before Tests or Quizzes	2.15
Evaluation	6.93
Reading	4.93
Worksheets and Study Guides	13.77
Laboratory Activities	9.93
Lecturing	14.09
Corrective Feedback on Materials	17.52
Viewing Videotape	6.61
Downtime (Students allowed to talk at beginning or end of period)	4.50
Total	100.00

FIG. 7.2   Percentage of total observation time by activity. (Total observation time = 3,180 minutes)

instructional pattern from unit to unit, he said, "I try to give a little content through the reading and lectures and then go on with it with the other stuff."

Students were aware of the variety in activities. On a day that I was in the building early for a convocation, I observed Mr. Weller's 2nd-hour earth science class. He was out of the room for a short while, so the students and I were talking. I asked them what they liked about earth science. One student said, "All the different things we do." The rest of the group added their assent. Students were also aware of the pattern from unit to unit. Megan said during an interview, "We do our reading in the book, then some other things, then we have a test."

Category #4: Use of Text

The Use of Text category explores how texts were used in Mr. Weller's classroom. The category has two properties: (a) Textbase and (b) Public and private use of the textbook.

Textbase is simply a catalog of all the printed text materials created by or given to the students. By the end of a unit of instruction, students had processed all or some of the following texts: (a) textbook chapters or sections, (b) answers to textbook questions, (c) lecture notes, (d) seat-work activities, (e) laboratories, (d) quizzes, and (e) notes from videos. Reference works are not included in the above list because I observed reference works being consulted on only one occasion to answer a question on a laboratory.

On the surface, this may look like a substantial base of text materials to process; however, the total amount of extended text processing was not great. Apart from the textbook reading at the beginning of each unit, the other materials required little extended processing. Most seat-work activities and laboratories were a few pages in length with mostly directions and short paragraphs of content information. Apart from written responses to questions, the only student generated writing was lecture notes. Thus, the need for writing extended connected text that revealed complex understanding of content concepts was lacking.

Public use of the textbook involved the textbook being brought into the mainstream of classroom interaction and construction of meaning. For example, Mr. Weller might refer to the textbook during a lecture or corrective feedback session, students might ask questions concerning textbook content, or they might use the book during small-group or laboratory activities. For example, in the following excerpt from a lecture, a student, Jim, asks Mr. Weller a question concerning a discrepancy detected between the textbook content and the content of Mr. Weller's lecture:

> Mr. Weller: California has had hundreds of earthquakes in modern times. It's a very active area around there.
> [Jim immediately raises his hand to get Mr. Weller's attention. Mr. Weller acknowledges Jim.]
> Jim: Didn't the book say something about. I mean, I thought the book said thousands of earthquakes in just a few days?
> Mr. Weller: That was after-shocks. Those come after an earthquake.
> Jim: Yeah, oh yeah. I see. I remember now.

Students asking such questions about textbook content occurred only four times during observations. Moreover, I observed the textbook become part of the public domain only 15 times during the course of the study. Ramifications of this small amount of public use of the textbook will be explored in the discussion section.

Private use of the textbook involved students using the textbook privately to construct meaning. For example, students reported reading the textbook during study hall to prepare for tests and quizzes. They also reported turning to the textbook, with mixed results, when they did not understand something Mr. Weller provided during class time. During an interview, I asked Teresa how important the textbook was to her. Her response illustrates her private use of the textbook:

> Well, it's pretty important sometimes. You know how I said the big words gets you confused [i.e., during class time] and I have to go up in the back of the book to look up the definition and that gets confusing.

When I asked her if she used the textbook when she studied for examinations, she replied:

> I read the book entirely. The chapter not the book. That came out wrong. Then I'll like see the definition and I'll try to memorize definitions. And I'll go back in the questions and problems and try to answer those. If I can't, I look it up.

Teresa's comments illustrate that for some students private use of the text was important. Such use of the textbook became important for me as well.

I began noticing within the first few weeks of observation that Mr. Weller seldom made reference to the textbook during class time; however, I found myself using the textbook quite often to complete worksheets, laboratories, and, like Teresa, when I reviewed for tests and quizzes. I doubted if I was the only person using the textbook in this manner, so I started looking around and asking questions.

I undertook a comparative analysis of textbook and lecture material. I compared top-level discourse structures (Meyer, Brandt, & Bluth, 1980) of lecture excerpts and corresponding textbook sections. The analysis revealed that Mr. Weller used the textbook to structure his lectures. He did not lecture directly out of the textbook; but he did, at times, draw from the content structure of the textbook as a seed for his lectures; yet he seldom referred to the textbook during the course of these lectures. When I asked him about this, he told me that he used the textbook as an outline. Thus, here was an instance of Mr. Weller's private use of the textbook.

Classroom observation contributed to fleshing out this category. One day in class, I witnessed an incident that exemplified the schism between private and public use of the textbook. Mike was an academically able student, and he was one of the few students who read the assigned textbook pages from beginning to end when the reading was assigned in class. Most students immediately found the first set of questions and started shuffling pages to find the answers, what Nicholson (1984) called "search and destroy." Mr. Weller was aware of this but did not know how to combat the problem.

Mike was a rare exception to the search and destroy rule. During an interview, he said that he was aware of how most students read the chapter and answered the questions but that he read the chapter all the way through. When all the other students were leafing through pages and writing answers immediately after the reading assignment had been given, Mike would be slouched in his seat reading with the book resting on his belly and the spine against the edge of the desk. Depending on the length of the chapter or the number of chapters assigned, he spent the entire hour reading. He told me that if he did not have time to do the questions in class, he did them in study hall. This technique proved effective for Mike. The following incident illustrates this point. It comes from fieldnotes that have been elaborated and edited for clarity and context:

> Today, Mr. Weller was lecturing and asked a question. He waited for a response, received none, so he called upon a student. This student gave an incorrect answer. This occurred two more times. While the other students responded and Mr. Weller rephrased his question, I saw Mike reach down and slide his textbook out from under his seat. He quickly opened it to the appropriate section, found the answer he was looking for, and raised his hand. Mr. Weller called upon him, and he gave the correct answer. I do not think Mr. Weller noticed Mike pulling the text out nor did he or Mike mention the textbook during their exchange of question and answer.

I asked Mike about this incident during an interview. He did not remember it, but explained that he probably remembered seeing the answer in the book and needed to look it up to make sure.

The incident serves to illustrate the schism in the classroom between private and public use of the textbook. Although Mr. Weller seldom referred to or displayed the textbook in the classroom, some students, like Mike and Teresa, would use the text privately to help them construct meaning and then employ that to their advantage in the classroom, whether it involved answering a lecture question or a test question.

To summarize, evidence showed that the textbook was isolated from the public domain of the classroom; however, it played a role, albeit a subtle one, in the classroom construction of meaning, mostly as a result of its private use. The following example illustrates how far removed from the public domain the textbook became. The excerpt comes from a combination of elaborated fieldnotes and transcription of audiotapes:

> Today, Mr. Weller instructed the students to look at a particular page in the textbook. Mark, a particularly jocose individual, immediately rejoined, "What's that?" Mr. Weller smiled and held up his text and said, "This thing, right here."

Mr. Weller became the primary purveyor of content. He wanted to be seen as a viable role model, so he conveyed the content to the students in humorous and palatable ways so they would buy into his brand of perceiving the natural world. In so doing, he pushed text and reading to the margins. Mark, being one of the more perceptive students in the class, recognized this fact.

There was another reason, however, behind the isolation of the textbook from the public domain of the classroom. The three earth science teachers in the department, including Mr. Weller, felt the textbook was too general for classroom purposes. Mr. Weller said the breadth of content coverage was adequate, but the topics were not covered with enough depth. He said the textbook was only good as introductory material and required extensive supplementation, exactly how he used the textbook in his classroom. He repeatedly said that he would like to have a better textbook. It is interesting to note that one of the other earth science teachers said that a weak text was not all that bad because the teacher has greater latitude in conducting the class. He believed that a strong text would have a greater tendency to dictate the scope and sequence of instruction. In other words, a strong text would insert itself more forcefully into the classroom construction of meaning.

Many of the students also felt the text was too general. For example, I asked Megan if she ever turned to the text for something she could not remember. She said, "Yeah, but usually they're (i.e. answers) kind of general."

Similar sentiments were expressed by Mike during an interview when I asked him if he used the text to study for tests. He said, "It's too broad. I mean it can hurt you more than it can help you." Even Teresa, who reported using the text quite a lot for study purposes, complained that it was vague and too general at times. I also found the text frustratingly superficial.

Complaints about the textbook, however, were not universal. Although they recognized its weaknesses, few students lodged complaints. On the contrary, some preferred a simple textbook. For example, when I asked Megan if she would like a more detailed textbook, she replied:

> I don't know about that. I like it better just as a study guide. I really do. Because when I read stuff it's harder for me to remember it sometimes if it's so specific that it gets boring then I won't remember anything. But textbooks like our earth science can be boring if you just start reading through them, but I mean as a study guide it's okay cause you don't really have to remember every single thing in it because it doesn't have the details and stuff. It's better to have someone say it and write it [i.e. take notes] and stuff instead of just reading it. (Interview)

The only student that opted for a more detailed textbook was Scott, the student discussed earlier as the negative case, an understandable desire in light of the fact that he drew upon the text for most everything he learned in earth science.

Mr. Weller's ambivalent attitude towards the textbook, like that of his earth science colleagues, filtered down to the students through myriad interactions in the classroom and heavily influenced the way in which the text was evaluated. When I asked the students how Mr. Weller felt about the textbook, many responded that he did not think much of it. For example, Jane said:

> I don't know. I think maybe he likes it, but, if he really liked it, he'd probably have us read it more. You know kind a want us to read it more. Really hit us to read it, but he doesn't. It's almost like he doesn't really care whether we do or not. So I figure that he's just pretty confident about what he's saying, and that's good enough for us. (Interview)

One can readily ascertain where Jane acquired most of her information in the class. Through a complex process of social interaction, teacher and students arrived at an interpretation of the quality of the textbook and the role that it would play within the classroom.

According to my observations and my experience with the textbook, interviews, and other measures, both the teachers' and the students' assessment of the textbook were correct. I compared the textbook to two other books on the market. All three were similar in their breadth of content coverage and lack of depth. I also administered a formal cloze procedure (Bormuth, 1968) to the 4th-hour students. All but one student scored at the independent level. The one outlier scored at the instructional level. Only one student said that the text was at times difficult to read; however, she scored at the independent level on the cloze procedure.

In summary, Mr. Weller constructed a teacher-centered classroom environment where he controlled the flow of information and became the primary source of information. Olson (1980, 1981, 1983) characterized this style of teaching as "high influence." Mr. Weller did not see himself in this way but his students did. When I mentioned that the students saw him as their primary source of information, he replied, "I hope that's not the case. I don't want that to be." His comment reveals complexities and contradictions that permeated this study that will be discussed in the following sections.

THE CULTURAL CONTEXT
OF READING AND TEXT USE

Mr. Weller reported, during conversations and interviews, that he felt reading was important and that he would like his earth science students to do more. So why did reading not play a larger part in his instructional agenda? The culture of Lincoln High School and the culture created within Mr. Weller's classroom did not support extended reading of multiple texts. The perceived need for tight control facilitated high influence teaching where independence from the teacher, which could have been fostered through reading and learning from text, was not positively reinforced. Furthermore, Mr. Weller's need to convey his caring and personable nature to his students in order for them to see him as a viable role model pushed him onto center stage, thus further displacing the need for extended reading. In short, Mr. Weller's controlling the flow of information became a primary agent of control, a primary means of achieving his goals, and a clear path to operationalizing his philosophy. Finally, the poor textbook, an assessment of which was socially constructed within the classroom, reinforced the lack of need to read.

Perhaps a better textbook would influence Mr. Weller's teaching and move him off center stage, thus allowing other texts to have voice in the classroom. This could happen in two ways. Mr. Weller could overtly give the text a larger role in the classroom, or the text could force itself into the classroom construction of meaning when students were empowered, as a consequence of their private use of a meatier textbook, to ask questions and add comments because of their additional knowledge. However, there is a potential pitfall here. If the text were too difficult for the students, then its private use might suffer, less reading would result, and students would be even more dependent on the teacher. Recall the lecture excerpt where Jim questioned Mr. Weller about the number of earthquakes California has experienced in modern times. Jim detected a discrepancy between what he had read in the textbook and what Mr. Weller was saying. The dialogue illustrates the textbook playing a role in the classroom construction of meaning. Perhaps, with a text containing greater content information and more engaging writing, students would formulate more questions like Jim's.

Given Mr. Weller's self-reports that reading was important and his desire to incorporate more reading into his classroom, I asked him why he did not supplement the weak text with other reading materials. Time and proximity were both factors. Mr. Weller believed there was already a lot of content to cover in the course, and finding time to go and locate additional materials was difficult. Duplication was another problem. The department had a limited paper budget so all faculty had to monitor their paper use. In short, it was more cost-effective in time, energy, and materials and more congruent with the culture of the school and his classroom for Mr. Weller to draw upon his extensive knowledge of earth science instead of seeking additional reading materials. Mr. Weller taught by telling his students what he wanted them to know (Sizer, 1985).

SUMMARY AND RECOMMENDATIONS

For secondary school reading, such findings have great import. First, impoverished textbooks, like the one used in Mr. Weller's classroom, have to improve (Schallert & Roser, 1989). Until textbooks are consistently written with greater depth of content coverage and a point of view that engages readers, the potential for teachers and students to ignore them will be great. The dialogue between Jim and Mr. Weller previously outlined illustrates how information in motivated students' hands can empower them to challenge the teacher. Without such information, they become powerless and passive.

Those concerned with content-area literacy instruction believe a diversity of reading materials should be offered to students (Moore, Readence, & Rickelman, 1992; Palmer & Stewart, 1997). This has been a belief of reading educators for over half a century (e.g., Gray, 1948); however, considering the culture of Lincoln High School and that of Mr. Weller's classroom, it is difficult for secondary school content teachers in similar circumstances to have the intrinsic motivation or desire to seek content-related literature to shore up a weak text. In the case of Mr. Weller, handling the numbers of students that he did each day; keeping up with the necessary paperwork that kept the class busy, moving forward, accountable, and in control; and projecting his personality into his teaching made it difficult for him to be concerned with putting a variety of reading materials on his instructional agenda.

Perhaps those of us concerned with secondary school reading should invest time in developing current anthologies of supplemental readings with detailed annotations from which a teacher could quickly draw. Evidence supporting this assertion came several months after the completion of this study. Mr. Weller told me how he and his colleagues were trying to accumulate a library of readily available reading materials that would be used during weekly reading periods. This statement serves to bring this paper full circle. In order to put reading and reading instruction on secondary school content teachers' agendas, both long-term observation in classrooms and long-term collaboration with teachers are required. Long-term observation reveals what is taught, how it is taught, and the cultural context of the teaching. Long-term collaboration helps teachers realize that multiple goals can be met even when reading plays a significant role in the classroom. In short, observation will inform subsequent collaboration.

LOOKING BACK AT MR. WELLER:
THEN AND NOW

But to look back from the stony plain along the road which led one to that place is not at all the same thing as walking on the road; the perspective, to say the very least, changes only with the journey; only when the road has, all abruptly and treacherously, and with an absoluteness that permits no argument, turned or dropped or risen is one able to see all that one could not have seen from any other place. (Baldwin, 1981, p. 161)

Baldwin eloquently described the power provided the perceiver as he or she looks back over territory already traversed. The perspective provided is different from that of the journey, yet curiously it remains constrained and contextualized by it. A retrospective look at Mr. Weller and his classroom produces similar shifts in perspective with concomitant changes in insight and interpretation. The hindsight that such a retrospective affords is rich with opportunity for critique of past, present, and future.

I look back on this study with a quaintness not unlike an experience I had as I remodeled an old house. I was tearing down an exterior wall when I came across old newspapers stuffed in the wall for insulation and draft abatement. As I opened the yellowed, crispy pages, advertisements and articles from the early part of this century came into view, and I was reminded how different things were and how people thought differently about themselves, their bodies, and their worlds. Revisiting this study and looking back over the years have been a similar experience. I can see how differently I thought about texts, secondary school content-area literacy, and teaching.

Symbolic interaction theory was and remains an excellent vehicle to explore classrooms (Stewart, Paradis, & Van Arsdale, 1995). As the study revealed, there was subtle negotiation that occurred in Mr. Weller's classroom that resulted in socially constructed and socially mediated definitions for text, reading, and knowledge. In keeping with SI theory, the behavior of Mr. Weller and his students toward text and reading reflected the definitions that had been socially constructed.

I look back on the data excerpts in this paper, the categories and properties, and how they were contextualized and see a lot more. The years allow me to see beyond the description of Mr. Weller's classroom to more fundamental issues. In addition to a mediated definition of literacy, social interaction in the classroom defined a culturally congruent epistemology that controlled students and marginalized and obviated their experience. When I look at Jim's brief dialogue with Mr. Weller concerning his confusion about earthquakes versus aftershocks and Jane's comment that she does not think Mr. Weller likes the textbook and " ... that he's just pretty confident about what he's saying, and that's good enough for us," I realize that what was operating in Mr. Weller's classroom was a classic transmission model of learning driven by an epistemology that defines knowledge as invariant and objective. On epistemology reflecting a single "naive realism" (Lincoln & Guba, 1985) that discounts multiple realities and the role that personal experience plays in constructing those realities.

In short, I see elements of critical theory and postmodernism in this retrospective journey of Monday morning quarterbacking. Except for their influencing his classroom choreography, Mr. Weller's students were disempowered in their learning. Because of a textbook that was too general, students who lacked knowledge about where to find more information, or more importantly students who lacked the need to know more information, Mr. Weller controlled the content and its delivery in the classroom. Objectified knowledge was the currency of the realm, and Mr. Weller was the bank teller and vault all rolled into one. His students had to conduct business at his window if they wanted to exchange their passive compliance for the currency (Bullough, 1987; Freire, 1993).

It is a subtle irony that on one hand Mr. Weller honestly wanted to influence his students' perception of the physical world around them, but on the other hand, the epistemology undergirding his instruction that objectified knowledge and disembodied it from actual experience directly conflicted with his desire to create in his students a personalized awe for the power and beauty of earth's processes. His philosophy was not just idle chatter. He truly wanted to affect his students' hearts and minds so that they would perceive their world in different ways. He wanted them to become excited about earth science and what it could teach them about their worlds. To accomplish this, he strove to make lasting impressions on them and worked hard to do so. He gave examples of what he talked about and showed pictures, made his lectures lively and enjoyable, and allowed his students significant time to work in small groups on activities that reinforced the content he taught. However, his needing to show himself as a viable role model and control his classroom kept him on center stage, which precluded his students from doing the in-depth study that may have helped them feel the fundamental forces at work all around them and how such forces shape virtually everything we do and who we are.

But this grandiose vision for what earth science instruction can and should be comes from the ivory tower of higher education and does not take into account the realities of Mr. Weller's workplace (O'Brien, Stewart, & Moje, 1995; see also O'Brien, Moje, & Stewart, chap. 2, this volume). Fifty-minute periods driven by bells, daily contact with and responsibility for over 125 students, knowledge constrained and defined by subject matter boundaries, and impotent teacher preparation that often serves to reinforce a specialist orientation to subject matter and its teaching obviate both teacher and students reaching deeply into the heart of earth science.

Mr. Weller's teaching was full of contradictions, but paradoxically logical within the context of his philosophy, classroom, and school (McNeil, 1988). On one hand, educators want students to be independent learners who self-direct and are intrinsically motivated. On the other hand, the realities of the workplace mandate relatively tight control that obviates a large amount of student self-direction. Some teachers lean more on one side than the other, but all operate within the boundaries defined by these contradictions. Mr. Weller was no exception. Because of the contradictions, he could only approximate his ideal. We can see this in his comments. When he heard that students saw him as their primary source of content information, he responded that he hoped that was not the case. He wanted to have more reading in his classroom, and he said on numerous occasions that he felt reading to be important, but the realities of his workplace did not support these feelings and desires. Mr. Weller's story reveals that in general contradictions tend to attenuate the ideal; and in the field of content-area literacy specifically, the contradictions lay bare the complexities of what on the surface appears to be a simple task—having students do more meaningful reading and writing in content classrooms.

These new perspectives of Mr. Weller and his classroom extricate me from a dilemma that I have been in ever since I first wrote about this study in 1989. As matter of fact, I have never published this study in its entirety because of this dilemma. I could never get beyond the language of deficit that always permeated what I wrote about Mr. Weller. It is in this chapter as well, and I still have twinges of guilt and doubt as the time draws near for me to drop this chapter in the mail to the editors and publisher. I never want to portray Mr. Weller in a negative light. He is a fine teacher and a fine person. Recently he was selected as a master teacher, given a 1-year sabbatical with full pay, and traveled his home state plus several surrounding states to mentor other earth science teachers. Obviously, he has much to offer the teaching profession. He also has much to offer students, and his students recognize this fact. They visited him during his planning period just to talk or to get help with assignments. Some came for help with coursework other than what Mr. Weller was teaching them, for example mathematics homework, and many of them came back to see him after they left his class or graduated. In one instance, he went out of his way for a female student to be his teaching assistant so that he could negotiate with her better attendance in school. He thought by getting her involved in school at a more personal level she would attend more often. His idea worked. By working with the student each day during his planning period, she started coming to school more often. His students in 4th hour, with the exception of Scott, enjoyed his class and looked forward to attending. Our schools would be better places if all teachers were as personable, motivated, and committed as Mr. Weller.

But from the narrow perspective of content literacy, Mr. Weller's classroom was not ideal. Thus, I have struggled all these years to characterize Mr. Weller fairly and to transcend the language of deficit, because whatever deficit there may be stems from different perspectives being taken on a single phenomenon. My perspective is no more valid than another. Postmodernism helps to more fully and fairly contextualize Mr. Weller and his classroom. Slattery (1995) spoke of radical eclecticism being a component of the postmodern condition. Within the relativity of the postmodern, diversity and the particular are celebrated. We must look at Mr. Weller and his classroom within this context. He is one teacher among many. He contributes to the educational enterprise in positive ways. His classroom is not all that much different from the many I have been in during the intervening decade. He is very good within the dominant pedagogical framework and epistemology operating in secondary schools. What we need then is to explore whether there is adequate diversity in our classrooms so that students receive teaching like that of Mr. Weller, teaching like that suggested by content-area literacy models, and many other forms of teaching as long as they are egalitarian, nondiscriminatory, and result in desired learning outcomes democratically negotiated by all stakeholders. So there is no need to point fingers, but there is need to deconstruct the larger context in which all of us operate. The question becomes: Is there need for greater diversity in teaching in our classrooms? If so, and if content-area literacy is one of the models we want to represent that diversity, then more work remains to be done.

Nearly 2 decades of research has shown that state-mandated content area literacy courses required for certification are an impotent force and fail to shift secondary school classrooms to more constructivist epistemologies where extended text processing becomes an important component. If content literacy is to be well represented amongst the many, then additional avenues of influence will be necessary including radically new models for infusion (O'Brien et al., 1995).

One bright spot on the horizon is the multitude of nonfiction trade books that have entered the market. If these become part of secondary teachers' agendas, the engaging writing and presentation of content in some of these books will increase the odds of these books being read and becoming a part of classroom discourse (Palmer & Stewart, 1997). Consequently, more voices will be available to be heard in classrooms. I mentioned earlier that those in the field of content-area literacy might devote energy to developing detailed annotated bibliographies specific to content areas and topics within those areas that teachers, like Mr. Weller, could readily access. I envision an interactive Web site where secondary school teachers could type in a topic and have listed an annotated bibliography of appropriate fiction and nonfiction trade books. With a click of a mouse on an annotation, a sample page of the text along with the table of contents would appear so the teacher could quickly ascertain the quality, appropriateness, and level of the text. Perhaps another click of the mouse would take the teacher to a page with ideas for lessons incorporating the texts. Of course, a Web page does not address the challenge of getting sufficient numbers of high quality texts into school libraries; but it is a start, and the field of secondary school content-area literacy needs such a start in order to be positioned for the next century.

Since I completed the study of Mr. Weller, there have been a number of similar studies exploring literacy in secondary school classrooms (e.g., Hinchman & Zalewski, 1996; Moje, 1996; Sturtevant, 1993a). They provide insightful and deep interpretations. In their insights and depth, they point to one overriding theme that content area literacy still has not addressed. Namely, that teaching is a highly individual, perhaps even idiosyncratic enterprise, and it is the complex interplay between teacher personality and the larger school culture that determines the role of text and reading. My study of Mr. Weller is no exception to this rule. The future of secondary school content-area literacy lies in our ability as scholars in the discipline and preparers of future teachers to articulate radical new models that influence teachers and the school and classroom contexts in which text, reading, and knowledge are defined. Without such new models, secondary school content-area literacy will continue to be marginalized in classrooms.

8

She Puts All
These Words In It:
Interpreting the Language of
Tenth-Grade Global Studies

Kathleen A. Hinchman
Syracuse University

Patricia Zalewski
Liverpool Central Schools

The "words" referred to in the title of this chapter were voiced as an epithet by Keisha, one of the students in Patricia Zalewski's 10th-grade global studies class. The words Keisha bemoaned were her teacher's, spoken to ask questions during classroom discussions about reading assignments. Keisha complained that, although she completed and understood such assignments, Pat asked questions in ways that created post-reading confusion for Keisha. The purpose of this chapter is to explore such literacy related constructions of meaning by students in Pat's classroom.

Informed by interpretivist and critical perspectives on the construction of meaning in social settings, our classroom case study positions the points of view of two teenaged informants, Keisha and Colin, in the foreground of our interpretations of literacy related activities in this setting. Our paper begins with an explanation of the genesis of our project, theoretical groundings, and methodology. Next, our descriptions of the classroom lives and language-related concerns of the two teenagers are woven together with an exploration of the social structures that seem to shape and be shaped by their words and actions. Finally, we consider the implications of our work for research and for classroom practice.

THEORETICAL PERSPECTIVES

Our Previous Work

We, the two authors of this piece, began our collaboration several years ago with a shared belief that meaning is constructed within social interactions (Blumer, 1969). We felt that by working together we could likely discern novel ways to enhance Pat's teaching (Cochran-Smith & Lytle, 1993). After many years of teaching global studies, Pat came to our work with the observation that many of her students struggled with reading, writing, and other aspects of discipline-specific language use. Following an absence from secondary school classrooms, Kathy brought a desire to understand better the convergence of students' and a teacher's perspectives regarding literacy in such a setting.

Our initial work involved us in reading about, and with Pat trying, widely published recommendations for promoting literacy across the secondary school curriculum (e.g., Alvermann & Phelps, 1998; Readence, Bean, & Baldwin, 1998; Vacca & Vacca, 1999). We also worked together with others on a multicase study to explore students' understandings of classroom discussion about text (Alvermann et al., 1996). In a related study, we explored how Pat's and her students' interactions revealed their construction of competing understandings of classroom literacy-related events (Hinchman & Zalewski, 1996). We noted that the sheer amount of imposed curriculum promoted speedy, narrow content coverage with traditional teacher-led lecture and follow-up discussion (Cazden, 1988; Mehan, 1979). Our projects left Pat working with others in her school to restructure curriculum, organizing the vast numbers of details to allow for deeper study of required topics and for evaluation with interactive, reflective, rubric-driven portfolios. She felt that such changes could allow her students and her to organize the large amounts of required information more effectively and to negotiate expectations more clearly.

Seeing Classrooms as Contexts for Critical Literacies

Even with such innovation, we remained worried that the larger context would preclude changes that would satisfy the needs of all students. We realized that social studies curricula have typically been critiqued as predominantly representing the views of the dominant culture (LaFrance, 1991; Noddings, 1992; Rooney, 1991), inhibiting engagement by those whose points of view are not represented. Moreover, despite curricular reorganization, there was still much content to cover, leaving little time for real consideration of issues from multiple perspectives. Such factors favor students who bring compatible insights or who are willing to suspend judgment as they hastily review required territory (Hinchman & Moje, 1998; O'Brien, Stewart, & Moje, 1995).

With this context in mind, we have come to appreciate those who describe individuals' construction of meaning in social settings in more hopeful ways, including theorists identified with sociolinguistic (e.g., Fairclough, 1989; Gee, 1996; New London Group, 1996) and feminist poststructural perspectives (e.g., Brodkey, 1992; Butler, 1993; Lather, 1991; Weedon, 1987). These perspectives theorize individuals who shape and are shaped by their positions as members of many social groups. Teachers and students are subjects who enact but can also disrupt oppressive practices and create social change within the context of their discipline-specific literacy enactments (Luke & Freebody, 1997).

Taking such a view suggests that individuals' perspectives within such contexts are important to understand as a basis for constructing more inclusive pedagogy (Hinchman, 1998). Like all teenagers, those in Pat's class were involved in efforts to establish a sense of themselves, their fit in a variety of in- and out-of-school social groups, and their power to act in these various settings (Dillon & Moje, 1998; Gee, 1996; Street, 1995). Our earlier searches for insights that held for all our student informants (Alvermann et al., 1996; Hinchman & Zalewski, 1996) precluded exploring their particularized perspectives. However, we now believe that such insights may be important to understanding and promoting critical classroom literacies in social studies.

PURPOSE

Beginning with our initial interpretivist perspectives, and adding our more recent interest in more critical views, the purpose of this case study was to reexamine Pat's classroom through the eyes of two of our teenaged informants, Keisha and Colin. Unlike our previous work, which considered the student's perspective in a way that resulted in a story of immutable social forces, our objective in this inquiry was to place particular students' points of view in the foreground of our interpretations of literacy in this setting. Our project drew on data from our earlier projects (Alvermann et al., 1996; Hinchman & Zalewski, 1996) to address the following questions: Who were Keisha and Colin? How did they enact literacy in global studies class? How were their enactments shaped by their social circumstances, and how in turn did their actions help to shape these same circumstances?

METHODOLOGY

Symbolic interactionist traditions informed our original collection of participant observation and in-depth interview data. Such traditions have usually been associated with efforts to understand the meaning of symbols as a setting's participants see them. This involves the inductive analysis of rich qualitative data (Blumer, 1969; Denzin, 1989).

Our more recent interest in critical literacies led us toward a feminist perspective to reconsider our data in novel and newly informative ways. According to Harding (1987b), a feminist standpoint addressed notions that (a) there is no universal experience by gender except as it is also bound to race, class, and culture, (b) even a single person represents various competing subjectivities, and (c) questions about how to change the conditions of a world involve considering the forces beyond it. Fine (1992) added that such research is "at once disruptive, transformative, and reflective; about understanding and about action; not about freezing the scene but always about change" (p. 227).

Such a hybrid of interactionist and feminist perspectives allowed us to consider a more complex view of meaning—one of multiple and partial truths—than has been thought to be suggested by interactionism alone (cf. Moje, Willes, & Fassio, chap. 9., this volume). More specifically, such a theoretically eclectic position (Biklen, 1995, p. ix) allowed us to consider two students' particular perspectives and the intersections of gender, race, class, and culture woven into their perspectives as a way to transform our view of Pat's class and what may be possible there.

Participants

The work represented by this chapter is best described as a single case study. The boundaries of this case were the walls of one of Pat's college preparatory global studies classes. Located in a 10,000 student, largely middle class suburban school district, the class had an enrollment of 10 males and 12 females. Most students appeared to be White, while two were African-American. Six students volunteered to serve as key informants for our original inquiry, and we talked with others during observations and in hallways to try to gain confidence in our ability to represent the students' perspective.

Foregrounding Two Students. A premise for this reanalysis was that foregrounding the perspectives of individual students may yield increased understandings of their complex social lives. We realized that in-depth exploration of a few students would be difficult for teachers usually charged with the instruction of 100 or so students per day, yet we felt that such analysis could be a valuable reminder of the social forces woven into the character of each of our students. As a result, we decided that it was important to select our two most voluble students for this analysis.

Of the six informants in our original inquiry, Keisha and Colin talked to us the most, giving us the richest insights into their way of thinking about school and Pat's class. Even more helpfully—although we do not mean to set up a simplistic, too dichotomized analysis—they were also the most different from one another in ways that addressed our interest in gender, race, class, and culture issues. One student, Keisha, was an African-American female and the other, Colin, was a White male. From dress, talk about family vacations, and extra-curricular activities like sports and music, we inferred that both students were middle class in this largely middle-class community, although we never queried this issue directly.

Researchers' Stance.   Our collaboration with each other was central to our ability to conduct the analysis we report here (Cochran-Smith & Lytle, 1993; Elliot, 1988; Erickson, 1989). Both of us are White females from working to middle class backgrounds. Our inquiry took place in one of Pat's global studies classes, and Kathy served as primary data collection agent, analyst, and author. Pat continues to teach new sections of the same 10th-grade class and a 12th-grade government elective, and Kathy works as a faculty member at a university near Pat's school, teaching classes in literacy education. Both of us are parents of children still at home, and both are involved in community service. We believe that because we occupy different positions relative to Pat's classroom world, our collaboration has enhanced our abilities to imagine alternative perspectives buried in students' words and actions. We have also helped each other to disrupt inclinations to compose facile explanations for others' complex problems.

Data Collection

Following symbolic interactionist traditions, Kathy gathered large amounts of rich qualitative data. Data included 8 months of either weekly or twice weekly participant observations in Pat's class, depending on the intersection of her and Pat's teaching schedules. Kathy also collected several videotaped samplings of students' small-group class discussions about text assignments, many audiotaped interviews of student informants, and documents associated with Pat's teaching of her class (e.g., Bogdan & Biklen, 1992; Denzin, 1989).

Interviews were collected from our volunteer key informants who met with Kathy for pizza during their lunch times. Class documents included discussion guides, assignment schedules, homework study guides, supplementary readings, quizzes, tests, and samples of students' work. Pat and Kathy wrote reflective memoranda before and during data collection to develop an understanding of how our respective lenses shaped our work.

Data Analysis

For this analysis, interview data—Keisha and Colin's actual words about their classroom words and actions—were the primary sources of data, while classroom observation, video transcripts, and documents were reviewed secondarily. We collected all the references in our data to each individual and reread them several times, seeking to construct a sense of each person overall, a sense for specific trends and themes that would seem important to a description of each individual's participation in Pat's class, and, as Lather (1991) and others suggested, a sense for the play of issues of gender, race, class, and culture within the context of their talk and action. Our analysis considered the themes in students' words and actions that seemed to answer our research questions regarding who they were and how literacy was woven into their interests. After a recursive process of reading all data sources in search of such trends and themes, preliminary categories were drafted, revised, and fitted together in a way that seemed coherent to us, and that formed the basis for the report in this chapter.

Because we were unable to return to Keisha and Colin for help with our more critical interpretations of their words, we grappled with how we represented the possible origins of their opinions and actions (Borland, 1991). We thought about what we knew of the two students while, at the same time, we interrogated our own tendencies toward simplistic, dualistic, and essentialist ways of explaining what happens (Berthoff, 1990; Davies, 1993). To combat these inclinations, we separately considered responses to the students' data and then combined our insights, discussing conflicting points of view as we composed this report. We tried to see that we allowed each student's view to emerge in all its variability and contradiction. Finally, we reflected on that which each of us brought to our reported interpretations that might explain, at least in part, our seeing in particular ways, and we used these reflections to qualify our interpretations further (Fuss, 1989). Even so, we realize that if others had listened to our students' voices they may have composed very different stories.

RESULTS

Keisha and Colin brought quite different points of view to the discipline-specific literacy in Pat's class. Each seemed to represent multiple and conflicting perspectives, grounded in their respective social worlds. In this section, we introduce what we know of Keisha and Colin, with special attention to what they say and do regarding literacy related concerns and to the social connections that seem woven into the fabric of these concerns.

Keisha

Who Was Keisha?   Keisha was a quiet, 15-year-old apparently middle class young woman in Pat's college preparatory class. She played in the traveling marching band and spoke of her parents and teachers with reverence and respect. She was also one of two students of African-American heritage in Pat's class of 22 students, thin, with longish brown hair and medium-brown skin. Importantly from the point of view of this inquiry, she was willing to do what was required to fit into what she saw as the parameters of this classroom community, and she was willing to talk with us about how she saw this fit. She always showed up for interviews when she promised she would, and she was willing to talk quietly but extensively about literacy and her activities in class.

Our observations suggested that Keisha would probably have been called a "nice girl" by anyone who saw her in this class, and, as Pat saw her, attentive and more than a little uncertain of her academic skills. She sat quietly each day, as though expecting the teacher to orchestrate classroom events. She offered no observable resistance to Pat's authority and spoke of her appreciation for Pat's expertise. While she confessed at one point that she did not complete reading assignments, she managed to submit almost all of the work that was required of her. She received passing grades for each marking period during the academic year, numerical averages made up of classwork, homework, and a variety of tests. Although she passed the course, she failed the state-produced final examination and ended up retaking the test in summer school to pass the course.

How Did Keisha Enact Literacy in Global Studies?   Keisha's priorities did not include an in-depth understanding of class material. She liked to collaborate with other students in small-group projects and discussions. But she only did this with as much disciplinary depth as was required to complete tasks and pass tests.

When we asked her about her need to read and understand directly, Keisha seemed to equate literacy in our queries with learning the single bits of technical vocabulary that she thought were best studied the night before a test. She counted vocabulary words for mnemonic help (e.g., 10 words, 10 definitions, remembered in literal relation to one another), and she noticed when all the words that she had studied were not on the test. She explained her study techniques:

> I look over the vocabulary and sometimes the notes we take from class I look over, because if I have other homework and if I try to do it a long time before the test, I forget. That's how I study for our vocabulary. I look at them a period before I take it, and I get like a 75 on it.

Other explanations hinted that she understood that the words were part of a larger context that could help her remember them, but that she did not always have the wherewithal to think through these relationships. After one in-class, student-led, small-group vocabulary review, she said, "I think there's an order (to an unordered list of vocabulary words about a particular historical event). That's what I have to look at tonight."

When we asked if she understood the information shared in this class, Keisha said, "Yeah, pretty much." Yet as the quotation at the beginning of this chapter suggested, Keisha saw Pat's wording as being quite hard to follow, needlessly complex compared to Keisha's understandings of content as she read, studied, and participated in class. It should be noted that Pat's language was mediated by years of work within this curriculum context. To help students know what was coming, the questions Pat used in class and on tests were taken from previous editions of the end-of-year statewide final examination. Keisha noted:

> Maybe a question would be simpler if she put it in simpler words. But she puts them in all the hard words. What does it say? She puts all these words in it, so you have no clue what you're talking about.

Perhaps Keisha's difficulty with the discourse is the reason that there was no instance in our fieldnotes of Keisha participating in whole-class discussions. But small-group discussions about assigned text reading were another matter, and she became quite engaged in these. Keisha knew that such small-group discussions, even when the teacher designed the tasks, helped her to gain additional access to the disciplinary discourse community. After one such conversation she reported on the manner in which she and her student colleagues had collaborated on completion of a discussion guide: "Well, we all tried to answer it ourselves, and then when we talked it over, we really had the same answer. But we put it in better words." She liked it when she was placed in a small group with students she knew: "I think it's better. Then you [really] talk." She thought it was a good discussion if everyone joined in equally. One discussion clip, involving Keisha with Tom and Teresa, hinted of Keisha's usually active participation in such interactions:

Keisha:	All right.
She read:	The different ethnic languages are ...
Tom:	Where the country is.
Keisha:	Yeah.
Tom:	Says something unintelligible as they all write.
Keisha:	The original countries.
Tom:	Yeah, OK.
Teresa:	They [the text] said they were what?
Keisha:	The original countries.
Tom:	Yeah, there you go.

She seemed equally engaged in most of the small-group discussions we observed, helping to construct answers and explanations with much engagement. She often served as group recorder, explaining, "They [the group] said I had the neatest hand writing."

Keisha confessed that she was not "much of a reader." She told us that, as of December, she had not yet begun to do out-of-school reading assignments. Perhaps she was looking up answers to homework questions or copying someone else's work because Pat's records suggested that she submitted most of her work. We asked her if she read otherwise during her spare time, and she replied, "If I'm bored." However, something in her reasoning or willingness to report on reading must have changed as the year progressed. She later reported that in-class work was easier to understand "when you read the book." She even suggested that she might appreciate reading stories related to particular historical periods, in the spirit in which they had addressed some aspects of Russian history by watching the movie *Nicholas and Alexandra*. She asked:

Why don't we read books? You know how in English we read books? Like some interesting book on Russia and then we took the quiz on it. It's [would be] easier because [otherwise] she does lectures on it and then Fridays we take the test, and I don't remember.

Perception of relevance was an issue for Keisha's discipline-specific literacy. In conversations with other students, she argued once that most of the reading within the parameters of this discipline did not seem relevant to her: "I can understand if it was our country—but who cares about Russia. I'm not going to go there." Her point suggested that she had not taken to heart the argument that the study of world-wide perspectives could add to one's sensitivity about the lives of others. She confessed that because of what she saw as dry content, she sometimes had difficulty making herself work as hard as she perhaps could or should, "Because if it's not interesting, it's hard for me to work all the time."

Yet there was something to suggest that once a topic was addressed in class, Keisha could feel differently about its relevance. Perhaps Pat was able to suggest something in terms with which Keisha agreed, or she was swept by Pat's own enthusiasm for the content. For instance, following their study of Russia, she noted:

> Some countries we do are so boring. Some countries I have no interest in learning about. I can understand Russia [as a country we should study]. I think we should only study countries that had something to do with the United States at one time.

Keisha was most concerned with literacy enactments that involved getting work done and grades, such as reading a text and answering questions. Although she was more interested and found more relevance when she thought she understood class content, understandings gleaned from such actions were not central to her concerns. She noted that students who were successful were those who did their work, describing one student as "secretly doing her homework"—secretly because Keisha could not tell the students who were the most successful just from their classroom actions and talk. She assumed responsibility for getting her own work done in response to these understandings of success:

> There is no excuse if I get a bad grade. It was my fault, I didn't have enough time to do everything.

We asked Keisha if she was successful in global studies, and her answer was consistent with the rest of her talk. That is, she talked about her grades, noting that she had difficulty with the literacy enactments required by homework assignments and tests:

> My homework average is an 89, but the tests I don't do good on. I do better on the homework and quizzes.

How Were Keisha's Enactments Shaped by Her Social Circumstances, and How, in Turn, Did Her Actions Help to Shape These Same Circumstances? As we described in our earlier analysis (Hinchman & Zalewski, 1996), Keisha implemented the sorts of literacy skills that have often been described in stories of schools in our age of industrialization. That is, she seemed to enact a production model's notion of making grades, rather than reaching to achieve the disciplinary understanding that the typical rhetoric of schooling suggests (Apple, 1993; Becker, Geer, & Hughes, 1995; Everhart, 1983). It may be argued by theoreticians concerned with development of independent learning strategies (Paris, Wasik, & Turner, 1991) that her focus on the completion of disconnected piecework precluded her development of conceptual understandings. Linguists (Gee, 1996) might argue that since Keisha worked in the vocabulary memorization portion of the assembly line, she could not be expected to develop enough discursive knowledge to feel confident in her participation in the discipline-specific discourse community.

But her story was more complex than a simple difference between teacher's and students' expectations or completion of piecework. Keisha's reports suggested contradictions within her enactments. She had a great willingness to assume responsibility and to develop elaborate study strategies, except that these were grade and not conceptually based. Her words hinted that she thought that more understanding might be desirable and possible. However, she did not seem to think of herself as in a position to construct such an understanding.

Although Keisha talked about this dilemma as the result of an adolescent time crunch, issues of gender, race, class, and culture may also be woven into her perspective. For instance, many of Keisha's behaviors could be explained as an enactment of the gendered school behaviors that have been observed as typical of many young women of the middle class (Sadker, Sadker, & Klein, 1991). For instance, Keisha seemed to desire to please the teacher, smiling in appreciation but not joining in with the student-joking that sometimes quietly occurred while Pat lectured. She rolled her eyes particularly at Colin, having apparently determined that his in-class behavior was somehow silly or not sanctioned by Pat. Her stated judgments of other students seemed harsh, overgeneralized versions of teacher-type critiques, as when she said, "Maria sat in the non-thinking group."

Keisha saw Pat sympathetically. She noted that, overall, Pat treated the students' efforts to understand with much support:

> The teacher will try to make it easier if it's hard and they know it's boring. Like the outlines we have to do. Like a certain amount of the texts we have to read.

I think when she looks at our homework, I don't know, the outline [she gives us] takes a lot of doing [work on Pat's part].

Keisha especially appreciated Pat's orchestration of small-group discussions about text assignments as a way for her to develop her understandings with the help of peers. She said that, "When we're all together in rows, we want to die," as a way of saying that listening to lectures or whole-class discussions and taking notes did not as easily invite her engagement. Keisha saw herself as an equal participant in this small-group talk, and the amount of her talk would suggest such equality.

However, Keisha often took the role of recorder in such groups, suggesting that perhaps the substance of her talk was not equal. When we mentioned this to Keisha, she bristled and said that her good spelling and neat handwriting made her the most qualified person for the job. Her embodied response suggests that she has some knowledge of the pros and cons in the constructions of gender that were inherent in such enactments (Finders, 1996). Perhaps she was conflicted about her own actions or with our insinuation of their possible sources. Of course the role also gave her the quiet power of having the last word, a subtle act of control in an otherwise consistent enactment of people-pleasing behaviors.

Keisha's request to read story versions of themes in global studies suggested a search for strategies to aid her own engagement. Indeed, her idea of reading stories matched frequent recommendations in the literature. As Bruner (1986) might suggest, she was probably asking for a more familiar discursive structure, narrative rather than the paradigmatic text more typical to this discipline at the high school level. Other perspectives suggest that such a preference for the narrative could have been an additional enactment of her constructions of a gendered self—girls are said to like stories more than exposition—in response to the demands of discipline-specific discourse (Christian-Smith, 1993; Gilbert, 1997; Mills, 1994).

Keisha's youthful enactments of traditional, if conflicted, constructions of gender likely shaped the way others responded to her. For instance, other students in her groups may have grown to depend on her abilities as a recorder, inadvertently yielding power to her in allowing her to be the one to transcribe their reports. Pat, too, may have responded to her enactments of gendered uncertainty by expecting only certain kinds of nice but not especially insightful responses from her class participation and submitted work.

Keisha worked hard on schoolwork in a way that suggested that participation in school was central to her view of herself (Gee & Crawford, 1998). Such an ethos might have been generated from her perception of the expectations of school culture and her desire to please those in authority. It also seemed consistent with what we knew of the expectations that Keisha brought from her home and community. She wanted to go to college, although she never really brought up particular aspirations. Her life outside of school was filled with school-sponsored extracurricular activities that, ironically, made it difficult for her to find the time to complete school assignments.

Keisha was a student of African-American heritage in a school whose population was predominately and obviously White. There were few students "like" Keisha in this regard. Yet she said nothing about race or ethnicity during our conversations or in any class discussions. Even when we asked about it, her response was to shrug her shoulders and mumble, "No, that doesn't matter." Our only hint that race might be an issue for Keisha was when Kathy showed her a videotape of an eighth-grade class in Athens, Georgia, whose population was primarily students of African-American heritage. Keisha sat up straight in her chair and reached to turn up the sound on the television set, even though she didn't say anything. Perhaps race was an issue that Keisha had put aside in the interests of fit or because she could do nothing about it. Perhaps race really was not an issue for Keisha. Finally, as others have suggested, perhaps race was an issue for her, but it was an issue about which she chose or had learned not to speak (Delpit, 1988; Willis, 1995).

Colin

Who Was Colin?   Like Keisha, Colin was also 15-years-old at the start of the school year. He was light skinned, thin, and plaid flannel-shirted in the manner of nearly all the young men in Pat's class. He was White in a class that was predominately White. He spoke often of his twin sister and parents, who were involved in community politics. Over our year together, Colin grew to look older and a bit rebellious, with brown hair in a bowl cut that he wore long on top with a ponytail tied at the back of his head. He wanted to go to college. Colin described himself as being interested in the topics subsumed under the large category known as "global studies." He was polite and engaging during interviews and other one-on-one interactions. He came to all interview appointments promptly and was willing to talk.

Early in the year, Colin demonstrated some interesting insights as a participant in whole-class discussions in Pat's class. However, throughout most of the year he struggled with Pat during these instructional sequences. A struggle between them was also suggested by his sporadic and often tardy submission of assignments. Even so, he participated in student-led, small-group discussions about text as the year progressed, always with some quiet joking and usually with a serious effort to talk with his colleagues about course content. Despite the fact that he did little outside assigned work, he could perform passably on tests. He was eventually transferred to another section of the class in a trade meant to resolve several students' behavior problems, including Colin's difficulties in this class. He passed the final examination but had not submitted enough work to pass the course. He ended up repeating the course.

How Did Colin Enact Literacy in Global Studies?   Colin believed he came into the class with much prior knowledge about and interest in class topics. Yet like Keisha, he complained that Pat's language about the topics was "too complex." He believed he already understood the course content from other experiences outside of class, explaining that he also watched the evening news and read *Time* magazine. About a particular lecture, he said:

> I learned all that, I knew it all, and I just went to one play [on the Middle East]. Yeah. I just went to one play and learned everything she said [during one class lecture].

His sense of his own world knowledge seemed to create a kind of Catch-22 situation for his relationship with Pat. That is, he thought he already knew whatever expertise that she had to share with him, however superficial this knowledge was for the needs at hand. He felt that her language made the work unnecessarily complex for what he saw as their purposes, not understanding the varying degrees of understanding that can be reflected in such discourse complexity.

Colin's difficulty within the discipline-specific discourse community was also reflected in his difficulty with class readings. He confessed that he didn't like the reading he had to do for global studies class, and that he found it more difficult than his every day reading. He explained:

> I don't like reading I have to read and think about. I have to read like four times. If I go sit down and read a magazine, something that I enjoy like *Sports Illustrated*, I can do that. But I don't understand the stuff we read about in class.

From the beginning of the school year, Colin seemed to have a reputation as the student who diverged from the teacher's expectations for classroom routines. Early on, he typically seemed quite engaged in whole-class discussions, contributing understandings in helpful ways. Our classroom observations from the early fall provided evidence of such engagement when Pat asked students about the meaning of the Code of Hammurabi:

> Colin: That you either obey or you get your hands blown off.
> Pat: It's very strict, isn't it?

Michael:	It'll scare people into obeying.
Pat:	It's an eye-for-an-eye kind of law, isn't it? They hold you accountable, don't they? If your house falls apart, you're the one responsible.
Colin:	So you always want to do your best.

He could be critical of Pat, especially when other students were around. He was especially vocal about the amount of time they were given to complete long-term projects. Yet, on some occasions he showed sympathy toward Pat, noting that she evidently thought a great deal about the ways she orchestrated classroom tasks and remarked, "I'd be the poorest teacher there ever was" because of his lack of organizational skills and attention to detail.

By the middle of the fall of our year together, Colin and Pat had developed serious differences in expectations. In one representative incident, Pat passed back quiz papers as students read their scores and remarked quietly to one another—until Colin looked at his paper and said, "You took off for capitalization? Do I have to write corrections for this?" Then he mumbled to himself, as though Pat could not hear, "I can't believe she took off for this," repeatedly until Pat walked to his desk and said, "You may go to the office and cool your jets for a few minutes and then come back." His participation in whole-class activities eventually lessened, and late in the school year he often put his head down on his desk as if to go to sleep—although his performance on tests suggested that he may have been listening even as he seemed observably resistant.

Early in the school year, Colin reported that he would rather work independently than in small groups. He seemed to also appreciate working on schoolwork at home, with his parents' help. He explained that in small-group discussions about text assignments he felt burdened by others who did not do what he saw as their "fair share." His report suggested that he may have had difficulty with the pace other students set, and that his parents did a better job of mediating his understandings than did his peers:

> Don't like that group stuff on the books because people are so phony. Like other people, they won't understand [that] if you read the question over, by the time you're done reading it, and let's say reading it over, by the time you've done two questions, they are ready to turn it in.

As the school year progressed, Colin saw more of a point to small-group discussion: "You understand more from someone your age that has the same background." He noted his perception of his own role in these groups: "I'm always arguing, trying to get a point across." He would not take on the role of secretary in these groups, and others agreed that he was not a viable candidate for this job. To this he took mock offense, and then he agreed: "Because I write slow? Me? But it [my handwriting] is neat. Oh yeah, I can't spell."

Colin seemed to like to disrupt both small- and large-group discussions. He teased a great deal, changing topics to get laughs, and nudging young women until they literally swatted him. He maintained a year-long competition with one young woman for control of their small-group talk about texts, noting that her version was always the one that was written down and reported. He argued that this happened "because she was a girl."

When we asked him what it took to be successful in Pat's class, Colin's answer was, "This year I've been doing all our homework"—this despite the fact that Pat's records indicated that only a limited amount of work had been submitted. The quotation hints that Colin understood the importance in this context of getting credit for homework assignments, as did Keisha. Still, Colin hinted of more concern for understanding when he talked about his knowledge of content, Colin also showed concern for the complexity of Pat's language, and complained about Pat's student teacher with the words, "We lost a lot because of the student teacher. He didn't cover the Renaissance very well."

How Were Colin's Enactments Shaped by His Social Circumstances, and How, in Turn Did His Actions Help to Shape These Same Circumstances? As was the case with Keisha, Colin's story seemed more complex than our other inquiry had been able to reveal. Despite the fact that Colin claimed to come to Pat's class with prior knowledge and interest in course content, he resisted completing the sorts of production-oriented literacy activities that Keisha was willing to do. He, like Keisha, thought Pat's language was unnecessarily complex. It might be argued that an unresolvable dissonance was created at the juncture of his familiarity with content, with his frustration with the greater sophistication of Pat's version of the content's discourse, and with his perception that school culture valued work over understanding. Perhaps such dissonance was responsible for his resistance to the class requirements.

Colin's reports suggested contradictions within his enactments of competing cultures. He cared about understanding, had a great enthusiasm for global studies, and could even perform passably on tests. Yet he did not care for an academic discourse that seemed, to him, needlessly complex and anchored in specifics. He did not understand that completing homework assignments might add to his understanding, and did not seem willing to produce it for production's sake.

Issues of gender, race, class, and culture can be said to be woven into his interpretation of classroom rules. Colin's exercise of power in this class may have been especially confused by the discipline-specific discourse community's other, quite convoluted gendered aspects. Noddings (1992), for instance, described social studies as a subject that has traditionally privileged a primarily White male view of history and politics. That is, such men wrote most of the history that is studied in schools today, and these interpretations are those that have been most often reported, until very recently.

Yet Colin was invited to engage in study of this curriculum by a female, who to be successful in the field is likely to have learned to read such texts according to the dominant view (Flynn & Schweickart, 1986). Grumet (1988) has been among those who have suggested that transmittal of such readings may make Pat, like many women teachers, an unwitting conduit of a dominant culture reading that, at the same time, devalues her interpretation simply because it was constructed by a female. Perhaps Colin positioned Pat as a female who literally had no actual business communicating as an expert within his realm. Indeed, such positioning may have been perceived by Pat at some level, shaping her response to Colin and causing increasing difficulty as their relationship progressed. There is some irony to be found in the idea that the claims to expertise that Pat made, transmitted by her use of particular ways of talking about her discipline, could have been the very elements of her discourse that Colin found most disruptive.

Colin did not complain directly about Pat's authority in the class. He did, however, complain about her use of the discipline's language—a discipline with which he thought he was already familiar. Colin made explicit reference to the fact that his constructions around gender colored his literacy related transactions in this class when he noted that he felt dominated by a particular young woman repeatedly in small-group discussions. His conflict in this area is evident in the fact that he had verbalized that he did not want to be the group recorder—this despite the fact that he recognized it as a position of control. His conflicted positioning of himself likely contributed to the reactions of other students who collaborated with him.

Like Keisha and many students who come from middle-class backgrounds in the United States (Gee & Crawford, 1998), success in school also seemed central to Colin's discussion of all that he did both in and out of school. His constructions included competing, unsuccessfully, for grades with his twin sister, and he worried about friends who quit school. His comfort with completing schoolwork at home suggested that his parents seemed to have constructed a family culture that was quite school oriented. His respectful talk about his parents' help with schoolwork supports this inference.

Yet, Colin's sense that his understanding of content was sufficient was not accurate. He did not complete all the work that was required for this class. He passed tests but did not excel, and this, combined with missing assignments, caused him to fail the course. Perhaps his construction of an intersection between his gendered sense of self and his relation to Pat and the school culture created such great dissonance for Colin that resistance was his only possible response. The notion that our culture usually privileges White, middle-class males like him may have added to his confusion over his efforts to transact successfully within this discourse community.

CONCLUSIONS

Keisha and Colin give us a much more complex view of the manner in which particular teenagers come together within the social context of discipline-specific, teacher-led study. They both spoke of understanding, generally, the content that was covered in class. However, both found Pat's language and the language of available printed texts unnecessarily complex. A desire to be successful in school was central to their constructions of identity. But neither participated in the discourse community in a way that yielded what would be perceived as success for them in this context. On one hand, Keisha enacted literacy behaviors that reflected word-by-word attention to the construction of knowledge in this classroom in deference to a production model. On the other hand, Colin believed the rhetoric that understanding was important but resisted the engagement that might yield entry into a more sophisticated discipline-specific discourse community. Their enactments shaped and were shaped by their entrance into this more complex discourse community, a community whose face was that of their female teacher, Pat. Their particular mixes of constructions of gender, race, class, and culture were woven throughout these enactments.

Our work in this inquiry suggests just how complicated it is when classrooms full of a teacher and teenaged students come together in pursuit of nuanced, discipline-specific literacy. Success comes from something more complex than completing work or gaining new understanding. The teacher's job could be said to be about enticing students like Keisha and Colin to reconstruct their understandings of certain aspects of their social worlds in order to develop a sense of fit and, eventually, fluency within this new community. Such entry requires the same sorts of immersion, experimentation, feedback, and critique that all such new language learning requires.

Students discern messages that invite them to participate in these transactions in particular ways. Only some of these messages may be known to those around them, including the teacher—even as their responses shape the teacher's practices in turn (Floriani, 1993; Prentiss, 1998). Their struggles to construct something they see as meaningful result in struggles for power with the teacher and other students. In our case study classroom, Keisha acquiesced while Colin resisted—and neither of these responses yielded a satisfactory solution. As Delpit (1988) suggested, the process is only that much more complicated when students come to our classroom transactions with enactments of gender, race, class, or culture that especially diverge from the classroom norm.

Our Particular Ways of Seeing

We should note here the limitations to our ways of seeing the social patterns in Keisha and Colin's discursive transactions within this classroom case study. Indeed, it is interesting to note that Colin and Kathy disagreed about who had control of his small-group battles with one of his female classmates. Kathy suggested that Colin was enacting the role of business executive fully in charge of dictating the whims of the group, and Colin claimed to have been severely crippled by the way in which the group was led to overlook his input. Would male researchers have seen these interactions the same way? We doubted it, and decided only to report the conflict without judging its source in any absolute way as a result.

Pat's interpretations of both students were tied to her sense of their responsibility in completing reading assignments meant to infuse their understandings of the subject. Most of her students did manage to complete such work, and Pat's interpretations were colored by these other successes. Keisha shared Pat's interpretation on one level and tried to do the work as assigned, although she had difficulty doing so with great understanding. Colin understood this interpretation, too, although he resisted it because of the convergence of his other understandings.

Kathy's interpretations were more concerned with why neither student's enactments yielded success by any of their definitions. Her interpretations were colored by a search for explanations—which some teachers may see as excuses for students making poor choices. Thus, each of our separate interpretations were compromised in our construction of this shared version of our classroom case study. Traditional notions of validity are undermined by such perspective-driven notions of reality. Instead, we are left with a general and well-qualified sense of the possible as our primary criterion for judging the trustworthiness of such reports and subsequent discussions (Lincoln, 1997).

IMPLICATIONS

Orner (1992) noted the importance in inviting "multiple, contradictory voices of teachers, writers, researchers, and administrators ... to speak" about education, about power, and about possibilities for change (p. 88).

This inquiry explored some of these voices and their competing and conflicted perspectives in an effort to chart a new course for ongoing literacy development. Pat used widely recommended teaching strategies, but they did not aid successful engagement by all of her students. Indeed, it may not be possible to design pre-, during-, and post-reading discussion or writing assignments of single texts that suit the inclinations of a whole class, particularly if there is no time to work through various students' critique and engagement due to the need to cover large amounts of material.

This study does not mean to suggest that structural constraints should prohibit action. At a minimum, teachers should consider orchestrating activities with an eye toward variation in students' participation, responding to their enactments of conceptual and social understandings in subsequent interactions. Better still would be an invitation to students to bring their varying perspectives to vocal, fair-minded critiques of texts representing multiple views. Teachers can be concerned with coming to understand the complex meanings being constructed in their own classrooms, as Pat did, and with talking with students about whether and how to disrupt them.

Of course, the calls for students' voices have been many of late, and we do not want to forget to add the teacher's expertise into the mix of those invited to speak (Ellsworth, 1989). Fecho (1998) and Oyler (1996) described new pedagogies that invite classrooms to be places of shared authority, where teachers' expertise is blended with students' ongoing pursuits of new learning. Phelan (1997), in turn, suggested that relationships among classroom participants be the core of such orchestrations—instead of pedagogical principles that work for most students and so are applied to all. Indeed, if our curricula contain information that is important to know, we can assume that ever-current adolescents will figure out this essence and go after it. And if they cannot, then we should begin to question our assumptions about what exists as the essence of our curricula.

Pat's ongoing curriculum development work has engaged in such querying, thus involving her in working with colleagues to revise content expectations and to implement responsive teaching strategies. At the same time, her school has moved to block scheduling, initiating longer, fewer classes that more easily allow for such in-depth, student-led study. The state's move toward assessment that considers conceptual, critical analysis of texts over detailed memory for facts has also fueled Pat's efforts to orchestrate a classroom that invites students to participate with more depth in this discipline-specific discourse community.

In classrooms like Pat's, teachers and students can learn to use their knowledge of each other to develop questions that will elicit purposeful agendas: What don't we understand about our own and each other's raced, classed, and gendered understandings? How may what the teacher and a single text explain about the nature and history of cultures be compared to alternative versions? Does the discourse of the course of study need to be as complex as it is at present? Are there yet undiscovered ways to invite more students to greater fluency within such discourse communities? The agenda for promoting literacy in social studies and across the curriculum may be much more effective than it has been when the specifics of this agenda are shared and become more personally meaningful to all of its constituencies.

9

Constructing and Negotiating Literacy in a Writer's Workshop: Literacy Teaching and Learning in the Seventh Grade

Elizabeth B. Moje
University of Michigan

Debra J. Willes
Granite Park Junior High School

Kris Fassio
University of Utah

This chapter presents our study of how literacy practices were negotiated and constructed in a junior high school English class as a teacher–researcher, two researcher–teachers, and 45 students put a writing workshop approach into practice for 1 year. Our research was situated in a local and particular context: two urban, seventh-grade literacy workshop classrooms comprised of 12- and 13-year-old students from diverse ethnic and cultural backgrounds. To understand the social negotiation and construction of literacy practices that occurred during this daily, 1-hour class, we sought to understand literacy practices of the participants (teacher, students, and researchers) in and out of the workshop. We did this by gathering data not only on students' in-workshop literacy practices, but also their out-of-workshop and out-of-class practices. Elizabeth and Debra also gathered data that allowed us to observe our own practice, and we kept journals of our experiences as a way of documenting our literacy beliefs and practices.

Because the classroom context revolved around the writer's workshop, we focused specifically on how students and teacher constructed and negotiated conceptions of literacy and of English class *in relation to the workshop approach*. Two broad research questions guided the research that we report here:

1. How do the various participants use, or practice, literacy within the context of the writer's workshop?
2. How are their practices constructed in classroom, disciplinary, school, community, and interpersonal contexts?

THEORIES AND RESEARCH LITERATURES THAT FRAME OUR WORK

This study is guided by the idea that learning literacy in school depends on and is shaped by the social and cultural beliefs one holds about the purposes and value of literacy enactments such as writing, as well as about the purposes and value of schooling. Further, we approach literacy as more than reading and writing. Specifically, we use Scribner and Cole's (1981) perspective that literacy is "a set of socially organized practices which make use of a symbol system and a technology for producing and disseminating it" (p. 236). Literacy also involves knowing how to use reading and writing in particular ways, at particular times, for particular purposes.

Barton (1991, 1994) made a further distinction between literacy events and literacy practices. Literacy events can be considered moments that include speaking, listening, reading, and writing. But literacy practices shape the ways people engage in and make meanings from literacy events, depending on how the events, are situated in particular social, cultural, and historical arrangements. In literacy events people draw on particular social practices that carry certain meanings and serve particular social purposes (cf. Santa Barbara Discourse Group, 1994). In a classroom, for example, a round-robin oral reading event may work as much—or more—to control student behaviors as it does to teach particular literacy processes. Similarly, as some theorists have argued, and as we will illustrate in this chapter, a whole-class group sharing of student writing in a writer's workshop may serve to regulate or normalize writing practices in ways that silence or stifle personal expression despite the intention of encouraging social interaction and collaboration (cf. Willis, 1995). The ways that these literacy events are constructed depend on the interactions—or social practices—within the classroom; interactions are informed by past, present, and future experiences, relationships, and goals both in and out of the classroom.

Although research on the literacy *processes* of reading and writing has contributed enormously to our understanding of how to teach literacy, less attention has been given to literacy as a set of social, cultural, political, and historical *practices* that are part of the cognitive processes of reading and writing. We argue that literacy teaching and learning in schools needs to be seen as sets of practices that are constructed during interactions within local and particular contexts—classrooms and schools—as well as in larger sociocultural, historical, and political contexts. Because the school is an institution, these practices can be seen as similar across many different classroom and school communities, but each school and classroom context is also unique due to particular interactions among particular teachers and students and to the particular contexts of the communities that surround the schools. Understanding this social construction and situatedness of literacy can be useful to teachers, researchers, and theorists as they work with students because they can use this understanding to think carefully about the practices they bring to literacy teaching or research and about the practices they expect young people to learn. As Street (1994a) argued, "the meaning and uses of literacy practices are related to specific cultural contexts; ... these practices are always associated with relations of power and ideology" (p. 139).

These perspectives on literacy shaped the development of our research questions and our methods of data collection. Because one of the questions in this study focused on how the participants' literacy practices reflected and influenced the reading–writing workshop pedagogy; as a result, we drew on expressivist writing theories, research, and practices espoused by Atwell (1987), Calkins (1994), Elbow (1976), and Graves (1983). According to these perspectives, workshop approaches are thought to improve not only students' reading and writing, but also their engagement with reading and writing and with other school activities because students are encouraged to take responsibility for and ownership of their literacy projects (Willinsky, 1991). In addition, workshop approaches, as conceptualized traditionally, are considered excellent ways for students to explore their own thinking and to express their knowledge, beliefs, and feelings about particular topics (Atwell, 1990; Calkins, 1994; Lensmire, 1994; Willinsky, 1991). There is, in fact, a good deal of support for the idea that the approaches encourage and celebrate diversity because children write and read from their diverse experiences.

Reading–writing workshop and other expressivist pedagogies have, however, been criticized from multiple perspectives in recent years (cf. O'Brien, Moje, & Stewart, chap. 2, this volume). In this chapter, we focus primarily on how participants interpreted and practiced the writer's workshop as more traditionally conceived (cf. Moje & Fassio, 1997 for an in-depth analysis of the social-action projects), but we raise questions about the implications of expressivist approaches for students' construction of literacy practices in and out of school. Consequently, our closing discussion includes a critique of the writer's workshop that asks how literacy as a *practice* is reflected and used in *process* approaches to literacy teaching and learning.

OUR METHODOLOGY AND METHODS

The methodology and interpretation in this study is guided by aspects of symbolic interactionist theory (Blumer, 1969; Mead, 1934) and by work done in the field of cultural studies (e.g. Fiske, 1989; Grossberg, 1995). Symbolic interactionism suggests that individuals define situations and negotiate meanings based on their interpretation of symbols while engaged in interactions with other human beings. However, symbolic interactionism explains human interaction and meaning-making in patterns and categories of action. Although we believe that general patterns are often relevant to our lives, we are leery of subscribing to a theory based on the assumption that some sort of truth can be understood by analysis of the observable world. Thus, we also turn to cultural studies perspectives, which draw on aspects of critical and postmodern theories to argue that people's practices and the meanings they make of them are shaped in various and sometimes contradictory ways as they interact with both the material and discursive world. A cultural studies perspective does not claim to present a truth—or even stable patterns—of people's lives, rather it attempts to understand the meanings that they make and to examine their everyday lives in their complexity and contradiction. More important, a cultural studies perspective seeks to link the micropractices in which people engage every day with the macrostructures and Discourses (Gee, 1996) that shape our lives. The combination of these two theoretical perspectives (cf. Denzin, 1992) supported our study of the complex and sometimes contradictory meanings classroom participants made about literacy within the context of their interactions in the writer's workshop.

Because this was a collaborative, action-oriented study, we initially thought of ourselves as coteachers and coresearchers. For reasons of school district accountability and research confidentiality, however, we identified Deb[1] as lead teacher and Elizabeth[2] as lead researcher. As a result, although we collaborated on planning, teaching, and data collection, Deb was ultimately responsible for planning, day-to-day teaching, and, particularly, for evaluating students. Elizabeth took responsibility for formal interviewing of students and for organizing and maintaining data collections. Elizabeth assisted in teacher conferences during the writing workshop on a regular basis, but taught the whole class only during some minilessons. Throughout the year, we moved in and out of these roles. In the second semester of the school year, Kris[3], a research assistant, joined the project. She visited the class once a week and collected field notes and conducted informal interviews in the two different classes we studied.

The data reported in this chapter were collected over the course of one school year. Deb, of course, spent each day in the classroom, but she did not record her reflections and observations on a daily basis. Elizabeth spent two days each week in the classroom; Kris visited the school once a week. Elizabeth observed and taught in two classes, and she and Deb often spent the lunch period (30 min) and Deb's consultation hour together. When not talking with Deb during lunch, Elizabeth spent time with the students either in the cafeteria or out of doors as they hung out in the school parking lots, lawns, or basketball courts. She also attended special school assemblies when possible.

Our data sources included fieldnotes of classroom observations; audiotaped (and some videotaped) recordings of classroom interactions; formal and informal interviews with Deb, the students, parents, and school administrators; electronic mail communications between Deb and Elizabeth; artifacts and documents such as students' writings, our planning notes, and class readings; and photographs. For data analysis, we used the constant comparative method (Glaser & Strauss, 1967; Strauss, 1987) as a tool for inductive analysis, and we used critical discourse analysis (Kress, 1989; Luke, 1995) as a tool for uncovering taken-for-granted assumptions embedded in discursive practices. These critical analyses of discourse helped us extend and specify the themes generated during constant comparative analysis.

Although we relied on the constant comparative method as a way to organize and think about our data, we reject many of the assumptions inherent in the theoretical underpinnings of this method. Like symbolic interactionism, constant comparative analysis assumes that stable patterns of behavior can be analyzed through the rigorous coding and categorization of data. Constant comparative analysis, drawing from the notion of "grounded theory," (Glaser & Strauss, 1967) seeks to let these patterns

---

[1]Deb is a European-American woman. This project initiated Deb's foray into workshop pedagogy although she had been using process-writing activities for many years.

[2]Elizabeth is a European-American woman who has taught high school but now teaches in a university setting and conducts secondary school, classroom-based research.

[3]Kris is a graduate student with many years of experience teaching young children.

emerge from the data. The theory implies that the researchers can—through rigorous coding procedures—leave behind their subjectivities to engage in an objective analysis of the world. We do not agree with this assumption and suggest, rather, that our analyses are an aspect of our particular situations and relationships in this classroom. Moreover, because of its emphasis on finding patterns, constant comparative analysis considers behaviors or people who do not fit into the analyzed patterns as "discrepant cases." We see these "discrepancies" as part of the complexity of the everyday lives and practices of the people in the study, and we believe that they must be considered part of the practices, rather than discrepancies from typical practice, as they would be discussed in a constant comparative approach. Thus, we used the steps of constant comparative analysis to organize and manage the voluminous data we collected, but we do not believe that following these steps yields one particular truth about the lives of the people in this study, nor did we seek only to find *stable* patterns and generalizations about this group of people, although we do present general themes of our analyses in the next section of the chapter. We believe these themes may have important implications for pedagogical practice, but we consider them to be partial, temporary, and open to contest.

We now turn to a discussion of these partial themes by first providing a brief snapshot of how students constructed particular literacy practices during the writer's workshop. Then, to illustrate how students saw literacy in different ways depending on the context for their literacy practices, we examine two of the students' perspectives and practices. We conclude the chapter by raising questions about the constructions of literacy that we saw in this classroom.

STUDENTS' CONSTRUCTIONS OF LITERACY IN THE WRITER'S WORKSHOP

We learned a great deal about the students' and our own conceptions of literacy, as well as about the reading–writing workshop when we put the workshop into practice and studied the process throughout the year. In this first section, we examine some general trends in students' perspectives and practices.

"To Teach You How to Speak Proper English": Literacy Practices in English Class

The students' initial constructions of English classroom literacy were evident from the classroom conversations on the first school day of school, as illustrated in this field note excerpt:

After the kids were settled, Deb began the class by saying that she was Ms. Willes. She asked the kids to sit according to a seating chart and then turned to the Daily Oral Language (DOL) activity, which consisted of a sentence written on the board:

"this here book making money could have been purchased lately but im not sure"

The class proceeded to offer changes to make the sentence grammatically correct. A number of students enthusiastically volunteered, while others sat and stared at the board.

When DOL was completed, Deb said that they needed to talk about class rules. Maria groaned. Deb ignored the groan, asked, "What have you done right so far this period?", and went on to solicit ideas from them about their responsibilities. After discussing her responsibilities as a teacher, Deb asked, "What's the biggest reason for an English class?"

Katie: To teach us how to talk.
Deb: We might do some of that in here, but not a lot of it.
Maria: To teach us how to speak proper English.
Deb: Hmmm ... Scott?
Scott: To teach us how to write.

In this exchange on the 1st day of class, Deb acknowledged that some aspect of English class focused on "how to talk," but she used Scott's comment as a springboard for introducing the workshop approach to reading and writing. She told the students that we were going to have them write every day. Although it was obvious that a number of the students thought that a focus on grammar, punctuation, and spelling might be the emphasis of the English class—underscored, perhaps, by the DOL activity in which they had just participated—they seemed open to a focus on writing. They seemed even more agreeable to the idea of choosing what they wanted to write about, as illustrated in this fieldnote excerpt, taken from the same class period:

Deb asked the kids to vote on whether they preferred to have their teachers give them topics to write about or to be able to choose topics. She asked them to think about that for a minute. Then she asked them to raise their hands if they preferred teacher-directed topics. Nobody raised a hand. She asked about student-directed topics. Each student raised her or his hand.

The students seemed to like the idea of choosing their own topics, but when Deb asked for ideas about what they might choose, only Trevor responded: He suggested writing about "dragons, unicorns, and wizards." When Deb asked for other volunteers and the class remained silent for a few minutes, Eugenio finally said, "Maybe most of the class is planning to write about something personal, and they don't want to share it with anybody."

Although we did not recognize it at the time—focused as we were on our teaching goal of brainstorming writing topics—Eugenio's response echoed concerns raised by some critics of workshop pedagogies, specifically, that the emphasis on sharing and publishing personal experiences may limit what students are willing to write (cf. Willis, 1995). As the two people in the classroom with the least to lose in terms of power relationships, we failed to realize that asking virtual strangers to volunteer personal experiences was folly. Our lack of awareness indicates both a failure to acknowledge the power relationships embedded in any social network, as well as our subconscious desire to have students write about mainstream experiences—those experiences to which we could relate. Had we really been hoping that the students would write about any and all experiences, we would have recognized that such experiences might be quite personal and that the students might have been hesitant to talk about those experiences in a group of relative strangers. Would we, even as the power brokers in the classroom, have told stories that might implicate ourselves in unsanctioned or embarrassing behaviors?

To encourage the brainstorming to continue, Elizabeth offered her own writing topic and asked the class for ideas about how to proceed with it. After a few minutes of discussing possibilities for Elizabeth's writing, Deb turned the conversation back to the students' topics. Suddenly a number of the students were full of ideas that seemed to reflect personal experiences. Their willingness to share may have stemmed from the more open feeling that was created as students gave Elizabeth suggestions, but it is clear that the students also began to cue in to the types of topics that we implicitly encouraged through our examples.

As the brainstorming continued, Deb told the class that all students needed to write from their personal experience during the first quarter. In effect, Deb's focus delimited how much choice would be allowed for all students within the framework of student autonomy. Despite this limitation and despite their earlier assumption that English class was about "how to speak proper English," the students accepted this negotiated definition of what literacy in English class would be about: writing personal experience stories. A focus on grammar, punctuation, and spelling took a supplemental position—via the DOL and editing of final drafts—to personal expression through writing. The definition included reading, but class readings early in the quarter were done primarily for the purpose of finding models of good writing.

Adding Detail and Dialogue:
The Negotiation of Literacy Practices

As coteachers, Deb's and Elizabeth's literacy beliefs and practices played a dramatic role in the construction and negotiation of classroom literacy practices. Early in the year, both Deb and Elizabeth taught a number of minilessons on the reading–writing workshop, with a particular focus on the writing process. We stressed the discourse of writer's workshop by (a) conducting minilessons on the art of conferring; (b) distributing progress records for the students to complete; and (c) requesting that students speak in the language of the writer's workshop when we took "status of the class" reports (cf. Atwell, 1987p). We also conducted minilessons on revision using a number of personal experience stories, some fictional short stories, and some contrived writing activities. Finally, we engaged in minilessons on the specifics of revision such as adding detail, dialogue, and themes to writing.

As a result of our various minilessons, we regularly observed all students talking in the language of writing process, attempting to add details and dialogue to their writing, and suggesting that others do so during peer conferences. They also suggested adding detail and dialogue when asked about the revision process during formal interviews. While we initially found the students willingness to take up these writing strategies and discourse, we realized with further analysis that literacy in English class was not constructed by the students or by us as communicating ideas, representing meaning, or entertaining others (although there were certainly instances of literacy being used for such purposes throughout the year) even though we ostensibly were committed to such practices. Instead, both students and teachers constructed literacy practices in English class as drafting, conferring, revising by adding details or dialogue, and publishing a final draft that would be read and graded by the teacher. Moreover, we all practiced literacy as a procedural activity in which students drafted pieces, identified weaknesses in the writing, and used stock writing strategies to eliminate those weaknesses. This construction of literacy in English class as a procedural activity constituted a particular literacy practice that both the students and we brought to the literacy events in the class.

This particular construction—a sort of assembly line practice of literacy—stemmed in part from our focus on teaching the process because we were so worried about students focusing solely on products and in part from students' conceptions of what one does in school and particularly in English class. Although this process approach to reading and writing was significantly different from what most of the students had experienced in English classes during previous school years, students defined and constructed the workshop approach in relation to their past English class experiences. Though we challenged some of these past practices through the workshop approach, we also normalized their constructions of English classroom literacy by privileging particular texts (narrative and personal experience writings) and writing strategies in the literary examples and activities we offered and modeled. Consequently, students viewed the workshop process as a new kind of classroom literacy that they had to learn, but they did not make it their own in significant ways. As we explain later, a large number of students maintained other literacy practices as separate and distinct from the reading–writing workshop.

LITERACIES FOR SCHOOL, LITERACIES FOR LIFE: LITERACY IN AND OUT OF CLASS

Throughout the year, we were struck by the differences in the students' beliefs about and practices of literacy in various contexts. The students we talked with asserted that they liked the reader's and writer's workshop approach because they could read and write about their own interests. They also mentioned specific things they had learned, such as how to add details or dialogue to make a story richer or more interesting.

Despite the students' claim that they enjoyed and learned from the writer's workshop, however, they viewed the writing that they did there as separate from the everyday writing of their lives. During minilessons, whole-class novel readings, passing time in the hallways, and lunch in the cafeteria, students wrote notes to each other, often in gang scripts and codes. They drew pictures and tagged (or wrote elaborate characters and scripts) their notebooks. But when asked to write during writing time, the same students wrote personal experience essays about classes, vacations, animals, or family members; fictional short stories; and romantic poems. Even when Elizabeth encouraged one young woman, Khek, to write a note to a friend as a way of getting her past a writer's block, Khek resisted the suggestions, perhaps because she saw Elizabeth's suggestion as a way of monitoring her note writing, or perhaps because it did not seem like an appropriate writing activity for the time period.

Similarly, at home and in the hallways students wrote entertaining and mocking—and sometimes violent or sexually explicit—raps, poems, and parodies, but they rarely wrote or read such pieces during the in-class writer's workshop time. Although one student wrote a fictional story called *Tragedy*, based on the actual shooting death of a good friend, more typical cases were those of Chile and Anthony. In the sections that follow, we highlight some of Chile's and Anthony's writings and discuss how they initially kept different literacy practices separate, but as the year progressed, began to integrate their in- and out-of-school practices.

Chile's Literacy Practices

Chile is a young Hispanic[4] woman who has lived in Salt Lake City all her life. At the time of the study she was 12-years-old. The youngest of five children, she lived at that time with her mother, three sisters, and a niece and nephew; a married brother lived nearby. In addition to strong family relationships, two other important parts of Chile's life are her local Hispanic Catholic church and neighborhood street gangs.

Although students affiliated with street gangs[5] are often characterized as resistant or at risk, Chile was cooperative and friendly in the English class. And, until near the end of the year, her grades in all her classes were above average. During interviews, Chile revealed that she had been enrolled in a gifted and talented program (called Extended Learning Program, or ELP, in Salt Lake City) while in elementary school. The only outward representations of her gang affiliations were her dress codes and her use of gang scripts when writing personal notes.

Chile wrote many of these personal notes to friends in and out of the classroom, but never during the time officially designated as writing time. The notes were scripted and coded with gang and other adolescent female conventions, such as elaborately folded pages (cf. Finders, 1996). These conventions, however, were not transported into her writing for the writer's workshop, despite the admonition to write from one's experience and interests. It is likely that Chile's failure to incorporate these codes and conventions into her school writing stemmed both from her desire to produce acceptable writings for the classroom and from her awareness that the codes and conventions of gang and youth cultures were particular communicative and expressive devices appropriate for particular contexts. It would not make sense, for example, to include gang scripts in a parody about the three little pigs meeting the Avon lady, one of Chile's most interesting writings of the year.

In informal interviews, Chile told Elizabeth a number of stories about street gang experiences as well as Hispanic–Mexican folklore passed down orally in her mother's family. She did not, however, choose to write these oral stories, perhaps because they were stories meant for telling; perhaps be-

---

[4]Chile's ancestry derived from both Spain and Mexico. Although I usually use Latino or Latina as an identifier, Chile preferred to be identified as Hispanic.

[5]Chile was not "jumped in to" or initiated into a gang, but she "kicked it" with gangsters, and she was loyal to particular sets.

cause, like Khek, she did not consider them appropriate written pieces for English class. Instead, Chile wrote a number of fictional or personal experience stories, including the parody of *The Three Little Pigs* and several stories about family experiences. Although her stories were well constructed and written with a rich voice, they carried no trace of her ethnicity. She did not weave the folk stories she told orally into her written work, even when her written pieces were about her family. Intertextual connections are certainly evident when one examines Chile's writing, but her written pieces do not contain the conscious intertextual moves of her oral stories. In one conversation, for example, Chile demonstrated her ability to play with storytelling and writing when she told Elizabeth about how she would weave together a Mexican folk tale of la Llorona with Shel Silverstein's poetry (cf. Moje, in press).

By contrast, Chile's workshop writings about her family usually consisted of the retelling of one event (such as discovering a cousin) or detailed descriptions of her family members. In these writings, she rarely made reference to family stories or events, or to ethnic or gender relationships that would connect the individuals. And, although Chile told Elizabeth a number of stories of gang practices, and was, according to the assistant principal, "deeply involved" with gangs, she never wrote about gang activity. Only when Chile had to choose a social action project at the end of the year did she use her knowledge of gangs in her written work, and even then she did not volunteer personal knowledge, but instead relied on books for her information.

Each of these data points can be analyzed in light of discourse theories (cf. Bakhtin, 1986; Fairclough, 1992; Kress, 1989). Specifically, Chile's textual and discursive practices can be understood in terms of the various genre in which Chile was writing, talking, or performing. According to Fairclough (1992), a genre can be considered a "relatively stable set of conventions that is associated with, and partly enacts, a socially ratified type of activity.... A genre implies not only a particular text type, but also particular processes of producing, distributing and consuming texts" (p. 126). Chile's writing, talking, and performing took on particular codes and conventions in light of the particular kinds of activities in which she engaged; when she shared a story about her family with Elizabeth, for example, she wove together oral folk tales and published poetry because the activity of talking, and specifically of talking to a researcher–teacher, called and allowed for such weaving together of texts.

The written texts that Chile constructed for the workshop, however, were cast in a different set of conventions and carried out for a different kind of socially ratified activity. In part because of her past experiences in English classes, and in part because of the way we had cast the writing of the workshop in terms of personal experience and fiction writing, Chile would not have seen folk stories as a relevant or appropriate genre. Similarly, the stories performed for the whole class spoke only of family vacations or experiences with family pets and were devoid of any mention of ethnicity, race, or culture. The processes of producing the written workshop texts also shaped what she included in those texts and how she wrote them. It is not unusual, then, that Chile's writing differed in and out of the workshop; according to discourse theory it would be startling if the texts she produced were not different. What is important, however, is that the workshop approach claims to build on diverse experiences—which should yield diverse genres and texts—and yet tends to privilege a few genres and texts, most of which derive from and work within activities ratified according to mainstream social and cultural norms (cf. Atwell, 1997).

As Chile's case implies, students often wrote nice or appropriate stories, suggesting that the reading–writing workshop served a kind of normalizing function (cf. Foucault, 1977), in which mainstream stories that revolved around certain kinds of topics were acceptable (cf. Finders, 1996; Lensmire, 1994; Willis, 1995). It is hardly surprising that Chile resisted writing about gangs; gang activity, after all, was heavily sanctioned in the school culture. Nevertheless, Chile's failure to write about something so predominant in her life and her focus on acceptable topics reveals an additional flaw in expressivist writing pedagogies: Few students will choose to write about their authentic experiences if those experiences are not sanctioned in school and classroom cultures.

Although this flaw has implications for the writing experiences of all students, most schools work within a middle-class, mainstream ideology; consequently, students who are not middle class and mainstream are the least likely to find their experiences valid or acceptable within the school culture and are, therefore, the least likely to write about their experiences. Not only does this stifle any learning that theoretically should occur as a result of self-expression (cf. Elbow, 1973a), but it also teaches students to subvert their social and cultural experiences to those of the dominant culture.

This issue is not unique to expressivist pedagogies; school and social culture defines and delimits any pedagogical approach (D. G. O'Brien, personal communication, June 14, 1998). This critique is important for expressivist pedagogies, however, because expressivist pedagogies have been offered as a way to meet the needs and engage the interests of diverse groups of students. Such claims fail to take into account the social and cultural norms of schools and society that shape the constructions of literacy practices that teachers and students bring to, negotiate, and reconstruct within classrooms.

There is, however, some potential for writing pedagogies derived from expressivist philosophies to make spaces for students to express themselves as social and cultural beings, as illustrated by our experience. Toward the middle of the year some of our students began to write personal experience stories that reflected some less mainstream themes such as cultural events, whereas others were about unsanctioned activities, such as gang banging or drinking alcohol. Students began to write about their experiences when they came to trust that we would not hold their writing subject to public scrutiny or to preconceived standards of acceptability. They also began to write and read more from their out-of-school experiences when we engaged in a pedagogy that encouraged students to consciously examine social, cultural, and political issues (cf. Moje & Fassio, 1997). In the following section, we use the case of Anthony (a pseudonym) to illustrate how both these unintended and intended modifications of the writer's workshop pedagogy seemed to influence Anthony's writing.

Anthony's Literacy Practices

Anthony was a 12-year-old boy who described his ethnicity as "Viet." He lived with his mother and two younger brothers in a nearby neighborhood, although he moved to the north side of town (and a new school district) at the end of the year. A mixture of English and Vietnamese was spoken in Anthony's home, and the family maintained strong ties with the Vietnamese community in Salt Lake City.

When Anthony first arrived in the seventh-grade English class, he seemed reticent or shy, but not uncooperative. Anthony dressed like most of the kids in the class at the beginning of the year; he would most often wear a T-shirt, oversized windbreaker, baggy pants, and a pair of Nike® tennis shoes. He was always present in class, he engaged in various activities, and he produced a number of written products. When reading class novels, he appeared to follow along, and he was ready to read if chosen by another student. He read with neither expression nor excitement, but he read clearly and fluently.

Anthony's first writing was a kind of journal entry of his First Day of School. In this piece, he wrote about what happened in each class, using descriptions such as, "That period was long and freaking boring." When he described a class as "alright," it seemed to be due to his friends' presence in the class. Virtually every class was labeled as long and boring because "all of the teachers would ever do was talk about stupid rules." Anthony described the English class as "alright," although that teacher (Deb) also "explained rules." Anthony's next writings were short pieces about finding a money-filled wallet and "kickin' it" with his friends at the local skating rink. Boredom was a theme in Anthony's early writings.

Not only did Anthony choose appropriate topics, but he also seemed to make an effort to apply the conventions of writing that we taught in minilessons. When responding to questions regarding what he liked about a class novel, Anthony wrote in his reader response journal: "How she tells a lot of detail about where she was from," and "How she adds conversation in her story." In such responses, Anthony was conforming to a particular conception of how to do English class, by answering the questions using the language of the writer's workshop.

In early December, a different Anthony began to appear in his writing. Assured that he would not have to share his piece in a group share, he started to write explicitly about his experiences with gangs. The piece Friends, written on December 11, 1995, begins:

> Friends. Friends are important. Everybody needs friends. You will be lonely if you didn't have no friends. Well, two weeks ago my friend got jumped by some gangsta's on his birthday on December second. [spelling and punctuation are intact]

The piece was quite graphic in its detail of the jumping incident—although he omitted letters from certain words to lessen their impact—and Anthony included dialogue in relating aspects of the incident:

> So we went to the bus stop we asked people what time the bus came this guy said, "That kid is f–cked up So I said, "You got a f–cking problem Then he said, "you want some?" Then I said, "Yeah, b–tch," and I threw my soda pop at him and caught the bus and he walked away.

Although Anthony negotiated his initial construction of appropriate literacy practices by choosing a risky topic and uncensored language, it is interesting to note how he incorporated punctuation conventions that we had stressed when discussing the use of dialogue in writing. Anthony applied quotation marks—punctuation that we had taught in a minilesson—but he neglected to use periods and other punctuation in his writing, punctuation that he had used correctly in other pieces. His attention to the conventions we had emphasized in class suggests that even as Anthony experimented with different topics, he also tried to maintain acceptable or appropriate genres and styles in the writing that he prepared for the workshop.

In his second term self-evaluation, Anthony wrote that a piece he had brought from outside of class, Gangsta's Prayer was his favorite piece of writing to that point in the year, "Because it's the only thing that is not a story it is a poem and i like the way it sounds, and how it rhymes." Although we have evidence that Anthony did not write the poem himself (this poem is well-known throughout United States), his choice of the poem as a representation of his writing indicates that he had become more comfortable with bringing an unsanctioned topic and a different genre to the writing workshop.

The remainder of Anthony's writings for the year carried the theme of gang activity (clearly not socially ratified activities), ranging from pieces about cruising in a friend's BMW to being chased by gangstas who carried sawed-off shotguns, and his final social action project focused on the theme of gang violence and graffiti. It was during the preparation of the project that Anthony's interest in tagging and graffiti became most evident. In a written piece, the group members addressed the issue of graffiti as a problem by linking it to violence and loss of property value, and they also highlighted the problem of confusing tagging—which they considered art—with gang graffiti. They used the posters to make the distinctions between the two forms clear. In this project, then, Anthony and his partners integrated nonschool literacy conventions and practices with school-based conventions and practices, although this integration required taking a risk by revealing personal knowledge of unsanctioned practices. Anthony and partners mitigated this risk, however, by conforming to socially ratified views of gangs in their writing and oral performances. conformed to socially accepted views of gangs (cf. Moje, in press). In a follow-up interview during the summer, Anthony said that he found the projects interesting and that he had learned from them. He felt that the most interesting and useful project was his own.

Based on our analyses, we suggest that students like Anthony expanded their constructions of classroom literacy practices and were willing to write more honest stories, essays, and projects for several reasons, at least three of which might be due to our influence as teachers and researchers. First, we publicly encouraged students to write what really happened in their lives. In one group-sharing session, for example, Giannetta read a story that she had written about a family party. In the story, Gina wrote about a fire erupting during the party; when someone in the class asked, "What did your parents say when they saw it?" Giannetta responded, "I can't write that ... [in a whisper] they were swearing!" Deb's subsequent exhortation to Giannetta not to clean up her writing for the classroom served as a green light for other writers in the class. Students may have begun to trust that they would not risk exposure by writing about some of their unsanctioned activities outside of school. They also may have felt that their varied cultural experiences would not be diminished and perhaps might even be valued. This negotiation of what was acceptable expanded constructions of literacy and appropriateness in the classroom.

Second, students found that they did not have to share their writing publicly unless they wanted to. Although we held group-share sessions, there was no "author's chair," (Graves & Hansen, 1983), nor were students required to share their work with the whole group. Until the presentation of his group project, Anthony, for example, never shared a written piece with anyone but Mike and Scott. This lack of emphasis on publishing may have reduced pressure to conform to a mainstream conception of good, appropriate, or normal social and cultural practices. Not only could students write about their experiences without risking teacher disapproval, but they felt secure that they would not be exposed to peer disapproval, as well. Ironically, this security came about as a result of our neglect of a major tenet of the reading–writing workshop: the publication, in some form, of individual stories.

Finally, the evaluation system that we established in the classroom may have also contributed to the changes we saw in students' writing over time. Although students were asked to record their progress and the types of writing they had done throughout the quarter, they were asked to select only one piece for a focused evaluation. Deb looked through and evaluated each student's entire notebook, but only read and commented in depth on one piece. As a result, students may have felt that they could write more freely on a large number of pieces, while writing in more appropriate ways for the focus piece. In contrast to our approach, advocates of workshop approaches suggest regular and in-depth evaluation of students' different writings. Although we worried that we should be evaluating more often and looking at a greater number of pieces, our interpretations suggest that a more sweeping evaluation process may have worked in much the same way as the publishing aspect of the workshop. That is, it may serve as a normalizing or regulatory process (Foucault, 1977) that silences students' experiences.

Even with the negotiation or mediation (cf. Smagorinsky & O'Donnell-Allen, 1998) of expressivist norms that we unintentionally engaged in, the constructions of literacy practice in the classroom remained rooted in larger social, cultural, and political practices that identified certain themes and styles of writing as appropriate for school and others as inappropriate or even dangerous. Although many of the students in this study were from low-income homes, they wrote stories with middle-class themes. And despite the diversity of ethnic and cultural groups in the classroom and a pronounced awareness of ethnicity, race, and culture among students and teachers at the school (students routinely differentiated kids who had the same name with the appellations such as, "White Nat" and "Black Nat," and teachers commented on students' ethnic backgrounds), students rarely wrote about ethnic or cultural experiences that were not White, European-American, and mainstream in orientation. Thus, we must ask questions about how to further reshape this literacy pedagogy to incorporate various literacy practices as well as processes.

HOW SHOULD STUDENTS' LITERACY PRACTICES INFORM PROCESS LITERACY PEDAGOGIES?

Our goal was to work with the social, family, and community literacies that students brought to the class, but we found that the reading–writing workshop pedagogy did not necessarily help us achieve that goal. We should not, perhaps, have been so surprised by such findings. The emphasis on experience in expressivist pedagogy like the writing workshop does not automatically encourage students to bring out-of-school practices to bear on their school literacy practices.

In expressivist pedagogies, students write individually from their experiences, and it is assumed within an expressivist process or workshop approach that students will feel comfortable sharing experiences with and getting feedback from peers. But unequal relations of power among students and between students and teachers—race, class, age, and gender differences, for example—shape the ways that students' experiences, or practices, are offered and received in the classroom (Finders, 1996; Lensmire, 1994; Oates, chap. 10, this volume). And, because students bring with them constructions of what counts as literacy in school and even in specific disciplines (Moje, 1996), they may also be hesitant to engage in practices that might be considered inappropriate in school settings or by school personnel, even if those are their everyday experiences.

We are in many ways responsible for the separation of literacy practices that we observed, because the models we provided were drawn from personal experience and fictional works that often embodied mainstream themes. Although expressivist pedagogies are useful in that they begin with student experiences, there is nothing in the pedagogy that explicitly challenges dominant and traditional assumptions about what is good or bad literacy (writing an essay, for example, versus writing graffiti) despite the claim that such pedagogy invites all readers and writers to participate. In fact, in many ways, such strategies as using literature as models for writing or publishing through whole-group sharing seem to emphasize constructions about particular literacies as good or appropriate for school—particularly English class—and others as more useful in different settings. As Dressman (1993) pointed out, expressivist pedagogies privilege personal expression over the kinds of literacy required for success in professional and disciplinary discourse communities.

As a result, like Lensmire (1994), we concluded that although we want to continue to offer students choice in establishing their reading and writing curriculum, we also have a responsibility to offer a variety of texts and experiences to students, not only as models for writing, but also as texts to analyze, question, and challenge (Moje, Thompson, Christiansen, & Zeitler, 1997). And we are now interested in further exploring alternative pedagogies that encourage students to draw on the literacies they use outside of school, to weave their social and academic literacies together, and to integrate their uses of literacy in the various disciplines. We were able to encourage some integration of social and academic literacies as a result of our unintended modifications of the literacy pedagogy, but we would like to—with the help of our students—develop pedagogies intended to foster connections among school, home, community, and adolescent peer-group literacy practices.

Such a reconceptualization of expressivist pedagogies will require that teachers and researchers give up the romantic notion (Rousseau, 1762/1974) that student choice must be foregrounded in a reading–writing workshop (cf. Atwell, 1997; Lensmire, 1994). We believe that teachers have a moral and ethical obligation to involve themselves in their students' choices, to encourage student experimentation with a variety of literacy practices, and to work with students to analyze and question how their experiences are part of a larger social system that may or may not work to their advantage. Even as we make this assertion, however, we recognize the tremendous demands such pedagogy would place on teachers. Our research has led us to ask questions about how such pedagogies can be put into practice, given the enormous material, emotional, and physical demands placed on teachers and students each day.

We must also acknowledge that although we advocate that teachers work within students' experiences, students may wish to keep their experiences—and their literacies—separate for any number of reasons. We should not assume that kids will want to bring their social literacies into the classroom. And students certainly do not need teachers to teach them how to engage in the literacies they value; they are obviously already skilled in those practices. More important, we wonder whether our appropriation of their literacies would be welcomed by students. If, for example, letter writing, tagging, or gang drawing were legitimized forms of representation, would the power of those practices be diminished for these students (cf. O'Brien, 1998)?

Thus, there are some limitations to a pedagogy based solely on students' experiences and literacies and, consequently, we have to be wary of simply encouraging students to bring these literacies into the classroom. Nevertheless, teachers and researchers can learn a great deal from studying the literacies that kids use in different contexts. We can see, for example, the oral tradition of storytelling that Chile has inherited as part of her family's language practices and the fluency and motivation with which Anthony wrote when he was vested in a particular topic or form. We can learn about the experiences that our students have had and find ways to generate responsive curricula and pedagogy based on those experiences (Moje et al., 1997). With a better understanding of the various perspectives on literacy that students bring to classrooms and of the many different literacies that are meaningful in adolescents' lives, we can envision curricula and pedagogy that will encourage students to use their literacies and experiences as tools for developing a variety of socially powerful, and personally satisfying, literacy skills.

10

Literacy as an Everyday Practice

Scott F. Oates
University of Wisconsin–Eau Claire

In *Remembering Writing, Remembering Reading* (1994), Deborah Brandt makes a distinction between literacy as a meaning-making activity[1] and the meaning people hold and construct for literacy. She notes that studies that have emphasized literacy as a meaning-making activity overlook literacy as a meaningful practice: "These investigations have mostly focused on reading and writing as processes of meaning-making … Only incidentally might these studies consider how people make meaning of reading and writing" (p. 460). This distinction raises several questions. What does it mean to consider the meaning people make of their literacy practices? What meanings do people have for their literacy and how does it influence their practices? Where do these meanings come from? And what significance might this view of literacy have in terms of learning and teaching, specifically in high school language arts classes? In this chapter, I investigate these questions, focusing on the meanings of the literacy practices in a 12th-grade English class and on the meanings and uses that two students from this class make of written language.

A literacy practice is meaningful because it is an enactment of social relations. For example, Heath's (1983) account of Trackton, a working-poor African-American community, illustrated that literacy practices are meaningful acts of being with people. Reading in Trackton was neither a solitary nor a private affair, but "a public group affair for almost all members of

---

[1]Brandt noted research going back to the mid-1980s that stressed how reading and writing are interdependent, knowledge-making activities (e.g., Elbow, 1993; Flower et al., 1990; Harste, & Woodward, & Burke, 1984; Langer, 1986; Nystrand, 1990; Tierney & Pearson, 1984).

Trackton from the youngest to the oldest" (Heath, 1983, p. 191). Consequently, to read alone conveyed meanings that were (potentially) disruptive to Trackton's everyday social life:

> Miss Lula sometimes read her Bible alone, and Annie Mae would sometimes quietly read magazines she brought home, but *to read alone was frowned upon, and individuals who did so were accused of being anti-social.* Aunt Bertha had a son who as a child would slip away from the cotton field and read under a tree. He is now a grown man with children, and he has obtained a college degree, but the community still tells tales about his peculiar boyhood habits of wanting to go off and read alone. *In general, reading alone, unless one is very old and religious marks an individual as someone who cannot make it socially.* (Heath, 1983, p. 191, italics added)

Heath's account suggested that literacy practices are not just ways of using words to make linguistic meanings, but that literacy practices are also ways to signify identity and maintain relationships according to the norms of a community. This point—that ways with words are also ways with people—is what I think sociolinguist Gee (1996) meant in his definition of literacy as *Discourse*:

> A *Discourse* is a socially accepted association among ways of using language, other symbolic expressions, and 'artifacts,' of thinking, feeling, believing, valuing, and acting that can be used to identify oneself as a member of a socially meaningful group or 'social network,' or to signal (that one is playing) a socially meaningful 'role'. (p. 131)

Gee's definition of literacy as Discourse suggested that reading in Trackton signals a person's membership (or lack of) in Trackton's social network, and moreover, that to participate in Trackton's Discourse is to assume a socially meaningful role. As Gee explained, assuming a role in a community means taking on a particular identity:

> Discourses are ways of being in the world, or forms of life which integrate words, acts, values, beliefs, attitudes, and social identities, as well as gestures, glances, body positions, and clothes. A *Discourse is a sort of identity kit* [italics added] which comes complete with the appropriate costume and instructions on how to act, talk, and often write, so as to take on a particular social role that others will recognize. (1996, p. 127)

Moje (1996), furthered my point by illustrating that classroom literacy practices are also Discourses. In her study of literacy in a high school chemistry class, Moje focused on the teacher's uses of literacy strategies to help her students break down, organize and synthesize complex ideas from the lectures, labs, and their readings. These strategies became meaningful, moreover, because of the teacher's humanist ethic. That is, the teacher offered the strategies as a gesture to "reach out to students, to try to make connections, establish rapport, and build relationships" (Moje, 1996, p. 187). Consequently, the literacy practices meant caring, respect, and allegiance, and the students' participation in these practices was emblematic of membership in the classroom culture of respect and care. When viewed as Discourse, the literacy practices of this chemistry classroom signified membership in a community that meant care, esteem, and allegiance.

I found in my research that the ways in which written language was used in English 12 could be viewed as a Discourse of crisis and esteem. By this I mean that students and teachers were positioned in a social network that was constructed in terms of faculty, administration, and counseling-staff beliefs that student esteem was in crisis, and that personal and academic hardship needed to be mitigated. The Discourse of crisis and esteem, as I will illustrate below, was the socially organizing theme in English 12, shaping not only the topics selected for reading and writing, but also the ways in which reading and writing became socially meaningful.

My study, however, was not limited to understanding only the Discourse of English 12. During this research, I found that students had their Discourses and that they relied on these to make sense and use of the literacy assignments in English 12. In other words, despite the appearance that the institutionally sanctioned Discourse of English 12 was uniform, the two case-study participants, Katy Pederson and Zeke Christiansen (all names are pseudonyms), carried out the assignments in terms of their identity kits and social networks. Katy's Discourse is one of intimacy and disclosure, as she uses written language to maintain intimate relationships with her mother, her girlfriends, her Heavenly Father, and with herself by writing about her feelings. Zeke, on the other hand, uses written language to assume a role in a Discourse of entitled authority. He both reads and writes as acts of rehearsing for a social network of young men authorized to make public proclamations about the morality, ethics, and responsibilities of peers, dating couples, his teachers, and his religious leaders.

My finding that Katy and Zeke drew from their Discourses to make sense and use of English 12 suggests, first of all, that the meaning of literacy practices is neither uniform nor stable. My point is underscored by social theorists and literacy researchers who have recently raised cautions about community-based views of social life and literacy[2]. Prior (1994), for exam-

---

[2]For example, social theorists (e.g., de Certeau, 1984; Fiske, 1989; Rosaldo, 1993; Smith, 1987) and literacy theorists (e.g., Dyson, 1995; Finders, 1997; New London Group, 1996; Pratt, 1991; Prior, 1994).

ple, explained that community-based views of literacy "which evoke an image of shared, cozy unity (or perhaps oppressive, authoritative unity) are not the only way to imagine social formations" (p. 486). Prior's point suggested that community-based views elide students' literacy practice, privileging instead institutional assumptions about the meanings and uses of written language. Overlooked, then, are the ways in which students draw from their Discourses to make sense and use of the Discourses in which they find themselves situated.

I believe that a bit of my literacy biography can elucidate why I think that it is important for literacy workers to attend to literacy practices as socially meaningful activities. My interest in the meanings that students construct and hold for literacy stems from my odyssey as a teacher turned researcher. I was a junior and senior high school English teacher through the 1980s, a full-time community college writing teacher in the early 90s, and finally a graduate student in literacy, rhetoric, and composition. I began teaching in the schools after finishing a bachelor's degree in English, eager to impart to students a love for reading and writing about literature. Reading and writing at that time were for me monolithic and unproblematic. They were for analyzing literature in order to present an insight into the human condition. Indeed, more than 10 years after I began teaching in the schools, these were the assumptions with which I entered graduate school with the goal of working in English education.

My assumption that literature-centered practices are monolithic was upended, though, when I left secondary school teaching to become a community college writing teacher and simultaneously became immersed in graduate coursework. I struggled with readings, writing, and teaching. I felt alien among my new peers. Experienced community college teachers and graduate students, it seemed to me, had a tacit knowledge about the purposes and ways of using texts, and I, without this knowledge, was socially, intellectually, and professionally on the margins. In retrospect, I understand that I was struggling with new literacy practices, and that the Discourse that I had gained proficiency in as a high school English teacher did not seamlessly transfer to these new contexts for being a student and a teacher.

Over a few months, I acquired knowledge of the practices of being a community college writing teacher and a graduate student, and what I gleaned informally has been the catalyst for my wanting to understand students' Discourses and the ways in which students engage with school Discourses. My difficulties, I discovered, could help me understand the struggles community college students displayed in the writing courses I taught. So as the students struggled, I queried them about how they understood what they were being asked to do, and about their view of why people analyze texts and write arguments. Many students, I found, were practiced with writing and sharing personal narratives about an autobiographically significant event. However, at the community college, personal experiences were no longer the text for analysis. Now, the privileged literacy practice was one of textual analysis and argumentation—coolly analytical and deliberately rhetorical. Students, I surmised, were struggling with unfamiliar kinds of texts and ideas, and, more so, they were confounded with the new kinds of social relationships these literacy practices enacted. That is, instead of assigning students to write about and share personal experiences, I was assigning them to construct an argumentative stance that meant openly disagreeing with authors, with their peers, and even with the authority structures that they had pledged allegiance to over their years of formal schooling.

As Prior's (1994) critique of community-based views of social life and literacy learning suggested, social formations (i.e., classrooms) can be a convergence of multiple Discourses. As an alternative to community-based views, anthropologist Rosaldo (1993) described the everyday as "disjointed" rather than as homogeneous. He explained that a person engages in "zones of differences [which are] … social worlds one passes through in daily life, a round that includes home, eating out, working hours, adventures in consumerland, and a range of relationships, from intimacy to collegiality and friendship to enmity" as well as the differences and contradiction in "gender, age, status, and distinctive life experience" (1993, pp. 29–30). Such a view—that practices are meaningful interpretations of social life, and that social life is disjointed—infers, then, that learning to use literacy is not simply a matter of learning the practice of a homogeneous community. Rather, learning an unfamiliar literacy practice is also a matter of engaging with and making sense of unfamiliar social relationships.

DATA COLLECTION AND ANALYSIS

The data that I report in this chapter is from my 5-month qualitative study of a regular 12th-grade language arts class titled *English 12: Literature and Language*.[3] The literature component of English 12 was a survey of British literature, presented in units organized around a historical period, such as the Anglo-Saxon period, the Medieval period, and so on. The language component consisted of a review of grammar, punctuation, and weekly vocabulary and spelling work derived from the literature assignments. By saying that English 12 was regular, I mean that the class carried no designation of being either an honors or a basic class. The students in English 12, for the

---

[3]This chapter is part of a larger study that includes case-study research into the literacy practices of community college and university students.

most part, did express an interest in going to a 4-year college, signing up to meet visiting admissions directors, accepting financial aid forms from counselors, etc. However, most of the students were behind in requirements for admission to the local universities (e.g., two years of foreign language; an extra year each of math, science and social studies).

The high school I studied, which I will call Capital City High, is located in downtown Salt Lake City. The people in the surrounding neighborhood and in the student body are predominantly members of the Mormon Church. Just a brief walk from the school are located a number of buildings and sites important to Mormons. Most notable of these sites is Temple Square, for which the Mormon faithful hold a deep reverence. At the time I conducted this study, both of the case-study participants actively participated in Mormon youth culture.[4]

I attended each meeting of a first period class from the end of August through the middle of January. For this analysis, I draw from my case-study work with Katy and Zeke. Both granted me access to their uses of literacy by allowing me to work with them in English 12, meeting with me outside of class to talk about literacy practices in other contexts, and bringing me copies of poems, letters, journals, and assignments from other classes.

I collected data using participant observer techniques (Spradley, 1980), and semiformal interviews. I collected written artifacts, such as essay assignments, poems, and copies of personal journal entries that students wanted to share with me, and I audiotaped all class sessions in order to detail my fieldnotes. I taped and transcribed all interviews. My aim in the interviews was to understand as much as I could about Katy's and Zeke's uses of written language in their everyday life. I also studied the beliefs, understandings, and meanings that informed Katy's and Zeke's uses of written language, as well as the relationships that influenced, were influenced by their literacy practices, or a combination of both.

For my analysis, I used the constant comparative method (Strauss & Corbin, 1990) to develop three categories for coding the data: (a) the *textual practice*, that is the meanings that a person makes with reading, writing, or both; (b) the *social practice*, that is, the way in which written language is used for a specific purpose in a specific context (i.e., Scribner & Cole, 1981); and (c) the *relational practice*, by which I mean the ways in which people interact and relate with each other in a literate act. These three codes overlapped

---

[4]For one period every day, the students are released to attend religious instruction of their choice. LDS students attend what is called *Seminary*, a class that is held in a church-owned building adjacent to every secondary school and college in Utah. The Mormon Church staffs the seminary with faculty and provides a curriculum for studying Mormon history, *The Book of Mormon*, *Doctrines and Covenants*, and *The Bible*. Non-LDS students may attend religious instruction of their choice; however, many non-LDS students simply elect to take an additional class in the regular curriculum of the high school.

each other in my analyses because the textual meanings a student produces are, simultaneously, a way of using literacy (a social practice) and a way of enacting social relationships (a relational practice).

THE DISCOURSE OF CRISIS AND ESTEEM

In the following, I further develop what I mean by a Discourse of crisis and esteem by analyzing a reading and writing task that I have selected because it typifies the textual, social, and relational practices in English 12. The saga *Beowulf* was the culminating text to an Anglo-Saxon study unit for which *The Failure Essay* was the major writing assignment. In the subsequent analysis, I illustrate that the students and the teacher, Ms. Allen, are positioned in a social network that views adolescents' esteem to be fragile and their lives to be in crisis. At the point of the following description, Ms. Allen has been reading *Beowulf* with the students for over a week. As the account from my fieldnotes illustrates, she reads aloud with enthusiasm and drama:

> The episode being read today is dramatic and gory. Beowulf has killed the monster's son, Grendel, and has now followed "the lady monster" into her underwater lair. Confronting Grendel's mother on her turf, Beowulf discovers that his weapons are useless and that his armor is beginning to fail him. He engages her in a pitched battle of tearing claws and stabbing teeth that wear him down.

Ms. Allen's reading has been a dramatic performance. All the students are watching her. Snapping and hissing the words, she approaches the climactic lines of this episode. Just when it seems that Beowulf might be killed, he finds the strength and will to snatch a magic sword from the wall and deliver a mighty blow to the "she-devil":

> And then, savage, now, angry
> And desperate, lifted it high over his head
> And struck with all the strength he had left.
> Caught her in the neck and cut it through,
> Broke bones and all. Her body fell
> To the floor, lifeless, the sword was wet
> With her blood, and Beowulf rejoiced at the sight.

Some students chortle "cool!" while others groan "gross." Ms. Allen goes on to complete the section—only a few more lines—that describe Beowulf's triumphant return to his men with the head of the monster.

This scene of Beowulf nearly succumbing to failure but finding the physical and emotional strength to prevail has introduced the parameters of the textual practice for the students' writing. That is, students are to emulate the theme of Beowulf's near failure by writing vividly about their own brush with failure. Prior to announcing the essay assignment, Ms. Allen amplifies this theme of potential disaster evolving into triumph:

> In this last battle with Grendel's mother, there is the possibility of failure. His helmet is damaged. She is biting him. There's that sense of mortality. He's not a god. He's not immortal. He begins to sense what failure is, but he has never failed. What I would like you to do in an essay—and this is really short, one page, is to discuss failure from a personal point of view.

In the context of Capital City High School, given that adults perceive student esteem to be fragile, the range of meanings on the theme of failure is tempered as Ms. Allen directs students to explore their experiences as a positive learning experience.[5] That is, any potential damage to student esteem caused by writing about a personal failure will be mitigated by the direction to write about what good is to be learned from their brushes with failure in the Failure Essay Assignment:

> Describe a time when you were concerned about failure.
> What would the consequences be if you were to fail?
> What does failure feel like?
> Can failure be turned into a learning experience?
> Is failure good for us?

Discourse, as Gee (1996) told us, identifies "socially acceptable" symbolic expressions. And indeed, the range of the textual practice (both in terms of what *Beowulf* means and what student essays can mean) is not controlled by the students. That is, despite the appearance that students are given the freedom to choose their own experience to write about, the socially acceptable topics, examples, and interpretations of experience for student writing are identified by Ms. Allen's direction for students to reflect on the experience as potentially good. Even more so, the parameters of the students' textual practice are defined by the glib tone and teasing examples Ms. Allen uses as she explains to students how to write the essay:

---

[5]The Discourse of crisis and esteem was not idiosyncratic to Ms. Allen's class. Indeed, the themes of adolescents in crisis and adults intervening to foster esteem were part of everyday interactions in English 12. Counselors came to class to talk about sexual harassment in the halls and the damages to both girls' and boys' esteem. The morning announcements lamented the football team's sudden loss in overtime. Graduating from high school was talked about as a potential crisis, unless students took adequate precautions. A school assembly featured a race relations team that would intervene when there was a racially charged crisis at the school. Moreover, there was the students' ongoing talk about the vicissitudes of peer life, dating, and jockeying for stature and esteem.

Describe a time when you were concerned about failure.

Failure in school, failure to make a play in football, failure to, well, you know how it is when you fail when you call up a girl (the males up front groan in unison) your heart is pounding, and you fail to get that date.

What would the consequences be if you were to fail?

So think back and forward. So what would happen—you football players got a game today—what happens if you fail to do your duty on the field? Go ahead and tell it.

What does failure feel like?

The sensation: think guys of calling that girl—and you too girls, calling up that guy. The anticipation of the heart, pounding; palms get a little sweaty; guys, you know your voice reverts to this ten-year-old and squeaks.

Okay, last two things to think about.

Can failure be turned into a learning experience?

Usually, especially if others learn from it.

And last question: *Is failure good for us?*

Indeed, the power of Discourse to identify the socially acceptable range of expressions was further indicated by the students' essays. Their texts displayed a tone similar to Ms. Allen's, and students emulated her contextualizing examples for the subjects of their essays (e.g., getting a date for the prom, acting masculine on a first deer hunt, playing football, etc.).

The Discourse of crisis and esteem was sustained also by social practices, that is the ways in which written language was used in English 12. Texts were not used to construct meanings about the text or to explore Anglo-Saxon culture. Instead, texts were used as templates for students to write about their experiences, feelings, and opinions. For example, the narrative of Beowulf's adventure (near failure followed by a disciplined self-rescue) is the same narrative structure assigned to students, that is to turn their near failure into a learning experience. The social practice in English 12, I thus suggest, was a practice of the self. Literacy was used as a springboard to students' personal experiences, and as a mirror on which they were to reflect about the meaning of their experiences with failure.

As a relational practice, The Failure Essay implicates literacy in powerful messages about identity kits and social relations. The practice of the self is simultaneously a display of the self to Ms. Allen and classmates. For example, several of the essays that students submitted were read aloud by Ms. Allen to the class. These readings were accompanied with Ms. Allen's commentary—not about the students' texts—but about the students' experiences and their interpretation of the good that they learned. To illustrate, some of the essays read aloud included a football player's narrative about almost fumbling in an important game, a cheerleader's fear of not being picked at cheerleader try-outs, and a regular student's experience getting a driver's license. In each case, the students were praised for not losing nerve or confidence under pressure, or despite a temporary setback. The relational practice thus constructs the teacher as a cultural parent who offers approval not of students' writing, but approval of the students. In other words, when students submitted their essays to be read, they were submitting themselves. Literacy, in English 12, means the self. Indeed, one student told me that when she wrote essays in English 12, she wanted to "show her [Ms. Allen] what a deep thinker I am. To show that I really know how to apply this stuff [the literature] to myself."

The Discourse of crisis and esteem in English 12 raises several concerns. Perhaps most pressing, given my choice of The Failure Essay to analyze, is the infantilizing teacher–student dyad. When a person is infantilized, it is assumed that she or he is incapable of determining her or his needs or directing the processes to obtain those needs. In English 12, Ms. Allen assumed that British literature was off-putting and too difficult for students to read alone; hence, she took the responsibility for reading and interpretation. Likewise, the texts that students were assigned to write were carefully directed to control troubling topics and to avoid unfamiliar text genres. Despite the appearance that students were authoring the meanings of their experiences with failure, they were being authored, directed that is, in terms of the socially acceptable range of textual, social and relational practices exemplified by Ms. Allen's reading of Beowulf, her commentary, and her explanation of the assignment.

A second problematic is the success of the Discourse of comfort and esteem. Both Katy and Zeke, who had struggled in their previous English classes, consistently received A grades and extolled how much they liked English 12. Zeke, for example, enthusiastically told me, "I like her class the best because she works so hard at making the stuff interesting. She makes the stuff about us." And indeed, Ms. Allen did design the course to be familiar to students in order to foster their success. Or, in other words, English 12 mitigated any potential disjoint between students' school, home, and community Discourses because the textual, social, and relational practices were familiar and common. Gee explained why this concerns me in the conclusion to his book, Social Linguistics and Literacies (1996). He argues that at the end of the 20th century, social life in America was a myriad of Discourses (or, to use Rosaldo's [1993] term, the everyday world is "disjointed") and that thus the aim of literacy learning should be to:

... allow students to juxtapose diverse Discourses to each other so that they can understand them.... Schools ought to allow students to acquire, not just learn about, Discourses that lead to effectiveness in their society ... and to imagine better and more socially just ways of being in the world. (p. 190)

The Discourse of crisis and esteem concerns me, because for the sake of bolstering students esteem, it denies opportunities for them to explore other Discourses, and it ignores the complex sociolinguistic realities that if they do not already engage, they likely soon will.

INTERDISCUSIVITY:
ENGAGING DIFFERENT DISCOURSES

The admonition that literacy education should foster the acquisition of Discourses implies, first of all, that Discourse is better thought of in plural terms. Gee explained that Discourses have a dynamic effect on each other: " ... other Discourses can effect in a variety of ways, what I think, do and say in any given Discourse. One's primary Discourse always affects one's use of secondary Discourses to some degree" (Gee, 1996, p. 167).[6] This suggests that when students are trying to understand the Discourse of a classroom they are constructing and interpreting the textual, social, and relational practices of the classroom in relation to their prior and ongoing Discourses. In the second half of this chapter, I focus on Katy's and Zeke's literacy practices, illustrating that they draw from their primary Discourses as they engage with, and make use of, English 12.

Engaging in multiple Discourses is what I call *interdiscursivity*, a term I borrow from Fairclough (1992). He meant that texts bear traces of other literacy practices and not just traces of other texts as intertextuality suggests (see Fairclough, 1992, pp. 124–130). My use of the term is to suggest the extratextual understandings of social and relational practices, implying the heterogeneity of a person's interpretations of the uses of literacy. I can illustrate my use of interdiscursivity with Finders' *Just Girls: Hidden Literacies and Life in Junior High* (1997), a study of the literate underlives of seventh-grade girls. As an example of Discourse, the girls used teen magazines and note-writing in class to sustain membership in their community. As an example of interdiscourse, the girls' literate underlife was lived in relation to adult-sanctioned literacy practices. Parents disapproved of the emphasis on

---

[6]However, as Elizabeth Moje has commented to me in conversation, as a person becomes proficient in multiple Discourses, it is difficult to locate the primary Discourse. The examples Gee drew on to illustrate his theory are of young children encountering for the first time a Discourse (the classroom) other than their home and neighborhood.

cosmetics and fashion in the magazines, and teachers forbade writing and passing notes in class. Moreover, the girls appropriated adult and popular themes in reaction to being treated like little girls by their parents and teachers. Acting on their interpretation of their life-world, the girls used fashion (via the teen magazines) and popular notions of the rebellious teenager to construct their Discourse (Finders, pp. 55–56).

Katy and Zeke, unlike the girls in Finders' study, did not fashion a literate underlife because they did not find English 12 to contradict the Discourses to which they held allegiance. Instead, they used their literacy to participate in Discourses sanctioned by their parents, church leaders, and Ms. Allen. As young adults who were anticipating graduation from high school, Katy's and Zeke's interests were taken up with topics of dating, going to college, and taking on the responsibilities of a young adult in the Mormon Church, topics and goals that were lauded by the adults in their lives. However, Katy's and Zeke's literacy practices were not simply a matter of following a script into adulthood. Though it may appear that the socioliterate landscape of Katy and Zeke is relatively seamless because they do not struggle with a disjoint between school and their Discourses, I illustrate subsequently they do indeed forge interdiscursive constructions among their Discourses and the Discourse of English 12.

Katy Pedersen: Discourses of Intimacy and Disclosure

Katy is the youngest child in a large, White Mormon family. Her brothers and sisters, all who attended the same high school as she, were out of the house and carrying out the lives of young Mormon adults—attending college, serving a mission for the LDS church, or marrying and starting a family. Katy was a popular senior girl. She was runner-up for homecoming queen, an outstanding performer in the high school's music and theater programs, and she was a leader in a peer counseling drug awareness program. She chose to not participate in the peer culture of fashion and cosmetics, often expressing to me in our interviews her disdain of "girls who perform for each other." Her early years of schooling had been marked with episodes of truancy that she attributed to depression.

Additionally, she told me that she was dyslexic and that I, as a researcher, probably would not want to talk to her much because she was not a good English student. When I asked her what she meant, she told me that she read slowly and was a bad speller. Both of those claims were true, but they hardly prevented her from using her literacy to maintain Discourses of intimacy and disclosure.

Intimacy and Disclosure in English 12.   The writing that Katy produced in Ms. Allen's class was consistently written in either the first or second person, giving her work a conversational tone, almost as if she were intimately speaking with someone about her feelings. To illustrate, the piece of writing that follows is from an activity assigned in English 12 where students were to read poems from the Victorian poetry section in the British literature anthology. They were instructed to select several of the poems and to write a half-page essay on each, telling what the poem was saying and responding personally to the poem's meaning. The following is Katy's response to a Dante Rossetti sonnet, *Silent Noon.* The topic of the poem is a summer afternoon spent lounging silently in a field with a beloved. Here is Katy's response to *Silent Noon:*

> The thing I like about poetry is that you can make it mean whatever for you. This poem was awesome cause I saw it as. All that he talked about was the lovers together. The grass was there place together so forth and so on. My favorite part however is when it says, *"Your eyes smile peace."* [Italics added] I would fall for any man whose eyes smile peace. WOW!!

Most noticeable about the text is that the informality of Katy's language bears traces of the slang of her youth culture: "awesome cause"; "so forth and so on;" "WOW!" Her diction suggests speaking that is also manifest in the broken sentence—"This poem was awesome because I saw it as"—which is followed by the next sentence like an overrunning thought: "All that he talks about was the lovers together". Moreover, her reading of Rossetti is personalized and intimate, as she discloses to her reader, Ms. Allen, what she would do in love: "I would fall for any man whose eyes smile peace." As a social and relational practice, Katy's reading and writing about poetry are unabashed reports of feelings to someone who is assumed to be trustworthy, a social and relational practice that she uses also in other contexts.

Katy's Discourse of Intimacy and Disclosure in Nonschool Contexts

Katy used written language to make disclosures of her feelings in places other than Ms. Allen's class. As a devout Mormon, Katy had been writing in journals since she was 8-years-old. Journal keeping, she told me, is an everyday activity for Mormons, and journals are given to children on their eighth birthday. "I started doing it," she told me, "because Church gave it to me." The purpose of the record, ideally, is to leave a legacy of moral examples for one's progeny. However, Katy uses her journal for a variety of other purposes in addition to recording her activities as a Mormon. As an example, one of our interviews focused on how her journal-keeping practices had changed over the years. She brought to the interview a box full of journals to show me the various themes of her writing over the years. Covers and pages were labeled in towering letters with the things that had been important to her: FEELINGS, POEMS, ACTING, CHURCH, FAMILY, MEMORIES, MOVIES. Additionally, Katy presented me with copies of her favorite poems that she had written in her journal over the last year. She wrote poems in her journal when she would go to Temple Square. She described how she would find a place in the gardens or near a fountain and "start writing about my feelings until they became a poem." The poems that she gave to me to read were about her loneliness, her religious faith, boyfriends, and her lack of self-confidence.

To illustrate, the poem below was written on a gray December day when she was feeling lonely and depressed after a Thanksgiving when all of her brothers and sisters were elsewhere. Similar to the Discourse of crisis and esteem of English 12, the textual meanings in Katy's poem describe a crisis that is followed by a rescue. (This appearance of the crisis–rescue theme in Katy's poem is suggestive of the pervasiveness of the Discourse of crisis and esteem that I found in Katy's peer culture.[7])

Feeling

How do I feel I ask myself
I hate it what ever it is
I have lost my drug [Katy's metaphor for having lost her boyfriend]
I have kidded myself
I wish I could feel pretty
I wish I felt the way so
little people make me feel in my life.
Why can't I be thankful
for the talents, gifts, and opportunities
I have
Instead of wishing I have the
gifts that others have received
The quote goes "if I could give
you one gift it would be that
you would picture yourself as the
wonderful person I picture you as."
Why can't I believe it

---

[7]I found out from interviews with other high school students that this crisis–rescue narrative was ubiquitous, appearing in videos that were popular, such as *The Dead Poet's Society*, and *Rudy*; in counseling, programs that presented adolescent life as a state of crisis; and in Mormon Seminary, were it was emphasized that God will provide emotional and physical resources in a time of crisis. Seminary is a program that LDS students attend daily.

Because this is life and it
isn't fair. And my biggest trial
is to except myself for what
I am.
                                        —Katy K. Pederson

Katy's poem suggests that the relational practice is no longer contingent on a trusted adult to receive the poem. Here, Katy is supervising and disciplining her self. That is, she is both the child in crisis and the supervising adult. Notice, for example, the self-discipline that follows the admission of despair and self-pity: she writes down her feelings for observation ("How do I feel I ask myself"), examines them ("I have lost my drug / I have kidded myself / I wish I could feel pretty"), and then provides a disciplined response ("Why can't I … I must except myself for who I am").

The final text that I present further indicates that Katy's literacy practices are interdiscursive, sustained by textual, social, and relational practices in everyday contexts other than school. The entry was not written by Katy—it was written in Katy's journal by her mother, DeeAnn. Katy told me that her mother regularly reads and writes in Katy's journals. She discovered the following poem–letter a few weeks prior to becoming a case study participant. Katy introduced the poem by telling me about finding it in her journal:

> And I was going through my journal, and she had wrote this one thing to me, it's kind of like a letter. Or like a poem. And she wrote it to me, and uhm, just how cool it was for me. And all this time, that my mom would write in my journal, and years later, well not years, but she will write it on a page that I haven't got to yet. So I find it, and it's all over in there.

In the following is the entry that DeeAnn made in Katy's journal. When Katy gave me a copy of this poem, she also included a written explanation of what the poem meant to her: "I found this in my journal my mom often writes inspiring notes in my journal so I find them. So [it] heals me". Katy's written explanation underscores the theme of crisis and rescue, and also that the practice of using written language to disclose feelings and maintain intimate relationships of nurturing.

Katy,
Always remember that you are precious to many people you are well loved and needed.
Always remember you are never alone because Heavenly Father knows your feelings, your needs, your fears and what he wants you to become.
Always remember you are beautiful all of you.
Especially your eyes and your deep heart.

Always remember to laugh easily it will carry you on bumpy days.
Always remember to love many people.
Love them well and carefully here lies your Joy.
Always remember to breath and touch nature, it will remind you to be grateful
so you can see your great treasures.
Remember to Pray—So you can hear Father whispering guidance and
comfort.
Remember to use your imagination to Create magic for yourself and
others—see the fairies.
Remember the gospel is the true path your feet will always have a place to go.
Remember me, for you are always mine and I am ever yours!

—DeeAnn Pedersen (Mom)

The textual practices of this poem–letter point to the Discourse of intimacy.
The use of Katy as a salutation and DeeAnn's signature at the end emphasizes the personalized nature of this communication; the immanence of crisis and emotional setbacks in Katy's life is mitigated by the familial reference
to the deity as "Father"; and the repetition of the parallel structure of "Always remember" acquires the resonance of a mother comforting a troubled
child. These elements, furthermore, echo the social and relational practices
of a parent–teacher giving advice and comfort to the child–pupil (e.g., "you
are loved and important"; "the greatest beauty is inside"; "God is watching
out for you"; etc.)

My analysis suggests that Katy's literacy practices functioned as intimate
disclosures to construct and sustain relationships of loyalty and trust. However, not all of Katy's texts were pitched as intimately as the examples I have
presented here. Much of her classroom writing was hastily completed, she
told me, with little thought or feeling. Nevertheless, even in these texts Katy
would assume a stance of intimacy and disclosure by drawing on clichés and
commonplaces as a gesture toward applying the class reading to her life.
While studying *Macbeth*, for example, Katy wrote: "She got what was coming. Anyone who would do what she did deserves to suffer. I could never do
what she did." Literacy, for Katy, was concomitant with carrying out personal relationships by sharing her interpretations of the meaning of one's
life. What varied for her was the authenticity of intimacy and disclosure that
was dependent on her interpretation of the context.

Zeke Christiansen:
The Discourse of Entitlement and Authority

Zeke also is a member of a large Mormon family, the second to the youngest
of six children. He enjoyed a family tradition at Capital City High School:
His parents and his maternal grandparents graduated from Capital City

High. Moreover, his parents, who grew up in the same neighborhood, were introduced to each other by the LDS bishop. The two expectations in Zeke's family were that sons would serve a mission for the LDS church, and that all the children would attend college. Zeke told me, "That's a real big one for my parents, because neither of my parents have a college degree. And it's really rough on them, especially having six kids." He did admit that he would be likely to attend the community college for a year or so in order to improve his grades. The previous year, he had failed a math class and had withdrawn from honors English after earning a D as his semester grade.

Over the 9 months that I was in touch with Zeke, his career ambitions ranged from psychology—wanting to know how people learn and are motivated—to wanting to become a schoolteacher. He attributed his interest and motivation to Mr. Tyler, a teacher for whom Zeke served as an aide, taking roll, grading tests, and running video equipment. Mr. Tyler had been at Capital City High for many years, having taught Zeke's father and brothers. "He's uhm, kind of like another tradition in our family." Zeke described school as "kickback for me." His classes did not require much homework or writing. His schedule consisted of assisting Mr. Tyler, Mormon seminary, two drafting classes, a choir class, a weight-training class, and Ms. Allen's English class, which he told me was his hardest class—not in terms of difficult material, but because Ms. Allen assigned a lot of activities and tasks to complete.

Zeke was also active in the LDS church, particularly pursuing leadership roles in Mormon youth culture. He assured me that he would "be called" to go on a mission for the LDS Church.[8] Every Sunday he led a group of men—called the priesthood—in a hymn for his church. His friends at school were leaders in Seminary, a situation that caused pain for Zeke since he was passed over for one of the leadership positions—unjustly he explained to me—and was thus excluded from participating in the social activities, such as planning meetings, that were reserved for the Seminary Council. This exclusion was particularly painful because he was interested in dating one of the girls who had been appointed to the Seminary Council. This event haunted Zeke, even after his graduation. Almost a year later, I ran into Zeke on a Saturday afternoon near Temple Square in downtown Salt Lake City. We chatted about his attendance at the local community college and his plans to go on his mission. Eventually, he asked me if I remembered about the girl he liked. I nodded, yes. Then, in a turn of self-deprecating irony, he confided in me that she was now going out with one of his friends who had been appointed to the Seminary Leadership Council.

---

[8]At the time I am preparing this chapter, 18 months after I worked with Zeke, he has sent me an invitation to his missionary farewell. Many Mormon males, and a few females, are called (if they are found worthy by church leaders) to go on a 2-year mission, where they proselytize for the LDS church and work with the elderly and needy in LDS communities. Zeke was called to Bordeaux, France.

Authority and Entitlement in Journals and Notebooks.
Zeke, like Katy, used his writing to explore his feelings and experiences. He kept a journal and a notebook. He also received a journal at the age of eight so that he could keep a record of his life. His uses of his journal were not as personalized as Katy's: He made entries about the day's events such as girls that he talked to, scriptures that he had studied in seminary class, or mission farewells.[9] Although he usually noted what he was feeling, he did not use the journal for exploring his feelings. Given that Zeke intended the journal to be read by his progeny, I speculate that he did not want to include entries that betrayed his frustrations, confusions, and loneliness. For this, he used his notebook of lined white paper that Zeke could tear out. Often, his detailed explorations of his feelings were written as fictional accounts of disclosing his affections to a girl. Zeke also used the notebook to sort out his frustrations with his male friends. In these pieces an authoritative, sometimes bitter tone emerges, as Zeke judges and criticizes his friends:

> And so, as the sun sets on yet another day in my pitiful life, I sit back and ponder the relationships I have with other people. My friends all seem to be getting on my nerves a lot lately. Steve is so full of himself that he hardly takes time to look down his nose at me to have a meaningful conversation. I stop to think about why this is and I realize that it is because I have stopped being as passive with him as I normally am. Steve really does have a problem with people telling him what to do.

Zeke was aware of this judgmental tone in his writing, criticizing himself for failing to be a more forgiving person instead of feeling bitter and angry. Nevertheless, the social practice of using written language to criticize the behavior of others surfaced in other contexts and relationships, including English 12.

Entitlement and Authority in English 12.   In many of Zeke's English class texts, he also practiced his authority to criticize. The following is an excerpt from an essay assignment where the students were directed to write a one-page essay commenting on an aphorism Ms. Allen offered the class: "The age of chivalry is never past, so long as there is a wrong left unredressed on earth." In his essay, Zeke assumes an authoritative stance as he defines and then criticizes the ethics of male–female relationships:

---

[9] A mission farewell is a send-off, held at the local Mormon church (called a ward house) for the young man or woman who is leaving home.

Common courtesy and politeness have taken the place of what is known as chivalry. I believe that in all of us is enough caring and love that keeps chivalry alive today. I know that when I see a lady, young or more mature, walking to a door or carrying something, I have an urge to try and help her but I am beat by another guy. I know that in some case I purposely don't help out a damsel in distress because then feelings are created by either side that mean trouble. I'm sure that these truths hold true inmost all cases. When people say that chivalry is dead it's because they expect everything done for them. Then when something is done for them they either fall in love with whomever did the good deed or they expect that person to [do] more and more. So in only some cases, chivalry is dead to those whom exploit nice guys into slave or someone to hassle about supposed love!

Zeke often developed this topic into a theme of the unfairness of romance and dating. Girls he liked either did not return his affections, or else there were interfering circumstances, such as another boyfriend. Zeke's concerns with romance and dating were particularly linked to his ambitions for a leadership role in Mormon youth culture. Being appointed by the adults in charge to a leadership role on the Seminary Council would have enhanced Zeke's status. Indeed, he saw himself as a chivalrous person who understood and followed the ethical codes for Mormon leadership, and as thus entitled to be a leader. However, because he was passed over, he believed that he was less attractive to the females he wanted to date. These themes—of injury, unfairness, and his entitlement to assume a position of leadership and attraction—play out in Zeke's textual, social, and relational practices in the context of his peer group and Seminary class.

Authority and Entitlement in the Seminary Class.   Z e k e ' s description of his reading and writing practices in his Seminary class indicate that there too he used written language to practice his authority. In this context, the authoritative uses of literacy were displayed and directed by the Seminary teacher. Seminary teachers—who go by Brother Clark or Sister Allen—highlight key verses for discussion and activities. For example, while studying verses from *The Book of Mormon* related to the creation, Zeke told me they were directed to make a clay human figure and then write down "where it lived, what it does, what it eats, what it does to protect itself." Zeke's studies of his scriptures were also guided by an LDS curriculum called Scripture Masters. In the interview excerpt that follows, notice the themes of authority in Zeke's description: Leaders of the LDS Church have designated the scriptures worthy of study, and through studying these, a young man—and some young women—may be worthy enough to be called to serve the LDS Church on a mission.

In the four years that we are here [in seminary] we study the Book of Mormon, the Doctrines and Covenants and [LDS] Church history, the New Testament and the Old Testament. In each of the four of those there are 25 scriptures that the leaders of the [LDS] Church have set aside for us to memorize as best we can. And it helps us out when we are on our mission and, uhm, just whenever, so we know more about the Church. It just kind of stresses the basics and the groundwork of the Church. It doesn't get into the deep and dark things.

Zeke's social practices consist of using religious texts when he is having troubles or when something is bothering him. "Like if I am having trouble overcoming different things, like against the standards of the Church." Related to this, a recurring theme in the verses Zeke showed and explained to me were accounts of God providing strength to overcome adversity. "Like there's one scripture that says the Lord won't put anything on us, won't test us with anything, won't give us any trial that we can't overcome whether by ourselves or with his help. So that helps me a lot." Some of these key scriptures that he showed to me were illustrated with color pictures that he had glued into the binding of the text. The pictures were, Zeke indicated, LDS Church illustrations of an important event in Mormon history. One illustration depicted a man with a thin leather headband, in a robe and sandals, standing on a wall high over a tumultuous, angry crowd. The man, a prophet of God, was attempting to speak to the crowd but archers were attempting to kill him. Zeke told me that this illustrated the power of God to protect the righteous from the wicked.

Forging School and Church Discourses.   These excerpts illustrate the imbrication of Zeke's textual, social and relational practices. First, Zeke's textual practices focused on themes of the ethics of friendships, the unjustness of power and love, and the promise of God to reward the righteous. Second, his social practices consisted of using these themes to organize and evaluate his frustrated experiences with dating and competition for leadership roles. Specifically, his social practice entailed using written language to develop and rehearse his opinions about the others in his social world, opinions that he derived from authoritative texts (i.e., the words of Mormon leaders), *The Bible* and *The Book of Mormon*, and his Seminary and Sunday School lessons. And third, Zeke's relational practice was a matter of participating in a social network that constructed young males as future civic and spiritual leaders. More specifically at stake for Zeke in terms of his relational practices, was the esteemed and status denied to him when he was passed over for a leadership position on the Seminary Council. To secure this position in his social network, he believed, would increase his currency within the social network of dating and romance.

While I was conducting this research, Zeke's desire to have his authority and entitlement recognized was fulfilled. In the early months of the school year, a controversy arose in one of the honors English classes concerning a textbook. The controversy concerned the depiction of a rape scene in a novel, to which a dozen students from the class protested being assigned to read. Though Zeke was not a member of the honors class, he had strong opinions, especially since the protesting students were peers from his church community. The controversy received considerable attention from local newspapers and television news programs, and Zeke participated by sending the following letter to the high school newspaper:

Students Shouldn't Have to Read Offensive Literature

I would like to address the issue of *The House of Spirits*, by Isabel Allende. My issue deals with the fact that students should have to read this book.

I understand that the ideas behind the book are to introduce students to different cultures, but whose culture does rape belong to? How are students supposed to learn about culture in details of rape and sex and other offending issues that are represented in the book. It is one thing to tell of a rape, but another to describe it in full and unabridged detail.

Another point to be made includes the argument that the ten students should not be able to change the curriculum of *their* [italics added] English class. Why is that the students cannot stand up for what they believe in?

In the past, single students have been able to change the curriculum because they were offended. Why is this case any different?

—Zeke Christiansen

Zeke's letter appeared in the school paper on a Friday, and on the following Sunday it was read aloud in the Young Women's meeting in the Mormon church he attended. At last, Zeke found himself in the limelight he sought, praised as an exemplary young man in his Mormon community, and particularly within the context of the girls' Sunday School meeting. As Zeke told me the following week, "Well, the girls in the Young Women's, their leader read it, and she brought it into class and made everybody read it. And so it kind of made me a celebrity at church."

This event illustrates several points about Zeke's textual, social and relational practices in terms of Discourse and interdiscourse. First, Zeke's letter enables him to galvanize his status in the Discourse of LDS youth culture. And unique to his practice is a strategic quality of how he uses written language to achieve his ends. By strategic, I mean that he achieves his goal (to gain recognition) by choosing to write about an issue that was not an immediate concern of his (he was not a member of the class) but that did have currency within the social network of his Mormon community. Related to this strategy—of using literacy in one context and gaining status in a different context, is the interdiscursivity of this event. First of all, the relational impact of the letter secures Zeke's social status in two separate contexts. His esteem is secured at both school and at church, most specifically among the young women. Second, Zeke applies to a school issue the textual and social practices he identifies with his LDS community. Or, in other words, Zeke draws on the practices of his social network as a male in Mormon youth culture in order to make sense and use of the social world in his classroom and school, assuming the stance of a person authorized to observe and evaluate the ethics and choices of others. Zeke's literacy, thus, is powerfully validated in the social context of his church relations.

A RADICAL CONCLUSION

radical: 1. of, relating to, or proceeding from a root; 2. marked by considerable departure from the usual or traditional.

As a conclusion to this chapter, I offer several considerations for social views of literacy. As the epigraph indicates, what I offer is somewhat radical. Although a social view of literacy, currently, is hardly a radical stance, I think that my findings do extend, in radical ways, thinking about social approaches to literacy and high school English. I organize these following remarks by the two meanings in the epigraph. First, I consider the social as the root of literacy, and second, I develop the implications of these remarks as I consider a departure from the usual or traditional in secondary school language arts classes.

In this chapter, I have sought to extend the social root of literacy to include social and relational practices as meaningful. Borrowing Gee's (1996) definition of literacy as Discourse, I have illustrated that people use written language to participate in a meaningful social formation. Furthermore, if part of the root of literacy is making meaning of one's social world, then, I have argued, textual meaning–making extends to the extratextual meanings of social networks and identity kits. Katy's and Zeke's ways of using written language, for example, were contingent on their interpretation of who they are (identity kit) in relation to their community (social network). The textual meanings each made of their writing and reading topics (romance, chivalry, depression, censorship) are nested in the meanings each holds for who she or he are in relation to her or his communities. This is to say, then, that the textual meanings are contingent on the meanings a person makes–holds for the social and relational practices he or she is engaging.

This argument decenters print language as the exclusive tool for making meaning and brings in focus the meanings people make of literacy practices. This view opens new ways to think about learning as a social activity and about classrooms as social environments. Classroom Discourses, such as English 12 for example, teach not only textual meanings about social life, but also the ways in which texts are used to carry out a particular form of social life. This view can enable us to analyze literacy practices as social genres and to evaluate the social ends and meanings of those genres. With this critical perspective, we can ask, for example, whether The Failure Essay teaches the textual, social, and relational practices and meanings that we want to foster.

My second set of radical comments concerns pedagogical implications of this view, particularly for high school language arts. Unfortunately, my analysis of the textual, social, and relational practices of The Failure Essay offers a negative example. Nevertheless, I believe that by analyzing classroom Discourse, we can begin to build a positive model. The key problem that I find underpinning the practices of English 12 is not so much the view that students are at risk, but rather the assumption about what kind of a social network should be provided to them as an intervention. In this case, the teacher and students were positioned in a network of emotional supervision, which supported the reading and writing practices of the Discourse of crisis and esteem. Specifically, literature was selected that could be used as a mirror in which students could reflect on the positive meaning of their life, which were then submitted to the supervising adult in a practice that conflated literacy with the essential self.

In this case, then, the uses of written language do not have currency beyond the social and relational practices with which students are already familiar. My point is conveyed by New London Group (1996), who argued that, given the ever increasing diversification and fragmentation of English-speaking countries, "full social participation" necessitates a "pedagogy of multiliteracies" (New London Group, pp. 60–61). Literacy education should prepare students to "interact effectively … with multiple languages, multiple English's, and communication patterns that more frequently cross cultural, community and national boundaries" (p. 64). English 12, I find, is an example of pedagogy and curriculum that effectively denies the conditions that the New London Group argues are immanent. Moreover, both Katy and Zeke, I also find, were able to appropriate English 12 to maintain rather than expand their interactions with other kinds of Discourse.

As I mentioned previously, the problematic key that my analysis indicates is the assumption about the social network in which student writing is to be practiced. What might happen, then, if English teachers were to imagine different kinds of contexts for using literacy in which students were to participate and learn? Such a line of questioning could lead away (and should, I argue) from traditional textual, social, and relational practices of high school English, such as they are represented by this case study. One point from which to proceed could begin by asking: What are the purposes of the uses of written language in a classroom? What social networks do these purposes presuppose? What purposes for using written language do students already know? What social networks do they already know how to participate in with written language? Such a line of questioning would be the first step toward designing curriculum that aims to guide students to study and learn the practices of new Discourses.

One way to illustrate my idea is to consider a literacy assignment that would create a different kind of classroom Discourse. While I was at the high school collecting this data, a Jewish student filed a lawsuit against the choir teacher for proselytizing in the class with music sacred to Mormons. The school and the community were inundated with texts about the issue—student letters in the student paper, letters from parents in the local papers, television news accounts, and newspaper editorials. Not surprisingly, the issue was hotly debated with little illumination of the definitions, principles, and assumptions about religious freedom, religious persecution, and civic life. And ironically, despite this flurry of literate activity in the community (which was, by the way, about the social world of the high school students) the topic was suppressed throughout the classrooms at Capital City High School. I suggest, however, that such a situation afforded an opportunity for students to study and practice a variety of Discourses. Students could be studying and writing in genres for various audiences (e.g., the school board and the city council) as well as writing in more traditional expository argument. Such a curriculum would, additionally, go beyond studying the textual meanings of arguments to include exploring how arguments are linked to social networks that are different forms of cultural and historical life experiences.

Finally, my analysis and example suggest an additional radical implication: A decentering of literary texts as exclusive in the secondary school language arts classroom. That is, a pedagogy that takes a view of literacy as Discourses and social practices would need to present students with opportunities to study and practice using texts other than literary genres. This is a particularly problematic implication, especially considering how crowded the literature curriculum has become with the struggle to included noncanonical and multicultural texts. Nevertheless, I argue for a language arts curriculum and pedagogy that is somewhat less about literature as Art and somewhat more about the art of using written language in new and unfamiliar Discourses.

In conclusion, I offer an appeal to those who find themselves to be critical of my proposal to decenter literature as the only text for literacy learning in high school English classes. If I understand the canon wars correctly, one of the issues is that literature furnishes students with cultural exemplars, that is, it furnishes readers with an interpretive lens for organizing experience and making ethical choices.[10] Guiding students to participate in new Discourses, I think, can profoundly engage students in using literacy to practice ethics. Rather than assigning students to make ethical textual meanings, we could teach students to make texts that have ethical effects. In other words, I advocate a rhetorical curriculum, one that uses literacy not only for the development and transmission of learning, but that uses written language as a social transaction that can organize and shape a person's everyday world. I do not think using written language in a classroom for social transactions other than the student displaying personalized interpretations of literature to the teacher is, finally, that radical. After all, Katy and Zeke were already using written language in their everyday lives to construct, maintain, and negotiate robust social relationships. My hope is that taking into account the everyday practices of students, school, and community can help us develop opportunities for students to use written language to engage and negotiate constructively with what they find to be unfamiliar.

---

[10]This assumption is shared by such odd bedfellows as Bloom in *The Closing of the American Mind* (1987) and Giroux in *Schooling and the Struggle for Public Life* (1988).

11

The Education of African-American Youth: Literacy Practices and Identity Representation in Church and School

Michelle M. Kelly
State University of New York at Cortland

LITERACY AND CULTURAL CONSCIOUSNESS

A group of six adolescent, African-American males sit in a circle in the multipurpose room of their Baptist church. Each holds a traditional African Jimbe drum between his knees. They gather together on the sunny, late winter, Saturday afternoon for a common purpose—a lesson in African drumming. All eyes turn to their instructor, an African-American man named Erik, who stands in their circle behind a tall Congo drum. Erik talks with the group about the role of drums in African-American culture:

> Drums are part of your culture. During slavery time they took all of these drums away and the only place that people had to gather together was in churches.... But they couldn't drum. Drumming is part of everything. But what they did instead of drumming; what they did was like hand clappin' and singin.' That's what they still do in churches today. When you hear somebody hand clappin', sometimes that hand clappin' is [these drums].

The boys involved in this drumming lesson learn different rhythms, call-and-response patterns, and the history and tones of the Congo and Jimbe drums, as well as the role of drums in African and African-American

239

culture. At the end of their lesson, Erik points out the importance of their session in the church basement:

> Well, now you gonna have the drums back in your church. Hopefully one day you'll be able to play good enough to be upstairs in the church, not just upstairs, but everywhere else too.

This lesson taught much more than patterns of rhythm. It helped these young African-American males understand their culture's connection to the drums and how the drums can still be found in the church today through hand clapping. Erik, the drumming instructor, viewed their ability to bring drums back into the church service as coming full circle as he stressed the importance of the youths' connections with the drums to their history and to their culture.

Through the lesson, the youths' historical and cultural understandings of what it means to be African American were strengthened and deepened. One might think of Erik's instructor role in this context as similar to the traditional African story teller, or *griot*, for he provided insight and introspection into some of the routine practices that occur in church, such as hand clapping. Erik helped the youth read part of their diaspora literacy by teaching them to "recognize the cultural signs of a past" (Busia, 1989, p. 197) and to understand the "vital importance of those traditions that carry meaning and history" (Busia, 1989, p. 204). Through the narratives shared during the drumming lesson, Erik showed the youth how they could reclaim their stories in a contemporary context. The teachings described in this drumming lesson were typical of what the youth experienced in church-sponsored activities.

PURPOSE OF THE CHAPTER

In this chapter, I present instances of how particular literacy events[1] in and out of school served to open up opportunities for development of a strong sense of historical and cultural identity as an African American. I describe and interpret literacy events at two sites.[2] The first is a set of church–community-based activities consisting of an African drumming group, an African-American dance troupe, and a Saturday School. This supplementary

---

[1]Literacy event is a phrase borrowed from Moss (1994b).

[2]As suggested by O'Brien, Moje, and Stewart (chap. 2, this volume), an expansion of the traditional notions of classroom and school is called for to include the literacy learning and practices that occur in sites such as home, church, and community organizations. Historically, these are rarely acknowledged in traditional school settings.

school is designed to support the academic content of the public school with tutoring and to enhance it with activities grounded in African and African-American history and culture. The second site is a public middle school, with a focus on English classes and extracurricular activities.

After describing some of the literacy events that take place during Sunday services and youth activities at church, I move to a case study of one young adolescent male involved in activities that use print forms of literacy in both Saturday School and his public school. This chapter aims to complicate traditional understandings of identity and literacy and to discuss multiple forms of culturally significant literacy practices as they relate to the identity practices of African-American youth. In addition, in the case study I specifically want to draw attention to the types of literacy practices that help one particular student claim a space for himself as a cultural being.

The following research questions guided the design of this chapter and analysis of data:

1. How are constructions of literacy framed in the different sites of participation?
2. What are the kinds of literacy practices that foster a positive sense of identity?
3. In what ways does this identity engender empowerment in African-American youth?

RESEARCHING LITERACY PRACTICES IN MULTIPLE COMMUNITIES

The data reported in this chapter were collected over the course of 1 year. Methods for data collection included participant observation; audiotaped formal and informal interviews with students, teachers, and community leaders; artifacts and documents; and videotaping.

For 3 1/2 years before this study was conceptualized, I worked with youth of all ages in a computer lab housed in Central City Baptist Church which has a predominantly African-American congregation and is located in Salt Lake City, Utah. The goal of the computer lab was to provide all church members—but especially the youth—opportunity and access to computers for their schoolwork, games, and word processing. During the last 6 months of my time spent in the computer lab, I also participated as a teacher in a church-based Saturday School program. One of the primary goals of the Saturday School program was to enhance traditional school subjects such as language arts, math, science, and history with an African-American perspective.

As part of the study, I attended all sessions of Saturday School for 1 year, and I continued to volunteer there for another 2 years after the completion of the study. Through the Saturday School I met students involved in the African drumming group and the African-American dance troupe. Some of these students became participants in this study.

Purposeful sampling—of a sort—was used to identify eight middle and junior high school age students as potential case study participants (Patton, 1990). The director of the Saturday School and I worked together to identify a pool of students as potential study participants. As we discussed students enrolled in Saturday School and looked over their files, we identified some students who were, for instance, academically successful; some who were not; some who were outgoing; and some who were not. All but one of the students identified were interested in participating in the study. I made it a point to introduce myself personally to each child's parent—their mother in all cases—in a face-to-face encounter. Each mother was enthusiastic about having her child participate. Most commented that they felt it would be a good opportunity for their children to express themselves. Because I had talked with the youth to get a sense of their interest before talking to their parents, several mothers also told me that their children seemed very excited about participating. Anthony, a pseudonym, whose case will be shared later in this chapter, was one of five Saturday School students who participated in the study. He was also a member of the African drumming group and the African-American dance troupe.

The years spent working with youth in the computer lab, my work as a Saturday School teacher, and my membership in the church enabled me to observe the practice sessions and several public performances of the African-American dance troupe and the African drumming groups. In addition to observing and participating in Saturday School, church services and other functions, I attended all public school classes and extracurricular activities with each student for 2 full weeks of 1 academic year. Students participated in three individual formal interviews; one of which was autobiographical. In addition to the interviews, I gave each student a small tape recorder and a supply of tapes so they could audiotape any thoughts they wanted to share with me outside of the interview structure.[3] All Saturday School teachers and each of the students' public school teachers, as well as school administrators, support staff, and church leaders were formally interviewed at least once.

---

[3]For a variety of reasons, student-generated tapes failed to be a successful form of data collection in this study. For example, one of Anthony's younger brothers, Charles, borrowed the tape recorder without Anthony's permission one day, took it to elementary school and played the tape for his classmates. The teacher overheard, and Charles, the tape recorder, and the tape ended up in the principal's office due to some of the language contained on the tape. This resulted in a school conference with Charles and his mother and the disappearance of the tape recorder.

I followed theoretical perspectives that highlighted the value of Afrocentric and culturally-based literacy practices (Asante, 1988, 1991; Busia, 1989; Gordon, 1993; King, 1992; King & Mitchell, 1990; Shujaa, 1994; Street, 1984, 1994a; Woodson, 1933). These perspectives allowed me to analyze the literacy practices of African-American youth in the many contexts of their everyday lives. I deconstructed these practices at the microlevel for instances of identity empowerment as an African-American in school and church. As adults in both contexts shared their perceptions of youth, distinct differences between the school personnel and church activity leaders emerged. These differences led me to problematize current conceptions of risk that are used in most public school contexts.

AT RISK: BY WHOSE DEFINITION AND IN WHAT CONTEXT?

Schools are often presented as isolated and autonomous structures that impact children's identities and successes. Much of the at-risk literature, as well as the current educational agenda of the federal government, emphasizes that each child must start school ready to learn. This rhetoric reflects a contemporary rephrasing of the cultural deficit position dating back to the 1960s (Fine, 1990, 1995; Lubeck & Garrett, 1990; Margonis, 1992; Swadener & Lubeck, 1995). For instance, Taylor (1987) posited that scholars studying racial issues have been mainly interested in the deprivation of the African-American community and its consequences. The underlying thought suggests that for some children the only learning that occurs in their lives is what happens at school, negating the rich cultural and community understandings all children bring to school.

In reality, the school is but one site of learning children encounter in their lives. The cultures of home, church, and community have a tremendous impact on the identity development of children and the literacy practices encountered in these sites. McLaughlin, Irby, and Langman (1994) and Heath and McLaughlin (1993) suggested that effective youth organizations offer many youth who are considered at risk the opportunities to achieve and maintain a sense of self that the public schools do not. In order to get a picture of African-American students in successful situations, these scholars suggest that we need to study children's participation in community organizations.

Just as children's school experiences cannot be separated from the rest of their lives, neither can family, church, or community experiences be viewed in isolation. Each context has expectations about who, what, and how children should be. The literacy practices associated with each community may be distinctly different on the surface but they are mutually constituted. By this I mean that a literacy event or practice does not occur in isolation: what is learned at home, church, or school has implications for what occurs in each of the other contexts. For instance, Anthony, whose case study is presented in this chapter, learned at a Sunday Service that his church pastor would visit South Africa, so he chose to use South Africa as the focus of his "Where in the World Is Carmen San Diego?" project for English class. A study of any learning context in isolation obscures how children mediate the interactions between and within multiple contexts to create and maintain a sense of self. In light of this position, the literacy practices presented here are described in two separate and culturally distinct contexts—church and school—but these contexts are examined in light of their intersections as well as their disjunctures. The following section examines the different world views in each context. The collective experience as it is conceptualized in Afrocentrism is foregrounded in activities at Central City Baptist.

INDIVIDUALISM AND AFROCENTRIC CONCEPTIONS OF COLLECTIVISM: DIFFERENT WORLD VIEWS IN CHURCH AND SCHOOL

In 1933, Woodson stated that the purpose of the American education project for African Americans was the maintenance of a status quo that suppresses them. "If you can control a man's thinking you do not have to worry about his action" (Woodson, 1933, pp. 84–85). One way schools are able to do this is by fostering and perpetuating the Eurocentric perspectives of rugged individualism and meritocracy. Both of these concepts privilege individual understandings or experiences over those of the group. This individual perspective flies in the face of Afrocentricity, which is described by Asante (1988, 1991, 1992) as the belief in a collective experience and in the centrality of Africans in postmodern history. The Afrocentric emphasis is on a collective, rather than an individual, will. Because schooling in the United States does not reflect such a perspective, the process perpetuates the existing power relations in society.

Asante has argued that "the emphasis on schooling and the de-emphasis on education have crippled the African American community. What is necessary is an orientation to knowledge that puts noble obligations ahead of material values" (1994, p. 395). Schooling, as described by Shujaa (1994) "is a process intended to perpetuate and maintain the society's existing power relations and the institutional structures that support these arrangements" (p. 15). Education, in contrast, is the process of transmitting the cultural codes, mores, and practices from one generation to the next (Shujaa, 1994). The activities carried out at Central City Baptist emphasize education over schooling and strive for a connectedness between all participants.

For example, the drumming lesson illustrated in the vignette at the beginning of this chapter makes such connections. Young drummers work to synchronize rhythms with each other, to connect with each other in the here-and-now, and to understand how the drums connect them with their ancestors. The patterns for learning in church are grounded in observation and experience, and patterns of teaching are active and physical. They are not confined to the traditional methods of the public schools. Youth and adults are encouraged to work interdependently and not at cross-purposes. Youth activities at church are structured to emphasize cooperation over competition, and the idea of mutual responsibility or helping each other out is valued. Most importantly, the culture of the learner is foregrounded and used as an avenue to connect with participants, whether through Sunday sermons or youth activities. This is not to say that Eurocentric perspectives did not exist in the context of the church. Both Eurocentric and Afrocentric perspectives shaped the types of literacy practices and texts used in the church and the school. The following section lays out the conception of literacy used in this study, broadly conceived as literacy for empowerment. This conception of literacy is grounded in a specific cultural context and includes two aspects: literacy as inherently connected to orality and diaspora literacy.

LITERACY AS A TOOL OF EMPOWERMENT

The notion that learners develop literacy practices for use in particular social contexts has strong support (see Gadsden, 1995; Heath, 1983; Moll, 1994; Street, 1994a; Taylor, 1989). Knowledge of practices that are relevant and understood in certain social contexts allow one to participate more fully in the events taking place in that context. Literacy as a tool of empowerment opens up possibilities for access and full participation in the social, political, and economic benefits of society (Slaughter-Defoe & Richards, 1995).

Literacy, as used in this chapter, is broadly conceived and considered in the context of its ability to empower youth in such a way that one's cultural and racialized identity is brought to the fore in positive ways. It refers specifically to the skills and representational signs that further the cultural and historical understandings of what it means to be a person of African descent living in the United States. As a tool of empowerment, the literacy practices described here helped to situate the individual as a member of a collective.

Literacy practices have the potential for personal empowerment and liberation when the practices are used to help individuals understand their own histories and cultural practices within communities.

Ladson-Billings (1992a) argued that literacy should be used as a liberatory tool and that literacy should be understood as a political act. The position that literacy is ultimately political has been similarly argued by Street (1984). He suggested that the practices and concepts we refer to as literacy in this society are "already embedded in an ideology and cannot be isolated or treated as 'neutral' or merely 'technical'" (p. 1). Street (1994a) termed this an 'ideological' model of literacy that "recognizes a multiplicity of literacies [and] that the meaning and uses of literacy practices are related to specific cultural contexts ... " (p. 139). In the public educational system in the United States, literacy is often understood as politically and culturally neutral and most commonly understood to encompass the skills of reading and writing. Traditional conceptions of literacy are usually limited to forms of print. In the context of the African-American church described in this study, however, print forms of literacy are minimized in many of the congregational and youth activities; yet there is evidence of literacy events involved in these activities—particularly literacy for empowerment of identity as described above.

Orality and Literacy
in the African-American Church

The drumming lesson involved neither reading nor writing in the traditional sense. Instead, the teaching style reflected the orality of African-American culture. The practices at Central City Baptist are similar to what Moss (1994b) found in her study of African-American preachers' sermons. In this study, I found that the use of written text was minimized. One or two verses of scripture at most, and often only a short phrase of a verse, served as the topic of sermons. Six of the eight pages in the bulletin contained the same information each week. The remaining two pages were updated as needed to offer brief announcements, a list of those in need of prayer, monthly wedding anniversaries, and scripture verses. Each service included one responsorial reading that represented the most formalized instance of textual reading at the service. Hymn books were available but most members knew the songs and did not need them. The other aspects of services, such as the sermon and call to Christian service, reflected an oral emphasis. This oral emphasis, again similar to Moss (1994b) findings, reflected an active participatory mode either through the dialogic call-and-response patterns or other forms of conversation. The majority of teaching and learning at this church occurs from and through an oral–aural mode.

What took place in many of the activities at church such as the drumming lesson, dance practice, and sermons made use of orality that is traditionally considered a nonliterate practice (Gee, 1994). I want to suggest that the understandings that the youth gained about their own cultural and historical identity from these activities informed and created an interest in pursuing these issues of African-American identity in the more traditional forms of literate practices—reading and writing. Moreover, the academic privileging of reading and writing as constituting acts of literacy may serve to devalue the contemporary and historical practices highly esteemed as representations of knowledge in other social contexts. In the African-American church in this study, there are many orally performed events on which literacy is dependent. Thus, whereas literacy is highly valued by the church community, in many instances it is integrally connected to orality.

Taylor (1989) argued that we should seek to understand the complexity of literacy behaviors:

> And our tasks as educators is to use these understandings to support and enhance children's learning opportunities, guiding them in both direct and indirect ways as they develop personal understandings of literacy that are both socially constructed and individually situated in the practical accomplishments of their everyday lives. (p. 186)

The idea that literacy practices are situated in particular social contexts is supported by Moll (1994). Literacy, for Moll (1994), is embedded in funds of knowledge that he described as essential information and strategies necessary to keep a household running smoothly. Central City Baptist Church is a social structure with particular practices and understandings or funds of knowledge that are carried out to help maintain its well-being. Much of that well-being is grounded in the preservation and support of the local African-American community and culture. Literacy practices are embedded in a social matrix and the types of literacy practices in a particular context cannot be neatly separated from the exchange of knowledge in that context. For this reason, literacy events in the African-American community should be expanded to include both interactions with print and traditions of orature. Ladson-Billings (1992a) also argued for "a broad conception of literacy that incorporates both literature and orature" (p. 387) in classrooms. This would enable African-American youth to participate in literacy practices in school that make sense to them and that connect with forms of orature they experience in church.

Diaspora Literacy

The drumming lesson provides an example of what Ladson-Billings (1992) described as "the existence of an African connection and consciousness (p. 379)" and, as such, increased the cultural and historical literacy of the youth involved in it. This literacy event became a liberatory tool as well a tool of empowerment. As a literacy event, it helped youth to make sense of the everyday practices in their cultural and spiritual lives and to situate those practices historically. Literacy, in this sense, helped to inform a sense of self and to shape identities.

Busia (1989) described "diaspora literacy" as a perspective on literacy that involves "an ability to read a variety of cultural signs of the lives of Africa's children at home and in the New World" (Busia, 1989, p. 197; see also Clark, 1991). To develop a sense of diaspora literacy "is to be able to see again the fragments that make up the whole, not as isolated individual and even redundant fragments, but as part of a creative and sustaining whole" (Busia, 1989, p. 197). Moreover, this perspective on literacy enables people to communicate or make representations using cultural signs. Diaspora literacy has the potential to aid the development of one's cultural knowledge and consciousness (King & Mitchell, 1990).

From my standpoint as researcher, the drumming lesson was a profound example of the power of diaspora literacy. The lesson was grounded in the everyday interests of the students—their drumming and learning new rhythms. It moved beyond basic skills to cultural and historical relevancy. The instructor helped the youth understand how African drumming connects to the experiences of enslaved Africans claiming a space for themselves through spiritual practices and to hand clapping, which continues to thrive in the church. The youth were connected to the drums in ways much larger than African drumming's contemporary popularity. The representations offered provided potential for increasing the students' cultural and critical consciousness as people of African descent.

The work that went on with youth in the African drumming group is just one example of the use of orature as part of literacy events and of diaspora literacy in the Black Baptist Church. The pastor's Sunday sermons routinely made connections to the topic or scripture for the day through use of personal stories about his growing up years on a small farm in the South. These connections served several purposes. The pastor's boyhood stories would always be met with "Amen", "Say it! Say it!", and heads nodding in agreement. The stories provided the older members the opportunity to publicly recognize their shared historical experiences. For the youth, the stories told the history of a recent past—one never found in their history or literature books at school. No matter where the church's older members had done their own growing up, the pastor's stories held the seeds of a diaspora literacy that allowed each person to make connections on some level and to reinforce their collective identity as African-Americans.

Learning to Read the Diaspora Experience in Dance Class.

The African-American dance troupe is another youth organization that, similar to the drumming group, worked to help youth develop a sense of diasporan identity. Much of the music used by the dance troupe had a political message. Renee, the troupe's founder and artistic director, was an accomplished artist in her own right and taught the meaning within each piece of music. If there were lyrics, she helped the dancers understand the historical and political message embedded in them. Each movement in dance had significance. Many of the dance moves themselves were a metaphor reflecting some aspect of the Black struggle in the United States and Africa. Renee pushed each dancer to understand what their bodies represented in each dance and then to clearly articulate that with their bodies in performance. Renee described her goals for the dance troupe in a letter introducing the project:

> It is my belief that the administration of these programs will enlighten the African American students of their history and enhance their public school education, as well as provide them the opportunity to excel in their education. It will also protect their identities through active involvement and participation.

Similar to dance groups described by Ball and Heath (1993), Renee worked to create a sense of community identity and connectedness for the youth in the dance troupe. She used dance practice as a time to teach youth, through the use of orature, about their histories, and she often shared her own personal stories about coming to know herself as an African-American. "I had to leave Utah to learn what it meant to be an African American. I didn't know anything about my history or my people until I went to college in Kansas." Renee often reminded the dancers of this when she worked with them and told them that she was teaching them all she knew so that they would know "who they are" while they were still young, and the message was not lost on the youth. Whenever we discussed some aspect of African-American history in Saturday School, someone would invariably state that "Miss Renee said she didn't know anything about her history until she went to college" in such a way that indicated a sense of pride in what the youth were learning at a young age. Through dance, lyrics, and story Renee created a space for youth to begin to make meaning in their own lives through diaspora literacy.

Studying the Diaspora Experience in Saturday School.
In many ways the structure of Saturday School paralleled that of the public school. Students were grouped according to age in classes and each class had its own team of teachers. Traditional print forms of literacy were used more in Saturday School than in any other youth activity at church but they were usually incorporated as parts of a larger project. Additionally, one of the Saturday School's goals was to reinforce skills learned in public school so activities involving reading and writing were a standard part of the Saturday School curriculum. The actual content of the curriculum differed from public school because lessons centered around the African and African-American experience. Helping youth develop positive identities as African-Americans was an important component of Saturday School because the teachers knew this was not happening in the public schools.

For example, the middle school through senior high school students studied African-American pioneers in Utah. Their exploration began with a visit to the genealogy library in downtown Salt Lake City where youth learned about the process involved in searching their ancestry. This included how to search county records, plantation records, and Freedman's Bureau records. They learned how searches would differ if an ancestor was a free person of African-American heritage or a slave. Students spent time looking up some of their more recent ancestors on the computerized genealogical programs and researching historical texts for information about African-American pioneers in Utah. Students used the research skills they learned in school but in a new way. It was the first time any of the youth used original historical documents in their research. They used these historical documents to research selected pioneers and to write reports about them.

During a field trip to the Utah Historical Society, the docents showed students antique photographs of African-Americans in Utah. The class borrowed a video called *Blacks in Utah* from the society. Students practiced their note-taking skills while they viewed the film and had a discussion about it afterward. Several church members' ancestors were descendants of pioneers portrayed in the film. This led to students setting up videotaped interviews with several of these church members, developing questions, and leading interviews.

This Saturday School project incorporated multiple methods to reinforce skills valued for academic success and to teach youth about the history of African-Americans in the state. The project used traditional forms of print literacy but also incorporated literacy for empowerment with the use of orature through the stories told in interviews and diaspora literacy in helping the youth discover a history of African Americans in the state that they never knew existed. When I asked the class what they learned in Saturday School, Anthony replied:

That thing we did on Black history in Utah. You know, I learned a lot. I didn't know so much about that but I could actually relate to it.

Through activities such as the drumming group, the dance troupe, and Saturday School, youth leaders in the church actively strived to create a community where youth had opportunities to engage in a variety of literacy activities. Youth education was a high priority activity in the church. Education that offered possibilities for the development of a positive sense of self and history as African-American was valued as much as education that brought traditional academic success. Interestingly, none of the public school teachers involved in this study was aware of the African drumming group, the African-American dance troupe, or the Saturday School. Nor were they aware of the extent to which the youth in the case studies were involved in church and other culturally relevant activities. This meant that it was up to the youth in this study to make connections between the two contexts of church and school. In the next section, I use a case study to describe some of the ways one young male brought together what he learned through church and school literacy practices.

CONSTRUCTING ANTHONY:
BUDDING SCHOLAR AT CHURCH:
AT-RISK AT SCHOOL

"Too much schooling, too little education," is what Shujaa (1994, p. 328) suggested is the case for African-American youth in most public schools. When I read this assertion I realized that I had seen much evidence of this during my 6 years of working with youth at Central City Baptist Church. Through their engagement in nonreligious, church-sponsored activities such as the drumming group, the dance troupe, and Saturday School, I saw a side of African-American youth that I had not experienced in 10 years of work as an elementary school teacher. For instance, I recorded these notes during the first class session of my work as an assistant teacher for African-American Social Studies in the Saturday School:

The second hour African-American history class was for the younger junior high school kids. It was a big class—nine students.... One of the male students really stood out to me. He came in, sat down, and held a clipboard with paper and pen on his lap. When the teacher, Brother Samuel, began to talk, this student was the only one writing things down. I thought to myself, "This kid is serious." (Fieldnotes, October 28, 1995)

This "kid" was Anthony. His knowledge of African-American history, the books he had read, his sophisticated level of articulating points and questions, and his enthusiasm for the class was unlike anything I had ever seen in a person that young. Anthony valued Saturday School because it is where he "learns what is happening in the community. Just like some of the stuff that you don't get to in public school." Saturday School helped him learn about African-American history and culture through both orature and literature.

Anthony used skills learned in public school at Saturday School. For example, he used the letter-writing skills he practiced in English class to write to the oldest living relative of one of Utah's African-American pioneers. He requested information for our Saturday School Project:

> We are from the Central City Baptist Church Saturday School Project in Salt Lake City, Utah. Mrs. Johnson mentioned you to us because we are gathering information on African-American history in Utah. We were wondering if you would send us information on your family history....

Anthony also incorporated research, reading, writing, and editing skills as students used historical documents to research selected pioneers and wrote reports about them. The following example was typical of how Anthony and other youth brought together knowledge and skills from public school and Saturday School:

> Anthony researched Elijah Abel, the first Black man ordained to the priesthood in the late 1800s by Mormon Church founder and prophet Joseph Smith. What fascinated Anthony were the inconsistencies in Mormon doctrine such as the one that occurred several years after Joseph Smith's death when Brigham Young had a revelation proclaiming that Black men were no longer eligible to hold the priesthood. This doctrine was yet again reversed in 1973 and all men, regardless of race, were eligible for the priesthood. I was sitting across from Anthony as he read about Elijah Abel in *The Negro Pioneer.* He would laugh and read sections aloud to me that he found contradicting. (Fieldnotes, May 11, 1996)

Skills learned from English class also helped him write this report. When Anthony gave me his report on Elijah Abel to look over, I read it and said:

> There's one question about this man, from what I've read about him, that's really important, that you haven't addressed. How could he have held the priesthood when the church said Black males weren't allowed to hold the priesthood? So this is what I'd like you to find out more about and include in your paper. (Fieldnotes, May 11, 1996)

He went back to work. A few minutes later he came back, excited, and said,

> Look, Michelle, this is what my English teacher taught us. You can either just cut your paper apart and tape the new section in, or you can make a mark [where you want to add text] and then come down here.... (Field Notes, May 11, 1996)

Anthony pulled out a second sheet of paper that had a corresponding number on it with the new text he wanted to insert to respond to my question. Thus, Anthony was able to incorporate editing skills in his Saturday School work.

Based on my work with Anthony in Saturday School, I assumed that he was an outstanding student in public school because he certainly possessed what seemed like all the necessary skills. He loved to read, and what he read informed his identity as African American. A talented athlete, he consciously chose not to emphasize sports in his life because he felt that a career in sports was an unrealistic goal and that it involved stereotyping of African-American males. Instead, he said, "I am learning more about myself and where I come from. I take it [studying Black history and culture] seriously.... I read books. I read books on Barbara Jordan, Malcolm X, whoever." Whenever his English teacher assigned in-class reading in the literature textbook, Anthony told me, "I just put my own book inside and read that instead." In addition to being an avid reader, Anthony was a critical thinker, participated in thoughtful and informed ways in discussions, and articulated a genuine desire to be successful academically: "I always want to get sharper in school and always improve in school." However, as I began to spend time as a participant observer in Anthony's school, I learned that his grades did not reflect his abilities.

Anthony attended a predominantly White middle school located in a middle- to upper-middle-class neighborhood. In many of his classes he was the only African American. None of the teachers or administrators at the school were African-American. Although identified by his English teacher, who was White, as at risk of failing in school, Anthony appropriated tools from school, such as reading and writing, for his own uses in pursuing an intellectual form of racial solidarity. Anthony also claimed a space for himself in school by focusing on issues of identity, race, and ethnicity in his writing assignments. In English class, he wrote about his family, his pastor, and other church leaders as well as the activities he was involved in at church. Outside of school, Anthony made a conscious effort to read books on African-American history, leaders, and novels by African-American authors. None of this reading was required for school.

In spite of his low grades in English, his teacher, Mrs. Boulton, saw a tremendous amount of potential in Anthony as evidenced in the following comments she made to me about him:

The thing that amazes me about him is *that* he hears and processes everything you say. You can see it going on through the eyes. Very seldom took a note, but he didn't have to. He is that [italics added] bright. If he could just channel it. And maybe it will come.... Oh, what report did he give.... I can't remember if it had to do with Utah history or what, but his understanding of it, his research, talking from it, from just notes he had taken from the article was phenomenal. He reads it and he knows it....

I asked Anthony why he got such poor grades in English when it was obviously he was a strong reader and writer, and he immediately stated his problems with the writing process. He just didn't want "to mess with all those different drafts because I don't write like that. I'd rather write a bunch of different papers than keep on goin' over the same one."[4] This is not to say that Anthony totally dismissed the writing process. In a persuasive letter writing assignment, for which he received an A, Anthony was able to bring together the steps of the writing process and his understanding of the importance of having a strong cultural identity to take an activist role in school politics. The next section describes Anthony's use of this writing assignment to argue for more culturally relevant activities in school.

The Black Student Union:
Bringing Church and School Learning Together

As part of a seventh-grade English persuasive writing requirement focusing on what students felt should be changed about the school, Anthony wrote a letter that worked to bring issues of race and ethnicity to a public space in the school. His letter to the principal requested time in the school day for a Black Student Union. Anthony wrote:

> The reason I'm writing you is because I'm really concerned about the minorities in our school, their education in their culture, and also how they fit in at school ... This program [I am proposing] would be quite helpful and educational. It would be called "The Black Student Union." It would help them learn more about their culture, and talk about issues that face the community, school, and them. We would help educate the school more about African American culture. We would do this by helping to organize cultural assemblies, and also getting the school involved in Black history month. We would also inform minorities about special scholarships for minorities and programs

---

[4]I am aware that these are issues for many youth, not just African-Americans. However, as Fordham (1996) explained, "I would point out that uniqueness is not a prerequisite for a practice to have a special meaning for one group of people" (p. 363). The writing process clearly had special meaning for Anthony and for the grade he earned in English class.

for the community like [the] African American Task Force, Hispanic Task Force, and many others.

My main goal is to meet once a week for an hour with all kinds of kids of African-American decent [sic] for one hour during school.

It is worth noting that of the selection of letters I read written by his classmates, Anthony's was the only one with a conscious political agenda. Letters I read written by other students requested things such as longer lunch breaks and more soda machines.

Anthony's study of African-American culture and history and his experiences in the church informed his interest in having a Black Student Union. In church, he listened to the pastor preach about taking responsibility and making the world a better place for everyone to live. He heard about Renee, the dance troupe and Saturday School director, taking action and intervening in school on behalf of many of the youth. In addition, Anthony's mother taught him about the importance of African-American solidarity. He explained to me that his mother told him and his eight siblings to love and support each other and to be a friend to each other. For once they walked out the door of their home, they would not be treated with care and love in a predominantly White community. Anthony pulled together and made use of what he learned from his mother and other church members in terms of developing and supporting a collective identity. What Anthony learned through all of these oral events informed his use of literacy events in school and he used open-ended assignments as an avenue for inserting his own identity into the curriculum.

The lessons from Anthony's mother and church imparted a sense of African-American solidarity, and Anthony saw the need to carry that sense of belonging through with his African American peers at school. His reasons for wanting to form a Black Student Union included a concern that his African-American friends at school—none of whom attended Central City Baptist—did not know who they were culturally. Anthony wanted other African Americans in the school to "get to know the Black side of themselves." Anthony's studies at Saturday School, his experiences in the drumming group and dance troupe, and his study of African-American literature and history provided him with the literacy, language, and cultural tools to recognize the need for a Black Student Union and to understand that his schoolmates did not have a strong sense of African-American history and culture.

Mrs. Boulton encouraged Anthony to give his letter to the principal, and Ms. Barbour, the principal, invited Anthony to her office to discuss his letter. He had this to say about the meeting:

So me and Miss Barbour were talking about startin' a Black Student Union up at Eastside and organizing cultural assemblies so minorities and White kids at our school can get educated about it too. Stuff like that. And meeting once a week with the Black kids in school just to talk about what's going on. What can help the school or whatever.

Through the combined efforts of Anthony, the principal, and his English teacher, a MESA (Math Science Engineering Achievement) Club and a Black Student Union were put in place the next year. Anthony was the student leader of the Black Student Union that met once a month during the school day and Ms. Barbour served as faculty advisor. For his ground-breaking work at school, the principal nominated Anthony for the state's annual Martin Luther King Jr. Youth Leadership Award. He was one of 14 youth statewide to be selected for the award in 1996.

MAKING SENSE OF ANTHONY'S SUCCESS WITH THE PERSUASIVE WRITING ASSIGNMENT

What might explain why Anthony brought his community self into the school on the occasion of this assignment? By this I mean that he took initiative, talked with the principal about his ideas, and he demonstrated his understanding of the personal as political in his words and actions. As a parallel question, I ask why he was able to complete and receive an A on this assignment when most of his English assignments went unfinished. I want to suggest that there is an interplay of at least three explanations. First, the assignment allowed him to make choices and he was able to connect it to his own life experiences. That is, he was able to draw on multiple orality and literacy events and experiences from both church and school. Anthony brought diaspora literacy and school literacy together in this assignment. It connected his school and community identities. Second, it allowed him to take action—to wear his activist hat, so to speak, and to bring the knowledge of his home and community to bear on the school context. Anthony was able to use his literacy skills for political purposes. Finally, the assignment had real life application and meant a possibility for change in ways that would directly impact students of color in the school. He chose to approach the assignment in a way that would openly make race an issue in the school and he challenged the school to recognize the identities of African-American students.

I would argue that Anthony did A-quality work on this assignment because it explicitly created a space for him to air issues that concerned him. Activist behaviors had been modeled for Anthony by adults in the church community, perhaps making it easier for him to move from the act of writing a letter to following it up with a personal visit to the principal. This was also a short writing assignment; one that Anthony could take through the steps of the writing process used by his teacher in a fairly short time. Additionally, the letter had a larger purpose than a grade and an audience beyond his teacher so the revision process could be seen as a practical step.

LESSONS ABOUT LITERACY FROM ANTHONY, HIS CHURCH, AND HIS SCHOOL

Through working with and watching Anthony and other young people, I have come to see the power of community, culture, history, spirituality, and shared oppression used in positive ways to create a framework for the development of a strong sense of self in African-American youth. The community's use of orature helped youth develop a diaspora literacy through such practices as dance, music, rhythm, storytelling, and personal history. These experiences provided students with a set of tools that seemed to encourage a flexibility and a creativity to help them move between community and school-based literacies.

Anthony articulated a complex understanding of himself and his identity as a member of a larger community in much of his spoken and written work in school. Through Anthony's involvement in the African drumming group and African-American dance troupe, he learned about African traditions. Through participation in church services and activities, Anthony learned about the historical significance of church in the African-American community. And through Saturday School, he learned about the role of African Americans in the settling and development of his state as well as the histories of older members of the community and their struggles. All of these experiences contributed to the development of a sense of self for Anthony that was highly literate in multiple ways. His sense of self exists, not in isolation, but in a complexly communal and historical sense. His sense of self is an on-going construction based in the negotiation of the multiple literacies that informed Anthony's everyday experiences. The understandings he gained through his participation in the African-American community guided his uses of school-sanctioned written literacy. Although the school did not specifically address Anthony's racial and cultural history and experiences, he was able to find spaces to articulate the knowledge ignored in school literacy but sanctioned by his community. Anthony was also able to use the tools he learned in school to further his own study of African-American history and culture through reading.

In this study, literacy takes on a broader and more complex meaning than the traditional school-sanctioned meaning of being able to read and write.

Literacy, for Anthony, involved understanding the self in context and having the tools to bridge multiple literacies and communities. In the case presented in this chapter, Anthony's literacies were used in an activist role. He successfully completed his assignment for English class by following directions and receiving an A, and he brought attention to the needs of African-American students in the school. Anthony's use of literacy was just one way the youth I have worked with used the representations acquired through community literacies to create a space for themselves in school. Anthony consciously sought out ways to bring his community literacies to the public middle school.

Shujaa (1994) argued that for many African-Americans education and schooling are two separate entities. "Schooling ties me to the social order framed by the nation-state. Education informs and locates my thinking within an African historical-cultural context" (Shujaa, 1994, p. 28). Unfortunately, in the public schools I visited, Shujaa's words rang true. School-based literacy in the sites I studied was limited in definition and presented as neutral. Fortunately, Anthony's involvement in the community programs at church helped him gain experience in larger and broader notions of literacy that he was able to use in school. This presents me with a problematic view of school and school-sanctioned literacy. Is it reasonable to expect African-American youth to do all the work of transgressing and crossing boundaries—to do the work necessary to connect the school and the community? And what of those African-American youth who do not have the opportunities that Anthony and others have as part of a strong, culturally rooted African-American community that actively works to create educational experiences for its children? We need to use information such as what has been generated by this study to learn how to bridge the gap between schooling and education.

Ladson-Billings' (1994) notion of culturally relevant teaching offered examples of how this can be done. She showed how teachers—both African-American and White—successfully taught young African-Americans with pedagogies that embraced multiple literacies and helped children make sense of school-based issues and texts by locating similar experiences in their own communities and the world. Teachers encouraged and supported students in using their understandings of history, culture, and power relations to make sense of school curricula. Teachers in Ladson-Billings' (1994) study used their grounding in the experiences and issues of the local African-American community to connect with their students' interests and needs as they developed curriculum and pedagogies.

Dewey (1938) also talked about the importance of a system of education that uses a curriculum beginning at the level of students' lived experiences. The teacher, who has the vision to lead students beyond this point, must create successive educative experiences that integrate with one another. Ladson-Billings' (1992a) argument for a culturally relevant curriculum presented similar criteria:. "Students are apprenticed into a learning community rather than taught isolated and unrelated skills ... [and] students' real life experiences are legitimated as part of the curriculum" (p. 387).

Open-ended assignments, such as the ones Anthony's teacher assigned, constitute a way of creating spaces for students' experiences to become part of the curriculum. However, teachers must go beyond making the assignments to using the knowledge generated by students in those assignments to develop the curriculum. This necessitates that teachers know something about the communities in which they teach, to help students make connections between their personal experiences and the larger community. Using students' lived experiences to generate curriculum and approaches to literacy also challenges teachers to critique the "colorblind" approach valued in most schools. A colorblind approach denies race as a salient aspect of a person's identity and privileges traditional conceptions of literacy and a monocultural curriculum.

Given that the majority of our nation's public school teachers are White and have little experience in other cultural and racial contexts, how do we go about broadening traditional understandings of literacy? This broadening would require not only expanding the list of the skills we define as leading to literacy, but would also call in question what constitutes literacy and the purposes for which different forms of literacy are useful. Broadening understanding of literacy requires that teachers learn about the roles of literacy in the communities in which they teach and that they incorporate social practices embedded in the real life experiences of youth as tools for learning.

III

Commentaries

12

Reading Gender and Positionality Into the Nine Case Studies: A Feminist Poststructuralist Perspective

Donna E. Alvermann
University of Georgia

The purpose of this chapter is to provide a response to the case studies presented in *Constructions of Literacy: Studies of Teaching and Learning in and Out of Secondary Schools*. In responding to the cases, I have chosen a feminist poststructuralist perspective in which to frame my commentary. This perspective, which I describe in the first section of the chapter, differs in its assumptions from the perspectives that the case authors drew on in framing their own work. But it is precisely this difference that opens up interesting possibilities for analyzing the findings that the authors have presented here—an analysis that I devote considerable time and space to in the second section of the chapter. Finally, in the last section of the chapter, I offer a critique and some suggestions for future research stemming from what I see as aspects of secondary literacy that need further addressing.

A FEMINIST POSTSTRUCTURALIST PERSPECTIVE

Feminist philosophers are not known for their high level of agreement over the basic tenets of any particular feminist perspective. Thus, whether it is a liberal, Marxist, radical, socialist, psychoanalytic, cultural, or poststructuralist feminist perspective that is the focus of discussion, one can be assured that a variety of views will surface. Before laying out one particular view of poststructural feminism—an approach that I found useful in synthesizing the findings of the case studies presented in this volume—I think it is informative to distinguish between the terms *postmodernism* and *poststructuralism*, often used interchangeably in the feminist literature, and then to describe how *cultural feminists* see themselves in relation to postmodern–poststructural feminists.

A Matter of Definitions

The broader of the two terms, postmodernism is being used in many academic fields (e.g., architecture, philosophy, sociology, education) to refer to a movement in advanced capitalist culture that seeks to dissolve normative, hierarchical distinctions and to textualize disciplines so that they "are treated as ... optional 'kinds of writing' or discourses" (Sarup, 1993, p. 132). Among feminists, postmodernism is frequently conflated with *poststructuralism*, which involves "a critique of metaphysics, of the concepts of causality, of identity, of the subject, and of truth" (Sarup, 1993, p. 3). Conflating the two terms leads to much confusion, as Weedon (1997) pointed out. In her view, this conflation often leads to polarizations in which feminists find themselves defined in terms of a particular world view rather than a set of political objectives (Weedon, 1997, p. 180).

Postmodern feminists, according to Tuana and Tong (1995), "regard the search for *woman's* voice and vision as yet another instantiation of 'phallocentric' thought—the kind of 'male thinking' that insists on telling *only* one, presumably true, story about reality" (p. 431). Rejecting the notion that it will ever be feasible or desirable for women to speak from one common standpoint, postmodern feminists point out that women's experiences differ across race, ethnic, cultural, and social class lines. They also point out the importance of celebrating this difference and for viewing any exclusion or marginalization that results from such difference as a positive state of affairs—one that places women in the enviable position of being able to criticize patriarchal norms, values, and practices. For postmodernist feminists, then, "difference, or Otherness, is much more than merely an oppressed, inferior condition; rather, it is a way of being, thinking, and speaking that allows for openness, plurality, and diversity" (Tuana & Tong, 1995, p. 431).

Feminists who identify with poststructural theories also posit difference as their primary concern. Drawing on influential French philosophers such as Derrida and Foucault, poststructural feminists deny the existence of any essential or authentic core to womanhood. In short, they deny any sense of biological determinism. To poststructural feminists, differences in women's experiences can be traced to how various social discourses, cultural prac-

tices, or both construct them. In Foucauldian terms, women are bodies "totally imprinted by history" (Foucault, 1984, p. 83). Or, as Luke and Gore
(1992) described this imprinting in terms of pedagogy, "texts, classrooms,
and identities are read in discursive inscriptions on material bod-
ies/subjectivities" (p. 4).

Despite the obvious appeal of postmodernist–poststructuralist thinking
about difference, some feminists, such as the cultural feminists (so named
because of their agenda to establish a female counter culture) express concern over the possibility that the absence of a common standpoint will leave
women politically and economically vulnerable (Echols, 1983). For example, cultural feminists worry that by emphasizing difference over certain essential traits that characterize womanhood in general, women will
jeopardize their chance to be heard on matters related to politics (abortion
rights, child care bills) and the workplace (equal pay for equal work, ad-
vancement policies). To quote Tuana and Tong (1995), "If feminism is to be
without any standpoint whatsoever, it becomes difficult to ground claims
about what is good for women or to engage in political action on behalf of
women" (p. 431).

My Identity Papers

In retrospect, it was Foucault's historical framing of what it means to be a
subject (in this case, *woman*, whose meaning is temporarily dependent on
the discursive context in which it is inscribed) that was my entryway into
the poststructural literature. As a history minor during my undergraduate
and master's level programs at the University of Texas–Austin in the mid- to
late1960s, I was well aware of the subordinate status of women throughout
recorded time. However, then, as later in my doctoral program at Syracuse
University in the late 1970s, I recall not being particularly drawn to the
women's movement in this country. Although I did not have the language
at the time to describe my lack of interest in the movement, since then I
have come to associate this disinterest with the essentialist nature of much
of early second-wave feminisms. I now understand that it was my resistance
to the essentialist belief "in an innate 'womanhood' to which we must all ad-
here lest we be deemed either inferior or not 'true' women" (Alcoff, 1995, p.
439) that kept me from joining in the many consciousness-raising activities
of the women's movement of the 1960s and 1970s. Instead, I joined the student movement of that period and learned through it the oppressions experienced due to race and class differences. My working-class background put
me much more in touch with the discourse of the civil rights movement
than with that of the women's movement, which was at the time comprised
largely of middle- and upper-class White women.

Until recently, I was quite content with the poststructural move to unfix meaning by questioning Saussure's (1974) logocentrism in which language is perceived as the location of social meaning through fixed signs. As the French poststructuralist Derrida (1976) demonstrated, there can be no fixed signifieds (concepts) because of the endless process of deferral in which signifiers (sound or written images) are open to challenge and redefinition depending on the social institutions and practices in which they are used. According to Weedon (1987), a poststructuralist feminist who uses the notion of unfixed meanings to address the power relations of everyday life:

> Language, in the form of an historically specific range of ways of giving meaning to social reality, offers us various discursive positions, including modes of femininity and masculinity, through which we can consciously live our lives. A glance at women's magazines, for example, reveals a range of often competing subject positions offered to women readers, from career woman to romantic heroine, from successful wife and mother to irresistible sexual object. These different positions which magazines construct in their various features, advertising, and fiction are part of the battle to determine the day to day practices of family life, education, work and leisure. How women understand the sexual division of labour, for example, whether in the home or in paid work, is crucial to its maintenance or transformation. (pp. 25–26)

Attuned to this poststructural way of perceiving language, I was more than a bit troubled when I began to read critiques of poststructural feminism in which the socially constructed nature of language was viewed as having a potentially deleterious effect on women's well being. As Alcoff (1995) noted:

> If gender is simply a social construct, the need and even the possibility of a feminist politics becomes immediately problematic. What can we demand in the name of women if "women" do not exist and demands in their name simply reinforce the myth that they do? How can we speak out against sexism as detrimental to the interests of women if the category is a fiction? How can we demand legal abortions, adequate child care, or wages based on comparable worth without invoking a concept of "woman"? (p. 443).

This critique and others like it (e.g., Collins, 1995; Riley, 1988) raised questions for me about the usefulness of poststructural feminism as a perspective. If the socially constructed category *gender* could potentially be erased from further political consideration, then why not race, class, age, and sexual orientation as well? That is, if underneath we are all the same (the classic liberal thesis), then what is to preclude the possibility that all individual particularities will be seen as irrelevant to issues of politics and justice? The answer to that question was addressed, at least partially, by Alcoff (1995) in her conception of gendered identity as positionality.

Alcoff's Concept of Positionality

Writing from a feminist poststructuralist perspective that attempts to deal with the paradoxical nature of language and the extremes of both cultural feminism and poststructuralism, Alcoff (1995) proposed a way to think about gender that removes the danger of perceiving it as simply a natural (a biological given) or irrelevant (a nominalism) category of analysis. Drawing on The Combahee River Collective's (1983) concept of *identity politics*, Alcoff argued that one's identity (race, class, gender, etc.) can be taken as a motivation for political action. Borrowing from the work of de Lauretis (1984), Alcoff also argued that language is not the sole source of meaning—that experience also counts. According to de Lauretis, it is one's *experience*, which she defined as "a complex of habits resulting from the semiotic interaction of 'outer world' and 'inner world,' the continuous engagement of a self or subject in social reality" (p. 182), that determines one's sense of self, one's subjectivity.

In explaining how this concept of subjectivity affords an individual a relative identity—one that changes with the constant shifting of historical, social, economic, and cultural conditions—and how when combined with the concept of identity politics, the two taken together form the concept of positionality, Alcoff (1995) wrote:

> If we combine the concept of identity politics with a conception of the subject as positionality, we can conceive of the subject as nonessentialized and emergent from a historical experience and yet retain our political ability to take gender as an important point of departure. Thus we can say at one and the same time that gender is not natural, biological, universal, ahistorical, or essential and yet still claim that gender is relevant because we are taking gender as a position from which to act politically. (p. 451)

It is the fluidity of Alcoff's concept of positionality that I find most appealing. For while positionality does not deny the construction of meaning through both language and experience, it also does not see such meaning as determinate for all time. Viewed from this perspective, "being a 'woman' is to take up a position within a moving historical context and to be able to choose what we make of this position and how we alter this context" (Alcoff, 1995, p. 452). The potential for altering whatever position we take up also renders less valid the argument of cultural feminists to return to what is basic or at the core of our identity.

Although avoiding an essentialist stance, the concept of positionality does not give up on the possibility of grounding a feminist politics; indeed, it opens up that possibility by celebrating difference and making certain that gender remains a viable category of analysis in Western intellectual circles where all too often one hears the liberal claim that underneath we are all the same. That same claim, stemming as it does from an allegedly ungendered humanism, can also be heard in matters related to race and class.

Intersections of Race, Class, and Gender

Race and class are among several other markers (e.g., age, sexual orientation, religion, ethnicity, and physical and psychological status) that typically intersect in studies where gender has been identified as the primary category of analysis. Although postmodern feminists are particularly interested in describing difference, their analyses have reflected for the most part a privileged class of well-educated Anglo-American or European women. But this situation is changing. African-American feminists, such as hooks (1989) and Collins (1995), wrote about the intersections of race, class, and gender in the academy. Spivak (1985) used deconstruction to decenter the hierarchical oppositions that underpin gender, race, and class oppression under colonialism. Lugones and Spelman (1995) dialogued about differences among Hispanic and Anglo feminists. And an edited volume by Tokarczyk and Fay (1993) explored the role of higher education at the intersection of class and gender.

Taken together, these examples of feminist work that have focused on the intersections of race, class, and gender provide ample evidence that "different discourses within the same language divide up the world and give it meaning in different ways which cannot be reduced to one another ... by an appeal to universally shared concepts reflecting a fixed reality" (Weedon, 1987, p. 22). For as Collins (1995) pointed out, a marginalized group not only perceives a different reality than that experienced by the dominant or mainstream group, it also interprets such a reality differently. This difference in perception and interpretation, especially as it is mediated by and through language, is at the heart of most feminist poststructuralist work. It is also central to the analysis and critique of the case studies that I offer in the final two sections of this chapter.

ANALYSIS OF CASE FINDINGS FROM A FEMINIST POSTSTRUCTURALIST PERSPECTIVE

In applying a feminist poststructuralist perspective to the findings presented here in the nine case studies of literacy teaching and learning in secondary classrooms, I am not aiming to increase or diminish the significance of the findings as they now stand. Rather, my purpose is simply to analyze this important body of work in a way that focuses on how power is exercised in certain classroom practices involving literacy and on the political struggles for changing how those practices are constructed.

Because this analysis requires that I attend to nine separate cases, I have chosen to group them in various ways for purposes of organization and emphasis. Sometimes such groupings appear discrete; at other times, they overlap. For example, when I discuss the material social relations that structure how students and teachers interact in discipline-specific classrooms, I group the studies by content area (science, social studies, math, and language arts). However, when discussing the range of existing discourses and the social power that they legitimize within particular classrooms, I group the cases according to students' seeming access to such discourses. Particularly in the latter instance, my groupings should be viewed as tentative. Not having the depth of knowledge that the case authors possess about their participants, I have had to rely on what was highlighted in their respective chapters. This limitation, coupled with the fact that I view the intersections of gender, race, and class (not to mention numerous other identity markers) through my own set of lenses, will become clear shortly. Perhaps the most to be hoped for in such an analysis is that it will generate a dialogue between individuals reading this chapter and those of us who have contributed to the volume in which it appears.

Social Relations that Structure
How Teachers and Students Interact

The assumptions that underpin how content literacy is acquired and used in discipline-specific classrooms in the United States consist of common sense notions of how schools, and particularly secondary school classrooms, are socially organized. More importantly, for the purpose of this chapter, it is the social meaning attached to such common sense notions (that inevitably privilege the most powerful group) that is of interest. This concept and the fact that power is exercised in the social relations teachers and students construct in their everyday classroom interactions are key to understanding the approach I have taken in analyzing the findings from the nine case studies presented here.

From a feminist poststructuralist perspective, "the common factor in the analysis of social organization, social meanings, [and] power ... is *language*.... [Language] is also the place where our sense of ourselves, our subjectivity, is *constructed*" (Weedon, 1987, p. 21, emphases in the original). Because this perspective assumes that subjectivity is constructed (socially produced) rather than genetically determined and that language (although not exclusively) is the site of political struggle, it seems reasonable to begin this analysis by looking at how teachers and students use language to mediate social relations involving literacy practices in discipline-specific classrooms.

Science.   In the three high school science classes described by Guzzetti, Stewart, and Dillon; O'Brien; and Volkmann (chaps. 6, 7, & 3, respectively, this volume), teachers used the language of the textbook, teacher-prepared study guides, or lecture notes, videos, and lab demonstrations to convey the kinds of knowledge that counted. In the Guzzetti case study, Miss Smitts lectured from sources that she privileged over those her students proffered. For example, when one of the boys in her Physical World class interrupted Miss Smitt's lecture on the mechanical advantage gained from using simple machines to offer information he had learned from his book on the Nile River, his contributions were countered first with a correction (30, not 100, years to build a pyramid) and later with a bid to hear another student's comment that followed up on her own belief about the 30-year time period. Although Mr. Williams, the other physics teacher in Guzzetti's (chap. 6, this volume) case study, was more open to student-generated ideas ("If no one knows for sure, then your comments are just as valid. That's what we do in science. We sift out ideas and find those that are valid."), he nonetheless used a debate-like format in whole-class discussions that favored male participation over female and sent the distinct message that argument was the preferred mode of discourse among "real" scientists.

In the Stewart (chap. 7, this volume) case study, Mr. Weller, a high school earth science teacher, controlled the flow of information to such an extent that the students saw him as their primary source of knowledge—a perception that bothered him, but which he took no steps to alter, perhaps because he equated controlling the content with controlling (managing) student behavior. Like Mr. Ruhl, the biology teacher in the Dillon et al. (chap. 6, this volume) case, Mr. Weller did not expect students to read their textbooks. In both their classrooms, the textbook was considered secondary to teacher-created texts (study guides in Mr. Ruhl's case and a resource file supplemented by his own store of personal knowledge in Mr. Weller's case). On one occasion when a student queried Mr. Weller about a discrepancy between what he heard his teacher state and what the textbook said (students did read their textbooks privately), Mr. Weller qualified his statement in such a way that the student acquiesced with a "Yeah, oh yeah. I see. I remember now."

Math.   In the Sturtevant, Duling, and Hall case study (chap. 4, this volume), Mr. Hall, a beginning ninth-grade algebra teacher, was also worried about classroom control. At one point in his 1st year of teaching, he contrasted his earlier career as a Commanding Officer in the Navy to his new found career in teaching. In his words, "I've run a 4,000 person organization before, and it's not nearly as intense as ... trying to figure how to orchestrate 25 kids." Unlike Mr. Weller and Mr. Ruhl, who relied on authoritative language and knowledge of their subject matter to manage students' behavior, Mr. Hall tried to establish a working relationship with his students by gauging their understanding of mathematics from what they wrote during various writing activities—a practice he had valued as a student teacher. This different use of language—to collect rather than to dispense knowledge—runs counter to the common sense notions of how secondary school teachers organize their classrooms. Thus, it is not surprising that Mr. Hall's students did not readily take up the position of knowers that he was trying to make available to them. They were simply unaccustomed to such positioning, given the discourse of schooling that they knew as "normal" or natural. Nor were they that sanguine about the required textbook for the course. Although Mr. Hall was initially pleased with the tremendous amount of applications and real life situations in the text, by springtime (after observing his applied level classes struggle with the text) he had capitulated to the common sense practice of giving students worksheets in lieu of textbook examples. Mr. Hall left the teaching profession after his second year, saying that he had had "incredibly naive" conceptions of what high school teaching would be like.

English Language Arts.   The case study authors of the four chapters devoted to the English language arts (Moje, Willes, & Fassio; Oates; O'Brien, Springs, Stith; Kelly; chaps. 9, 10, 5, & 11, respectively, this volume) appear primarily concerned with language use that is capable of reflecting difference in social relations. For example, Moje et al., (chap. 9, this volume) opted to interpret discrepant cases as part of the "normal" practice of everyday interactions in Deb Willes's seventh-grade writer's workshop. Rather than relegate such differences to the discrepant case category, they viewed these differences as informative of the way students exercised power in writer's workshop. Thus, Chile's reluctance to write about the gang activities in which she was involved gave rise to considering how expressivist pedagogies, such as writing workshop, encourage students who are positioned outside the dominant classroom culture to subvert their experiences to those of the dominant culture; and similarly, how it was only after Anthony felt assured he would not have to share his writing publicly that he began to use gangsta language in his stories. Although both Chile and Anthony found spaces within Ms. Willes's writing workshop to express their personal experiences (Chile orally shared a number of gang stories with Moje), neither adolescent deviated from the traditional writing conventions they associated with school writing—the one exception being when Anthony used tagging and graffiti in his end-of-the-year social action project. Moje and her colleagues interpreted the students' preference for maintaining a difference between personal and workshop language as evidence of their willingness to buy into the hegemonic practices associated with school writing.

In the O'Brien et al. (chap. 5, this volume) case study of low-achieving students enrolled in a high-tech literacy lab, which was designated a regular English class at Jefferson High School, Donny and Ashley used a documentary style of composing in which the written text served only as background for the more engaging and emotion-filled visual images. This use of the documentary, which compensated for the two adolescents' lack of technical sophistication in school writing, is a good example of how literacy practices that support difference in students' use of language enable them to exercise power in constructing everyday social relationships with their teachers and peers. In this particular instance, stemming from an assignment in which students in the literacy lab were to explore the issue of TV violence, Donny and Ashley coauthored a multimedia project that used intertextual links to a video frame of *Beavis and Butthead*, a scanned magazine photo of Jessica Matthews (a victim of a fire reportedly inspired by a *Beavis and Butthead* scene), two photos of Michael Shingledecker (a teenager who unsuccessfully tried to imitate a stunt featured in the movie, *The Program*), a scanned text of the Shingledecker tragedy, a discussion of the *Ren and Stimpy* cartoon's negative impact on children, and a plea to parents to monitor their children's TV viewing habits. Using icons from popular culture, Donny and Ashley successfully communicate their concern about TV violence. They also communicate that they are literate in ways not always visible when the criteria supported by the hegemonic practices of print literacy are applied to their work as the sole means of evaluation.

The case studies of Oates (chap. 10, this volume) and Kelly (chap. 11, this volume) are particularly interesting when juxtaposed as two separate but related snapshots of the mediating force of language within a culture heavily influenced by the Church of the Latter Day Saints (LDS). In the case of Katy and Zeke, Oates illustrates how the discursive practices of Ms. Allen's 12th-grade high school literature class, influenced as they were by the LDS Church and Mormon family life, played a significant role in students' social relations both in and out of school. Describing the literacy practices in Ms. Allen's room as expressivist and constituted in what he terms a "Discourse of crisis and esteem," Oates provides examples of how Katy and Zeke were deprived of the opportunity to make sense of (and ultimately take charge of) their own life experiences. Writing as a person outside the LDS Church, Oates argues, among other points, that the different

social uses to which each of these two young people put their literacy practices configured them as gendered objects. That is, Katy used her literacy to
maintain relationships and an identity of intimacy and disclosure, whereas
Zeke used his literacy to claim and exercise the power and authority reserved for young men in the Mormon culture.

In Kelly's (chap. 11, this volume) case of Anthony, a 13-year-old African-American growing up as a member of Salt Lake City's Central City Baptist Church, she documents how this seventh-grader integrated what he had
learned about the history and culture of his race through church activities
with what he learned about the power of the code (print literacy) from Mrs.
Boulton, his English teacher. Although Anthony had been labeled *at risk* by
the school that he attended in a predominantly White middle- to upper-middle class neighborhood, in his church he was regarded by the adults as a young
intellectual who held great promise for positive youth leadership. Although it
is true that Anthony claimed a space for himself by writing about issues of race
and identity in a school where he was frequently the only African-American
in his classes, it is also true that he received low grades in Mrs. Boulton's English class because he failed to complete all the steps in the writing process.
From Anthony's perspective, he just did not want "to mess with all those different drafts because I don't write like that. I'd rather write a bunch of different papers than keep on goin' over the same one." However, motivated as he
was by the social action projects undertaken by members of his church, Anthony was able to find value in what Mrs. Boulton attempted to teach him
about the writing process when he engaged in a seventh-grade English persuasive letter-writing requirement that let him assume an activist role in school
politics. Encouraged by his teacher, Anthony gave his letter to the school principal, with whom he later met for the purpose of developing a plan for putting
his proposed idea of a Black Student Union into place the following year. With
this example of how language (and in particular, a single letter writing project)
led to the establishment of a social organization (the Black Student Union) for
mediating social relations among different races, ethnicities, and cultures, Kelly
successfully demonstrates the importance of attending to differences in literacy
practices and their potential for exercising power. For had Anthony's teacher
only been concerned with his adhering to the five steps of the writing process, it
is doubtful she would have recognized his ability to write persuasively on an issue that mattered deeply to him on a personal level.

Social Studies.   In the Hinchman and Zalewski case study (chap. 8,
this volume), Keisha and Colin showed great concern over what they perceived as the difficulty of the language Pat Zalewski used to frame her lectures or to ask discipline-specific questions about the course content, global

studies. Keisha appeared to equate literacy as enacted in Ms. Zalewski's class with learning the meanings of the various terms (words) associated with global studies. By focusing her efforts on learning the technical vocabulary in the required readings, Keisha missed the larger concepts that held the discipline together. While she was not ignorant of this fact, she showed little inclination to construct the larger meaning. In Hinchman's and Zalewski's eyes, however, a more encompassing explanation for the difficulty Keisha experienced as a student could be traced to her gendered behaviors. They viewed her as exhibiting many of the stereotypes associated with young, middle-class adolescent women (e.g., the desire to please in social situations, to respect her teachers and not question their motivations, to sit back and take a less aggressive role in class discussions than her male peers)—factors that they saw as possibly hindering Keisha's understanding of course content and her ability to pass the difficult and highly competitive year-end, state-mandated exam in global studies.

In contrast to Keisha, Colin was less sympathetic to his teacher's perceived need to use difficult vocabulary. He believed that Ms. Zalewski unnecessarily complicated a subject about which he thought he knew a great deal. To Colin's way of thinking, global studies could be learned from watching the evening news, reading *Time* magazine, attending drama productions on politically sensitive issues, and so on. Also, in contrast to Keisha, Colin openly challenged Ms. Zalewski and his peers in ways that led to serious confrontations, several of which highlighted the push and pull involved in exercising power in a classroom where language was viewed as both a site of struggle and a mediator of social relations.

Summary.   Overall, based on the data available in the nine case studies presented here, there appears little reason to suspect that teachers in the various content areas were generally intent on unfixing meaning, a concept central to most feminist poststructuralist projects and one that questions Saussure's logocentrism. With the exception of the teachers in three of the nine cases (Moje et al.; O'Brien et al.; Sturtevant et al.; chaps. 9, 5, & 4, respectively, this volume), the pedagogies engaged in by the other six seemed fairly traditional in that they could be described as teacher- or content-centered, although certainly not devoid of concern and a care for students. Quite the contrary. In fact the argument could be made that in today's assessment driven curricula, one of the ways a teacher can express her or his concern for students is through delivering information in a manner that will enable them to pass state-mandated exams. On the other hand, it should go without saying, that student-centered pedagogies are also interested in students doing well on such exams; it is not an either–or situation.

What this first part of the analysis shows, in terms of a general theme, I believe, is that language does indeed mediate the social relations of discipline-specific classrooms. In all nine cases, and in varying ways, language was shown to be the site through which both teachers and students constructed a sense of themselves. It was also a site of political struggles—struggles made even more complex by the intersection of issues related to gender, race, culture, and social class status. It is these issues, embedded as they are in the discursive practices of content-area literacy, that provide the focus of part two of the analysis that follows. There, also, the reader will find the concept of positionality (Alcoff, 1995) revisited—this time in terms of its usefulness for exploring differences in discursive practices.

Discourses and the Social Power They Legitimize

As pointed out in an earlier section of this chapter, a marginalized group not only perceives a different reality than that experienced by the dominant or mainstream group, it also interprets such a reality differently. This difference in perception and interpretation plays a major role in how marginalized groups understand various Discourses (Gee, 1996) and the social power they legitimize. Furthermore, the experiences of individuals within these groups will be far from homogeneous. For example, how a particular individual interprets a sexist remark by another individual will depend on that individual's beliefs about femininity or masculinity, and more generally, how she or he is positioned in one or more Discourses (e. g., family, school, work, church, and so on). It will also depend on the context in which the remark is made, who made it, why, and with what possible gain in mind. Having access to this kind of information, however, does not guarantee that the same individual will respond in the same way to a similar remark made later on in a similar context. For as Weedon (1987) reminded us, "Unlike humanism, which implies a conscious, knowing, unified, rational subject, poststructuralism theorizes subjectivity as a site of disunity and conflict, central to the process of political change and to preserving the status quo" (p. 21).

This feminist poststructuralist concept of subjectivity has implications for how I interpreted the way power was exercised in certain classroom practices involving literacy in the nine case studies presented here, and for how I analyzed the political struggles in which teachers and students were engaged in their attempt to change the way those practices were constructed. For instance, because I believe like Weedon (1987) that there exists a "thinking, feeling subject and social agent, capable of resistance and innovations produced out of the clash between contradictory subject positions and practices" (p. 125), I chose examples from the different case studies that allowed me to illustrate this kind of subject. I also chose examples that permitted me to show this kind of agency at work across a range of Discourses (school, family, church, and community organizations) and issues (gender, race, culture, and social class status). One final qualifier: separating the Discourses as I have subsequently done is for ease of organization only. I do not believe that Discourses function in isolation of each other. Instead, I know that my membership in one Discourse influences my sense of self and positioning in another (similar or competing) Discourse.

School. Perhaps one of the clearest examples of a power struggle involving a school literacy practice and a student was that of Colin and Ms. Zalewski, his 10th-grade global studies teacher (Hinchman & Zalewski, chap. 8, this volume). Although other cases (e.g., Dillon et al., chap. 3, this volume; Guzzetti, chap. 6, this volume) hinted at gender's mediating role in struggles between students and their teachers, none theorized a relationship as conflicted as Colin's and his teacher's. Colin, who had a reputation among his classmates for being critical of Ms. Zalewski, positioned himself in contradictory ways. At times, he could be quite vocal about his displeasure in the way Ms. Zalewski graded his work or used what he considered to be unnecessarily complex vocabulary to get her point across. At other times, he would confide in the university researcher (Hinchman) a certain marvel at Ms. Zalewski's organizational skills. Conflicted about his own subject positions as a student, Colin sometimes sent the message that he found Ms. Zalewski's particular way of talking about her discipline—an expertise that he did not possess—as totally outside what he determined was appropriate. The struggle was not one-sided; Ms. Zalewski let it be known that Colin did not meet her expectations on more than one occasion. In an attempt to understand this struggle, Hinchman and Zalewski (chap. 8, this volume) proposed an explanation that read gender into the equation. I find their explanation plausible and supported, in fact, by the gendered interactions Colin had with members of his study group. Believing that one of the young women in his group purposely silenced his every move to be a valued participant, Colin complained that she got away with this kind of behavior simply "because she was a girl." The fact that Colin constructed himself as an unsuccessful competitor with his sister, especially when it came to matters of academic prowess, may also have colored how he read his interactions with the young woman in his study group, and with Ms. Zalewski, as well.

Another site of struggle—this one motivated by a culture of control—involved the discursive practice that Mr. Weller (see Stewart, chap. 7, this volume) referred to as "keeping those generals busy." His remark, made in reference to the practice of giving low-achieving students in the general track a copious amount of paper-and-pencil seatwork to keep them occupied and out of trouble, reflected the school's hidden curriculum. According to Mr. Reed, one of the teachers interviewed at Lincoln High, the school could be characterized in the following way: "Mass education so that kids don't start to think that they are individuals and can do whatever they want and have their own opinions because nobody wants the late 60s and early 70s again." Although Mr. Weller and his colleagues tried to compensate for this sentiment by being good role models and caring teachers, nonetheless, "It was difficult," as one of his coworkers noted, "to separate the police function from the teaching function even after the classroom door was closed." And indeed, this seemed to describe the situation in Mr. Weller's room, too. For even though he projected a personable and caring demeanor through his sense of humor and flair for the dramatic, Mr. Weller organized his classroom literacy practices in a way that assured he maintained strict control of his students. Ironically, Mr. Weller's primary goal in teaching earth science ("for students to have a heightened awareness of their natural surroundings") was largely unobtainable given the school's hidden curriculum. The situation left little room for productive struggle, and the students seemed to sense as much. Of all the students in Mr. Weller's fourth-period class, only Scott challenged his teacher's authoritarian ways, and in the end just barely passed the course.

Doing school in Mr. Ruhl's biology class (see Dillon et al., chap. 3, this volume) equated to involving oneself in what might be described as a culture of struggle. Talking or struggling aloud, Mr. Ruhl believed, prepared the students to think critically about the answers they would eventually record in their study guides, which he went to great pains to prepare, and which he viewed as the primary focus of all small-group work. For the most part, however, students found ways to change the practice of struggling together. Either they completed the guides ahead of time (typically at home, despite Mr. Ruhl's direction to work together on the guides during class time) or they surreptitiously used their textbook to find the answers to the questions on the guides. Sharing, which often consisted of directly copying from one another, ensured a product (a completed guide) although it short-circuited the process. Inasmuch as it was the process that Mr. Ruhl valued, the students by and large had found a way to change a literacy practice that was a site of struggle (no pun intended) for them.

Family.   Discursive practices within families at the lower, middle, and upper levels of the socioeconomic ladder vary considerably, as does the social power legitimized by such practices. Perhaps nowhere is this more clearly illustrated than in the two case studies reported by O'Brien et al. (chap. 5, this volume) and Guzzetti (chap. 6, this volume). With nearly one-third of the Literacy Lab students coming from families whose incomes placed them at the lower end of the socioeconomic scale, O'Brien and his coauthors set out to develop a literacy program that would compensate, at least partially, for the school's policy of labeling these students as being at risk of failing due to family and environmental factors beyond the school's control. Thus, the site of political struggle at Lafayette's Jefferson High School was the Literacy Lab program, itself, rather than any specific reading and writing practices within it. The action that O'Brien et al. took in developing such a program essentially disrupted the institutionalized view that classes typically designated as remedial in nature for lower socioeconomic status (SES) students are supportive and provide the necessary challenge for so-called at-risk students to pull themselves up by the proverbial boot straps. In stark contrast to what one might expect to find in an English class for low-achieving students, the Literacy Lab provided students who for most of their school years had been labeled inept at comprehending printed texts with opportunities to construct meaning differently through multiple forms of media representation. Thus, in some ways it could be argued that a formerly marginalized group of low-achieving high school students found the means for expressing difference in a way that worked to their advantage—an exercise of power rarely afforded students whose low social class status marks them as outliers.

The students in Mr. Williams's Physics and Honors Physics classes (see Guzzetti, chap. 6, this volume) represented a culturally diverse group of juniors and seniors who came from families classified as upper-middle to middle-upper class. Socially, economically, and educationally advantaged (e.g., Oz's father was a physicist, and Oz himself had lived outside the United States), these two groups of students benefitted from growing up in families who wielded considerable power when it came to interacting with the school. For example, a parent request was all that was required to move a student from Physics to Honors Physics. Where power struggles existed in Mr. Williams's two sections of high school physics, they were usually tied to issues of gender, not social class status, although family values were still traceable. One instance in particular stands out in the Guzzetti case study. In an attempt to resolve a situation where the girls rarely spoke up in groups comprised of both males and females, or were viewed as incompetent by the boys when it came to recording data and writing up lab reports, Mr. Williams changed his classroom practice for holding discussions and assigning students to lab groups. He experimented with the idea of same-sex grouping. This proved beneficial for the girls when they were in small-group settings, but it did not lead to increased participation in whole-class discussions. The implications Guzzetti drew from this study resonate with what I found in my own work; that is, upper-middle to middle-upper class adolescents admit that gender bias is the "norm" in most classroom discussions and that attempts to change the norm are not worth the risk of losing social standing (for females) or privileged status and power (for males). As noted earlier, preserving the status quo is one of two outcomes (the other being change) that may be expected when attempts are made to disrupt ingrained discursive practices that privilege the group already in power. It is especially difficult to effect change when hegemonic beliefs about what constitutes femininity and masculinity are being questioned, as in the Guzzetti case.

Church.   Issues of gender and race are inextricably linked in the two cases reported by Kelly and Oates (chaps. 1 & 10, respectively, this volume). For Anthony, a sense of social agency, modeled after what he saw as highly valued discursive practices in his church and in church-related community activities (e.g, Saturday School, drumming, and dance groups), was the springboard he needed to go from at-risk middle school learner to social activist and organizer of the first Black Student Union in his school. Although it would be easy to designate Anthony's resistance to the five-step writing process as the site of struggle in this case study, I prefer to think of such a site as being situated in a different and larger arena. Enlarging on an idea that I learned from reading Kelly's case study of Anthony, I would like to begin a discussion that includes the following questions for starters: Is it fair, or even reasonable, to expect African-American youth to initiate single-handedly the work that needs to be done in transgressing and crossing boundaries? Might we not expect to see the schools in which the Anthonys of this world find themselves enrolled also taking on some responsibility for connecting students' lives outside of school to their lives inside the place we call school? For me, these questions seem to be the real site of political struggle—a struggle not unlike the one O'Brien and his colleagues (chap. 2, this volume) took on in developing a literacy program for so-called at-risk students in Lafayette, Indiana.

Although the concepts of social agency and power struggle seem lost or at least temporarily hidden from view in Zeke's case (see Oates, chap. 10, this volume), I do see other parallels in Anthony's and Zeke's lives. For instance, both adolescents are members of churches that recognize the potential for influencing young people's educations and lives in directions that go beyond the spiritual. Specifically, the discursive practices of the two churches (Baptist and Mormon) reflect an awareness that literacy entails using written language in culturally sanctioned ways—ways that necessitate learning to read the texts of such discursive practices for the social power enacted in them. Another parallel is that both Anthony and Zeke benefit from their placement on the left hand side (the more powerful side) of the male–female binary. Although this gendered advantage is more implicit than explicit in Anthony's case (at least as described in Kelly's [chap. 11, this volume] characterization of Salt Lake City's Central City Baptist Church), there can be no doubt that Zeke's positioning in both school and church Discourses is privileged due to his having been born male, not female.

Community Organizations.   The discursive practices of Saturday Schools, Seminary Council, and youth gangs might seem rather unrelated under most conditions. In analyzing the nine cases of this volume, however, I found what seems to signal some common threads among a number of the studies. For instance, in the cases of Anthony and Zeke, as they intersected with Moje et al.'s (chap. 9, this volume) case, I found an interesting parallel in the cultural struggles that each of the three cases documented. In Anthony's case (see Kelly, chap 11, this volume), the cultural struggle for an African-American Black presence in a city founded by the followers of the Church of the Latter Day Saints (LDS) was the focus of a project that began with a visit to the genealogy library in downtown Salt Lake City and culminated with a field trip to the Utah Historical Society. In Zeke's case (see Oates, chap. 10, this volume), his exclusion from a leadership position in Seminary Council, an organization linked to the LDS Church, was a painful reminder that such exclusions often carry a personal, as well as cultural, penalty. Only after he had successfully published a piece in the school's newspaper that garnered the attention of the Young (Mormon) Women's organization was he able to recoup some of his lost esteem. And, in Moje et al.'s (chap. 9, this volume)case, the cultural struggle stemmed from several gang affiliated youths' refusal to bring the personal into their school writing until a literacy practice known as group sharing was dropped as a requirement for participation.

In each of these three cases, a partial resolution to the struggles associated with what feminist poststructuralists call *identity politics* revealed just how complex and deeply ingrained these struggles are. They are also widespread, though they look different under different conditions, and in some instances seem to disappear altogether. For example, while Anthony used his identity as motivation for political action in establishing his school's first Black Student Union, Keisha, one of only two African-American students in Ms. Zalewski's global studies class (Hinchman & Zalewski, chap. 9, this volume), never mentioned race or ethnicity in a year-long study that presented her with numerous opportunities to do so during individual interviews with the researcher. Neither did Chile, a 12-year-old Hispanic girl, in

Moje et al.'s (chap. 9, this volume) case study—at least not in her written stories. Although the stories Chile wrote were carefully structured and followed the norm expected for school writing, they were missing the rich, ethnic details of family life and folklore that were present in the stories she shared orally with Moje. What these different ways of doing identity politics suggests is that, as Weedon (1987) argued, we cannot assume that:

> material structures such as family, education and the [community], which constitute and discipline our sense of ourselves both conscious and unconscious, can be changed merely at the level of language. Discursive practices are embedded in material power relations which also require transformation for change to be realized. (p. 106)

Summary.   Combining the concept of identity politics with the concept of positionality (Alcoff, 1995) provided me with a rationale for choosing examples from the nine case studies that illustrate how people's differences in perception and interpretation can account for different understandings of various Discourses and the social power they legitimize. This feminist poststructuralist move, though useful in focusing on the political struggles for changing (or maintaining) the status quo, is not without controversy. Those who take issue with the concept of the subject as positionality do so on the grounds that it supports a relativist position. However, as Alcoff (1996) pointed out, her concept of positionality does not invite unbridled relativism, or the so-called ideal state of disinterested tolerance.

Like Alcoff (1996), I am skeptical of unbridled relativism for the very reason that "in the guise of promoting mutual respect, [disinterested tolerance] renders real respect impossible" (p. 181). As Alcoff (1996) explained, "the liberal attitude of treating others with such deference and delicacy that one never voices one's own views or criticisms is patronizing and condescending, and reveals a lack of respect" (p. 183). It seems to me what Alcoff is striving for in her concept of positionality invites discussion of the possibility that one might revise one's own beliefs and practices after considering the differences encountered in listening to another's point of view. This openness to the other is not a license to practice disinterested tolerance. Neither, however, is it a clarion call to search for universals (the argument that at the bottom we are all the same) to avoid absolute relativism. As Alcoff (1996) asserted:

> Relativism is better avoided by a piecemeal approach than by a global attempt to devise absolute standards once and for all. That is, it is better avoided by small-scale discussions and joint projects through which differences can be explored and understood by all parties. (p. 183)

Finally, it seems to me that the case studies analyzed in *Constructions of Literacy: Studies of Teaching and Learning In and Out of Secondary Schools* are good examples of the discussions and projects to which Alcoff alludes. By providing us with nine cases through which differences in literacy practices can be explored, the authors leave little doubt about the importance of looking for points of coherence while continuing to respect the otherness in other people's views.

A CRITIQUE AND SOME SUGGESTIONS FOR FUTURE RESEARCH

Writing a critique of the nine case studies in this volume from one particular feminist poststructuralist perspective offered me a chance to think about how the cases might have looked if the authors originally had chosen to frame their work using this same perspective. Thinking in terms of what if rather than what was also left me unencumbered. I was free to shed my usual reviewer role, which in the academic community typically involves commenting on a manuscript's theoretical perspective, methodology, and interpretation. Casting off the reviewer role seemed appropriate in this instance for several reasons. First, the authors wrote from many different perspectives, a definite plus for the book, but problematic for me if I were to attempt to organize my remarks in a way that showed some measure of depth and yet stayed within the page limits. Second, I felt the case studies presented extremely useful insights as they stood, and I doubted seriously that any remarks I might make after the fact would be of much worth to the authors. Finally, the idea of concentrating on how a feminist poststructuralist perspective might have framed the cases differently appealed to me because of what I might learn about this particular perspective's own strengths and shortcomings.

In dividing this final section of the chapter into two parts, I focus first on the what ifs alluded to in the previous paragraph. After that, I end with some suggestions for future research based on what I learned from applying the what if approach to the case studies as a whole. These suggestions, while framed within a feminist poststructuralist perspective, are not intended to privilege that perspective over all others. Thus, they will best serve their purpose if they generate interest in further inquiry into adolescent literacy from multiple and competing perspectives.

What If ... ?

As I read the cases, I picked up scraps of conversation between the authors and their intended audiences that reminded me of how differently, or similarly, situated their theoretical perspectives were from my own. In some cases, gender was neither discussed nor mentioned in passing (unless I were to include the mention of how many boys and girls participated in a study, which from my perspective would be an example of sex category, not gender). Because gender is a primary category of analysis in poststructural feminisms (including the version of poststructural feminism to which I personally subscribe), its absence in a case also reminded me that by agreeing to do a self-conscious feminist reading of the nine studies, it was incumbent upon me to stay alert to missed opportunities for exploring issues of gender. Or, as Pearce (1997) would put it, my agreed-upon feminist reading of the manuscript insured that there would be no time for feminism to be "off duty" (p. 3). And so, pen in hand, my scribbled notes in the margin of the case manuscript would begin to take on the shape of a study redesigned and reinterpreted from a feminist poststructuralist perspective. Granted, some of the new case frameworks that I imagined were not much in the way of improvement over the earlier design. But others excited me, and I found myself wondering if my next study might not look a lot like the one I had just scribbled into existence in the margins of the particular case manuscript I was reading. Where the feminist poststructuralist perspective seemed to come in most handily and have the greatest potential was in cases where looking at the gendering of meaning production would have enhanced our understanding of how female and male adolescent readers take up or resist a particular text's positioning of them. This, understood within Alcoff's (1995) conception of positionality, would have created a space for exploring more than just the essentialized behaviors of the two sexes. It would also have permitted a more in-depth analysis of the intersections between gender and race, class, and culture. Such intersections become more visible when analyzed within a conception of positionality that accords an individual a relative, or fluid, identity—one that changes with the constant shifting of historical, social, economic, and cultural conditions.

Another what if that occurred to me as I read and reread the nine case studies in this volume stemmed from the numerous times that I noted the frequency with which the exercise of power in particular literacy practices was implied, but not made explicit. This observation suggested to me that had the researcher been working from a feminist poststructuralist perspective, he or she would likely have tried to untangle some of the assumptions underlying these practices. Viewed from my perspective, such an untangling was needed. For left unexamined, the assumptions would only further inscribe what might seem on the surface to be common-sense reasons for maintaining the status quo. This possibility was particularly troubling to me when the literacy practices involved were those that depended primarily on hegemonic beliefs about femininity and masculinity for their existence. At the

same time, I can imagine how heavy handed it might seem to some researchers to write from a feminist poststructuralist perspective about literacy practices that anyone can "see" simply reflect "the way things are"—"the norm".
Disrupting the norm is never comfortable. Yet I would argue that we have
little choice but to do so if we wish to have a say in how we represent ourselves (and by extension, our literacy practices).

Finally, as I read various case descriptions of teachers' perceptions and interpretations of particular literacy practices and how these contrasted with
students' perceptions and interpretations, I wondered about the limitations
this dualistic way of thinking imposed on the data. What if the same data
were analyzed from a feminist poststructuralist perspective? Might I expect
to come away with a very different understanding of the teachers, the students, and the literacy practices themselves? More than rhetorical in nature, this question inquires into the usefulness of representing the
participants in our research as possessing contradictory subject positions.
For example, what would be gained by depicting participants' subjectivities
as sites of "disunity and conflict" (Weedon, 1987, p. 21) rather than as
all-knowing, unchanging, and rational? On the gain side, I expect we might
discover, as others have before us (e.g., Davis, Sumara, & Kieren, 1996;
Sumara, 1996; Varela, Thompson, & Rosch, 1991), that "although it seems
to each of us that we are somehow autonomous and independent beings, we
are, in fact, woven into the world that we perceive as 'other'" (Davis et al.,
1996, p. 158). Revealing the contradictory subject positions of both teacher
and student might lead to an understanding of how each inhabits the other's
world. It might also show the false naturalness of some common assumptions underlying certain contested literacy practices. At the very least, as I
have argued elsewhere (Alvermann, 1998), such a move would be a step toward destabilizing the teacher–student binary that presently exists.

Suggestions for Future Research

In future research involving adolescents, their literacies, and their teachers,
I would like to see more attention paid to gender as a category of analysis.
Although biological differences exist between the two genders, it is the
meanings that we give to those differences, not the gender categories themselves, that are of interest here. Such meanings are socially produced
through language within a range of conflicting Discourses (Gee, 1996). Examining such Discourses to learn how language mediates the social relations of discipline-specific classrooms and their respective literacy practices
would add immeasurably to what we currently know about teaching and
learning at the secondary school level. It would also focus much needed at-

tention on how power is exercised in certain classroom practices involving literacy and on the political struggles for changing how those practices are constructed.

A second aspect of teaching and learning in the secondary school that needs to be addressed further in the research literature has to do with problematizing what too often pass for common-sense explanations about how literacy is to be taught and used. Marginalized groups of students, in particular, fall victim to these too-easy explanations. Research is needed that will allow us as teachers and teacher educators to understand in greater depth why the literacy practices that we value may be perceived and interpreted in very different ways by individuals who through choice or circumstance are outside the dominant or mainstream culture.

Finally, I believe there is need for research that may lead us to rethink how we structure our knowledge of ourselves and our students, especially in terms of the categories we use. Pairing categories so that one is presented as being more natural and desirable than the other is the result of centuries of Western thinking (Kenny, 1994). As burdensome as these categories can be for those positioned as subordinate other, it is doubtful we could get along without using them to help us think, classify, and order our everyday world. Just as importantly, categories can be politically useful. They provide ways for naming and calling attention to certain patterns of activity that consistently privilege one group or cultural practice over another (Davies, 1996). For example, without the category named student in the teacher–student binary, adolescents' perspectives on literacy would remain invisible and thus indistinguishable from those of the dominant group (*teachers*). Yet, despite their usefulness, the categories remain problematic. Their mere existence continues to reinforce notions of the inevitability of certain groups of people and literacy practices being positioned as more (or less) powerful than other groups. They also inscribe notions of what is "normal" and therefore more valued or admired. Research that is designed to challenge our presumptions about the naturalness of such groupings would be welcome, as would inquiry into the Discourses (Gee, 1996) that produce and maintain them. As Weedon (1987) reminded us, without access to (and understanding of) how we construct and are constructed by such Discourses, we are destined to presume a neutral model of literacy teaching and learning, one free of biases and power relations.

13

Boundaries on Construction of Literacy in Secondary Classrooms: Envisioning Reading and Writing in a Democratic and Just Society

David Bloome
Vanderbilt University

The chapters in this volume, combined with other recent books on second-ary school literacy (e.g., Alvermann, Hinchman, Moore, Phelps, & Waff, 1998; Beach & Hynds, 1990) and literacy in nonacademic settings (e.g., Hamilton, Barton & Ivanic, 1994; Lankshear, 1996; Prinsloo & Breir, 1996; Shuman, 1986), call for reactions that go beyond the traditional education questions of effectiveness. For at least two decades, the fields of classroom research and reading and writing research have, in general, been mired in seeking more effective ways to teaching reading and writing, defined almost exclusively by test scores. One result of that obsession has been a failure to examine the substance of what is being read or written, of what social rela-tionships are being taught and learned, and what cultural ideologies are be-ing promulgated. With the marginalization of left-wing politics in the United States. and elsewhere, and with the marginalization of schooling in-formed by cultural and social critique, education including literacy educa-tion has been simplistically defined as access to the existing economic structure. Reading and writing at the secondary school level has been defined in terms of its effectiveness in helping students acquire academic knowledge and skills measured by tests and as needed for access. Gone was even the pretext that secondary school education had a transformative social agenda to create a more just and equitable society as multicultural education, bilingual education, cultural and ethnic studies, sex education, community studies, ungraded curricula, writing process, women's studies, whole language, gay and lesbian studies, studies of contemporary literature by people of color, and other progressive directions, all came under attack and were either eliminated, marginalized, or forced underground. The chapters in this book refuse to be contained within the framework of effectiveness. Necessarily then, a response to the chapters in this book must be political.

The range of topics, theoretical issues, settings, and perspectives represented in the chapters in this volume is impressive because of the critique it presents of traditional conceptions of reading and writing in secondary schools. Beginning with and taking for granted a conception of reading and writing as social processes, the chapters in this volume present a culture critique revealing the ways in which literacy practices in secondary schools have been used to construct knowledge, personhood, social relationships, social and cultural identity, gender, race, class, and schooling. Furthermore, in most chapters, the authors have described ways that students, teachers, and communities (both school and nonschool communities) have resisted the imposition of constructions of literacy that have limited human potential and shown how literacy practices have been reconstituted to open up spaces for students and meanings otherwise marginalized.

And yet, there is an unarticulated element in these chapters that, at least as I see it, is important to foreground. This unarticulated element is a vision of what reading and writing might be in a democratic and just society. I believe that, as a field, we are far from having such an articulated vision.

We do have visions of resistant literacy practices (e.g., Andrade, 1998; O'Brien, Springs & Stith, chap. 5, this volume; Schaafsma, 1998), of subrosa and vernacular literacies (see Conquergood, 1997; Gilmore, 1987; Tabouret-Keller, Le Page, Gardner-Chloros, & Varro, 1997), of community literacy practices that affirm students who are dehumanized in school settings (e.g., Egan-Robertson, 1998; Luke, O'Brien, & Comber, 1994; G. Moss, 1989; Schaafsma, 1998), and of literacy pedagogies that assist students in becoming critically reflective on the worlds in which they live (e.g., Freire & Macedo, 1987; Macedo, 1996; Mercado, 1998; Torres, 1998; Willis, 1997). Both in this volume and elsewhere, there are visions of literacy practices and of literacy instruction that provide students with a better understanding of oppressive economic, social, political, and linguistic relations and that engage students in activities that transform these oppressive relations, if not permanently at least temporarily (e.g., Egan-Robertson, 1998; Freire & Macedo, 1987; Montero-Sieburth, 1998; Morgan, 1997; Searle, 1998; Shor, 1980, 1992; Wallace, 1992; Walsh, 1991). However, these descriptions and visions of reading and writing practices and of instructional practices, do not in themselves articulate a vision of reading, writing, or language in a democratic and just society. It may be the case that it is premature to attempt to envision what literacy practices would be like in a democratic and just society; nonetheless, in this chapter I present four issues that I believe need to be considered in developing a vision of reading and writing in a democratic society. These four issues are:

1. A shift from technocratic models of literacy to ideological models.
2. A shift from conceptions of literacy to conceptions of literacies.
3. The rolling back of the market economy from its intrusion into social institutions and social domains outside the boundaries of the traditional business world.
4. The flattening of the hierarchy in domains and practices reading and writing.

I have stated these aforementioned four issues in the language of critique. But they can also be stated in more affirming language:

1. Recognition of the close connection between social, cultural, and political dynamics and literacy practices, including the ways that literacy practices can be transformative.
2. Acknowledgment and appreciation of the many diverse ways that people use and understand reading and writing, reflecting the multiple worlds in which they participate.
3. An emphasis on the value of family, community, and personal contexts determined by the quality of social relationships rather than by their dollar value.
4. An appreciation of what has been called local literacies and the reading and writing done by ordinary people in their everyday lives.

These four issues are not the only ones that need to be considered in envisioning reading and writing in a democratic and just society, but given the limitations of space, I highlight these four and can only briefly discuss each.

RECOGNITION OF THE CLOSE CONNECTION BETWEEN SOCIAL, CULTURAL, AND POLITICAL DYNAMICS AND LITERACY PRACTICES

Reading and writing events can be viewed as involving at least two social contexts. The first involves the social interaction of authors[1] and readers[2] (Bruce, 1981), the second involves the social interaction of the people involved in the actual situation in which the reading or writing is occurring (see Bloome, 1983, 1987; Green, 1990; Heath, 1982a; Maybin & Moss, 1993). Thus, in a literature lesson in a secondary school, there is the interaction of the author of the piece of literature with the student reader, and, there is the social interaction of the teacher and the students with each other during the reading lesson. As the chapters in this volume make clear, it is always the case that the first social context (author–reader) is always embedded in and influenced by the second social context (in situ participants) since it is this second context that constitutes the literacy event. Even when a person is reading alone (e.g., during silent reading or at a carrel in the library), it is still the case that there are in situ social relationships, especially given the difficulty of finding and maintaining social and physical space for being alone. In others words, even when alone, reading and writing are social events.

Viewing reading and writing as social events is different than simply locating reading and writing in social contexts. If reading and writing are viewed as located in social contexts, then it may be claimed that reading and writing are fundamentally psychological processes mediated by social factors. For example, cognitive views of reading and writing have suggested that the background knowledge and various other psychological factors influence how readers interpret written texts and what and how writers write. As such, cognitive views of the reading and writing process can be viewed as iterations of the traditional transmission model of reading and writing (writers communicate their ideas to readers) but with an acknowledgment that there is static inherent in the system due to mediating social factors. Similarly, reader-response models (Rosenblatt, 1978) have postulated a transaction between a reader and a text, potentially mediated by social factors (Cai,

---

[1]By author I mean both the person who wrote the text as well as all of those people and institutions involved in producing the text (e.g., publishers) and in placing it in front of the reader (e.g., marketing people, textbook selection committees, and teachers).

[2]From a theoretical perspective, determining who the reader is depends on who is asking the question. From the point of view of the author, the reader may include all of those people who make up the line of consumption (e.g., editors, marketers, textbook selection committees, book reviewers, and student readers). From the point of view of the student, the reader is him or herself. For the purposes of the discussion here I am taking the point of view of the student.

1997). While acknowledging cultural differences and rejecting a transmission model, the difficulty with such reader-response theories is the assumption nonetheless that reading is fundamentally psychological in nature. By contrast, to view reading and writing as social processes (rather than merely located in a social context) is to argue that reading and writing cannot be reduced to an essentialism or to a set of psychological processes. What reading and writing are is what we make them to be.

Yet, to view reading and writing as social processes requires moving beyond simplistic applications of social constructionism. The meaningfulness of any social event, including reading events, is not just a set of shared cognitive constructs that have been socially constructed. Social interaction does not take place in neutral contexts (see Brodkey, 1987; A. Lee, 1996; Luke 1988; for discussions on this issue with regard to literacy instruction). When people interact with each other, which is what happens when people engage in reading and writing, they act on the world and they do so materially and historically (O'Brien, Moje & Stewart, chap. 2, this volume; Moje, Willes, & Fassio, chap. 9, this volume), and this is so even when the substance of their interactions and actions is language (cf. Bakhtin, 1953/1986; Volosinov, 1929/1973). It is because social interaction is material and historical that reading and writing always involve a social and cultural ideology (for further discussion see Street, 1984, 1994a, 1995). As McDermott (1999) noted, culture is not an environment of the mind. Stated less abstractly, when students and teachers engage in a literature lesson, for example, how they interact with each other (who says what to whom, how they configure themselves, what meanings, values, identities, they assign to what people do and say, etc.) has real (i.e., material) consequences for the students and the teacher, including restructuring their social organization, who gets what privileges and who is marginalized, and what behaviors, values, knowledge, visions, language, and feelings are viewed as legitimate, deviant, or threatening (Baker & Luke, 1991; Green & Weade, 1990).

Examining the distinctions among viewing reading and writing as psychological processes, as located in a social context, as social constructions, or as social processes that are material and historical, is not just an academic exercise. These distinctions provide an awareness of what and how reading and writing events are constituted, what their consequences may be, and how they are part of broader social and cultural processes. Examining the distinctions provides a way to engage in critique of attempts to impose essentialist definitions of reading. In other words, to claim that reading and writing are just a set of decontextualizable skills or cognitive processes (what Street, 1984, called an autonomous model of literacy) is to attempt to impose a particular social, cultural, and political agenda without announcing or acknowledging the attempt as being part of such an agenda. For example, if reading and writing are defined as a set of particular decontextualizable skills, those people who do not acquire them can be defined as less worthy of various opportunities and rewards available from our society, and the claim can be made that their lost opportunities are the result of their own qualities rather than the result of social, cultural, and political processes. Their marginalization and the denial of even basic human resources can be justified as a matter of merit determined objectively, rather than recognized as symbolic violence (cf. Bourdieu, 1977). Consider a further example, if reading is defined as a particular set of cognitive processes acquired through practice, education, or apprenticeship, then a hierarchy can be established with regard to the authority for determining the meaning of any particular text (e.g., the meaning of a legal document or a poem), without having to acknowledge that the authority for that interpretation is a matter of social, cultural, and political privilege. In order to get a different interpretation viewed as legitimate requires justification within the terms established by those with authority, and is difficult to do. Such justifications, although legitimizing a different interpretation, at the same time legitimize the hierarchy of authority for interpretation. It is, of course, more likely that those who hold alternative interpretations are liable to be viewed as less competent, less able, and potentially, socially deviant.

Viewing reading and writing as social processes has profound implications for research on reading and writing and for education. If reading and writing are not monolithic practices, then it is no longer possible to locate precursors of reading and writing achievement in biological or neurological factors. Similarly, it is also not possible to isolate social and cultural factors (e.g., socioeconomic status) and use those factors as predictors of reading and writing achievement. Indeed, the notion of identifying an isolated factor or set of factors as determinants of how students might engage in reading and writing is a non sequitor from the perspective of reading and writing as social processes. Who gets to engage in which literacy practices, how those practices are adopted and adapted, when, for what purposes, with whom, and with what consequences, is necessarily an ongoing social, cultural, and political process; and the study of that ongoing process is necessarily a descriptive and interpretive one, rather than a mathematical task of creating an algorithm. The educational task is less one of giving reading and writing to students—as if it were a commodity for sale or barter—than of creating environments in which a broad range of reading and writing practices are available and can be employed in pursuit of real goals of value both to school and nonschool communities. In such environments, reading and writing are not static practices, previously established and engaged in for the purpose of acquiring expertise with the established practice, but rather emphasis is placed on the dual processes of adopting and adapting extant literacy practices, during and for their uses. Street (1995) called such engagement in literacy practices, taking hold of literacy, foregrounding what people do to literacy in making it part of their lives.

In summary, to claim that reading and writing are essentially a specific set of decontextualizable psychological skills and processes, is to engage in a kind of social, cultural, and political hegemony; to view reading and writing as fundamentally social processes (and to act on that view) is to undermine that hegemony.

ACKNOWLEDGMENT AND APPRECIATION OF THE DIVERSE WAYS THAT PEOPLE USE AND UNDERSTAND READING AND WRITING

For nearly three decades, researchers have been documenting the diverse ways that people use reading and writing. They have conducted studies across cultures (e.g., Hartley, 1994; Heath, 1983; B. S. Moss, 1994a; Scollon & Scollon, 1981), across academic, work, and home/community domains (e.g., Farr & Guerra, 1995; Foster, 1992; Heath, 1982b; Kelly, this volume; Saxena, 1994; Willett & Bloome, 1992), as gendered social practices (e.g., Finders, 1997; Guzzetti, chap. 6, this volume; Karach & Roach, 1994; Solsken, 1993), among others. These studies have made clear that how people use reading and writing (and spoken language) is an extension of their cultures, the fields in which they are working, or both. Variation in how people read and write includes what, where, when, how, and with whom they read and write, and what roles reading and writing play and what material consequences reading and writing have in their collective lives.

One implication of recognizing variation in how people use written language is that cross-cultural differences can be identified and miscommunications and misevaluations can be reduced. This is especially important in the early grades where educators, parents, and students, may make assessments of a student's academic potential, and such assessments may have a lasting impact (e.g., Michaels, 1981; Collins, 1987). Yet, concern for cultural differences in how people use written language is also important at the middle and high school level. Students' families and communities are still important influences on their lives and on how they use written language. Bridges can be built between how spoken and written language is used in their communities to how it is used in academic contexts, without denigrating either set of ways of using written language (e.g., C. Lee, 1997; Mahiri, 1991, 1994; Moje, Willes & Fassio, chap. 9, this volume).

Since at least 1962 (see Cazden, John, & Hymes, 1962), educational researchers have called on teachers and other educators to be sensitive to cultural variations in how people use language and literacy and to design instructional programs that would not punish people for such differences. However the development and implementation of instructional models that incorporate such diversity has been rare (for examples see Au, 1980; Curry & Bloome, 1998; Elsasser & John-Steiner, 1977; Evans, 1997; Irvine & Elsasser, 1988; Ladson-Billings, 1992b; Lee, 1997; Moje, Willes & Fassio, chap. 9, this volume).

The reluctance of teachers to develop and use such models may be due to a concern for providing students with access to what has been called the "cultures of power," (Delpit, 1995), ways of using reading and writing that provide access to dominant society. The access rationale provides an easy justification for needing to only give lip service to diversity as a fundamental quality of literacy practices.[3] Yet, there is no inherent contradiction between creating educational environments that are inclusive of a broad and culturally diverse range of ways to engage in and use written language, and in gaining access to dominant society; unless they are made to be contradictory (Guerra, 1997).

In my view, changes in the political climate in the United States in the late 1980s and 1990s have made it no longer necessary, for those who would prefer, to not even give lipservice to diversity. Schools focus attention on giving students access to academic and economic opportunities defined primarily in terms of test scores and similar markers. The result is an odd situation in which educators could acknowledge diversity, but have no need or mandate to recognize or incorporate it into instruction or into educational goals, indeed the mandate is just the opposite. And yet, it is still the case that students from communities that have not traditionally been well-served by the schools, continue not to gain access despite the emphasis on access.

It can be argued that a singular emphasis on access is an emphasis on assimilation to the culture of dominant society, perhaps requiring some students to give up their home and community cultural identity (Clark & Ivanic, 1997; Ivanic, 1994). Whereas dual emphases on access and on diversity in ways of using written (and spoken) language allows accommodation of multiple cultures and complex but integrated social and cultural identities without necessarily sacrificing one for the other (e.g., Hesford, 1997).

The failure to both acknowledge and incorporate a diversity of literacy practices across cultures and social domains into instructional programs has

---

[3]Although Delpit (1995) called for educators to attend to providing students of color access to the culture of power, her argument does not necessarily negate attention also to students' cultural background or pedagogical approaches that accommodate such differences. Rather, it is interpretations and uses of Delpit's argument that has often reduced a concern for cultural difference to lipservice or has set a concern for cultural difference as oppositional to gaining access.

two downsides beyond the terrible loss of students who would otherwise do well in school but who instead either "sleep through school" (Siddle-Walker, 1992) or drop out (Fine, 1991). First, it limits the possibilities for building creative uses of reading and writing. As students learn about others' ways of using reading and writing, they have opportunities to adopt and adapt those ways of reading and writing to enrich their own lives. Second, failure to acknowledge the importance of diverse literacy practices creates a social and cultural hierarchy of literacy practices, placing particular academic literacy practices on top and other literacy practices from both school and nonschool domains at various steps below. This hierarchy is taken up in the next section.

FLATTENING THE HIERARCHY OF WRITING

In our research on the literacy practices of people who wrote for the Mass-Observation Project in the United Kingdom (a people's ethnography and history of life in Britain), we found that most of the people we interviewed did not view themselves as "writers" although they did a lot of writing in their lives (Sheridan, Street, & Bloome, in press). Writers were those people who held particular positions in society that designated them as writers: published novelists, journalists, academics, etc. We found that many of the people we interviewed aspired to be writers, and some wrote for the Mass-Observation Project to practice their writing. Their views do not seem much different than the views of the general public or of schools. In brief, a hierarchy exists. There are those designated as writers, and the rest of us who might aspire to be writers. Such a hierarchy, in my view, is not a matter of competency versus lack of competence. Rather, it is a matter of social structure and organization that provides only a few positions for designated writers. Schools play an important role in maintaining this hierarchy through choices in what literature is read (what counts as writing worth reading), through its emphasis on formal grammar, and by restricting writing in school to academic writing. I will briefly discuss each item.

Recent debate on what literature should make up the canon read in literature classes has focused on whether to include literature by people of color, women, and more recent authors who have not traditionally been part of the canon versus limiting the canon to the Great Books authored primarily by European and Euro-American males that have traditionally made up the canon. From one perspective, this debate is about recognition that great literature exists across cultures and peoples, and that in a pluralistic society such as the United States, limiting the canon to works primarily from one group gives a distorted picture of the literary legacy and suggests that only people from one race and gender are likely to produce great literature. However, from another perspective, it is the existence of a canon at all (whether or not it contains a diverse literary heritage) that supports a writing hierarchy by dividing writing into that worth reading and other. Unrecognized is the wide range of writing that goes on in people's lives, the stories they write[4] and tell to each other, the numerous community writing groups, etc. Perhaps more importantly, the difficulty of getting one's writing included in the canon—or recognized by any other of society's mechanisms for designating what's worth reading (e.g., having a book published)—has made it unlikely that many people will even engage in writing stories, histories, poems, and similar works for others to read. Their literary efforts are mostly limited to told stories, and despite academic studies of oral stories and histories, oral stories rarely become part of the literary canon. Indeed, it is not unreasonable to claim that the emergence of rap is a reaction to the limited opportunities for ordinary people to be included as authors or to have their voices heard (although the recent commercialization of rap has tended to make it more of an elite enterprise and therefore has tended to incorporate it into the hierarchy of writing and writers).

The emphasis on teaching formal grammar also supports a hierarchy of writing (Collins, 1991). The teaching of grammar is often viewed by educators and the general public as requisite to be able to write. Students who do not succeed in formal grammar instruction may not be given access to extended writing instruction.[5] When teachers evaluate student writing, they often focus on the use of formal grammar and on formal organizational characteristics (and similarly with many standardized writing tests). The result is to elevate success with formal grammar as a gatekeeping mechanism that determines who is capable of contending to be a writer. Because formal grammar is most similar to Standard English dialect, there is a built-in advantage for native speakers of Standard English dialect and a built-in obstacle for those who are not. The relationship of student success in formal grammar instruction to writing extended texts worth reading is, at best, uncertain. Nonetheless, such success plays a gatekeeping role and may even result in many students internalizing the belief that they are not capable of

---

[4]One of our findings in our study of literacy practices and the Mass-Observation Project was the large amount of writing that people did in their lives including the writing of stories, histories, autobiographies, poems, essays, etc.

[5]Students who do poorly in formal grammar instruction may receive low grades in their English classes and not be eligible to take creative writing classes or advanced English classes where opportunities for writing extended texts are usually located.

creating writing worth reading (and perhaps also they are not capable of us-ing language well, creating shame in how they speak).

A third way that schools promote a hierarchy of writing is through a re-stricted range of writing opportunities and genres (Applebee, 1984a). In brief, writing in schools is limited to academic writing, particularly the aca-demic essay or report. Opportunities for creative writing may occur occa-sionally under special circumstances but they do not constitute a major writing activity. Furthermore, even creative writing is often limited to styles associated with academic writing. Yet, opportunities for the writing of extended academic texts are limited, with writing for most secondary students being rare. Mostly students engage in the writing of brief re-sponses and worksheets. The result is to limit who may contend to be a writer to a very small group of students who both meet the criteria estab-lished by the school and pursue additional school and nonschool opportu-nities to learn how to write in a manner that will get them recognized as a writer.

Through these three strategies, educational programs may be sending an implicit message about the lack of value of nonacademic literacy prac-tices. This creates a double-bind for students. Academic literacy practices often lack substance, and when they do include substance, there is little reason to attend to the substance or view it as having much importance (Applebee, 1984a; Street, 1994b; Street & Street, 1991). For example, students often have to copy assignments from textbooks or answer ques-tions at the end of a textbook chapter. What matters is completing the as-signment and getting the correct answer, not the substance of the text; it is a phatic exercise (Bloome, Puro, & Theodorou, 1989). The result is that the literacy practices presented as having value have no substance, and the literacy practices that have substance (family and community prac-tices) have no value. Although this is not what pundits, politicians, and the general public mean when they talk of a literacy crisis, such a situation would seem to be one.

There are numerous directions for flattening the hierarchy of writing. In many neighborhoods and communities, ordinary people meet in writing groups, produce their own stories and texts and share them with each other. Many people engage in extended letter writing, with letters often containing numerous pages and the exchange of letters lasting over many years. Com-munity publishing groups make the works of local people available to others, and ethnic organizations may encourage their members to write about their families and histories, collecting them for use by future generations (e.g., see Horowitz, 1998; Kugelmass & Boyardin, 1983; on the writing of Jewish me-morial books, discussed in depth later). Instead of organizing writing in-struction around the goal of writing education to create an elite corps of writers,[6] schools could organize around the goal of engaging all students in the writing of stories, histories, and autobiographies, to be shared within local communities of peers, families, and similar others. That is, schools could take on the goal of changing the conception of what a writer is and what writing is, and they could engage students in writing and reading practices that would value the writing that others did and not just the writing of an elite corps. But doing so would require schools to challenge the organization and structure of writing in nonschool contexts, particularly in the cultures of power, but it is a challenge they may be neither inclined to undertake nor prepared for.

AN EMPHASIS ON THE VALUE OF FAMILY, COMMUNITY, AND PERSONAL CONTEXTS DETERMINED BY THE QUALITY OF SOCIAL RELATIONSHIPS RATHER THAN BY DOLLAR VALUE

In 1957, Hoggart argued that mass production and the proliferation of mass media directed at Britain's working class after World War II were implicated in eroding the traditional values and meanings of working-class life in Britain. Despite the hardships of working-class life that were potentially being made easy through mass production and the mass media, there was nonetheless alarm in the potential of the uses of literacy as they were being enacted for a hollowing out of family and community life, and in the growing potential that a sense of self-worth and esteem of others would not be defined beyond the acquisition of material goods and occupational and social status.

Despite editorials and commentary by pundits, politicians, and others on the political extreme right decrying the decline of the family and community, and despite Hoggart's warnings, recent studies by Barton and Hamilton (1998), Knobel (1999), among others, suggested that there is little evidence of a hollowing out of family and community life among the working class or ordinary people in general; and even if there were, it is unlikely that the cause of such hollowing out would be literacy practices per se. Nonetheless, a number of social and cultural critics have raised concerns about the encroachment of the market economy into other domains of social life, such as the family, school, and community (e.g., Bloome, 1997; Lankshear & McLaren, 1993).

---

[6]The claim here is not that schools create an elite corps of writers on their own initiative, but rather that schools take on that task as a result of expectations and tasks that they have been given by other social institutions and through a widely held social ideology defining reading and writing practices. For schools to do otherwise, they would have to resist powerful forces from many sectors of society that expect schools to accept and accomplish those tasks and that role.

Elsewhere I have described in detail various illustrations of how the market economy is redefining social institutions beyond the traditional boundaries of commerce (Bloome, 1997). Rather than view families as sites of loving relationships among adults and children, and seeking to strengthen those relationships, families are advised to view themselves as economic units. They are advised to establish a budget, develop a portfolio, take advantage of tax loop holes and related opportunities, limit financial and tax liabilities, and teach their children about investing at an early age. Purchasing a family home becomes a matter of investing in real estate (as opposed to joining and building a community), and neighborhood associations focus their attention on maintaining the market value for houses in their neighborhood.

The encroachment of the market economy into education redefines what happens in schools as an economic investment for the future. Children are told that what they are being taught will get them a good job in the future and provide them access to various economic opportunities. Whether such an equation is true or not (see Brandau & Collins, 1994), it has become the folk wisdom believed by educators, parents, and the general public. The involvement of Chambers of Commerce and business leaders in formulating educational policies, and in designing educational systems based on business models, has become taken for granted as both legitimate and as a public service. As schooling becomes defined by its market value, parental involvement in their children's education becomes an investment. Parents of young children are advised to read to their children nightly because it will increase their children's reading achievement, rather than because they are opportunities for strengthening loving relationships. Stories are not read for their wonder and imagination, but for the development of phonemic awareness. Similarly, parents of adolescents are asked to monitor their children's homework and attendance so that their children will get good grades and have access to better educational and economic opportunities. Stated differently, parents are asked to be study hall proctors and truancy police, roles that do not necessarily build loving relationships between adults and children. Parents are not asked to discuss what students are reading for the purpose of helping students engage in critique, rather on those rare occasions when parents are asked to engage in such activities, it is to insure students' comprehension.

Consider an attendance policy at a local urban school district in Tennessee. Students are allowed to miss only 7 days during an academic semester, including both excused and unexcused absences (e.g., absences for religious holidays count as part of the 7). Students who miss more than 7 days are either failed or have to attend Saturday school. Students have 3 days to make up any work missed during an absence, otherwise they receive the grade of zero for that work. There is a similar policy with regard to school tardiness. The rationale for the policy is twofold; students cannot learn when they are not in school, and, adolescents get into trouble when they are not in school. The result of this policy, as claimed by school officials, has been an increase in attendance especially at those schools that previously has low attendance rates. However, other results have been to set families against the schools. Parents often send sick children to school out of fear of the attendance policy. For those families that rely on their adolescent children to help with maintaining the family (perhaps through assistance with child care, elder care, or finances), an important means of support has been taken from them and parents must choose between family needs and the negative consequences of the school policy. In its initial implementation, middle-class families taking their adolescents on college visits were not excused and they had to curtail such activities; however, through formal and informal policies such trips have become school activities and are not necessarily counted as absences.

What is at issue is how schooling and family–community life are being defined. Schools have become an extension of the business community, and families and communities are being asked to redefine themselves as support systems for the schools. What is worrisome is not the role of schools in providing access to the business sector of society; rather it is the unidimensionalizing of schools and families in terms of such access. It is the failure of schools to view themselves as support systems to families and communities, in addition to their roles as providing access to the economic sector of society. In such a social, cultural, and political context, reading and writing become ways of structuring social relationships among teachers, students, and parents in regard to the encroachment of the market economy into schools and families. Students read and write to gain the credentials that will give them the economic opportunities available, and there is little or no space or time for reading and writing that fulfills any other agenda.

And yet, as de Certeau (1984) pointed out, ordinary people are very adept at dodging and transforming the encroachments of a market economy into their lives. In the next section, I discuss the reading and writing that people do to fulfill many needs in their everyday lives that eschew the encroachment of the market economy.

AN APPRECIATION OF WHAT HAS BEEN CALLED LOCAL LITERACIES AND THE READING AND WRITING DONE BY ORDINARY PEOPLE IN THEIR EVERYDAY LIVES

Studies of reading and writing in people's everyday lives (e.g., Barton & Hamilton, 1998; Barton & Ivanic, 1991; Hamilton, Barton & Ivanic, 1994; Horowitz, 1998; Knobel, 1999; Oates, chap. 2, this volume; Sheridan et al., in press), undercut the prevalent view of an illiterate and aliterate society. These studies also show that ordinary people use reading and writing for a broad range of purposes that create meaningful and caring relationships, that affect change in their local situations, and that contribute to change in broader social and cultural contexts. The uses of reading and writing are not circumscribed wholly by the encroachment of the market economy. There is a lot to learn about the uses and nature of reading and writing in the lives of ordinary people that can inform directions for reading and writing education in secondary schools.

In their study of a working-class community in northern England, Barton and Hamilton found that many of the people they studied used reading and writing to participate in local interest and political groups, to pursue interests beyond work or civic duty, or a combination of both (e.g., bird watching, studying World War II, collecting, crafts of various kinds, allotment gardens).

In our study of people writing for the Mass-Observation Project (Sheridan et al., in press), we came across ordinary people who used writing to transform (or attempt to transform) their communities and families. Yet, many of these same people would never consider themselves to be writers and much of their writing is invisible to pundits and politicians who claim a literacy crisis (Barton, Bloome, Sheridan & Street, 1993). For example, Mrs. Friend wrote extensive letters to a broad range of family members and friends. Her letters were often 12 pages long and she wrote several each day. Through these letters she maintained family and friendship relationships even though people had moved away. A quick look at her home would never suggest a writer's workshop. She wrote often in the evening when she and her husband would sit in the living room. Hidden in cabinets and in various furniture were her supplies and files that she would take out while her husband watched television. In addition to these letters, she had begun a novel. Another person we interviewed, Mr. Reed, was a former construction worker, disabled by back injuries, who lived in an economically depressed section of London. His home was very crowded and he had many tough circumstances in his family. He had suffered several hurtful indignities in his life, primarily because of his working-class status. Nonetheless, he found time and energy to write poetry as part of a local community group. He shared his poetry and the writing process with his family and the people he knew. There was no economic gain to this poetry writing, its effect was to transform who he was and who the people in his community were from merely being nameless victims of an economic system, to having the full range of human emotions and a sense of agency (despite obstacles and limitations on what might be accomplished).

Appreciation for local literacies goes beyond what people individually and in families do. It extends to the various community writing projects. In many communities, in the United States and elsewhere, ordinary people come together to establish a community writing project that may take the form of publishing local histories, autobiographies, political treatises, etc. Sometimes these books are sold in local bookstores or in community centers. In some cases, local teachers have taken on such projects, enlisting students in writing about their local communities and then publishing books or magazines that make what they have learned about their communities visible and public (e.g., Egan-Robertson, 1998; Schaafsma, 1998). Sometimes such projects are overtly political, in the sense of affirming local culture and people. There are also other projects that sit on the fence between establishment institutions (such as universities) on one hand and ordinary people and local communities on the other. The Mass-Observation Project in the United Kingdom is one such project in which academics at the University of Sussex coordinate a people's history and ethnography project, inviting ordinary people to write about particular aspects of life in the United Kingdom.

Another community project is the writing of Yisker Bikher, Jewish Memorial books written after World War II to commemorate and preserve the Jewish communities that had existed in Europe prior to their destruction by the Nazis. Landsmanshaftn (Jewish Community and Immigrant Groups in the U.S., Israel, and South America, organized around previous inhabitants of a particular community) would make a call to their members to write about their previous and now destroyed city, town, or village, and a history would be written. Sometimes a landsmanshaftn would also hire a professional writer or historian to help with the task. Often, the books were written first in Yiddish or Hebrew, and later translated to English so that future generations could read them. The creation of Yisker Bikher can loosely be traced back to the writing of pinkesim, a sort of diary that might be kept by the burial society of a Jewish community or by other notables, that recorded the history of the community. Pinkesim were also kept by individuals about their businesses or families. The writing of Yisker Bikher can be traced loosely back to memorial books written in response to previous pogroms (attempts at the mass murdering of the Jewish people). The writing of Yisker Bikher also seems to be related to the efforts of Jewish organizations in pre-Holocaust Europe to engage ordinary Jewish people in writing about their lives. But in the final analysis, the writing of the Yisker Bikher was a creative adaptation of previous writing genres both from Jewish history and elsewhere, firmly grounded in the culture and ideology of the landsmanshaftn.

It is not that the Mass-Observation Project or the writing of Yisker Bikher should be duplicated by others, but rather that there is a lot of writing that goes on in everyday life and by ordinary people that is often invisible to schools, academics, journalists, and dominant society in general. This writing has a long, rich history that people and educators can build on and can adapt to address the needs and interests of ordinary people now and in the future. It does not sit lower in a hierarchy of writing, but rather, side-by-side with any writing.

The questions that acknowledgment and appreciation of these local literacies raise for schools concern the models and definitions of reading and writing promulgated in schools. To what degree do schools engage students in models of reading and writing that would encourage them to participate in the kinds of local literacies previously described? If reading and writing are defined primarily or exclusively as tools for gaining access to dominant society (and more particularly, to the economic sector of dominant society), how will students ever learn about ways of using writing and reading that have transformative potential in the social, cultural, and political spheres that also make up the worlds in which they live? How will students ever learn about the literacy histories and legacies they have within their local communities? How will they ever own their reading and writing? And how will schools ever get beyond the creation of a few authors who use writing to create worlds, and a multitude of scribes who merely copy down and pass on the writing of others (cf. Wolf & Perry, 1988)?

FINAL COMMENTS

I have listed four issues that, among others, need to be considered in moving toward a vision of reading and writing in a democratic and just society. Like others, I have argued that the ways in which reading and writing are constituted contribute to and reflect social and cultural ideologies that legitimize inequitable power relationships, the hegemony of a market economy, and all of the pain, suffering, and lost dreams that are a part of such ideologies. To date, the field has provided a language of critique (e.g., Janks & Ivanic, 1992) and directions for reading and writing education that resist the imposition of hierarchical and hegemonic ideologies and their effects (e.g., Benton, Hamilton, & Padmore, 1994; De & Gregory, 1997; Egan-Robertson & Bloome, 1998; Foster, 1995; Kutz & Roskelly, 1991; Moll & Diaz, 1987; Soliday, 1997; Yeager, Floriani & Green, 1998). In my view, these directions along with acknowledgment of the social, cultural, and political nature of reading and writing, the appreciation for diversity of literacies and for what people and communities do with reading and writing in their everyday lives, and provide a basis for beginning to envision reading and writing in a democratic and just society. The chapters in this volume are part of the language of critique, illustrate resistant literacy practices both in classroom and nonclassroom settings, and help build a foundation that may lead to a vision of reading and writing in a democratic and just society. The unidimensionalization of school reading and writing education, as gaining access to dominant society and its emphasis on effectiveness, needs to be replaced by a broader and multidimensional concept of the uses and meanings of reading and writing. One that builds on the reading and writing that ordinary people do in their everyday lives, and one that takes as fundamental that everyone is a writer with a thousand stories worth reading. Such an acknowledgment and transformation cannot occur only in classrooms, but it cannot occur if it does not happen in classrooms.

ACKNOWLEDGMENTS

I gratefully acknowledge the assistance of Stephanie Powers, who helped with editorial and related aspects of this manuscript. Whatever flaws remain in the manuscript are my sole responsibility.

REFERENCES

Alcoff, L. (1989). Justifying feminist social science. In N. Tauna (Ed.). *Feminism and science.* Bloomington: Indiana University.

Alcoff, L. (1995). Cultural feminism versus post-structuralism: The identity crisis in feminist theory. In N. Tuana & R. Tong (Eds.), *Feminism and philosophy* (pp. 434–456). Boulder, CO: Westview Press.

Alcoff, L. M. (1996). *Real knowing: New versions of the coherence theory.* Ithaca, NY: Cornell University Press.

Alexander, P. A. (1997). Mapping the multidimensional nature of domain learning: The interplay of cognitive, motivational, and strategic forces. In M. L. Maehr & P. R. Pintrich (Eds.), *Advances in motivation and achievement* (Vol. 10). Greenwich, CT: JAI.

Allington, R. L., & McGill-Franzen, A. (1993). Placing children at risk: Schools respond to reading problems. In R. Donmoyer & R. Kos (Eds.), *At-risk students: Portraits, Policies, programs, and practices* (pp. 197–217). Albany: State University of New York Press.

Alvermann, D. E. (1993, December). Student voice in class discussion: A feminist poststructuralist perspective. In *Expanding the possibilities: How feminist theories inform traditions and positions in reader response, classroom discussion and critical thinking.* Meeting of the National Reading Conference, Charleston, SC.

Alvermann, D. E. (1995/1996). Peer-led discussions: Whose interests are served? *Journal of Adolescent and Adult Literacy, 39,* 282–289.

Alvermann, D. E. (1998). Imagining the possibilities. In D. E. Alvermann, K. A. Hinchman, D. W. Moore, S. F. Phelps, & D. R. Waff (Eds.), *Reconceptualizing the literacies in adolescents' lives* (pp. 353–372). Mahwah, NJ: Lawrence Erlbaum Associates.

Alvermann, D. E., & Commeyras, M. (1994). Gender, text and discussion: Expanding the possibilities. In R. Garner & P. Alexander (Eds.), *Beliefs about text and instruction with text* (pp. 183–199). Hillsdale, NJ: Lawrence Erlbaum Associates.

Alvermann, D. E., Commeyras, M., Young, J. P., Randall, S., & Hinson, D. (1997). Interrupting gendered discursive practices in classroom talk about texts: Easy to think about, difficult to do. *Journal of Literacy Research, 29,* 73–104.

Alvermann, D. E., & Dillon, D. R. (1991). Response: Ways of knowing are ways of seeing—A response to Roller. *Reading Research Quarterly, 26,* 329–333.

Alvermann, D. E., Dillon, D., & O'Brien, D. (1987). *Using discussion to promote reading comprehension.* Newark, DE: International Reading Association.

Alvermann, D. E., & Guthrie, J. T. (1993). *Themes and directions of the National Reading Research Center* (Perspectives in Reading Research No. 1).Universities of Georgia and Maryland, National Reading Research Center.

Alvermann, D., Hinchman, K., Moore, D., Phelps, S., & Waff, D. (Eds.). (1998). *Reconceptualizing the literacies in adolescents' lives.* Mahwah, NJ: Lawrence Erlbaum Associates.

Alvermann, D. E., & Moore, D. W. (1991). Secondary school reading. In R. Barr, M. L. Kamil, P. B. Mosenthal & P. D. Pearson (Eds.), *Handbook of reading research Vol. II* (pp. 951–983). New York: Longman.

Alvermann, D. E., O'Brien, D. G., & Dillon, D. R. (1990). What teachers do when they say they're having discussions of content reading assignments. *Reading Research Quarterly, 24,* 295–322.

Alvermann, D. E., & Phelps, S. F. (1998). *Content reading and literacy: Succeeding in today's diverse classrooms* (2nd ed.). Boston: Allyn & Bacon.

Alvermann, D. E., & Swafford, J. (1989). Do content area strategies have a research base? *Journal of Reading, 32,* 388–394.

Alvermann, D. E., Young, J. P., Weaver, D., Hinchman, K. A., Moore, D., Phelps, S., Thrash, E., & Zalewski, P. (1996). Middle and high school students' perceptions of how they experience text-based discussions: A multi-case study. *Reading Research Quarterly, 31,* 244–267.

American Association of University Women. (1992). *How schools shortchange girls: A study of major findings on girls and education.* Washington, DC: Author.

Anderman, E. M., & Maehr, M. L. (1994). Motivation and schooling in the middle grades. *Reviews of Educational Research, 64,* 287–389.

Anders, P. L., & Evans, K. S. (1994). Relationships between teachers' beliefs and their instructional practice in reading. In R. Garner & P. A. Alexander (Eds.), *Beliefs about text and instruction with text* (pp. 137–153). Hillsdale, NJ: Lawrence Erlbaum Associates.

Anders, P. L., & Guzzetti, B. J. (1996). *Literacy instruction in the content areas.* Fort Worth, TX: Harcourt Brace College Publishers.

Anderson, R. C., & Biddle, W. B. (1975). On asking people questions about what they are reading. In G. Bower (Ed.), *Psychology of learning and motivation* (Vol. 9, pp. 89–132). New York: Academic Press.

Anderson, R. C., & Pearson, P. D. (1984). A schema-theoretic view of basic processes in reading comprehension. In P. D. Pearson, R. Barr, M. L. Kamil, & P. Mosenthal (Eds.), *Handbook of reading research* (pp. 225–253). New York: Longman.

Anderson, T. H., & West, C. K. (1995). Commentary: An analysis of a qualitative investigation: A matter of whether to believe. *Reading Research Quarterly, 30,* 562–569.

Anderson, V. A., & Roit, M. (1993). Planning and implementing collaborative planning instruction for delayed readers in grades 6–10. *Elementary School Journal, 94,* 121–137.

Andrade, R. (1998). Life in elementary school: Children's ethnographic reflections. In A. Egan-Robertson & D. Bloome (Eds.), *Students as researchers of culture and language in their own communities* (pp. 93–115). Cresskill, NJ: Hampton Press.

Anyon, J. (1980). Social class and school knowledge. *Curriculum Inquiry, 11,* 1–42.

Anyon, J. (1994). The retreat of Marxism and socialist feminism: Postmodern and poststructuralist theories in education. *Curriculum Inquiry, 24,* 115–134.

Apple, M. (1988). *Teachers & Texts: A political economy of class & gender relations in education.* New York: Routledge.

Apple, M. (1993). *Official knowledge.* New York: Routledge.

Apple, M. W. (1986). *Teachers and texts: The political economy of class and gender relations in education.* Boston: Routledge & Kegan Paul.

Apple, M. W. (1996). *Cultural politics and education.* New York: Teachers College Press.

Apple, M. W., & Christian-Smith, L. (1991) The politics of the textbook. In M. W. Apple & L. Christian-Smith (Eds.), *The politics of the textbook* (pp. 1–21. New York: Routledge.

Applebee, A. N. (1981). *Writing in the secondary school.* Urbana, IL: National Council of Teachers of English.

Applebee, A. (1984a). *Contexts for learning to write: Studies of secondary school instruction.* Norwood, NJ: Ablex.

Applebee, A. N. (1984b). Writing and reasoning. *American Educational Research Journal, 54,* 577–596.

Armstrong, J., Dubert, L., & Drabik, M. (1995, November). *Improving the likelihood of content literacy strategy use.* Paper presented at the National Reading Conference, New Orleans, LA.

Aronowitz, S., & Giroux, H. A. (1991). *Postmodern education.* Minneapolis: University of Minnesota Press.

Artley, A. S. (1968). *Trends and practices in secondary reading.* Newark, DE: International Reading Association.

Asante, M. K. (1988). *Afrocentricity.* Trenton, NJ: Africa World Press, Inc.

Asante, M. K. (1991). The Afrocentric idea in education. *Journal of Negro Education, 60,* 170–180.

Asante, M. K. (1992). Afrocentric systematics. *Black Issues in Higher Education, 9,* 16–17.

Asante, M. K. (1994). The Afrocentric project in education. In M. J. Shujaa (Ed.), *Too much schooling, too little education: A paradox of Black life in White societies* (pp. 395–398). Trenton, NJ: Africa World Press, Inc.

Athanases, S. Z. (1998). Diverse learners, diverse texts: Exploring identity and difference through literacy encounters. *Journal of Literacy Research, 30,* 273–296.

Atwell, N. (1987). *In the middle.* Portsmouth, NH: Heinemann.

Atwell, N. (1990). *Coming to know.* Portsmouth, NH: Heinemann.

Atwell, N. (1997). Cultivating our garden. *The Council Chronicle, 6*(5), 16.

Au, K. (1980). Participation structures in a reading lesson with Hawaiian children. *Anthropology and Education Quarterly, 11*(2), 91–115.

Ayres, L. P. (1913). *Laggards in our schools.* New York: Survey Associates.

Baker, C., & Luke, C. (Eds.). (1991). *Toward a critical sociology of reading pedagogy.* Philadelphia: John Benjamins.

Bakhtin, M. M. (1986). *Speech genres and other late essays.* (V. W. McGee, Trans.; C. Emerson & M. Holquist, Eds.). Austin: University of Texas Press. (original work published 1953)

Baldwin, J. (1981). *Go tell it on the mountain.* New York: Dell.

Baldwin, R. S., Readence, J. E., Schumm, J. S., Konopak, J. P., Konopak, B. C., & Klingner, J. K. (1992). Forty years of NRC publications: 1952–1991. *Journal of Reading Behavior, 25,* 505–532.

Ball, A., & Heath, S. B. (1993). Dances of identity: Finding an ethnic self in the arts. In S. B. Heath and M. McLaughlin (Eds.), *Identity and inner city youth: Beyond ethnicity and gender* (pp. 69–93). New York: Teachers College Press.

Ball, S. J., & Lacey, C. (1984). Subject disciplines as the opportunity for a group action: A measured critique of subject sub-cultures. In A. Hargreaves & P. Woods (Eds.), *Classrooms and staffrooms: The sociology of teachers and teaching* (pp. 234–244). Milton Keynes, Great Britain: Open University Press.

Barbieri, M. (1995). *Sounds from the heart.* Portsmouth, NH: Heinemann.

Barnes, D. (1990). Oral language and learning. In S. R. D. Hynds (Ed.), *Perspectives on talk and learning* (pp. 41–54). Urbana, IL: National Council of Teachers of English.

Barnes, D., Britton, J., & Rosen, H. (1971). *Language, the learner, and the school.* Harmondsworth, England: Penguin.

Barron, R. F., & Stone, V. F. (1974). The effect of student-generated graphic post organizers upon learning vocabulary relationships. In P. L. Nacke (Ed.), *Interaction: Research and practice in college adult reading* (pp. 172–175). Twenty-third Yearbook of the National Reading Conference. Clemson, SC: National Reading Conference.

Barton, D. (1991). The social nature of writing. In D. Barton & R. Ivanic (Eds.), *Writing in the community* (pp. 1–13). Newbury Park, CA: Sage.

Barton, D. (1994). *Literacy: An introduction to the ecology of written language.* Oxford, England: Blackwell.

Barton, D., Bloome, D., Sheridan, D., & Street, B. (1993). *Ordinary people writing: The Lancaster & Sussex writing research projects* (Working Paper #51). Lancaster, England: Centre for Language in Social Life.

Barton, D., & Hamilton, M. (1998). *Local literacies.* London: Routledge & Kegan Paul.

Barton, D., & Ivanic, R. (Eds.). (1991). *Writing in the community.* Newbury Park, CA: Sage.

Baudrillard, J. (1988). *Selected works.* (M. Poster, Ed. & Trans.). Cambridge: Polity Press.

Beach, R. (1992). Adopting multiple stances in conducting literacy research. In R. Beach, J. L. Green, M. L. Kamil, & T. Shanahan (Eds.), *Multidisciplinary perspectives on literacy research* (pp. 91–110). Urbana, IL: National Conference on Research in English/National Council of Teachers of English.

Beach, R., Green, J. L., Kamil, M. L., & Shanahan, T. (Eds.). (1992). *Multidisciplinary perspectives on literacy research.* Urbana, IL: National Conference on Research in English/National Council of Teachers of English.

Beach, R., & Hynds, S. (Eds.). (1990). *Developing discourse practices in adolescence and adulthood.* Norwood, NJ: Ablex.

Bean, T. W., & Readence, J. E. (1989). Content area reading: Current state of the art. In D. Lapp, J. Flood, & N. Farnan (Eds.), *Content area reading and learning* (pp. 14–23). Englewood Cliffs, NJ: Prentice-Hall.

Beason, L. (1993). Feedback and revision in writing across the curriculum classes. *Research in the Teaching of English, 27,* 395–418.

Beck, I. L., McKeown, M. G., Worthy, J., Sandora, C. A., & Kucan, L. (1996). Questioning the author: A yearlong classroom implementation to engage students with texts. *Elementary School Journal, 96,* 385–414.

Becker, H., Geer, B., & Hughes, E. (1995). *Making the grade: The academic side of college life.* New Brunswick, NJ: Transaction Publishing.

Bellack, A. A., Kliebard, H. M., Hyman, R. T., & Smith, F. L., Jr. (1966). *The language of the classroom.* New York: Teachers College Press.

Benton, S., Hamilton, M., & Padmore, S. (1994). Breaking and remaking the rules. In M. Hamilton, D. Barton, & R. Ivanic (Eds.), *Worlds of literacy* (pp. 258–264). Clevedon: Multilingual Matters.

Berger, A., & Robinson, H. A. (Eds.). (1982). *Secondary school reading.* Urbana, IL: ERIC Clearinghouse on Reading and Communication Skills and National Conference on Research in English.

Berger, P. L., & Luckmann, T. (1967). *The social construction of reality.* Garden City, NY: Doubleday.

Berlin, J. (1987). *Rhetoric and reality: Writing instruction in American colleges, 1900–1985.* Urbana, IL: National Council of Teachers of English.

Berthoff, A. E. (1990). Killer dichotomies: Reading in/reading out. In K. Ronald & H. Roskelly (Eds.), *Farther along: Transforming dichotomies in rhetoric and composition* (pp. 12–24). Portsmouth, NH: Heinemann.

Biklen, S. K. (1995). *School work: Gender and the cultural construction of teaching.* New York: Teachers College Press.

Bing, J. M., & Bergvall, V. L. (1997). The question of questions: Beyond binary thinking. In V. L. Bergvall, J. M. Bing, & A. F. Freed (Eds.), *Rethinking language and gender research.* London: Addison-Wesley Longman.

Bitting, P. F., Cordeiro, P. A., & Baptiste, H. P. (1992). Philosophical and conceptual issues related to students at risk. In H. C. Waxman, J. W. d. Felix, J. E. Anderson, & H. P. Baptiste (Eds.), *Students at risk in at-risk schools* (pp. 17–32). Newbury Park, CA: Corwin.

Bloom, A. (1987). *The closing of the American mind.* NY: Simon & Schuster.

Bloome, D. (1983). Reading as a social process. In B. Hutson (Ed.), *Advances in reading / language research,* Vol. 2. (pp. 165–196). Greenwich, CT: JAI.

Bloome, D. (1985). Reading as a social process. *Language Arts, 62,* 134–142.

Bloome, D. (Ed.). (1987a). *Literacy and schooling.* Norwood, NJ: Ablex.

Bloome, D. (1987b). Reading as a social process in a middle school classroom. In D. Bloome (Ed.), *Literacy and schooling* (pp. 123–149). Norwood, NJ: Ablex.

Bloome, D. (1989a). Beyond access: An ethnographic study of reading and writing in a seventh grade classroom. In D. Bloome (Ed.), *Classrooms and literacy* (pp. 53–104). Norwood, NJ: Ablex.

Bloome, D. (Ed). (1989b). *Classrooms and literacy.* Norwood, NJ: Ablex.

Bloome, D. (1991). Anthropology and research on teaching the English language arts. In J. Flood, J. M. Jensen, D. Lapp, & J. R. Squire (Eds.), *Handbook of research on teaching the English language arts* (pp. 46–56). New York: Macmillan.

Bloome, D. (1997). This is literacy: Three challenges for teachers of reading and writing. *Australian Journal Of Language And Literacy, 20*(2), 107–115.

Bloome, D., & Bailey, F. (1992). From linguistics and education, a direction for the study of language and literacy. In R. Beach, J. Green, M. Kamil, & T. Shanahan (Eds.), *Multiple disciplinary perspectives on language and literacy research* (pp. 181–210). Urbana, IL: NCRE and NCTE.

Bloome, D., & Egan-Robertson, A. (1993). The social construction of intertextuality in classroom reading and writing lessons. *Reading Research Quarterly, 28,* 305–333.

Bloome, D., & Green, J. (1984). Directions in the sociolinguistic study of reading. In P. D. Pearson (Ed.), *Handbook of reading research* (Vol. 1, pp. 395–421). New York: Longman.

Bloome, D., Puro, P., & Theodorou, E. (1989). Procedural display and classroom lessons. *Curriculum Inquiry, 19*(3), 265–291.

Blumer, H. (1969). *Symbolic interactionism: Perspective and method.* Englewood Cliffs, NJ: Prentice-Hall.

Bogdan, R. C., & Biklen, S. K. (1992). *Qualitative research for education: An introduction to theory and methods* (2nd ed.). Boston: Allyn & Bacon.

Borland, K. (1991). "That's not what I said": Interpretive conflict in oral narrative research. In S. B. Gluck & D. Patai (Eds.), *Women's words: The feminist practice of oral history* (pp. 63–75). New York: Routledge.

Bormuth, J. (1968). Cloze test readability: Criterion scores. *Journal of Educational Measurement, 5,* 189–196.

Bourdieu, P. (1977). *Outline of a theory of practice.* Cambridge, England: Cambridge University Press.

Boyer, E. L. (1983). *High school: A report on secondary education in America.* New York: Colophon.

Brandau, D. M., & Collins, J. (1994). Texts, social relations, and work-based skepticism about schooling: An ethnographic analysis. *Anthropology and Education Quarterly, 25,* 2, 118–136.

Brandt, D. (1994). Remembering writing, remembering reading. *College Composition and Communication, 45,* 459–479.

Britton, J., Burgess, T., Martin, N., McLeod, A., & Rosen, H. (1975). *The development of writing abilities (11–18).* London: Macmillan Education Ltd. for the Schools Council.

Brodkey, L. (1987). *Academic writing as social practice.* Philadelphia: Temple University Press.

Brodkey, L. (1992). Articulating poststructural theory in research on literacy. In R. Beach, J. L. Green, M. L. Kamil, & T. Shanahan (Eds.), *Multidisciplinary perspectives on literacy research* (pp. 293–318). Urbana, IL: National Conference on Research in English and National Council of Teachers of English.

Bromley, H. (1998). Introduction: Data-driven democracy? Social assessments of educational computing. In H. Bromley & M. W. Apple (Eds.), *Education/Technology/Power: Educational computing as a social practice* (pp. 1–25). Albany: State University of New York.

Bromley, H., & Apple, M. W. (Eds.). (1998). *Education/technology/power.* Albany: State University of New York Press.

Brown, J. S., Collins, A., & Duguid, P. (1989). Situated cognition and the culture of learning. *Educational Researcher, 18,* 32–42.

Bruce, B. (1981). A social interaction model of reading. *Discourse Processes, 4,* 273–311.

Bruner, J. (1986). *Actual minds, possible worlds.* Cambridge, MA: Harvard University Press.

Buckingham, D., & Sefton-Green, J. (1994). *Cultural studies goes to school.* London: Taylor & Francis.

Bullock, A. (1975). *A language for life.* (Report of the Committee of Inquiry Appointed by the Secretary of State for Education and Science). London: Her Majesty's Stationery Office.

Bullough, R. (1987). School knowledge, power, and human experience. *The Educational Forum, 51,* 259–274.

Bullough, R. (1989). First year teacher; A case study. New York Teachers College Press.

Busia, A. P. A. (1989). What is your nation?: Reconnecting Africa and her diaspora through Paule Marshall's *Praisesong for the Widow.* In C. A. Wall (Ed.), *Changing our own words: Essays on criticism, theory, and writing by black women* (pp. 196–211). New Brunswick, NJ: Rutgers University Press.

Butler, J. (1993). *Bodies that matter: On the discursive limits of "sex."* New York: Routledge.

Cai, M. (1997). Reader-response theory and the politics of multi-cultural literature. In T. Rogers & A. Soter (Eds.), *Reading across cultures: Teaching literature in a diverse society* (pp. 199–212). New York: Teachers College Press.

Calkins, L. M. (1994). *The art of teaching writing.* Portsmouth, NH: Heinemann.

Cazden, C. (1986). Classroom discourse. In M. Wittrock (Ed.), *The handbook of research on teaching* (Vol. 3, pp. 432–464). New York: Macmillan.

Cazden, C. (1988). *Classroom discourse: The language of teaching and learning.* Portsmouth, NH: Heinemann.

Cazden, C., John, V., & Hymes, D. (Eds.). (1962). *Functions of language in the classroom.* New York: Teachers College Press.

ChristianSmith, L. (Ed.). (1993). *Texts of desire: Essays on fiction, femininity, and schooling.* Washington, DC: Falmer.

Christie, F. (1989). *Language education.* London: Oxford University Press.

Clark, R., & Ivanic, R. (1997). *The Politics of Writing.* London, Routledge & Kegan Paul.

Clark, V. (1991). Developing diaspora literacy and *marasa* consciousness. In H. Spillers (Ed.), *Comparative American identities* (pp. 41–61). New York: Routledge.

Cochran-Smith, M., & Lytle, S. (1993). *Inside outside: Teacher research and knowledge.* New York: Teachers College Press.

Cohen, J., Christman, J., & Gold, E. (1998). Critical literacy and school reform: "So much to do in so little time.'" In D. E. Alvermann, K. A. Hinchman, D. W. Moore, S. Phelps, & D. Waff (Eds.), *Reconceptualizing the literacies in adolescents' lives* (pp. 303–324). Mahwah, NJ: Lawrence Erlbaum Associates.

Collins, J. (1987). Using cohesion analysis to understand access to knowledge. In D. Bloome (Ed.), *Literacy and schooling* (pp. 70–97). Norwood, NJ: Ablex.

Collins, J. (1991). Hegemonic practice: Literacy and standard language in public education. In C. Mitchell & K. Lueiles (Eds.), *Rewriting literacy: Culture and the discourse of the other* (pp. 229–254). New York: Benjamin & Garvey.

Collins, N. D., & Collins, J. R. (1992). A crack in time: A student traversing paradigms. *Journal of Reading Behavior, 24,* 403–411.

Collins, P. H. (1995). The social construction of Black feminist thought. In N. Tuana & R. Tong (Eds.), *Feminism and philosophy* (pp. 526–547). Boulder, CO: Westview Press.

The Combahee River Collective. (1983). The Combahee River Collective statement. In B. Smith (Ed.), *Home girls: A Black feminist anthology* (pp. 272–282). New York: Kitchen Table Press.

Cone, J. (1994). Appearing acts: Creating readers in a high school English class. *Harvard Educational Review, 64,* 450–473.

Conley, M. (1988, May). Summary and closing comments. In M. W. Conley (Chair), *Directions for research and practice in secondary school reading.* Symposium conducted at the meeting of the International Reading Association, Toronto, Canada.

Conquergood, D. (1997). Street literacy. In J. Flood, S, Heath, & D. Lapp (Eds.), *Handbook of research on teaching literacy through the communicative and visual arts* (pp. 354–375). New York: Simon & Schuster .

Constas, M. A. (1998). Deciphering postmodern educational research. *Educational Researcher, 27*(9), 36–41.

Cook-Gumperz, J. (1986). *The social construction of literacy.* New York: Cambridge University Press.

Covington, M. V. (1992). *Making the grade: A self-worth perspective on motivation and school reform.* New York: Cambridge University Press.

Craik, F. I. M., & Lockhart, R. S. (1972). Levels of processing: A framework for memory research. *Journal of Verbal Learning and Verbal Behavior, 11,* 671–684.

Crawford, T., Kelly, G. J., & Brown, C. (1999, March). *Ways of knowing beyond facts and laws of science: An ethnographic investigation of student engagement in scientific practices.* Paper presented at the annual meeting of the National Association of Research in Science Teaching, Boston, MA.

Creswell, J. W. (1998). *Qualitative inquiry and research design: Choosing among five traditions.* Thousand Oaks, CA: Sage.

Cuban, L. (1984). *How teachers taught.* New York: Longman.

Cuban, L. (1986). Persistent instruction: Another look at constancy in the classroom. *Phi Delta Kappan, 68*(1), 7–11.

Cuban, L. (1989). The 'at-risk' label and the problem of urban reform. *Phi Delta Kappan, 70*, 780–784, 799–801.

Cunningham, J. W., & Fitzgerald, J. (1996). Epistemology and reading. *Reading Research Quarterly, 31*, 36–60.

Curry, T., & Bloome, D. (1998). Learning to write by writing ethnography. In A. Egan-Robertson & D. Bloome (Eds.), *Students as researchers of culture and language in their own communities* (pp. 37–58). Cresskill, NJ: Hampton Press.

Cusick, P. *The egalitarian ideal and the American high school: Studies of three schools.* New York: Longman.

Davies, B. (1993). Beyond dualism and towards multiple subjectivities. In L. Christian-Smith (Ed.), *Texts of desire*. London: Falmer.

Davies, B. (1996). *Power/knowledge/desire*. Canberra, Australia: Department of Employment, Education, Training, and Youth Affairs.

Davis, A. B., Sumara, D. J., & Kieren, T. E. (1996). Cognition, co-emergence, curriculum. *Journal of Curriculum Studies, 28*, 151–169.

De, E. N., & Gregory, D. U. (1997). Decolonizing the classroom: Freshman composition in a multicultural setting. In C. Severino, J. Guerra, & J. Butler (Eds.), *Writing in multicultural settings* (pp. 118–132). New York: The Modern Language Association of America.

de Certeau, M. (1984). *The practice of everyday life*. Berkeley: University of California Press.

Delamont, S. (1983). *Interaction in the classroom* (2nd ed.). London: Methuen.

de Lauretis, T. (1984). *Alice doesn't*. Bloomington: Indiana University Press.

Delpit, L. D. (1988). The silenced dialogue: Pedagogy and power in educating other people's children. *Harvard Educational Review, 58*, 280–298.

Delpit, L. (1995). *Other people's children: Cultural conflict in the classroom*. New York: New Press.

Demory, P. (1994). Intertextuality. In A. C. Purves (Ed.), *Encyclopedia of English studies and language arts* (Vol. 1, pp. 663–665). New York: Scholastic.

Denzin, N. K. (1978). *The research act*. New York: McGraw-Hill.

Denzin, N. K. (1989). *Interpretive interactionism*. Thousand Oaks, CA: Sage.

Denzin, N. K. (1992). *Symbolic interaction and cultural studies*. Cambridge, MA: Blackwell.

Derrida, J. (1976). *Of grammatology*. [G. Spivak, Trans.] Baltimore: Johns Hopkins University Press.

Dewey, J. (1938). *Experience & education*. New York: Macmillan.

Dillon, D. (1990). Introduction to language across the curriculum. *Language Arts, 67*, 7–9.

Dillon, D. R. (1989). Showing them that I want them to learn and that I care about who they are: A microethnography of the social organization of a secondary low-track English-reading classroom. *American Educational Research Journal, 26*, 227–259.

Dillon, D. R., & Moje, E. B. (1998). Listening to the talk of adolescent girls: Lessons about literacy, school, and life. In D. E. Alvermann, K. A. Hinchman, D. W. Moore, S. Phelps, & D. Waff (Eds.), *Reconceptualizing adolescent literacies* (pp. 193–224). Mahwah, NJ: Lawrence Erlbaum Associates.

Dillon, D. R., O'Brien, D. G., Moje, E. B., & Stewart, R. A. (1994). Literacy learning in science classrooms: A cross-case analysis of three qualitative studies. *Journal of Research in Science Teaching 31*, 345–362.

Dillon, D. R., O'Brien, D. G., & Ruhl, J. (1988, December). *The construction of the social organization in one secondary content classroom. An ethnographic study of a biology teacher and his academic-track students.* Paper presented at the annual meeting of the National Reading Conference, Tucson, AZ.

Dillon, J. T. (1983). Cognitive complexity and duration of classroom speech. *Instructional Science, 12*, 59–66.

Donmoyer, R. (1996). Editorial: Educational research in an era of paradigm proliferation: What's a journal editor to do? *Educational Researcher, 25*(2), 19–25.

Donmoyer, R., & Kos, R. (1993). At-risk students: Insights from/about research. In R. Donmoyer & R. Kos (Eds.), *At-risk students: Portraits, policies, programs, and practices* (pp. 7–35). Albany: State University of New York Press.

Dressman, M. (1993). Lionizing lone wolves: The cultural romantics of literacy workshops. *Curriculum Inquiry, 23,* 245–263.

DuBois, B. L., & Crouch, I. (1975). The question of tag questions in women's speech: They don't really use more of them, do they? *Language in Society, 4,* 289–294.

Durst, R. K., & Newell, G. E. (1989). The uses of function: James Britton's category system and research on writing. *American Educational Research Journal, 59,* 375–394.

Dweck, C. S., & Leggett, E. L. (1988). A social-cognitive approach to motivation and personality. *Psychological Review, 95,* 256–273.

Dyson, A. H. (1989). *Multiple worlds of child writers: Friends learning to write.* New York: Teachers College Press.

Dyson, A. H. (1995). Writing children: Reinventing the development of childhood literacy. *Written Communication, 12,* 4–46.

Dyson, A. H., & Freedman, S. W. (1991). Writing. In J. Flood, J. M. Jensen, D. Lapp, & J. R. Squire (Eds.), *Handbook of research on teaching the English language arts* (pp. 754–774). New York: Macmillan.

Echols, A. (1983). The new feminism of yin and yang. In A. Snitow, C. Stansell, & S. Thompson (Eds.), *Powers of desire: The politics of sexuality* (pp. 430–459). New York: Monthly Review Press.

Eco, U. (1984). *Semiotics and the philosophy of language.* Bloomington: Indiana University Press.

Edelsky, C. (1979). Question intonation and sex role. *Language in Society, 8,* 15–32.

Edelsky, C. (1981). Who's got the floor? *Language in Society, 10,* 383–421.

Edwards, A. D., & Furlong, V. J. (1976). *The language of teaching.* London: Heinemann.

Egan-Robertson, A. (1998). "We must ask our questions and tell our stories": Writing ethnography and constructing personhood. In A. Egan-Robertson & D. Bloome (Eds.), *Students as researchers of culture and language in their own communities* (pp. 261–284). Cresskill, NJ: Hampton Press.

Egan-Robertson, A., & Bloome, D. (Eds.). (1998). *Students as researchers of culture and language in their own communities.* Cresskill, NJ: Hampton Press.

Elbow, P. (1976). *Writing without teachers.* New York: Oxford University Press.

Elbow, P. (1993). The war between reading and writing and how to end it. *Rhetoric Review, 12,* 5–24.

Elliot, J. (1988). Educational research and outsider–insider relations. *International Journal of Qualitative Studies in Education, 1,* 155–166.

Ellsworth, E. (1989). Why doesn't this feel empowering? Working through the repressive myths of critical pedagogy. *Harvard Education Review, 59,* 297–324.

Elsasser, N., & John-Steiner, V. (1977). An interactionist approach to advancing literacy. *Harvard Educational Review, 47*(3), 451–465.

Epstein, J. S. (1998). Introduction: Generation X, youth culture, and identity. In J. S. Epstein (Ed.), *Youth culture: Identity in a postmodern world* (pp. 1–23). Malden, MA: Blackwell.

Erickson, F. (1984). What makes school ethnography 'ethnographic'? *Anthropology & Education Quarterly, 15,* 51–66.

Erickson, F. (1986). Qualitative methods in research on teaching. In M. C. Wittrock (Ed.), *Handbook of research on teaching* (Vol. 3, pp. 119–161). New York: Macmillan.

Erickson, F. (1989). Research currents: Learning and collaboration in teaching. *Language Arts, 66,* 430–432.

Erickson, F., & Shultz, J. (1981). When is a context?: Some issues and methods in the analysis of social competence. In J. Green & C. Wallat (Eds.), *Ethnography and language in educational settings* (pp. 147–160). Norwood, NJ: Ablex.

Erickson, F., & Wilson, J. (1982). *Sights and sounds of life in schools: A resource guide to film and videotape for research and education* (Research Series No. 125). East Lansing, MI: Institute for Research on Teaching, College of Education.

Evans, H. (1997). An Afrocentric multicultural writing project. In C. Severino, J. Guerra, & J. Butler (Eds.), *Writing in multicultural settings* (pp. 273–286). New York: The Modern Language Association of America.

Evans, K., Alvermann, D. E., & Anders, P. L. (1998). Literature discussion groups: An examination of gender roles. *Reading Research and Instruction, 37*(2), 107–113.

Evans, K. S. (1996). A closer look at literature discussion groups: The influence of gender on student response and discourse. *The New Advocate, 9,* 183–196.

Everhart, R. (1983). *Reading, writing, and resistance: Adolescence and labour in a junior high school.* Boston: Routledge & Kegan Paul.

Evertson, C., & Green, J. (1986). Observation as inquiry and method. In M. Wittrock (Ed.), *The handbook of research on teaching* (Vol. 3, pp. 162–214). New York: Macmillan.

Fairclough, N. (1989). *Language and power.* London: Longman.

Fairclough, N. (1992). *Discourse and social change.* Cambridge, England: Polity Press.

Farr, M., & Guerra, J. (1995). Literacy in the community: A study of Mexicano Families in Chicago. *Discourse Processes, 19*(1), 7–19.

Farrell, R. T., & Cirrincione, J. M. (1984). State certification requirements in reading for content area teachers. *Journal of Reading, 28,* 152–158.

Fay, B. (1987). *Critical social science.* Ithaca, NY: Cornell University Press.

Fecho, R. (1998). Crossing boundaries of race in a critical literacy classroom. In D. E. Alvermann, K. A. Hinchman, D. W. Moore, S. Phelps, & D. Waff (Eds.), *Reconceptualizing the literacies in adolescents' lives* (pp. 75–102). Mahwah, NJ: Lawrence Erlbaum Associates.

Finders, M. (1996). "Just girls": Literacy and allegiance in junior high school. *Written Communication, 13,* 93–129.

Finders, M. (1997). *Just girls: Hidden literacies and life in junior high.* New York: Teachers College Press.

Fine, M. (1990). Making controversy: Who is "at risk"? *Journal of Urban and Cultural Studies, 1*(1), 555–568.

Fine, M. (1991). *Framing dropouts: Notes on the politics of an urban public high school.* Albany: State University of New York Press.

Fine, M. (1992). *Disruptive voices: The possibilities of feminist research.* Ann Arbor, MI: University of Michigan Press.

Fine, M. (1995). The politics of who's "at risk." In B. B. Swadener & S. Lubeck (Eds.), *Children and families "at promise": Deconstructing the discourse of risk* (pp. 76–94). Albany, NY: State University of New York Press.

Fiske, J. (1989). *Understanding popular culture.* London: Routledge.

Fleischer, C. (1994). Researching teacher-research: A practitioner's perspective. *English Education, 26*(2), 86–124.

Floriani, A. (1993). Negotiating what counts: Roles and relationships, texts and contexts, content and meaning. *Linguistics and Education, 5,* 241–273.

Florio, S., & Clark, C. (1984). *Comprehension instruction: Perspectives and suggestions.* New York: Longman.

Flower, L., Stein, V., Ackerman, J., Kantz, M. J., McCormick, K. and Peck, W. C. (1990). *Reading-to-write: Exploring a cognitive and social process.* New York: Oxford University Press.

Flynn, E., & Schweickart, P. (Eds.). (1986). *Gender and reading: Essays on readers, texts, and contexts.* Baltimore: Johns Hopkins University Press.

Foertsch, M. A. (1992). *Reading in and out of school: Factors influencing the literacy achievement of American students in grades 4, 8, and 12 in 1988 and 1990.* Washington, DC: National Center for Educational Statistics.

Fordham, S. (1996). *Blacked out.* New York: Routledge.

Foster, M. (1992). Sociolinguistics and the African-American community: Implications for literacy. *Theory Into Practice, 31*(4), 303–310.

Foster, M. (1995). Talking that talk: The language of control, curriculum, and critique. *Language and Education, 7,* 129–150.

Foucault, M. (1972). *The archaeology of knowledge and the discourse on language*. New York: Pantheon.

Foucault, M. (1977). Discipline and punish: The birth of a prison (2nd ed).

Foucault, M. (1980). *Power/knowledge: Selected interviews and other writings*. (C. Gordon, Ed., C. Gordon, L. Marshall, J. Mepham, & K. Soper, Trans.). New York: Pantheon.

Foucault, M. (1984). Nietzsche, genealogy, history. In P. Rabinow (Ed.), *The Foucault reader* (pp. 76–100). New York: Pantheon.

Freire, P. (1993). *Pedagogy of the oppressed*. New York: Continuum.

Freire, P., & Macedo, D. (1987). *Literacy: Reading the word and the world*. New York: Bergin & Garvey.

Fulwiler, T. (1987). *Teaching with writing*. Portsmouth, NH: Boynton/Cook.

Fulwiler, T. (1988). Evaluating writing across the curriculum programs. In S. H. McLeod (Ed.), *Strengthening programs for writing across the curriculum* (pp. 61–75). San Francisco: Jossey-Bass.

Fuss, D. (1989). *Essentially speaking*. New York: Routledge.

Gadsden, V. L. (1995). Introduction: Literacy and African American youth: Legacy and youth. In V. L. Gadsden & D. A. Wagner (Eds.), *Literacy among African American youth: Issues in learning, teaching, and schooling* (pp. 1–12). Cresskill, NJ: Hampton Press.

Gage, N. (1989). The paradigm wars and their aftermath: A "historical" sketch of research and teaching since 1989. *Educational Researcher, 18*(7), 4–10.

Gallas, K. (1995). *Talking their way into science: Hearing children's questions and theories, responding with curricula*. New York: Teachers College Press.

Garcia, R., & de Felix, J. W. (1995). The dropout issue in school reform. In H. C. Waxman, J. W. de Felix, J. E. Anderson, & H. P. Baptiste Jr. (Eds.), *Students at risk in at-risk schools*. Newbury Park, CA: Sage.

Garcia, G., Pearson, P. D., & Jimenez, R. T. (1994). *The at-risk situation: A synthesis of reading research* (Special Report). Urbana–Champaign: University of Illinois, Center for the Study of Reading.

Gee, J. P. (1993). Postmodernism and literacies. In C. Lankshear & P. L. McLaren (Eds.), *Critical literacy: Politics, praxis, and the postmodern* (pp. 271–295). Albany: State University of New York Press.

Gee, J. P. (1994). Orality and literacy: From *The Savage Mind* to *Ways with Words*. In J. Maybin (Ed.), *Language and literacy in social practice* (pp. 168–192). Philadelphia: The Open University.

Gee, J. P. (1996). *Social linguistics and literacies: Ideology in discourses*. (2nd ed.). London: The Falmer Press.

Gee, J. P., & Crawford, V. M. (1998). Two kinds of teenagers: Language, identity, and social class. In D. E. Alvermann, K. A. Hinchman, D. W. Moore, S. Phelps, & D. Waff (Eds.), *Reconceptualizing the literacies in adolescents' lives* (pp. 225–246). Mahwah, NJ: Lawrence Erlbaum Associates.

Gee, J. P., Michaels, S., & O'Connor, M. (1992). Discourse analysis. In M. D. LeCompte, W. L. Millroy, & J. Preissle (Eds.). *The handbook of qualitative research in education* (pp. 227–291). San Diego, CA: Academic Press.

Gergen, K. J. (1985). The social constructionist movement in modern psychology. *American Psychologist, 40*, 266–275.

Gehrke, N. J., Knapp, M. S., & Sirotnik, K. A. (1992). In search of school curriculum. In C. Grant (Ed.), *Review of research in education* (pp. 51–110). Washington, DC: American Education Research Association.

Gilbert, P. (1997). Discourses on gender and literacy: Changing the stories. In S. Muspratt, A. Luke, & P. Freebody (Eds.), *Constructing critical literacies* (pp. 69–76). Cresskill, NJ: Hampton Press.

Gilmore, P. (1987). Sulking, stepping, and tracking: The effects of attitude assessment on access to literacy. In D. Bloome (Ed.), *Literacy and schooling* (pp. 99–120). Norwood, NJ: Ablex.

Giroux, H. (1988a). *Schooling and the struggle for public life*. Minneapolis: University of Minnesota Press.

Giroux, H. A. (1988b). *Teachers as intellectuals: Toward a critical pedagogy of learning.* Granby, MA: Bergin & Garvey.

Giroux, H. A. (1992). *Border crossings.* New York: Routledge.

Glaser, B., & Strauss, A. (1967). *The discovery of grounded theory: Strategies for qualitative research.* New York: Aldine.

Glaser, B., & Strauss, A. (1978). *Advances in the methodology of grounded theory.* Mill Valley, CA: The Sociology Press.

Glatthorn, A. (1994). Postholing in the humanities. In A. C. Purves (Ed.), *Encyclopedia of English studies and language arts* (Vol. 2, p. 933). New York: Scholastic.

Goetz, J., & LeCompte, M. (1984). *Ethnography and qualitative design in educational research.* Orlando, FL: Academic Press.

Gold, Y. (1996). Beginning teacher support: Attrition, mentoring, and induction. In J. Sikula (Ed.), *Handbook of research on teacher education* (2nd ed., pp. 548–594). New York: Simon & Schuster.

Goodlad, J. I. (1984). *A place called school: Prospects for the future.* New York: McGraw-Hill.

Goodson, I. F. (1983). *School subjects and curriculum change.* London: Croom Helm.

Goodson, I. F. (1994). *Studying curriculum.* New York: Teachers College Press.

Goodson, I. F., & Anstead, C. J. (1994). Subject status and curriculum change: Local commercial education, 1920–1940. In I. F. Goodson (Ed.), *Studying curriculum* (pp. 82–95). New York: Teachers College Press.

Gordon, B. M. (1993). African-American cultural knowledge and liberatory education: Dilemmas, problems, and potentials in a postmodern American society. *Urban education, 27,* 448–470.

Graff, H. (1987). *The legacies of literacy: Continuities and contradictions in western culture and society.* Bloomington: Indiana University Press.

Graves, D. (1983). *Writing: Teachers and children at work.* Portsmouth, NH: Heinemann.

Graves, D., & Hansen, J. (1983). The author's chair. *Language Arts, 60,* 176–183.

Graves, M. F., Cooke, C. L., & LaBerge, M. J. (1983). Effects of previewing difficult short stories on low ability junior high school students' comprehension, recall, and attitudes. *Reading Research Quarterly, 18,* 262–276.

Gray, V. (1993). *The write tool to teach algebra.* Berkeley, CA: Key Curriculum Press.

Gray, W. (1948). Nature and scope of a sound reading program. In N. B. Henry (Ed.), *Reading in the high school and college, 47th Yearbook of the National Society for the Study of Education* (pp. 46–68). Chicago: University of Chicago Press.

Green, J. (1990). Reading is a social process. *Social context of literacy: Selected papers from the 15th Australian Reading Association Conference.* Canberra, Australia: ACT Department of Education.

Green, J., & Weade, G. (1990). The social construction of classroom reading: Beyond method. *Australian Journal of Reading, 13*(4), 326–336.

Green, J. L. (1983a). Exploring classroom discourse: Linguistic perspectives on teaching–learning processes. *Educational Psychologist, 18,* 180–199.

Green, J. L. (1983b). Teaching as a linguistic process: A state of the art. In E. Gordon (Ed.), *Review of research in education* (Vol. 10, pp. 151–254). Washington, DC: American Educational Research Association.

Green, J. L. (1992). Multiple perspectives: Issues and directions. In R. Beach, J. L. Green, M. L. Kamil, & T. Shanahan (Eds.), *Multidisciplinary perspectives on literacy research* (pp. 19–33). Urbana, IL: National Conference on Research in English/National Council of Teachers of English.

Green, J. L., & Meyer, L. A. (1990). The embeddedness of reading in classroom life: Reading as a situated process. In C. Baker & A. Luke (Eds.), *Toward a critical sociology of reading* (pp. 141–160). Philadelphia: Johns Benjamin.

Gritsavage, M. (1997a, March). *Gender, culture and literacy: Comparing students' reflections and change by age and sex.* Paper presented at the annual meeting of the American Educational Research Association, Chicago, Illinois.

Gritsavage, M. (1997b, May). *Examining dominance in discourse in the graduate course, Gender, Culture and Literacy*. Unpublished manuscript, Arizona State University at Tempe.

Grossberg, L. (1995). Cultural studies: What's in a name? (One more time). *Taboo: The Journal of Culture and Education, I*, 1–37.

Grossman, P. L., & Stodolsky, S. S. (1995). Content as context: The role of school subjects in secondary school teaching. *Educational Researcher, 24*, 5–11, 23.

Grumet, M. (1988). *Bitter milk: Women and teaching*. New York: Routledge.

Grumet, M. R. (1990). On daffodils that come before the swallow dares. In E. W. Eisner, & A. Peshkin (Eds.), *Qualitative inquiry in education: The continuing debate* (pp. 101–120). New York: Teachers College Press.

Guba, E., & Lincoln, Y. (1994). Competing paradigms in qualitative research. In N. Denzin & Y. Lincoln (Eds.), *Handbook of qualitative research* (pp. 105–117). Thousand Oaks, CA: Sage.

Guerra, J. (1997). The place of intercultural literacy in the writing classroom. In C. Severino, J. Guerra, & J. Butler (Eds.), *Writing in multicultural settings* (pp. 248–260). New York: The Modern Language Association of America.

Gumperz, J. J. (1977). Conversational inference and classroom learning. In J. Green & C. Wallat (Eds.), *Ethnography and language in school settings* (pp. 3–23). Norwood, NJ: Ablex.

Guthrie, J. T., Bennett, L., & McGough, K. (1994). *Concept-oriented reading instruction: An integrated curriculum to develop motivations and strategies for reading* (Reading Research Report no. 10). Universities of Georgia and Maryland, National Reading Research Center.

Guthrie, J. T., McCann, A., Hynd, C., & Stahl, S. (1997). Classroom contexts promoting literacy engagement. In J. Flood, S. B. Heath, & D. Lapp (Eds.), *Handbook of research on teaching literacy through the communicative and visual arts* (pp. 753– 762). New York: Macmillan.

Guthrie, J. T., & Wigfield, A. (Eds.). (1997). *Reading engagement: Motivating readers through integrated instruction*. Newark, DE: International Reading Association.

Gutiérrez, K., Rymes, B., & Larson, J. (1995). Script, counterscript, and underlife in the classroom: James Brown versus Brown v. Board of Education. *Harvard Educational Review, 65*, 445–471.

Guzzetti, B. J. (1997, April). *Gender, culture and literacy: Comparing students' reflections and change by demographics and ethnicity*. Paper presented at the annual meeting of the American Educational Research Association, Chicago, IL.

Haggard, M. R. (1988). Developing critical thinking with the Directed Reading–Thinking Activity. *The Reading Teacher, 41*, 526–533.

Halliday, M. A. K. (1985). Context of situation. In M. A. K. Halliday & R. Hasan (Eds.), *Language, context, and text: Aspects of language in a social-semiotic perspective* (pp. 3–14). Victoria, Australia: Deakin University Press.

Halliday, M. A. K., & Hasan, R. (1976). *Cohesion in English*. London: Longman.

Hamilton, M., Barton, D., & Ivanic, R. (Eds.). (1994). *Worlds of literacy*. Clevedon: Multilingual Matters.

Hampel, R. L. (1986). *The last little citadel: American high schools since 1940*. Boston: Houghton Mifflin.

Harding, S. (1987a). *Feminism and methodology*. Bloomington: Indiana University.

Harding, S. (1987b). Introduction: Is there a feminist method? In S. Harding (Ed.), *Feminism and methodology* (pp. 1–14). Bloomington: Indiana University Press.

Hargreaves, A. (1994). Critical introduction, Studying Curriculum (pp. 1–11). New York: Teachers College Press.

Harste, J., Woodward, V. A., Burke, C. L. (1984). *Language stories and literacy lessons*. Portsmouth, NH: Heinemann.

Hartley, T. (1994). Generations of literacy among women in a bilingual community. In M. Hamilton, D. Barton, & R. Ivanic (Eds.), *Worlds of literacy* (pp. 29–40). Clevedon: Multilingual Matters.

Hartman, D. 1997, September). *Doing things with text: Mapping the textural practices of two African-American male high school students*. Paper presented at the Fall Forum of the National Academy of Education, Boulder, CO.

Hasan, R. (1995). The conception of context in text. In P. H. Fries & M. Gregory (Eds.), *Discourse in society: Systematic functional perspectives (meaning and choice in language: Studies for Michael Halliday), Vol. L in advances in discourses* (pp. 183–283). Norwood, NJ: Ablex.

Hayes, D. A. (1987). The potential for directing study in combined reading and writing activity. *Journal of Reading Behavior, 19,* 333–352.

Hayes, J. R. (1992). A psychological perspective applied to literary studies. In R. Beach, J. L. Green, M. L. Kamil, & T. Shanahan (Eds.), *Multidisciplinary perspectives on literacy research* (pp. 125–139). Urbana, IL: National Conference on Research in English/National Council of Teachers of English.

Healy, M. K., & Barr, M. (1991). Language across the curriculum. In J. Flood, J. M. Jensen, D. Lapp, & J. R. Squire (Eds.), *Handbook of research on teaching the English language arts* (pp. 820–826). New York: Macmillan.

Heap, J. L. (1992). Ethnomethodology and the possibility of a metaperspective on literacy research. In R. Beach, J. L. Green, M. L. Kamil, & T. Shanahan (Eds.), *Multidisciplinary perspectives on literacy research* (pp. 35–56). Urbana, IL: National Conference on Research in English/National Council of Teachers of English.

Heath, S. (1982a). Protean shapes in literacy events: Ever-shifting oral and literate traditions. In D. Tannen (Ed.), *Spoken and written language: Exploring orality and literacy.* Norwood, NJ: Ablex.

Heath, S. (1982b). What no bedtime story means: Narrative skills at home and at school. *Language in society, 11,* 1, 49–76.

Heath, S. B. (1983). *Ways with words.* Cambridge, England: Cambridge University Press.

Heath, S. B., & McLaughlin, M. (1993). Building identities for inner-city youth. In S. B. Heath and M. McLaughlin (Eds.), *Identity and inner city youth: Beyond ethnicity and gender* (pp. 1–12). New York: Teachers College Press.

Henry, A. (1998). "Speaking up" and "speaking out": Examining "voice" in a reading/writing program with adolescent African-Caribbean girls. *Journal of Literacy Research, 30,* 233–252.

Herber, H. (1988, May). Knowing why: Rationale and goals for secondary school reading. In M. W. Conley (Chair), *Directions for research and practice in secondary school reading.* Symposium conducted at the meeting of the International Reading Association, Toronto, Canada.

Herber, H. L. (1978). *Teaching reading in content areas* (2nd ed.). Englewood Cliffs, NJ: Prentice-Hall.

Herber, H. L., & Herber, J. N. (1993). *Teaching in content areas.* Needham Heights, MA: Allyn & Bacon.

Hesford, W. (1997). Writing identities: The essence of difference in multicultural classrooms. In C. Severino, J. Guerra, & J. Butler (Eds.), *Writing in multicultural settings* (pp. 133–149). New York: The Modern Language Association of America.

Heshusius, L., & Ballard, K. (1996). *From positivism to interpretivism and beyond.* New York: Teachers College Press.

Hicks, D. (1995/1996). Discourse, learning, and teaching. In M. W. Apple (Ed.), *Review of research in education* (Vol. 21, pp. 49–95). Washington, DC: American Educational Research Association.

Hillocks, G. (1986). *Research on written composition.* Urbana, IL: National Conference on Research in English, Eric Clearinghouse on Reading and Communication Skills.

Hinchman, K. (1985). Reading and the plans of secondary teachers: A qualitative study. In J. A. Niles & R. V. Lalik (Eds.), *Issues in literacy: A research perspective, Thirty-fourth Yearbook of the National Reading Conference* (pp. 251–256). Rochester, NY: The National Reading Conference.

Hinchman, K. (1987). The textbook and three content-area teachers. *Reading Research and Instruction, 26,* 247–263.

Hinchman, K. A. (1998). Reconstructing our understandings of adolescents' participation in classroom literacy events: Learning to look through other eyes. In D. E. Alvermann, K. A. Hinchman, D. W. Moore, S. Phelps, & D. Waff (Eds.), *Reconceptualizing adolescent literacies* (pp. 173–192). Mahwah, NJ: Lawrence Erlbaum Associates.

Hinchman, K. A., & Moje, E. (1998). Conversations: Locating the social and political in secondary school literacy. *Reading Research Quarterly, 33,* 117–128.

Hinchman, K. A. & Zalewski, P. (1996). Reading for success in a tenth-grade global-studies class: A qualitative study. *Journal of Literacy Research, 28,* 91–106.

Hobbs, R. (1997). Literacy for an information age. In J. Flood, S. B. Heath, & D. Lapp (Eds.), *Handbook of research on teaching literacy through the communicative and visual arts* (pp. 7–14). New York: Simon & Schuster.

Hoggart, R. (1957). *The uses of literacy. Changing patterns in English mass culture.* Fair Lawn, NJ: Essential Books.

Holmes Group. (1990). *Tomorrow's schools: Principles for design of professional development schools.* East Lansing, MI: Author.

Holt-Reynolds, D. (1992). Personal history-based beliefs as relevant prior knowledge in course work. *American Educational Research Journal, 29,* 325–349.

Holt-Reynolds, D. (1999). Good readers, good teachers? Subject matter expertise as a challenge in learning to teach. *Harvard Educational Review, 69,* 29–50.

hooks, b. (1989). *Talking back: Thinking feminist, thinking black.* Boston: South End Press.

hooks, b. (1994). *Teaching to transgress: Education as the practice of freedom.* New York: Routledge.

Horowitz, R. (1998). *Literacy and cultural transmission in the reading, writing, and rewriting of Jewish memorial books.* San Francisco: Austin & Winfield.

Howe, K., & Eisenhart, M. (1990). Standards for qualitative (and quantitative) research: A prolegomenon. *Educational Researcher, 19*(4), 2–9.

Hymes, D. (1972). Toward ethnographies of communication: The analysis of communicative events. In P. Paolo Giglio (Ed.), *Language and social context* (pp. 21–44). New York: Penguin.

Hynd, C. R., McNish, M., Qian, G., Keith, M., & Lay, K. (1994). *Learning counter-intuitive physics principles: The effects of text and educational environment* (Reading Research Report No. 16). Athens, GA: NRRC, Universities of Georgia and Maryland.

Hynds, S. (1997). *On the brink: Negotiating literature and life with adolescents.* New York: Teachers College Press.

Ilsley, P. J., & Stahl, N. A. (1993). Reconceptualizing the language of adult literacy. *Journal of Reading, 37,* 20–27.

International Reading Association/National Council of Teachers of English (1996). *Standards for the English Language Arts.* Newark, DE: Author.

Irvine, P., & Elsasser, N. (1988). The ecology of literacy: Negotiating writing standards in a Caribbean setting. In D. Rubin & B. Rafoth (Eds.), *The social construction of written communication* (pp. 304–320). Norwood, NJ: Ablex.

Ivanic, R. (1994). I is for interpersonal: Discoursal construction of writer identities and the teaching of writing. *Linguistics and Education, 6*(1), 3–17.

Jacob, E. (1987). Qualitative research traditions: A review. *Review of Educational Research, 57*(1), 1–50.

Jacob, E. (1999). *Cooperative learning in context: Case studies of an educational innovation.* Albany: State University of New York Press.

Jaeger, R. M. (Ed.). (1997). *Complementary methods for research in education* (2nd ed.). Washington, DC: American Educational Research Association.

Jakobson, R. (1960). Linguistics and poetics. In T. A. Sebeok (Ed.), *Style in language.* New York: Wiley

Janks, H., & Ivanic, R. (1992). Critical discourse awareness and emancipatory discourse. In N. Fairclough (Ed.), *Critical language awareness* (pp. 305–331). London: Longman.

Johnson, S. M. (1990). The primacy and potential of high school departments. In M. B. McLaughlin, J. E. Talbert, & N. Bascia (Eds), *The Contexts of teaching in secondary schools: Teachers' realities* (pp. 167–184). New York: Teachers College Press.

Jones, M. G., & Wheatley, J. (1990). Gender differences in teacher–student interactions in science classrooms. *Journal of Research in Science Teaching, 27*(9), 861–874.

Kagan, D. M. (1992). Professional growth among preservice and beginning teachers. *Review of Educational Research, 62,* 129–69.

Kahle, J. B., & Lakes, M. K. (1983). The myth of equality in science classrooms. *Journal of Research in Science Teaching, 20,* 131–140.

Karach, A., & Roach, D. (1994). Collaborative writing, consciousness raising and practical feminist ethics. In M. Hamilton, D. Barton, & R. Ivanic (Eds.), *Worlds of literacy* (pp. 237–246). Clevedon: Multilingual Matters.

Katz, M. (1971). *Class, bureaucracy, and schools: The illusion of educational change in America.* New York: Praeger.

Kelly, G. J., & Green, J. (1998). The social nature of knowing: Toward a sociocultural perspective on conceptual change and knowledge construction. In B. Guzzetti & C. Hynd (Eds.), *Theoretical perspectives on conceptual chance.* Mahwah, NJ: Lawrence Erlbaum Associates.

Kenny, A. (Ed.). (1994). *The Oxford history of western philosophy.* New York: Oxford University Press.

Kerlinger, F. N. (1964). *Foundations for behavioral research: Educational and psychological inquiry.* New York: Holt, Rinehart & Winston.

Kincheloe, J. L., & McLaren, P. L. (1994). Rethinking critical theory and qualitative inquiry. In N. K. Denzin & Y. S. Lincoln (Eds.), *Handbook of qualitative research* (pp. 138–157). Thousand Oaks, CA: Sage.

Kindsvatter, R., Wilen, W., & Ishler, M. (1991). *Dynamics of effective teaching* (2nd ed.). New York: Longman.

King, J. E. (1992). Diaspora literacy and consciousness in the struggle against miseducation in the Black community. *Journal of Negro Education, 61,* 317–340.

King, J. E., & Mitchell, C. A. (1990). *Black mothers to sons: Juxtaposing African American literature with social practice.* New York: Peter Lang.

Knobel, M. (1999). *Everyday literacies; Students, discourse and social practice.* New York: Peter Lang.

Knowles, J. G. (1992). Models for understanding pre-service and beginning teachers' biographies: Illustrations from case studies. In I. F. Goodson (Ed.), *Studying teachers' lives* (pp. 99–152). New York: Teachers College Press.

Kress, G. (1989). *Linguistic processes in sociocultural practice.* (2nd ed.). Oxford, England: Oxford University Press.

Krockover, G. H., & Shepardson, D. F. (1995). The missing links in gender equity research. *Journal of Research in Science Teaching, 32,* 223–224.

Kugelmass, J., & Boyardin, J. (1983). *From a ruined garden: The memorial books of Polish Jewry.* New York: Schocken Books.

Kumagai, J. (1995). Do single-sex classes help girls succeed in physics? *Physics Today,* 73–74.

Kutz, E., & Roskelly, H. (1991). *An unquiet pedagogy: Transforming practice in the English classroom.* Portsmouth, NH: Heinemann.

Kyle, S. (1996, May). *How do adolescent African-American female students express themselves in classroom discussions?* Unpublished manuscript, Arizona State University at Tempe.

Ladson-Billings, G. (1992a). Liberatory consequences of literacy: A case of culturally relevant instruction for African American students. *Journal of Negro Education, 61*(3), 378–391.

Ladson-Billings, G. (1992b). Reading between the lines and beyond the pages: A culturally-relevant approach to literacy teaching. *Theory Into Practice, 31*(4), 312–320.

Ladson-Billings, G. (1994). *The dreamkeepers.* San Francisco: Jossey-Bass.

LaFrance, M. (1991). School for scandal: Different educational experiences for females and males. *Gender and Education, 3,* 3–13.

Lakoff, G., & Johnson, M. (1980). *Metaphors we live by.* Chicago: University of Chicago Press.

Langer, J. A. (1984). Literacy instruction in American schools: Problems and perspectives. *American Journal of Education, 93,* 107–132.

Langer, J. A. (1986). *Children reading and writing: Structures and strategies.* Norwood, NJ: Ablex.

Langer, J. A., & Applebee, A. N. (1986). Reading and writing instruction: Toward a theory of teaching and learning. In E. Z. Rothkopf (Ed.), *Review of research in education* (Vol. 13, pp. 171–194). Washington, DC: American Educational Research Association.

Langer, J. A., & Applebee, A. N. (1987). *How writing shapes thinking.* Urbana, IL: National Council of Teachers of English.

Lankshear, C. (1996). Self-direction & empowerment; Critical language awareness & 'The new work order.' In P. O'Connor (Ed.), *Thinking work.* Sydney, Australia: Adult Literacy and Basic Skills Coalition.

Lankshear, C., & McLaren, P. (Eds.). (1993). *Critical literacy: Politics, praxis, and the postmodern.* Albany: State University of New York Press.

Lather, P. (1991). *Getting smart: feminist research and pedagogy with/in the postmodern.* New York: Routledge.

Lather, P. (1992). Critical frames in educational research: Feminist and post-structural perspectives. *Theory into Practice, 31,* 87–99.

Lee, A. (1996). *Gender, literacy, curriculum: Re-writing school geography.* London: Taylor & Francis.

Lee, C. (1997). Bridging home and school literacies: Models for culturally responsive teaching, a case for African-American English. In J. Flood, S. Heath, & D, Lapp (Eds.), *Handbook of research on teaching literacy through the communicative and visual arts* (pp. 334–345). New York: Simon & Schuster.

Lee, V. E., Bryk, A. S., & Smith, J. B. (1993). The organization of effective secondary schools. In Darling-Hammond (Ed.), *Review of research in education* (Vol. 19, pp. 171–267).

Lemke, J. L. (1990). *Talking science: Language, learning, and values.* Norwood, NJ: Ablex.

Lensmire, T. (1994). *When children write: Critical revisions of the writing process.* New York: Teachers College Press.

Lesley, M. (1997). The difficult dance of critical literacy. *Journal of Adolescent and Adult Literacy, 40,* 420–424.

Lewis, A. (1990). Remembering the forgotten half. *Phi Delta Kappan, 71,* 748–749.

Lieberman, A., & Miler, L. (1992). *Teachers: Their world and their work.* New York: Teachers College Press.

Lincoln, Y. (1997). What constitutes quality in interpretive research? In C. K. Kinzer, K. A. Hinchman, & D. J. Leu (Eds.), *Inquiries in literacy theory and practice* (pp. 54–68). Chicago: National Reading Conference.

Lincoln, Y. S., & Guba, E. G. (1985). *Naturalistic inquiry.* Beverly Hills, CA: Sage.

Lubeck, S., & Garrett, P. (1990). The social construction of the "at risk" child. *British Journal of Sociology of Education, 11*(3), 327–340.

Lugones, M. C., & Spelman, E. V. (1995). Have we got a theory for you! Feminist theory, cultural imperialism and the demand for "the woman's voice." In N. Tuana & R. Tong (Eds.), *Feminism and philosophy* (pp. 494–507). Boulder, CO: Westview Press.

Luke, A. (1988). The non-neutrality of literacy instruction: A critical introduction. *Australian Journal of Reading, 11*(2), 79–83.

Luke, A. (1993). Stories of social regulation: The micropolitics of classroom narrative. In B. Green (Ed.), *The insistence of the letter: Literacy studies and curriculum theorizing* (pp. 137–153). London: Falmer.

Luke, A. (1995/1996). Text and discourse in education: An introduction to critical discourse analysis. In M. W. Apple (Ed.), *Review of research in education* (Vol. 21, pp. 3–48). Washington, DC: American Educational Research Association.

Luke, A., & Freebody, P. (1997). Critical literacy and the question of normativity: An introduction. In S. Muspratt, A. Luke, & P. Freebody (Eds.), *Constructing critical literacies* (pp. 1–18). Cresskill, NJ: Hampton Press.

Luke, A., O'Brien, J., & Comber, B. (1994). Making community texts objects of study. *Australian Journal of Language and Literacy, 17*(2), 139–149.

Luke, C. (1993). Television curriculum and popular literacy: Feminine identity politics and family discourse. In B. Green (Ed.), *The insistence of the letter: Literacy studies and curriculum theorizing* (pp. 175–194). Pittsburgh: University of Pittsburgh Press.

Luke, C., & Gore, J. (1992). Introduction. In C. Luke & J. Gore (Eds.), *Feminisms and critical pedagogy* (pp. 1–14). New York: Routledge.

Luster, B., Varelas, M., Wenzel, S., & Liao, J. (1997, March). *Gender issues in the construction of scientific knowledge: Inquiry into a sixth-grade urban classroom.* Paper presented at the annual meeting of the American Educational Research Association, Chicago, IL.

Macedo, D. (1996). Literacy for stupidification: The pedagogy of big lies. In P. Leistyna, A. Woodrum, & S. Sherblom (Eds.), *Breaking free: The transformative power of critical pedagogy* (pp. 31–58). Cambridge, MA: Harvard Educational Review.

MacLeod, J. (1987). *Ain't no makin' it: Leveled aspirations in a low-income neighborhood.* Boulder, CO: Westview Press.

MacLeod, J. (1995). *Ain't no makin' it: Aspirations and attainment in a low-income neighborhood.* Boulder, CO: Westview Press.

Mahiri, J. (1991). Discourse in sports: Language and literacy features of preadolescent African American males in a youth basketball program. *Journal of Negro Education, 60*(3), 305–313.

Mahiri, J. (1994). Reading rites and sports: Motivation for adaptive literacy of young African-American males. In B. Moss (Ed.), *Literacy across communities* (pp. 121–146). Cresskill, NJ: Hampton Press.

Marcus, G. E. (1986). Contemporary problems of ethnography. In J. Clifford & G. E. Marcus (Eds.), *Writing culture* (pp. 165–193). Berkeley, CA: University of California Press.

Margonis, F. (1992). The cooptation of "at risk": Paradoxes of policy criticism. *Teachers college record, 94*(2), 343–364.

Martin, N. (1983). Language across the curriculum. A paradox and its potential for change. In N. Martin (Ed.), *Mostly about writing: Selected essays* (pp. 100–110). Portsmouth, NH: Boynton/Cook.

Maybin, J., & Moss, G. (1993). Talk about texts: Reading as a social event. *Journal of Reading Research, 16*(2), 138–147.

McCombs, B. L. (1996). Alternative perspectives on motivation. In L. Baker, P. Afflerbach, & D. Reinking (Eds.), *Developing engaged readers in school and home communities* (pp. 67–87). Mahwah, NJ: Lawrence Erlbaum Associates.

McDermott, R. (1999). Culture is not an environment of the mind. *The Journal of the Learning Sciences, 8*(1), 157–169.

McGinley, W., & Kamberelis, G. (1996). Maniac Magee and Ragtime Tumpie: Children negotiating self and world through reading and writing. *Research in the Teaching of English, 30,* 75–113.

McLaren, P. (1989). *Life in schools.* New York: Longman.

McLaughlin, M., Irby, M., & Langman, J. (1994). *Urban sanctuaries: Neighborhood organizations in the lives and futures of inner-city youth.* San Francisco: Jossey-Bass.

McLaughlin, M. W., & Talbert, J. E. (1990). The contexts in question: The secondary school workplace. In M. W. McLaughlin, J. E. Talbert, & N. Bascia (Eds.), *The contexts of teaching in secondary schools: Teachers' realities* (pp. 1–14). New York: Teachers College Press.

McLaughlin, M. W., Talbert, J. E., & Bascia, N. (Eds.). (1990). *The contexts of teaching in secondary schools: The secondary school workplace.* New York: Teachers College Press.

McNeil, L. (1988). *Contradictions of control: School structure and school knowledge.* New York: Routledge.

Mead, G. H. (1934). *Mind, self, and society.* Chicago: University of Chicago Press.

Medley, D., & Mitzel, H. (1963). Measuring classroom behavior by systematic observation. In N. L. Gage (Ed.), *Handbook of research on teaching* (pp. 247–328). Chicago: Rand McNally.

Mehan, H. (1979). *Learning lessons: Social organization in the classroom.* Cambridge, MA: Harvard University Press.

Mercado, C. (1998). When young people from marginalized communities enter the world of ethnographic research—Scribing, planning, reflecting and sharing. In A. Egan-Robertson & D. Bloome (Eds.), *Students as researchers of culture and language in their own communities.* Cresskill, NJ: Hampton Press.

Mercer, N. (1992). Culture, context and the construction of knowledge in the classroom. In P. Light & G. Butterworth (Eds.), *Context and cognition: Ways of learning and knowing* (pp. 28–46). Hillsdale, NJ: Lawrence Erlbaum Associates.

Merriam, S. (1998). *Qualitative research and case study applications in education*. San Francisco: Jossey-Bass.

Merriam, S. B. (1988). *Case student research in education, a qualitative approach*. San Francisco: Jossey-Bass.

Messaris, P. (1997). Introduction. In J. Flood, S. B. Heath, & D Lapp (Eds.), *Handbook of research on teaching literacy through the communicative and visual arts* (pp. 3–5). New York: Macmillian.

Meyer, B., Brandt, D., Bluth, G. (1980). Use of top-level structure in text: Key for reading comprehension of ninth-grade students. *Reading Research Quarterly, 16,* 72–103.

Michaels, S. (1981). "Sharing time": Children's narrative styles and differential access to literacy. *Language in Society, 10*(3), 423–442.

Michaels, S. M., & O'Connor, M. C. (1990, Summer). *Literacy as reasoning within multiple discourses.* Paper presented at the Council for Chief State School Officers 1990 Summer Institute, Newton, MA. Restructuring Learning.

Miles, M., & Huberman, A. (1994). *Qualitative data analysis: An expanded sourcebook (2nd ed.).* Thousand Oaks, CA: Sage.

Mills, S. (1994). *Gendering the reader.* New York: Harvester Wheatsheaf.

Mikulecky, L. (1978). *Aliteracy and the changing view of reading goals.* (ERIC Documentation Reproduction Service No. ED157052)

Mikulecky, L., & Drew, R. (1991). Basic literacy in the workplace. In R. Barr, M. L. Kamil, P. Mosenthal, & P. D. Pearson (Eds.), *Handbook of reading research: Volume II* (pp. 669–689). New York: Longman.

Moje, E. B. (1993, December). *Life experiences and teacher knowledge: How a content teacher decides to use literacy strategies.* Paper presented at the annual meeting of the National Reading Conference, Charleston, SC.

Moje, E. B. (1996). "I teach students, not subjects": Teacher–student relationships as contexts for secondary literacy. *Reading Research Quarterly, 31,* 172–195.

Moje, E. B. (1997). Exploring discourse, subjectivity, and knowledge in chemistry class. *Journal of Classroom Interaction, 32,* 35–44.

Moje, E. B. (in press). *To be part of the story: The literacy practices of "gangsta" adolescents.* Teachers College Record.

Moje, E. B., Brozo, W. G., & Haas, J. (1994). Portfolios in a high school classroom: Challenges to change. *Reading Research and Instruction, 33,* 275–292.

Moje, E. B., Fassio, K. (1997, December). *Re-visioning the writer's workshop.* Paper presented at the annual meeting of the National Reading Conference, Scottsdale, AZ.

Moje, E. B., & Handy, D. (1995). Using literacy to modify traditional assessments: Alternatives for teaching and assessing content understanding. *Journal of Reading, 38,* 612–625.

Moje, E. B., & Shepardson, D. P. (1998). Social interactions and children's changing understanding of electric circuits: Exploring unequal power relations in "peer" learning groups. In B. Guzzetti & C. Hynd (Eds.), *Theoretical perspectives on conceptual change.* Mahwah, NJ: Lawrence Erlbaum Associates.

Moje, E. B., & Thompson, A. (1996, September). *Sociocultural practices and learning to write in school.* Paper presented at the 2nd conference for socio-cultural research: Vygotsky-Piaget, Geneva, Switzerland.

Moje, E. B., Thompson, A., Christiansen, R., & Zeitler, E. (1997, March). *"Just kicken' it": Literacy as sociocultural practice in an urban middle school.* Paper presented at the annual meeting of the American Educational Research Association, Chicago, IL.

Moll, L., & Diaz, R. (1987). Teaching writing as communication; The use of ethnographic findings in classroom practice. In D. Bloome (Ed.), *Literacy and schooling* (pp. 193–221). Norwood, NJ: Ablex.

Moll, L. C. (1994). Literacy research in community and classrooms: A sociocultural approach. In R. B. Ruddell, M. R. Ruddell & H. Singer (Eds.), *Theoretical models and processes of reading* (pp. 179–207). Newark, DE: International Reading Association.

Montero-Sieburth, M. (1998). Reclaiming indigenous cultures: Student-developed oral histories of Talamanca, Costa Rica. In A. Egan-Robertson & D. Bloome (Eds.), *Students as researchers of culture and language in their own communities* (pp. 217–242). Cresskill, NJ: Hampton Press.

Moore, D. W. (1988, May). Directions for research and practice in secondary schools. In M. W. Conley (Chair), *Directions for research and practice in secondary school reading.* Symposium conducted at the Annual Meeting of the International Reading Association, Toronto, Canada.

Moore, D. W. (1996). Contexts for literacy in secondary schools. In D. J. Leu, C. K. Kinzer, & K. A. Hinchman (Eds.), *Literacies for the 21st century: Research and practice* (pp. 15–46). Forty-fifth Yearbook of the National Reading Council. Chicago: National Reading Conference.

Moore, D. W. (1997). Some complexities of gendered talk about texts. *Journal of Literacy Research, 29,* 507–530.

Moore, D. W. (1998). Metaphors for secondary reading: Choosing one or choosing several. *NASSP Bulletin, 82*(600), 10–15.

Moore, D. W., Readence, J. E., & Rickelman, R. J. (1983). An historical exploration of content area reading instruction. *Reading Research Quarterly, 18,* 419–438.

Morgan, W. (1997). *Critical literacy in the classroom: The art of the possible.* London: Routledge.

Moore, D. W., Readence, J. E., & Rickelman, R. J. (1992). An historical exploration of content area reading instruction. In E. Dishner, T. Bean, J. Readence & D. Moore (Eds.), Reading in the content areas: Improving classroom instruction (3rd ed., pp. 5–29). Dubuque, IA: Kendall/Hunt.

Morse, L. W., & Handley, H. M. (1985). Listening to adolescents: Gender differences in science classroom interaction. In L. C. Wilkinson & C. B. Marrett (Eds.), *Gender influences in classroom interaction* (pp. 37–56). New York: Academic Press.

Mosenthal, P. (1993). Understanding agenda setting in reading research. In A. P. Sweet & J. I. Anderson (Eds.), *Reading research into the year 2000* (pp. 115–129). Hillsdale, NJ: Lawrence Erlbaum Associates.

Moss, B. (Ed.). (1994a). *Literacy across communities.* Cresskill, NJ: Hampton Press.

Moss, B. J. (1994b). Creating a community: Literacy events in African-American churches. In B. J. Moss (Ed.), *Literacy across communities* (pp. 147–178). Cresskill, NJ: Hampton Press.

Moss, G. (1989). *Un/popular fictions.* London: Virago.

Myers, J. (1992). The social contexts of school and personal literacy. *Reading Research Quarterly, 27,* 296–333.

Myers, J. (1995). The value-laden assumptions of our interpretive practices. *Reading Research Quarterly, 30,* 582–587.

National Council of Teachers of Mathematics (1989). *Curriculum and evaluation standards for teaching mathematics.* Reston, VA: The Council.

Natoli, J., & Hutcheon, L. (1993). Introduction: Reading a postmodern reader. In J. Natoli & L. Hutcheon (Eds.), *A postmodern reader* (pp. vii–xiii). Albany: State University of New York Press.

NBC News Dateline, *Failing in fairness.* New York,: NBC News.

New London Group. (1996). A pedagogy of multiliteracies: Designing social futures. *Harvard Educational Review, 66,* 60–92.

Newell, G. E. (1984). Learning from writing in two content areas: A case study/protocol analysis of writing to learn. *Research in the Teaching of English, 18,* 265–287.

Nicholls, J. G. (1989). *The competitive ethos and democratic education.* Cambridge, MA: Harvard University Press.

Nicholson, T. (1984). Experts and novices: A study of reading in the high school classroom. *Reading Research Quarterly, 19*(4), 436–451.

Noddings, N. (1992). Social studies and feminism. *Theory and Research in Social Education, 20*(3), 230–241.

Noll, E. (1998). Experiencing literacy in and out of school: Case studies of two American Indian youths. *Journal of Literacy Research, 30,* 205–232.

North, S. M. (1987). *The making of knowledge in composition.* Upper Montclair, NJ: Boynton/Cook.

Nystrand, M. (1990). Sharing words: The effects of reading on developing writers. *Written Communication, 7*, 3–24.

O'Brien, D. G. (1988). Secondary preservice teachers' resistance to content reading instruction: A proposal for a broader rationale. In J. E. Readence & R. S. Baldwin (Eds.), *Dialogues in literacy research* (pp. 237–243). Thirty-seventh yearbook of the National Reading Conference. Chicago: National Reading Conference.

O'Brien, D. G. (1998). Multiple literacies in a high-school program for "at-risk" adolescents. In D. E. Alvermann, K. A. Hinchman, D. W. Moore, S. F. Phelps, & D. R. Waff (Eds.), *Reconceptualizing the literacies in adolescents' lives* (pp. 27–50). Mahwah, NJ: Lawrence Erlbaum Associates.

O'Brien, D. G., & Dillon, D. R. (1994, December). *Benefits of school–university collaboration in constructing a schoolwide literacy program.* Paper presented at the Annual Meeting, National Reading Conference, San Diego, CA.

O'Brien, D. G., & Dillon, D. R. (1995, April). *Engagement and disengagement in a high school literacy program: Classroom contexts and students' academic and life histories.* Paper presented at the Annual Meeting, American Educational Research Association, San Francisco, CA.

O'Brien, D. G., Dillon, D. R., Wellinski, S. A., Springs, R., & Stith, D. (1997). *Engaging "At-Risk" High School Students* (Perspectives in Reading Research, No. 12). University of Georgia and Maryland: National Reading Research Center.

O'Brien, D. G., & Stewart, R. A. (1990). Preservice teachers' perspectives on why every teacher is not a teacher of reading: A qualitative analysis. *Journal of Reading Behavior, 22*, 101–127.

O'Brien, D. G., Stewart, R. A., & Moje, E. B. (1995). Why content literacy is difficult to infuse into the secondary curriculum: Strategies, goals, and classroom realities. *Reading Research Quarterly, 30*, 442–463.

Ogle, D. (1986). K-W-L: A teaching model that develops active reading of expository text. *The Reading Teacher, 39*, 564–570.

Ogle, D. (1994). Webbing. In A. C. Purves (Ed.), *Encyclopedia of English studies and language arts* (Vol. 2, pp. 1256–1257). New York: Scholastic.

Olson, J. (1980). Teacher constructs and curriculum change. *Journal of Curriculum Studies, 12*, 1–11.

Olson, J. (1981). Teacher influence in the classroom: A context for understanding curriculum translation. *Instructional Science, 10*, 259–275.

Olson, J. (1983, April). *Mr. Swift and the clock: Understanding teacher influence in the science classroom.* Paper presented at the Annual Meeting of the American Educational Research Association, Montreal, Canada.

Orellana, M. F. (1995). Literacy as a gendered social practice: Tasks, texts, talk and take-up. *Reading Research Quarterly, 30*(4), 674–706.

Orner, M. (1992). Interrupting the calls for student voice in "liberatory" education: A feminist poststructural perspective. In C. Luke & J. Gore (Eds.), *Feminisms and critical pedagogy* (pp. 74–89). New York: Routledge.

Ortony, A. (Ed.). (1993). *Metaphor and thought* (2nd ed.). New York: Cambridge University Press.

Oyler, C. (1996). *Making room for students: Sharing teacher authority in room 104.* New York: Teachers College Press.

Pajares, M. F. (1992). Teachers' beliefs and educational research: Cleaning up a messy construct. *Review of Educational Research, 62*, 307–332.

Palinscar, A. S., & Brown, A. L. (1984). Reciprocal teaching of comprehension-fostering and comprehension-monitoring activities. *Cognition and Instruction, 2*, 117–175.

Palmer, R., & Stewart, R. (1997). Nonfiction trade books in content area instruction: Realities and potential. *Journal of Adolescent and Adult Literacy, 40*(8), 630–641.

Pappas, C. C., & Pettegrew, B. S. (1998). The role of genre in the psycholinguistic guessing game of reading. *Language Arts, 75*, 36–44.

Paris, S. G., Wasik, E. A., & Turner, J. C. (1991). The development of strategic readers. In R. Barr, M. L. Kamil, P. B. Mosenthal & P. D. Pearson (Eds.), *Handbook of reading research* (Vol. 2, pp. 609–640). New York: Longman.

Patterson, A. (1995). Reading research methodology and the *Reading Research Quarterly*. *Reading Research Quarterly, 30,* 290–298.

Patterson, L., Santa, C. M., Short, K. B., & Smith, K. (Eds.). (1993). *Teachers are researchers.* Newark, DE: International Reading Association.

Patton, M. Q. (1990). *Qualitative evaluation and research methods* (2nd ed.). Newbury Park, CA: Sage.

Pearce, L. (1997). *Feminism and the politics of reading.* London: Arnold.

Pearson, P. D. (1992). Reading. In M. C. Alkin (Ed.), *Encyclopedia of educational research* (6th ed., Vol. 3, pp. 1075–1085). New York: Macmillan.

Phelan, A. (1997). When the mirror cracked: The discourse of reflection in preservice teacher education. In K. Watson (Ed.), *Dilemmas in teaching and teacher education* (pp. 169–178). London: Cassell.

Phillips, S. (1972). Participant structures and communicative competence: Warm Springs children in community and classroom. In C. B. Cazden, V. P. John, & D. Hymes (Eds.), *Functions of language in the classroom* (pp. 370–394). New York: Teachers College Press.

Pinar, W. F. (Ed.). (1988). *Contemporary curriculum discourses.* Scottsdale, AR: Gorsuch Scarisbrick.

Pinar, W. F., Reynolds, W. M., Slattery, P., & Taubman, P. M. (Eds). (1996). *Understanding Curriculum.* New York: Peter Lang.

Pintrich, P. R., & Schunk, D. H. (1996). *Motivation in education.* Englewood Cliffs, NJ: Merrill.

Popkewitz, T. S. (1991). *A political sociology of educational reform.* New York: Teachers College Press.

Posner, G. F. (1988). Models of curriculum planning. In L. E. Beyer & M. W. Apple (Eds.), *The curriculum: Problems, politics, and possibilities* (pp. 77–97). Albany: State University of New York Press. Boston: Houghton Mifflin.

Powell, A. G., Farrar, E., & Cohen, D K. (1985). *The shopping mall high school: Winners and losers in the educational marketplace.*

Pratt, M. L. (1991). Arts of the contact zone. *Profession, 91,* 33–40.

Prentiss, T. (1995). Constructing literacy practices: An analysis of student lived and perceived experiences in high school English. *Journal of Classroom Interaction, 30*(2), 27–39.

Prentiss, T. (1998). Teachers and students mutually influencing each others' literacy practices: A focus on the students' role. In D. E. Alvermann, K. A. Hinchman, D. W. Moore, S. Phelps, & D. Waff (Eds.), *Reconceptualizing the literacies in adolescents' lives* (pp. 103–128). Mahwah, NJ: Lawrence Erlbaum Associates.

Prinsloo, M., & Breir, M. (1996). *The social uses of literacy: Theory and practice in contemporary South Africa.* Bertsham, South Africa: Sached Books.

Prior, P. (1994). Response, revision, disciplinarity: A microhistory of a dissertation prospectus in sociology. *Written Communication, 11,* 483–533.

Pugach, M. C. (1995). Twice victims: The struggle to educate children in urban schools and the reform of special education and Chapter 1. In M. C. Wang & M. C. Reynolds (Eds.), *Making a difference for students at risk* (pp. 27–60). Thousand Oakes, CA: Corwin.

Purves, A. C. (1991). The textual contract: Literacy as common knowledge and conventional wisdom. In E. M. Jennings & A. C. Purves (Eds.), *Literate systems and individual lives* (pp. 51–69). Albany: State University of New York Press.

Pyne, S. J. (1998). *How the canyon became Grand.* New York: Viking.

Ralph, J. (1989). Improving education for the disadvantaged: Do we know whom to help? *Phi Delta Kappan, 70,* 395–401.

Ratekin, N., Simpson, M. L., Alvermann, D. E., & Dishner, E. K. (1985). Why teachers resist content reading instruction. *Journal of Reading, 28,* 432–437.

Readence, J. E., Bean, T., & Baldwin, R. S. (1998). *Content area literacy: An integrated approach.* Dubuque, IA: Kendall/Hunt.

Readence, J. E., & Moore, D. W. (1983). Why questions? An historical perspective on standarized reading comprehension tests. *Journal of Reading, 26,* 306–313.

Reddy, M. J. (1993). The conduit metaphor: A case of frame conflict in our language about language. In A. Ortony (Ed.), *Metaphor and thought* (2nd ed., pp. 164–201). New York: Cambridge University Press.

Reinking, D., Labbo, L., & McKenna, M. (1997). Navigating the changing landscape of literacy: Current theory and research in computer-based reading and writing. In J. Flood, S. B. Heath, & D. Lapp (Eds.), *Research on teaching literacy through the communicative and visual arts* (pp. 77–92). New York: Simon & Schuster.

Rieck, B. (1977). How content teachers telegraph messages against reading. *Journal of Reading, 20,* 646–648.

Riley, D. (1988). *"Am I that name? Feminism and the category of women in history.* Minneapolis: University of Minnesota Press.

Robinson, R. P. (1941). *Effective study.* New York: Harper & Row.

Roller, C. M. (1991). Commentary: Research in the classroom—How will we ever know? *Reading Research Quarterly, 26,* 325–328.

Rooney, P. (1991). Gendered reason: Sex metaphor and conceptions of reason. *Hypatia, 6,* 77–103.

Rosaldo, R. (1993). *Culture and truth: The remaking of social analysis.* Boston, MA: Beacon Press.

Rosenblatt, L. (1978). *The reader, the text, and the poem: The transactional theory of literary work.* Carbondale: Southern Illinois University Press.

Rosenholtz, S. (1989). *Teacher's workplace: The social organization of schools.* New York: Longman.

Rosenshine, B., & Furst, N. (1973). The use of direct observation to study teaching. In R. M. W. Travers (Ed.), *Second handbook of research on teaching* (pp. 122–183). Chicago: Rand McNally.

Rousseau, J. J. (1974). *Emile.* B. Foxley, trans. London: Dent (original work published 1762).

Rubin, D. L. (Ed.). (1995). *Composing social identity in written language.* Hillside, NJ: Lawrence Erlbaum Associates.

Rushkoff, D. (1996). *Media virus.* New York: Ballantine.

Rusnak, G. E. (1994). Bridging the comprehension gap. *Journal of Reading, 37,* 678–679.

Sadker, M., & Sadker, D. (1994). *Failing at fairness: How America's schools cheat girls.* New York: Scribner's.

Sadker, M., Sadker, D., & Klein, S. (1991). The issue of gender in elementary and secondary education. In G. Grant (Ed.), *Review of Research in Education* (Vol. 17, pp. 269–334). Washington, DC: American Educational Research Association.

Saks, A. L. (1996). Viewpoints: Should novels count as dissertations in education? *Research in the Teaching of English, 30,* 403–427.

Santa Barbara Discourse Group. (1994). Constructing literacy in classrooms: Literate action as social accomplishment. In R. B. Ruddell, M. R. Ruddell, & H. Singer (Eds.), *Theoretical models and processes of reading* (4th ed., pp. 124–154). Newark, DE: International Reading Association.

Sarup, M. (1993). *An introductory guide to post-structuralism and postmodernism* (2nd ed.). Athens: The University of Georgia Press.

Saussure, F. de (1974). *A course in general linguistics.* London: Fontana.

Saxena, M. (1994). Literacies among Punjabis in Southall. In M. Hamilton, D. Barton & R. Ivanic (Eds.), *Worlds of literacy* (pp. 195–214). Clevedon, England: Multilingual Matters.

Schaafsma, D. (1998). Telling stories with Ms. Rose Bell: Students as authors of critical narratives and fiction. In A. Egan-Robertson & D. Bloome (Eds.), *Students as researchers of culture and language in their own communities* (pp. 243–260). Cresskill, NJ: Hampton Press.

Schallert, D., & Roser, N. (1989). The role of reading in content area instruction. In D. Lapp, J. Flood, & N. Farnan (Eds.), *Content Area Reading and Learning: Instructional Strategies* (pp. 25–33). Englewood Cliffs, NJ: Prentice-Hall.

Schultz, K. (1996). Between school and work: The literacies of urban adolescent females. *Anthropology and Education Quarterly, 27,* 517–544.

Schumacher, G. M., & Nash, J. G. (1991). Conceptualizing and measuring knowledge due to writing. *Research in the Teaching of English, 25,* 67–96.

Schwandt, T. A. (1994). Constructivist, interpretivist approaches to human inquiry. In N. K. Denzin & Y. S. Lincoln (Eds.), *Handbook of qualitative research* (pp. 118–137). Thousand Oaks, CA: Sage.

Scollon, R., & Scollon, S. (1981). *Narrative/literacy and face in interethnic communication.* Norwood, NJ: Ablex.

Scribner, S., & Cole, M. (1981). *The psychology of literacy.* Cambridge, MA: Harvard University Press.

Searle, C. (1998). *None but our words: Critical literacy in classroom and community.* Philadelphia: Open University Press.

Secretary's Commission on Achieving Necessary Skills. (1991). *What work requires of schools: A SCANS report for America 2000.* Washington, DC: Department of Labor.

Sedlak, M. W., Wheeler, C. W., Pullin, D. C., & Cusick, P. A. (1986). *Selling students short: Classroom bargains and academic reform in the American high school.* New York: Teachers College Press.

Sheridan, D., Street, B., & Bloome, D. (in press). *Writing ourselves: Literacy practices and the Mass-Observation Project.* Cresskill, NJ: Hampton Press.

Shor, I. (1980). *Critical teaching and everyday life.* Boston: South End Press.

Shor, I. (1992). *Empowering education: Critical teaching for social change.* Chicago: University of Chicago Press.

Shujaa, M. J. (1994). *Too much schooling, too little education: A paradox of Black life in White societies.* Trenton, NJ: Africa World Press, Inc.

Shulman, L. S. (1987). Knowledge and teaching: Foundations of the new reform. *Harvard Educational Review, 57,* 17–38.

Shuman, A. (1986). *Storytelling rights.* Cambridge, England: Cambridge University Press.

Siddle-Walker, E. (1992). Falling asleep and failure among African-American students: Rethinking assumptions about process teaching. *Theory Into Practice, 31*(4), 321–327.

Siedow, M., Memory, D., & Bristow, P. (1985). *Inservice education for content area teachers.* Newark, DE: International Reading Association.

Siegel, M. (1995). More than words: The generative power of transmediation for learning. *Canadian Journal of Education, 20,* 455–475.

Simpson, M. L. (1986). PORPE: Writing strategy for studying and learning in the content areas. *Journal of Reading, 29,* 407–414.

Sinclair, J. M., & Coulthard, R. M. (1975). *Towards an analysis of discourse: The English used by teachers and pupils.* London: Oxford University Press.

Sinetar, M. (1987). *Do what you love, the money will follow: Discovering your right livelihood.* New York: Dell.

Sizer, T. R. (1985). *Horace's compromise: The dilemma of the American high school.* Boston: Houghton Mifflin.

Sizer, T. R. (1992). *Horace's school: Redesigning the American high school.* Boston: Houghton Mifflin.

Sizer, T. R. (1996). *Horace's hope.* Boston: Houghton Mifflin.

Slattery, P. (1995). *Curriculum development in the postmodern era.* New York: Garland.

Slaughter-Defoe, D. T., & Richards, H. (1995). Literacy for empowerment: The case of Black males. In V. L. Gadsden & D. A. Wagner (Eds.), *Literacy among African-American youth* (pp. 125–148). Cresskill, NJ: Hampton Press.

Smagorinsky, P., & O'Donnell-Allen, C. (1998). Reading as mediated and mediating action: Composing meaning for literature through multimedia interpretive texts. *Reading Research Quarterly, 33,* 198–227.

Smist, J. M., Archambault, F. X., & Owen, S. V. (1997, March). *Gender and ethnic differences in attitude toward science and seined self-efficacy among high school students.* Paper presented at the annual meeting of the American Educational Research Association, Chicago, Illinois.

Smith, D. E. (1987). *The everyday world as problematic: A feminist sociology.* Boston: Northeastern University Press.

Smith, F., & Feathers, K. (1983a). Teacher and student perceptions of content area reading. *Journal of Reading, 26,* 348–354.

Smith, F., & Feathers, K. (1983b). The role of reading in content classrooms: Assumption vs. reality. *Journal of Reading, 27,* 262–267.

Smith, J. (1997). The stories educational researchers tell about themselves. *Educational Researcher, 26*(5), 4–11.

Smith, J., & Heshusius, L. (1986). Closing down the conversation: The end of the qualitative–quantitative debate among educational inquirers. *Educational Researcher, 15*(1), 4–12.

Soliday, M. (1997). The politics of difference: Toward a pedagogy of reciprocity. In C. Severino, J. Guerra, & J. Butler (Eds.), *Writing in multicultural settings* (pp. 261–272). New York: The Modern Language Association of America.

Solsken, J. (1993). *Schools, literacy, gender and work in families and in school.* Norwood, NJ: Ablex.

Soltis, J. F. (1992). Inquiry paradigms. In M. C. Alkin (Ed.), *Encyclopedia of educational research* (6th ed., Vol. 2, pp. 620–622). New York: Macmillan.

Spear-Swerling, L., & Sternberg, R. J. (1996). *Off track: When poor readers become learning disabled.* Boulder, CO: Westview Press.

Sperling, M., & Woodlief, L. (1997). Two classrooms, two writing communities: Urban and suburban tenth-graders learn to write. *Research in the Teaching of English, 31,* 205–239.

Spivak, G. (1985). Three women's texts and a critique of imperialism. *Critical Inquiry, 12,* 243–261.

Spivey, N. N. (1997). *The constructivist metaphor.* San Diego, CA: Academic Press.

Spradley, J. P. (1980). *Participant observation.* Orlando, FL: Harcourt Brace Jovanich.

Stake, R. E. (1994). Case studies. In N. K. Denzin & Y. S. Lincoln (Eds.), *Handbook of qualitative research* (pp. 236–247). Thousand Oaks, CA: Sage.

Stanley, L., & Wise, S. (1993). *Breaking out again: Feminist ontology and epistemology.* London: Routledge.

Stanovich, K. (1990). A call for the end to the paradigm wars in reading research. *Journal of Reading Behavior, 22,* 221–231.

Stewart, R. (1990a). A microethnography of a secondary science classroom: A focus on textbooks and reading (Doctoral dissertation, Purdue University, 1990). *Dissertation Abstracts International, 50,* 35–40A.

Stewart, R. (1990b). Factors influencing preservice teachers' resistance to content area reading instruction. *Reading Research and Instruction, 29*(4), 55–63.

Stewart, R., & O'Brien, D. (1989). Resistance to content area reading: A focus on preservice teachers. *Journal of Reading, 32,* 396–401.

Stewart, R., Paradis, E., & Van Arsdale, M. (1995). Mrs. Van's story: An exploration of the meaning changes in a teacher's professional life. In K. Hinchman, D. Leu, & C. Kinzer (Eds.), *Perspectives on Literacy Research and Practice, Forty-fourth Yearbook of the National Reading Conference* (pp. 438–447). Chicago: National Reading Conference, Inc.

Strauss, A., & Corbin, J. (1990). *Basics of qualitative research: Grounded theory procedures and techniques.* Thousand Oaks, CA: Sage.

Strauss, A. S. (1987). *Qualitative analysis for social scientists.* Cambridge, England: Cambridge University Press.

Street, B. & Street, J. (1991). The schooling of literacy. In D. Barton & R. Ivanic (Eds.), *Writing in the community* (pp. 143–166). London: Sage.

Street, B. V. (1984). *Literacy in theory and practice.* Cambridge, England: Cambridge University Press.

Street, B. V. (1994a). Cross cultural perspectives on literacy. In J. Maybin (Ed.), *Language and literacy in social practice* (pp. 139–150). Clevedon, England: Open University.

Street, B. V. (1994b). Struggles over the meaning(s) of literacy. In M. Hamilton, D. Barton, & R. Ivanic (Eds.), *Worlds of literacy* (pp. 15–20). Clevedon: Multilingual Matters.

Street, B. V. (1995). *Social literacies: Critical approaches to literacy in development, ethnography, and education.* New York: Longman.

Street, J. C., & Street, B. V. (1995). The schooling of literacy. In P. Murphy, M. Selinger, J. Bourne, & M. Briggs (Eds.), *Subject learning in the primary curriculum: Issues in English, science, and math* (pp. 75–88). New York: Routledge.

Sturtevant, E. G. (1992). Content literacy in high school social studies: Two case studies in a multicultural setting. (Doctoral dissertation, Kent State University, 1992). *Dissertation Abstracts International, 53*–04A, p. 1119.

Sturtevant, E. (1993a). Content literacy in high school social studies: A focus on one teacher's beliefs and decisions about classroom discussions. In T. Rasinski & N. Padak (Eds.), *Inquiries in literacy learning and instruction* (pp. 3–12). Pittsburg, KS: College Reading Association.

Sturtevant, E. G. (1993b, November). *Non-traditional secondary teachers' beliefs about content area literacy strategies.* Paper presented at the College Reading Association Annual Meeting, Richmond, VA.

Sturtevant, E. G. (1994, November). *Language and literacy activities in content instruction: A comparison of the advice given to mathematics teachers by literacy and math teacher educators.* Paper presented at the College Reading Association Annual Conference, New Orleans, LA.

Sturtevant, E. G. (1996a). Lifetime influences on the literacy-related instructional beliefs of experienced high school history teachers: Two comparative case studies. *Journal of Literacy Research, 28,* 227–257.

Sturtevant, E. G. (1996b). Beyond the content literacy course: Influences on beginning mathematics teachers' uses of literacy in student teaching. In D. J. Leu, C. K. Kinzer, & K. A. Hinchman (Eds.), *Literacies for the 21st century: Research and practice.* Forty-fifth yearbook of the National Reading Conference. Chicago: National Reading Conference.

Sturtevant, E. G. (1997). Teaching contexts and literacy decisions in mathematics and science: A focus on three beginning teachers during years one and two. In C. K. Kinzer, K. Hinchman, & D. J. Leu (Eds.), *Inquiries in literacy theory and practice: The forty-sixth yearbook of the National Reading Conference* (pp. 237–249). Chicago: The National Reading Conference.

Sturtevant, E. G., Deal, D., Duling, V., Guth, N., Tiss, J., Castellani, J., & Haid, L. (1997, December). *Content literacy and five beginning mathematics and science teachers: The final report of a four-year longitudinal study.* Paper presented at the National Reading Conference, Scottsdale, AR.

Suhor, C. (1994). Semiotics. In A. C. Purves (Ed.), *Encyclopedia of English studies and language arts* (Vol. 2, pp. 1068–1070). New York: Scholastic.

Sumara, D. J. (1996). *Private readings in public.* New York: Peter Lang.

Swadener, B. B., & Lubeck, S. (1995). The social construction of children and families "at risk": An introduction. In B. B. Swadener & S. Lubeck (Eds.), *Children and families "at promise": Deconstructing the discourse of risk* (pp. 1–14). Albany: State University of New York Press.

Swann, J. (1988). Talk control: An illustration from the classroom of problems in analyzing male dominance of conversation, p. 125–140. In J. Coates & D. Cameron (Eds.), *Women in their communities* (pp. 125–140). London: Longman.

Tabouret-Keller, A., Le Page, R. B., Gardner-Chloros, P., & Varro, G. (Eds.). (1997). *Vernacular literacy: A re-evaluation.* Oxford, England: Oxford University Press.

Tannen, D. (1992). How men and women use language differently in their lives and in the classroom. *Chronicle of Higher Education, 32,* 3–6.

Taylor, D. (1989). Toward a unified theory of literacy learning and instructional practices. *Phi Delta Kappan, 71*(3) 184–193.

Taylor, R. L. (1987). The study of Black people: A survey of empirical and theoretical models. *Urban research review, 11*(2), 11–15.

Tharpe, R. G., & Gallimore, R. (1988). *Rousing minds to life: Teaching, learning, and schooling in social context.* New York: Cambridge University Press.

Thorndike, E. L. (1917). Reading as reasoning: A study of mistakes in paragraph reading. *Journal of Educational Psychology, 8,* 276–282.

Tierney, R., Carter, M., & Desai, L. (1991). *Portfolio assessment in the reading–writing classroom.* Norwood, MA: Christopher-Gordon.

Tierney, R., & Pearson, P. D. (1984). Towards a composing model of reading. In J. M. Jensen (Ed.), *Reading and composing.* Urbana, IL: ERIC Clearinghouse on Reading and Communication Skills.

Tierney, R. J., & Pierson, P. D. (1992). A revisionist perspective on "Learning to Learn from Text: A Framework for Improving Classroom Practice." In E. K. Dishner, T. W. Bean, J. E. Readence & D. W. Moore (Eds.), *Reading in the content areas: Improving classroom instruction* (pp. 82–86). Dubuque, IA: Kendall/Hunt.

Tierney, R. J. (1997). Learning with multiple symbol systems: Possibilities, realities, paradigm shifts and developmental considerations. In J. Flood, S. B. Heath, & D. Lapp (Eds.), *Research on teaching literacy through the communicative and visual arts* (pp. 286–298). New York: Simon & Schuster.

Tierney, R. J., & Shanahan, T. (1991). Research on the reading–writing relationship: Interactions, transactions, and outcomes. In R. Barr, M. L. Kamil, P. Mosenthal, & P. D. Pearson (Eds.), *Handbook of reading research* (Vol. 2, pp. 246–280). New York: Longman.

Tobin, K. (1988). Differential engagement of males and females in high school science. *International Journal of Science Education, 10,* 239–252.

Tobin, K., & Garnett, P. (1987). Gender related differences in science activities. *Science Education, 71*(1), 91–103.

Tokarczyk, M. M., & Fay, E. A. (Eds.). (1993). *Working-class women in the academy.* Amherst: The University of Massachusetts Press.

Torres, M. (1998). Celebrations and letters home: Research as an ongoing conversation among students, parents, and teacher. In A. Egan-Robertson & D. Bloome (Eds.), *Students as researchers of culture and language in their own communities* (pp. 59–68). Cresskill, NJ: Hampton Press.

Tromel-Plotz, S. (1985, December). *Women's conversational culture: Rupturing patriarchal discourse.* Unpublished manuscript, Roskilde Universitetscenter, Roskilde, Denmark.

Tuana, N., & Tong, R. (1995). *Feminism and philosophy.* Boulder, CO: Westview Press.

Usher, R., & Edwards, R. (1994). *Postmodernism and education.* London: Routledge & Kegan Paul.

Vacca, R. T. (1975). The development of a functional reading strategy: Implications for content area reading instruction. *Journal of Educational Research, 69,* 108–112.

Vacca, R. T., & Linek, W. M. (1992). Writing to learn. In J. W. Irwin & M. A. Doyle (Eds.), *Reading/writing connections: Learning from research* (pp. 145–159). Newark, DE: International Reading Association.

Vacca, R. T., & Vacca, J. L. (1993). *Content area reading* (4th ed.). New York: HarperCollins.

Vacca, R. T., & Vacca, J. L. (1996). *Content area reading* (5th ed.). New York: HarperCollins.

Vacca, R. T., & Vacca, J. L. (1999). *Content area reading* (6th ed.). NY: Longman.

Van Fleet, A. (1979). Learning to teach: The cultural transmission analogy. *Journal of Teacher Education, 35,* 281–289.

van Manen, M. (1990). *Researching lived experience.* New York: State University of New York Press.

Varela, F., Thompson, E., & Rosch, E. (1991). *The embodied mind: Cognitive science and human experience.* Cambridge: MIT Press.

Vaughan, J. (1977). A scale to measure attitudes toward teaching reading in content classrooms. *Journal of Reading, 20,* 605–609.

Volosinov, V. N. (1973). *Marxism and the philosophy of language* (L. Matejka & I. Titunik, Trans.) Cambridge, MA: Harvard University Press. (original work published 1929)

Vygotsky, L. S. (1978). *Mind in society.* Cambridge, MA: Harvard University Press.

Wallace, C. (1992). Critical literacy awareness in the EFL classroom. In N. Fairclough (Ed.), *Critical language awareness* (pp. 59–92). London: Longman.

Walsh, C. (Ed.). (1991). *Literacy as praxis.* Norwood, NJ: Ablex.

Wang, M. C. Reynolds, M. C., & Walberg, H. J. (1995). Introduction: Inner-City Students at the Margins. In M. C. Wang & M. C. Reynolds (Eds.), *Making a difference for students at risk* (pp.1–26). Thousand Oaks, CA: Sage.

Waxman, H. C. (1992). Introduction: Reversing the cycle of educational failure for students in at-risk school environments. In H. C. Waxman, J. W. d. Felix, J. E. Anderson & H. P. B. Jr. (Eds.), *Students at risk in at-risk schools* (pp. 1–9). Newbury Park, CA: Sage.

Weedon, C. (1987). *Feminist practice and poststructural theory.* Oxford, England: Basil Blackwell.

Weedon, C. (1997). *Feminist practice and poststructuralist theory* (2nd ed.). Oxford, England: Blackwell.

Weiler, K. (1988). *Women teaching for change: Gender, class and power.* New York: Bergen & Carvey.

Whorf, B. L. (1956). *Language, thought, and reality.* Cambridge, MA: MIT Press.

Willett, J., & Bloome, D. (1992). Literacy, language, school and community: A community-centered perspective. In C. Hedley & A. Carrasquillo (Eds.), *Whole language and the bilingual learner* (pp. 35–57). Norwood, NJ: Ablex.

Willinsky, J. (1990). *The new literacy.* New York: Routledge.

Willinsky, J. (1991). *The triumph of literature—The fate of literacy: English in the secondary school curriculum.* New York: Teachers College Press.

Willis, A. I. (1995). Reading the world of school literacy: Contextualizing the experience of a young African American male. *Harvard Educational Review, 65,* 30–49.

Willis, A. (1997). Exploring multicultural literature as cultural production. In T. Rogers & A. Soter (Eds.), *Reading across cultures: Teaching literature in a diverse society* (pp. 135–160). New York: Teachers College Press.

Wolcott, H. F. (1992). Posturing in qualitative research. In M. D. LeCompte, W. L. Millroy, & J. Preissle (Eds.), *The handbook of qualitative research in education* (pp. 3–52). San Diego: Academic Press.

Wolf, D., & Perry, M. (1988). Becoming literate: Beyond scribes and clerks. *Theory Into Practice, 27,* 1, 44–52.

Woods, P. (1992). Symbolic interactionism. In M. LeCompte, W. Millroy, & J. Priessle (Eds.), *The handbook of qualitative research in education* (pp. 338–404). San Diego, CA: Academic Press.

Woodson, C. G. (1933). *The mis-education of the Negro.* Hampton, VA: U. B. & U.S. Communications Systems.

Yeager, B., Floriani, A., & Green, J. (1998). Learning to see learning in the classroom. In A. Egan-Robertson & D. Bloome (Eds.), *Students as researchers of culture and language in their own communities* (pp. 115–140). Cresskill, NJ: Hampton Press.

Yore, L. (1986, March). *What research says about science textbooks, science reading and science reading instruction: A research agenda.* Paper presented at the Annual Meeting of the National Association for Research in Science Teaching, San Francisco, CA. (ERIC Document Reproduction Service No. ED 269 243).

Yore, L. (1987, April). Secondary science teachers' attitudes towards, knowledge about and classroom uses of science reading and science textbooks. Paper presented at the Annual Meeting of the National Association for Research in Science Teaching, Washington, DC.

Yore, L. (1991). Secondary science teachers' attitudes and beliefs about science reading and science textbooks. *Journal of Research in Science Teaching, 28,* 55–72.

Yore, L., & Denning, D. (1989, March). Implementing change in secondary science reading and textbook usage: A desired image, a current profile, and a plan of change. Paper presented at the Annual Meeting of the National Association for Research in Science Teaching, San Francisco, CA.

Young, A., & Fulwiler, T. (Eds.). (1986). *Writing across the disciplines: Research into practice.* Upper Montclair, NJ: Boynton/Cook.

Zaharlick, A., & Green, J. L. (1991). Ethnographic research. In J. Flood, J. M. Jensen, D. Lapp, & J. Squire (Eds.), *Handbook of research on teaching the English language arts* (pp. 202–225). New York: Macmillan.

Author Index

Locators annotated with *n* indicate notes.

A

Ackerman, J., 213n, 313
Alcoff, L., 129, 265, 266, 267, 275, 281, 283, 305
Alcoff, L. M., 281, 305
Alexander, P. A., 81, 305
Allington, R. L., 107, 305
Alvermann, D., 106, 110, 287, 305
Alvermann, D. E., 3, 7, 8, 11, 16, 17, 22, 23, 30,
    34, 35, 42, 44, 51, 52, 54, 59, 80, 81,
    82, 84, 105, 106, 107, 125, 127, 138,
    145, 146, 148, 172, 173, 284, 305,
    306, 313, 325
Alvermann, E. M., 109, 306
American Association of University Women,
    125, 306
Anders, P. L., 79, 125, 138, 306, 313
Anderson, R. C., 22, 24, 306
Anderson, T. H., 3, 306
Anderson, V. A., 12, 306
Andrade, R., 288, 306
Anstead, C. J., 33, 315
Anyon, J., 16, 306
Apple, M., 29, 181, 306
Apple, M. W., 29, 122, 306, 309
Applebee, A., 297, 306
Applebee, A. N., 5, 24, 52, 53, 54, 59, 306, 319,
    320
Archambault, F. X., 128, 327
Armstrong, J., 80, 306
Aronowitz, S., 37, 306
Artley, A. S., 7, 306
Asante, M. K., 243, 244, 306, 307
Athanases, S. Z., 46, 307

Atwell, N., 35, 195, 201, 205, 211, 307
Au, K., 294, 307
Ayres, L. P., 19, 307

B

Bailey, F., 57, 73, 74, 308
Baker, C., 291, 307
Baker, C. L., 316
Bakhtin, M. M., 204, 291, 307
Baldwin, J., 165, 307
Baldwin, R. S., 7, 172, 307, 325
Ball, A., 249, 307
Ball, S. J., 33, 307
Ballard, K., 10, 317
Baptiste, H. P., 108, 308
Barbieri, M., 13, 307
Barnes, D., 9, 74, 307
Barr, M., 54, 55, 317
Barron, R. F., 7, 307
Barton, D., 40, 106, 110, 112, 194, 287, 298,
    300, 301, 307, 316
Bascia, N., 55, 321
Baudrillard, J., 46, 47, 307
Beach, R., 3, 21, 287, 307
Bean, T., 172, 325
Bean, T. W., 52, 308
Beason, L., 52, 54, 308
Beck, I. L., 12, 308
Becker, H., 181, 308
Bellack, A. A., 7, 308
Bennett, L., 107, 109, 316
Benton, S, 303, 308
Berger, A., 7, 308

Subject Index

Locators annotated with *f* indicate figures.
Locators annotated with *n* indicate notes.
Locators annotated with *t* indicate tables.

A